Handbook of Computer Networks and Communications

Volume II

Handbook of Computer Networks and Communications
Volume II

Edited by **Akira Hanako**

CLANRYE INTERNATIONAL

New Jersey

Published by Clanrye International,
55 Van Reypen Street,
Jersey City, NJ 07306, USA
www.clanryeinternational.com

Handbook of Computer Networks and Communications
Volume II
Edited by Akira Hanako

© 2015 Clanrye International

International Standard Book Number: 978-1-63240-263-9 (Hardback)

Printed in the United States of America.

Contents

Preface

A communication is a method to exchange data of different types which is encoded and then transferred through wired connection, or wireless connection, a communication can be one to one, many to one, and many to many. A computer network on the other hand is a data network or data connection which allows two computer systems to exchange data.

Network computers when originate data, establish routes, and then exchange data followed by terminating the link; are known as network nodes. One of the most common examples of computer network is internet, and internet's applications such as World Wide Web (WWW), printers, messaging applications, cash cards use, etc. Computer networks can be applied in different physical media with different approaches.

This book studies the different computer networks used in different applications and for different purposes for the communications. This book contains some topics which study the problems in computer networks and communication processes, and these topics will prove to be good read for all those who are working in the field of communication setups and computer networks.

I would like to thank all the contributing authors who have put in their hard work and time in these researches. I also wish to acknowledge the extraordinary efforts of the publishing team in helping me at every step.

Editor

A Survey on Multipacket Reception for Wireless Random Access Networks

Jia-Liang Lu,[1] Wei Shu,[1] and Min-You Wu[2]

[1] *Department of Computer Science & Engineering, Shanghai Jiao Tong University, Shanghai 200240, China*
[2] *Department of Electrical & Computer Engineering, The University of New Mexico, Albuquerque, NM 87131-0001, USA*

Correspondence should be addressed to Jia-Liang Lu, jialiang.lu@sjtu.edu.cn

Academic Editor: Yang Yang

Multipacket reception (MPR) is the capability of simultaneous decoding of more than one packet from multiple concurrent transmissions. Continuous investigations on increasing the reception capability are giving new scientific contributions. In this paper, we provide an overview of MPR-related research work covering (1) the theoretically proved impacts and advantages of using MPR from a channel perspective to network capacity and throughput; (2) the various technologies that enable MPR from transmitter, transreceiver, and receiver perspectives; (3) previous work on protocol improvement to better exploit MPR. Indeed, MPR approaches have been applied in modern wireless mobile systems but the focus of this paper is to discuss MPR in random access wireless networks. Using MPR in such multihop environments calls for new adaptation on protocols, especially a cross-layer approach. To this end, we detail a scheduling method that targets full utilization of MPR capability.

1. Introduction

In the past decade, wireless technologies have become key technologies, offering mobile and flexible communications for industries, enterprises and individuals. Unlike a wired network where various kinds of physical connection, over copper, or fiber optics are used, nodes in a wireless network send information to each other sharing the common medium, air. An analogy to the problem is that people want to communicate with each other during a meeting in a room. The key is how to organize the conversations in this small room to let people get as much information as they can. This organization is known as medium access control. The most common assumption is that if several people talk at the same time, their voices will all be perturbed and communication will fail. There are two models for this common phenomenon. (1) From a channel-based point of view, the room is a single communication channel and the key is to enable multiple signals to occupy this channel. There are three basic types of techniques: Time-Division Multiple Access (TDMA), Frequency-Division Multiple Access (FDMA), and Code-Division Multiple Access (CDMA). (2) From a packet-based point of view, the room is the medium, and any simultaneous transmissions will cause collisions. Traditional medium access controls based on the collision model are viewed as collision recovery (e.g., Aloha), collision avoidance (e.g., CSMA/CA), or collision-free (Token Ring) techniques.

Different methods of analysis are used for different networks; a channel-based approach is often used for telecommunication systems such as wireless mobile systems, while a packet-based approach has been intensively investigated in computer networks such as wireless random access networks. However, the design of modern communicating systems involves both approaches. The signal processing techniques [3–7] in channel access enable a receiver to decode simultaneous signals from different transmitters. The notion of Multipacket reception (MPR) was also introduced in some of these works [4, 5] and is applied in telecommunication systems. It was in [6] that MPR was first discussed for the slotted Aloha protocol and for a random access wireless network.

Why does this have a large impact? MPR subverts the fundamental assumption of a wireless random access network, the collision model. Under the collision model, the capacity of a wireless network is limited mainly by the concurrent packet transmissions. Simultaneous transmissions lead to useless collisions and a significant degradation of network throughput, and retransmissions often make the situation even worse. All these disadvantages are related to the receiver capability of Single Packet Reception (SPR). But MPR can totally overturn the collision model by receiving the lost packet in a collision.

After several proposals on channel and medium access protocols on MPR [6–8, 22] were presented in the 90's, [23] was a seminal paper, the first to examine MPR, as an interaction between the physical and medium access control layers for a wireless random access network. The MPR node model used in [23] was derived from [6]. The MPR capability of a node is modeled by an MPR matrix with conditional probability $R_{n,k}$ that k packets are correctly received given that n packets are transmitted.

$$R = \begin{pmatrix} R_{1,0} & R_{1,1} & & & \\ R_{2,0} & R_{2,1} & R_{2,2} & & \\ R_{3,0} & R_{3,1} & R_{3,2} & R_{3,3} & \\ \vdots & \vdots & \vdots & \vdots & \ddots \end{pmatrix}. \tag{1}$$

The fundamental change of this model compared to the collision model is that the reception can be described by conditional probabilities instead of deterministic failure when simultaneous transmissions occur.

An interesting observation on the recent work on MPR is that significant results have been obtained on the capacity and throughput analysis based on the MPR model, while the enabling MPR technologies are rarely mentioned in these papers. Many studies are based on an assumption that receivers are able to extract, in some optimal way, the signals from multiple transmitters despite the interference with one another. We find an increase of confusion in MPR techniques and how to use MPR techniques. We think that it comes from the gap of channel-based approach and packet-based approach.

One of the purposes of this survey is to clarify MPR enabling techniques by classifying them into transmitter, trans-receiver, and receiver perspectives (Section 3). We expect this survey would help researchers working in related areas to make more realistic hypothesis with the MPR model. The second purpose is to discuss how to use MPR. MPR can bring significant improvement in capacity and throughput (Section 2) but it needs to cope with MAC and the networking layer to achieve real improvement. We will discuss major work on MAC and networking protocol design to exploit MPR (Section 4) and in the same part we detail a scheduling method that targets full utilization of MPR capability using a cross-layer approach.

2. Impacts of MPR

The MPR matrix given in (1) describes the capability of a receiver through a channel. The weakest MPR is equivalent to a conventional collision channel R_0, while the strongest

MPR R_1 corresponds to the case that all transmitted packets are perfectly received and separated:

$$R_0 = \begin{pmatrix} 0 & 1 & & & \\ 1 & 0 & 0 & & \\ 1 & 0 & 0 & 0 & \\ \vdots & \vdots & \vdots & \vdots & \ddots \end{pmatrix},$$

$$R_1 = \begin{pmatrix} 0 & 1 & & & \\ 0 & 0 & 1 & 0 & \\ 0 & 0 & 0 & 1 & \\ \vdots & \vdots & \vdots & \vdots & \ddots \end{pmatrix}. \tag{2}$$

In between, the form of the MPR matrix depends on the channel conditions, capture models, and signal separation algorithms [23]. This MPR matrix was initially proposed to model a multiple reception channel and today it is the usual model for a receiver from the packet access point of view.

2.1. One-Hop Throughput. Let's first discuss the throughput on a node. In [8], the number of successfully received packets in a time slot is defined as the one-hop throughput. It is the MPR channel capacity from the channel-based point of view. It is easy to understand that when we take an arbitrary node, the number of packets that are allowed to go through the node describes exactly the receiver channel characteristics. The average throughput is upper bounded by

$$\eta = \sup_{i=1}^{n} R_n, \tag{3}$$

where

$$R_n = \sum_{k=1}^{n} k R_{n,k}. \tag{4}$$

R_n is the expected number of correctly received packets given that n packets are transmitted. η is defined as the capacity of the MPR channel.

The above statement is validated under saturation traffic. When we consider a Poisson distribution of the intervals between packet arrivals, the following formula should be considered:

$$\eta_{\text{Aloha}} = \sup_{\lambda \geq 0} e^{-\lambda} \sum_{i=1}^{n} \frac{\lambda^i}{i!} R_i. \tag{5}$$

The maximum stable one-hop throughput of a MPR node with n neighbors using Aloha-like protocols is given by [6]. According to (5), the maximum one-hop throughput of the conventional collision model can be obtained as $\eta_{\text{Aloha}} = \sup_{\lambda \geq 0} e^{-\lambda} \lambda$ by taking $R_1 = 1$ and $R_i = 0, i > 1$. R_i is therefore the only factor that impacts the one-hop throughput in MPR model over conventional collision model.

2.2. Spatial Throughput. The spatial throughput is used to move the focus from one arbitrary node to a packet radio network node. In [9], the authors consider such a network with nodes spatially distributed in the plane according to a

Poisson process with parameter λ. A set of assumptions is adopted from [4] to extend the spatial throughput analysis to networks with MPR nodes.

Given the probability p of a node transmitting at a given time slot (in Slotted Aloha), the probability that one node r receives x packets is

$$P[X = x] = P[X = x \mid A]P[A], \tag{6}$$

where A is the event that r does not transmit; therefore $P[A]$ equals $(1 - p)$. $P[X = x|A]$ depends on the probability $P[T]$ of the event T that a sender t transmits in the time slot and the density of the senders, hence the following expression:

$$P[X = x \mid A] = \sum_{n=0}^{\infty} \sum_{k=x}^{n} \binom{k}{x} P[T]^x (1 - P[T])^{k-x}$$
$$\times R_{n,k} \frac{(\lambda p \pi r_0^2)^n}{n!} e^{-\lambda p \pi r_0^2}, \tag{7}$$

where r_0 is the transmission range and $R_{n,k}$ is the conditional probability in the MPR matrix (1). According to Equations (6) and (7), the probability distribution function of X can be obtained. The spatial throughput on receiver r is immediately obtained by taking the expectation of X:

$$E[X] = \sum_{x=1}^{\infty} xP[X = x]. \tag{8}$$

If there are N nodes in the network, the local throughput, S, of the network is

$$S = NE[X]. \tag{9}$$

The spatial local throughput with different values of k is summarized in Figure 1, in which we observe as expected that the MPR feature improves the maximum achievable local throughput. The improvement ratio is close to a liner function of k.

2.3. Capacity. Since 2007, a series of results on capacity improvement by protocol architectures that exploit MPR has been published in [10–12]. Extensive results for k-MPR and a combination of MPR, multichannel, and multiinterface can be found in [13, 24]. Hereafter, Θ, O, and Ω stand, respectively, for a tight bound, upper bound and lower bound.

Given n as the number of nodes in the network, Garcia-Luna-Aceves et al. [10] have shown that a 3D random MPR-based wireless network has a capacity gain of $\Theta(\log n)$. And MPR is proved to achieve a better capacity improvement for wireless ad hoc networks than Network Coding (NC) when the network experiences a single-source multicast and multipair unicasts.

Also assuming that all the transmissions within receiving range can be decoded, they [11] further prove that MPR does increase the order of the transport capacity of random wireless ad hoc networks for multi-pair unicast applications by a factor of $\Theta(\log(\log n))$ under the SINR (Signal to Interference plus Noise Ratio) model.

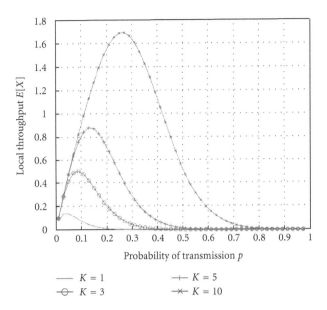

FIGURE 1: Local throughput in packets/timeslot for the simple model of multipacket.

In [12], energy efficiency is taken into account as a factor to increase the capacity of the network. They showed that $\lambda(n) = \Theta(R(n)^{(1-2/\alpha)}/n^{1/\alpha})$ bits per second constitutes a tight upper and lower bound for the throughput capacity of random wireless ad hoc networks, where $\alpha > 2$ is the path loss parameter in the physical model, n is the total number of nodes in the network, and $R(n)$ is the MPR receiver range. The MPR achieves a capacity gain of at least $\Theta((\log n)^{((\alpha-2)/2\alpha)})$ when $R(n) = \Theta(\sqrt{\log n/n})$ compared to Gupta and Kumar's result.

Several important results on the improvement of k-MPR over collision-based wireless networks (1-MPR) are given in [13].

(i) For an arbitrary k-MPR network, the capacity gain over 1-MPR networks is $\Theta(\sqrt{k})$, when $k = O(n)$.

(ii) The capacity is $\Theta(W_n)$ bit-meter/sec and the network is scalable, when $k = \Omega(n)$.

(iii) For random k-MPR networks, the capacity upper bound and lower bound match and the capacity gain over 1-MPR networks is $\Theta(k)$ when $k = O(\sqrt{\log n})$.

(iv) Even the lower bound has a capacity gain of $\Theta(\sqrt{\log n})$ when $k = \Omega(n)$.

In [25], Wang et al. summarize their work on MPR by presenting a unifying approach for the computation of throughput capacity of wireless ad hoc networks under all data traffic patterns including unicast, multicast, broadcast, and anycast. They use an (n, m, k)-cast formulation, where n, m, and k denote the number of nodes in the network, the number of destinations for each communication group, and the actual number of communication group members that receive the information, respectively. The protocol model in [11] is used. They show that the per source-destination

(n, m, k)-cast throughput capacity $C_{m,k}(n)$ is tightly bounded by $\Theta(R(n)\sqrt{m}/k)$, $\Theta(1/k)$, and $\Theta(R^2(n))$ w.h.p when $m = O(R^{-2}(n))$, $\Omega(k) = R^{-2}(n) = O(m)$, and $k = \Omega(R^{-2}(n))$, respectively. The most important fact that they proved is that for the minimum value of the received range $(R(n) = \Omega(\sqrt{\log n/n}))$ required to guarantee network connectivity; the (n, m, k)-cast throughput capacity with MPR has a gain of $\Theta(\log n)$ compared to the throughput attained with SPR. In Table 1, we recapitulate the theoretical capacity results related to MPR.

2.4. Stability. The majority of capacity and throughput calculations assume that the network is saturated. It is very important in this condition to analyze the stability. The stability relies on whether a maximum stable throughput is reachable, that is, whether the probability of packet buffer overflow can be made arbitrarily small by making the buffer size sufficiently large. In [5], Ghez et al. give two important theorems for the Slotted Aloha network with MPR,

(1) If Rn has a limit $R = \lim_{n \to \infty} R_n$, then the system is stable for all arrival distributions such that $\lambda < R$ and is unstable for $\lambda > R$.

(2) The system is stable for $\lambda < \lim\inf_{n \to \infty} R_n$ and unstable for $\lambda > \lim\sup_{n \to \infty} Rn$.

In [26], a general asymmetric MPR model is introduced and the medium-access control (MAC) capacity region is specified. It is shown that the stability region undergoes a phase transition from a concave region to a convex polyhedral region as the MPR capability improves in a two-user system. Furthermore, it is shown that persistent Aloha is also optimal for the symmetric MPR model in a wide range of MPR regimes.

From these two theorems, it is clear that if the number of simultaneous transmissions is greater than the average MPR capacity, the system cannot achieve a maximum stable throughput. Therefore, to exploit MPR, scheduling should still be used among the transmitters. Some recent papers which begin to address this problem [2, 19] will be discussed in Section 4.2.

Dua [27] analyzed a one-dimensional Markov chain which captures the evolution of the queue of a typical transmitter in isolation in an MPR system. Both static channels under ideal power control and fading channels under ideal slow power control are studied. He provides sufficient conditions under which the system converges to a unique steady state. And the average delay per packet for an MPR network is given by

$$D = \frac{\eta - \Delta \cdot p}{p(\Delta - \eta)}, \tag{10}$$

where η is the effective probability of transmission for a transmitter in steady state Δ is the actual probability for a transmitter with a nonempty queue.

In [28, 29], the analytical equations for the characteristics of a relay node's queue such as average queue length and stability conditions are studied for the throughput per user.

The authors consider a network with N users sources, one relay node with MPR, and a single destination node with MPR as well. By modeling the relay node's queue with a one-dimension Markov Chain, they show that the throughput with N source nodes with a relay node is N times the throughput without a relay: $\mu_{\text{total}} = N\mu$, and the throughput is stable if the transmission probability of the relay is bigger than a reference probability $Q_{0\min}$ that can be computed with the stability condition of the Markov chain.

3. How to Realize MPR

Significant improvements to both throughput and capacity of a wireless network can be obtained with MPR. There are a number of techniques which allow simultaneous decoding of packets on a receiver but in many papers MPR is said to be realized with CDMA or MIMO. The appearance of these notions together with MPR brings some ambiguities to the understanding of MPR enabling techniques. Examples such as CDMA and MIMO cover a wide range of techniques in signal processing and wireless systems. Give the current research achievements around MPR, it is worthwhile to set up a clear classification of MPR technologies and to exclude misleading notions. To this end, we give a classification based on transmitter perspective, trans-receiver perspective, and receiver perspective.

3.1. Transmitter Perspective. The first class of techniques that enable MPR require a significant effort by the transmitter. Examples such as CDMA and OFDMA fall into this class. CDMA allows multiple users to be multiplexed over the same wireless channel by employing a coding scheme where each transmitter is assigned a code. The baseband signal is multiplexed with a spreading code running at a much higher rate. The spreading code is a pseudorandom code, and all codes used for one channel are orthogonal. Therefore, on the receiver side, an unwanted signal will be eliminated by the cross-correlation decode, and only the relevant signals are conserved. This technique allows the receiver to decode multiple data streams with the different codes that are known a priori. The ability to decode multiple data packets depends on the selection of code. For example, the orthogonality is the key that allows the receiver to decode the set of simultaneous arrived signals, and this is done on the transmitter side.

OFDMA competes with CDMA as a major multi-access technique. It is used to increase the wireless channel efficiency based on multicarrier modulation methods (in IEEE802.11 a,g,n). For each packet, several data streams are transmitted over the subcarrier frequencies as many slowlymodulated narrow-band signals rather than one rapidlymodulated wide-band signal. In OFDMA, the transmitters of a receiver are assigned different OFDM subchannels. Since the sub-channels do not interfere with each other, MPR is enabled on a frequency basis. In [30], the authors describe a many-to-many communication in which the transmissions are divided in frequency to allow the receiver to decode the packets. Again, OFDMA enables MPR with a great effort for the transmitter in sub-channel selection. Furthermore, it

TABLE 1: Theoretical results on the capacity.

Metric	Condition	SPR	MPR	Works
One-hop throughput (upper bound)	Slotted aloha	$\sup\limits_{\lambda\geq 0} e^{-\lambda}$	$\sup\limits_{\lambda\geq 0} e^{-\lambda}\sum\limits_{i=1}^{n}\dfrac{\lambda^i}{i!}R_i$	[8]
Spatial throughput	Slotted aloha	$\sum\limits_{x=1}^{\infty} P[X=x]$	$P[X=1]$	[9]
Throughput (tight bound) per source-destination	Protocol model (graph model)	$\Theta\left(\sqrt{\dfrac{1}{n}}\right)$	$\Theta\left(\sqrt[3]{\dfrac{\log n}{n}}\right)$	[10]
Throughput (lower bound) per source-destination	Physical model (SINR model)	$\Theta\left(\dfrac{1}{\sqrt{n\log n}}\right)$	$\Theta\left(\dfrac{\log(\log n)}{\sqrt{n\log n}}\right)$	[11]
Throughput (tight bound) per source-destination	Multiflow SINR model	$\Theta\left(\sqrt{\dfrac{1}{n}}\right)$	$\Theta\left(\dfrac{(\log n)^{(1/2)-(1/\alpha)}}{\sqrt{n}}\right)$	[12]
Network throughput (tight bound)	k-MPR (arbitrary networks)	$\Theta(\sqrt{n})$	$\Theta(\sqrt{kn}), k=O(n)$ $\Theta(n), k=\Omega(n)$	[13]
Network throughput (lower bound)	k-MPR (random networks)	$\Theta(\sqrt{\dfrac{n}{\log n}})$	$\Omega\left(k\sqrt{\dfrac{n}{\log n}}\right), k=O\left(\sqrt{\log n}\right)$ $\Omega(\sqrt{n}), k=\Omega(\sqrt{\log n})$	[13]

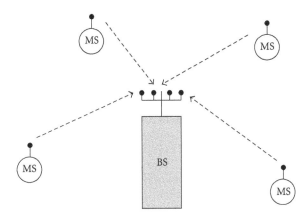

FIGURE 2: The BS is MPR in a MIMO system with multiple antennas.

is a pseudo-MPR capability, because the bandwidth is also divided at the same time, when the radio channel is divided into sub-channels.

3.2. Transreceiver Perspective. In this class of techniques, to enable MPR, transmitters and receivers should cooperate on some operations. Multiantenna MIMO system [14] can achieve MPR by exploiting the spatial diversity of the transmissions. In such a system, each antenna corresponds to a different channel characteristic $H(t)$. A packet sent through one antenna can be easily distinguished from one sent with another antenna by channel estimators. In case of a cellular or AP-based wireless network, the communication between Mobile Station (MS) and Base Station (BS) is based on the MPR capability of the BS (Figure 2). The realization of MPR in a multi-antenna MIMO system requires both transmitters and receivers to implement specific functionalities. That is how it differs from pure transmitter-based techniques.

Another type of technique that could in principle be used for MPR is signal separation. The problem of packet separation can be formulated as one of signal separation in a MIMO system. In [31], the authors present Known Modulus Algorithms (KMA) to allow packet separation in asynchronous ad hoc networks. In the algorithm, a transmitter needs to send a constant modulus signal multiplied by an amplitude modulating code known at the receiver and an antenna array is used on the receiver side which can detect and filter out the desired user among the other interfering signals with the help of this modulation code. The modulation code can be a random binary sequence determined either by the transmitter or the receiver. In [32], a variation of KMA, Algebraic KMA (AKMA), is proposed based on a matrix perturbation analysis. Other signal separation techniques based on a Constant Modulus Algorithm (CMA) or Multiple Modulus Algorithm (MMA) [33] require blind equalization and are usually not efficient for MPR.

In [34], the authors propose to use polynomial phase-modulating sequences to provide MPR capability. The algorithm exploits the fact that the baseband signal exhibits cyclostationarity properties, which are induced at the transmitters after modulation with polynomial phase sequences. So the proposed modulation does not expand the bandwidth and can be considered as a *color code* to distinguish packets from different users.

Some resource allocation base techniques fall also in this class. It is mainly based on a network-assisted approach. The network-assisted diversity is firstly introduced in [35] as a technique to separate the collided packets. The collided packets are kept in memory rather than being discarded and are later combined with future retransmissions to extract all the collided information packets. The proposed method is suitable for multiplexing variable-bit-rate sources without affecting the physical layer bit rate parameter of each source. In [36], a bit-map-assisted dynamic queue (BMDQ) protocol is presented. In the proposed protocol, the traffic in the channel is viewed as a flow of transmission periods, each of which has a bit-map slot for user detection so that accurate knowledge of active users can be obtained. To summarize, resource allocation reuses signal processing principles on packet level.

3.3. Receiver Perspective. Next, we present a class of techniques that involve only the receiver for decoding several packets simultaneously. Compared to the previous two classes, this class of solutions comes closer to the ideal of MPR, to shift the responsibility from transmitters to receivers.

The Match Filter (MF) approach is widely used for single user detection. Even though it is not optimal when multiple users are present, still a receiver can use a bank of Match Filters [9] to decode packets coded with spreading codes that need not even be orthogonal.

Techniques used to separate signals for Multiuser Detection (MUD) are more applicable for MPR. That is why many papers [2, 10–12] on network capacity with MPR cited it as the technique to realize MPR. It is a way to alleviate Multiple Access Interference (MAI) during the simultaneous transmissions on the same channel.

An optimal MUD detector refers to maximum likelihood sequence estimation (MLSE) [37] which requires knowledge of all transmitters' spreading codes (e.g., base stations in a cellular CDMA system). This optimal detector is too complicated for practical application although it has excellent performance. One of the reasons, given in [38], is that cellular system is centrally controlled and always has synchronization among different users to some extent. However, in distributed wireless networks, it is quite difficult to apply signal processing techniques to separate the asynchronous transmissions. Therefore, MLSE is not a candidate for MPR.

In suboptimal MUD techniques, two approaches can be identified, namely, linear and nonlinear MUD. In linear MUD, a linear transformation is applied to the soft outputs of the conventional detector in order to produce a new set of decision variables with MAI greatly decoupled. Two most cited linear multiuser detectors are decorrelated detectors [39] and the Minimum Mean Square Error (MMSE) detector [9]. They are generally complex but yield an optimal value of the near-far resistance performance metric.

On the other hand, non-linear MUDs use interference estimators and remove the interference from the received signal before detection. They are much simpler but have an inferior performance compared to linear MUD. Multistage Interference Cancellation (IC) is one of the most interesting in this category, where cancellation can be carried out either successively (SIC) or in parallel (PIC).

For SIC, the multi-user's signals are demodulated and cancelled from the strongest to the weakest according to their received signal power. References [2, 10–12] assume the receiver node utilizes MUD and SIC to decode multiple packets. It is a misleading phrase, because SIC is a method in MUD. Indeed, it may be the most practical way to realize MPR given the current state of the art.

For PIC, without the exact knowledge of the interfering bits, their estimates in the previous stage are used instead. To enhance the performance of PIC, a multistage approach is often adopted, in which the detector at nth stage uses the bit decision from the $(n-1)$th stage. In theory, PIC could support more simultaneous packets from different users, but a perfect power control is necessary. In practice, it is shown

in [40] that in a single of a 2-path Rayleigh fading channel, 2-stage PIC, and SIC have very close performance.

In Figure 3, the techniques that are applied for MPR are summarized with a tree classification. Again, many of these techniques were applied to mobile communication systems such as cellular networks; for wireless random access network only a subset of techniques is possible due to the distributed random channel access nature. Among the three classes, our view is that the receiver-based techniques are more applicable for wireless random access networks. They also meet the objective of the introduction of MPR in a wireless random access network, which is shifting the responsibility from the transmitters to the receivers.

3.4. Enabling MPR in a Wireless LAN. The techniques described in the previous section work for random access wireless networks. However, there is a class of technologies which are specific to WLANs based on an access point (AP).

In [1], Zheng et al. consider the uplink MPR in a WLAN, that is, from client station to AP. The AP has M antennas, while each client station has only one antenna Figure 4.

Based on this model, Zhang et al. investigate a number of topics on MPR in WLANs: [41] gives a delay analysis; [42] studies the impact of capacity improvement with MPR in a WLAN; [43] proposes a multiround contention random-access protocol to increase the channel utilization; [44] extends the investigation to the nonsaturation case and shows that super-linear scaling also holds for two newly defined situations, networks with with bounded mean delay, and bounded delay jitter. The focus of this survey is general wireless random access networks; therefore, the above works focusing particularly on WLANs will not be further detailed.

In [14], an MPR-based MAC protocol with adaptive resource allocation is proposed for a MIMO/OFDM-based WLAN. The idea of MPR is applied through a request-to-send/clear-to-send-(RTS/CTS-) based MAC protocol along with MUD to resolve the collision problem. A realistic collision model is employed, taking into consideration the PHY layer parameters such as channel information, space-time-coded beam-forming, and multiuser detection, as well as subcarrier, bit, and power allocation. Several numerical results show that this PHY-MAC cross-layer optimization enhances the throughput of the system, because MPR can greatly reduce the probability of collisions.

In [15], contention resolution algorithms are proposed for MPR in a slotted Aloha WLAN. These algorithms require centralized information, the retransmission probability computed by the base station. Based on this information, the algorithm chooses the optimal retransmission probability to maximize the expectation of the system throughput conditioned on the number of retransmitting terminals.

Table 2 lists the realization of MPR in a WLAN.

4. Protocols with MPR

As discussed in the previous section, a set of technologies enable MPR capability for wireless nodes, and each has easy and hard parts in practice. MPR has also been proven to

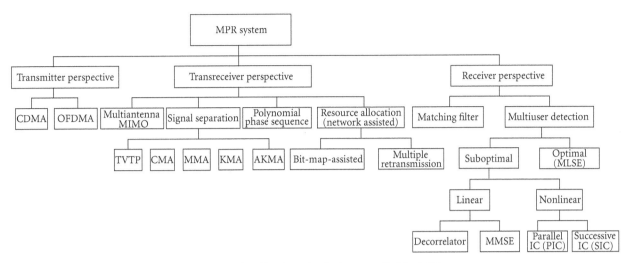

FIGURE 3: Classification of techniques applied for MPR.

TABLE 2: WLAN with MPR.

Protocol	MPR realization	MPR adaptation	Performance results	Works
Zheng's	Multiple antennas on AP	Modified CTS	Maximum throughput scale with k (k-MPR)	[1]
Huang's	MIMO with multiple antennas	Allocation scheme	5.2 packets/ms (with MIMO) 3.1 packets/ms (SPR)	[14]
DFT IFT	Spreading-centralized control by AP	Contention resolution	77.3% of theoretical throughput 69.7%	[15]

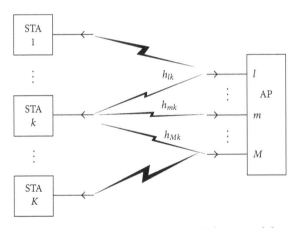

FIGURE 4: System configuration for uplink MPR in [1].

improve the network capacity in various works reviewed in Section 2. At the same time, MPR introduces greater challenges in network protocol design, and it requires closer interactions between the layers of the wireless network. We consider the design and analysis of MAC and networking protocols which employ adaptations to fully utilize MPR capability.

4.1. MAC with MPR. Mergen and Tong [8] proposed a multiple-access protocol based on receiver controlled transmission (RCT). RCT is a hybrid scheduled and random access MAC, which applies scheduling to determine the receiving nodes and then the transmitters for each receiving

node. RCT aims to maximize local throughput by granting an appropriate subset of users so that the varying levels of MPR capability are exploited. The simulation results show that using RCT with MPR achieves almost double the local throughput of the slotted Aloha protocol. Although this first work pointed out that adaptation on the MAC layer is necessary to fully exploit MPR capability, the proposed scheduling works with predefined network topologies and is hard to extend to general ad hoc networks.

Later in [16], Zhao and Tong designed a multiqueue service room (MQSR) protocol, which exploits MPR capability to handle users with different quality of service constraints. For each slot, the number of users is computed to maximize the expected number of successfully received packets. The performance of MQSR is compared with slotted Aloha and URN [3] with 2-MPR. The URN protocol manages to optimally adapt to the network load. In Figure 5, both MQSR and URN can extend the network capacity. But MQSR approaches the maximum throughput upon the transmission probability $P = 0.5$, while URN and slotted Aloha achieve their maximum throughput when P close to 1.

Yu and Giannakis associate a contention tree algorithm with SIC to propose SICTA in [45]. They aim to create a collision resolution access protocol, from the packet point of view. It turns out to be an interesting approach for MPR. Performance metrics including throughput and delay are analyzed to establish that SICTA outperforms existing contention tree algorithms reaching 0.693 in stable throughput.

Celik et al. point out in [17, 46] that the near-far problem reminds an important factor which degrades the throughput and the fairness in a wireless network even with

TABLE 3: MAC with MPR.

Protocol	MPR adaptation	Performance results	Works
RCT	Scheduling, reception feedback	4.7 packet/slot (MPR) 2.5 packet/slot (SPR)	[8]
MQSR	Estimation of the state of users	Max throughput with $P = 0.5$ (MPR) Max throughput with $P = 1$ (optimal SPR)	[16]
GDP	Switching between two transmission probabilities	Improved overall throughput and fairness	[17]
CMGPQ	Cooperative multigroup priority queuing	30% improvement on throughput under light load ($P < 0.6$)	[18]

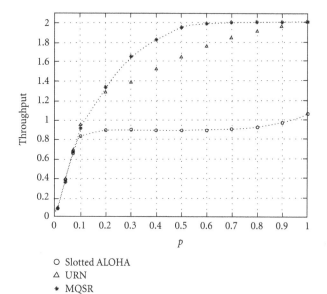

○ Slotted ALOHA
△ URN
∗ MQSR

FIGURE 5: Throughput of MQSR.

MPR capability. To overcome this problem, they added an alternative model to the MAC protocol in which a node decreases its transmission probability following success and increases it following failure. This approach makes no sense in the conventional collision model, but was proved to outperform the standard model in terms of both throughput and fairness in a network with MPR capability. They also present a modified contention window technique as the easier implementation of GDP protocol. The most important contribution of [17, 46] is that a MAC protocol designed for MPR may diverge from the traditional backoff mechanisms in random access.

Reference [18] proposed a dynamic multi-group priority queueing protocol to exploit the cooperative diversity for improving the system throughput. Cooperative diversity is a well-established notion in MIMO systems; it can be also applied on MAC protocol design for MPR. The proposed cooperative multi-group priority queueing MAC protocol has two independent parts, one in the base station and the other in the wireless nodes, so it is based on a server-client model, which is not scalable.

4.2. Network-Layer Adaptation. Wang and Garcia-Luna-Aceves analyzed the performance upper bound of joint routing and scheduling for wireless ad hoc networks that

embrace interference by using MPR [2]. They propose a polynomial-time heuristic algorithm to approximate the optimal solution which consists of route selection followed by link scheduling. By maximizing the number of node-disjoint multipaths, the throughput can better approximate the performance upper bound (Table 3). A simple example to illustrate is given in Figure 6.

In case Figure 6(b), two links can be scheduled to transmit in each time slot and fully exploit the MPR capability.

The routing and link scheduling in MPR is still an open topic. To fully exploit MPR, appropriate routing algorithm and scheduling schemes should be designed. A set of parameters could be optimized, such as schedule length or number of simultaneous paths in the network.

In [19], Crichigno et al. address the minimum length scheduling problem in one-hop multiaccess networks. They define the capacity region as the closure of the convex hull of a set of rate vectors. Figure 7 gives an example of the capacity region extension of 2-MPR over a single user channel. The function $\varphi i(P/\eta)$ denotes the channel capacity for a given reception power P and a given channel noise η. The upper bound capacity is achieved at sum rate, and the length of a schedule is minimized when concurrent transmitters operate at these sum points. They propose a linear program for the Minimum Length Scheduling Problem (MLSP) which their representation defines.

Reference [20] studies the neighbor discovery algorithm by incorporate multi-packet reception capability. Jeon and Ephremides consider neighbor discovery by incorporating MPR and Physical-Layer signal processing. They adopt the viewpoint of random set theory (RST) to propose a method for estimating the set of transmitting neighbors.

Almost simultaneously, Zeng et al. studied the time for achieving neighbor discovery on an arbitrary node with MPR [21]. For an idealized MPR network, the time for all the nodes to discover their respective neighbors is $\Theta(\ln n)$ when a simple Aloha-like algorithm is used. With a more realistic k-MPR model, they show that the time to discover all neighbors is $\Theta(n \ln n/k)$. Table 4 lists the discussed works related to networking. A trend of a cross-layer approach to better exploit the MPR advantages is introduced by these works. In the next part, we detail an example realized on a network with scheduling.

4.3. Scheduling for Multihop Routing with MPR. Reference [2] proposed to maximize the number of node-disjoint

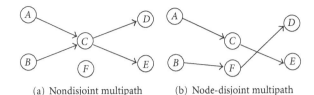

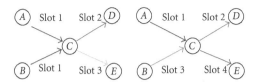

FIGURE 8: node-disjoint multipath is not optimal for MPR.

(a) Nondisjoint multipath   (b) Node-disjoint multipath

FIGURE 6: Influence of node-disjoint routing on link scheduling in [2].

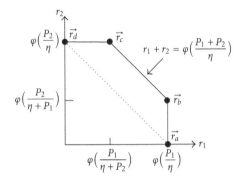

FIGURE 7: Capacity region of a multiaccess channel for a receiver node receiving data from two simultaneous transmitters.

TABLE 4: Networking with MPR.

Protocol	Problem	Works
Wang's	Joint routing and scheduling	[2]
HS for LP-MLSP	Maximum length of scheduling	[19]
RST-based estimation	Neighbor discover	[20]
Zeng's	Neighbor discover	[21]

multi-paths with joint routing and scheduling, but by using node-disjoint paths, at any time slot, each receiver only receives one packet for relaying. The intermediate nodes in routing paths cannot be effective MPR receivers. Figure 8 gives an example with two data flows (A to D via C, and B to E via C). Ideally, C could benefit from its 2-MPR to receive simultaneously from A and B at slot 1 and use the next two slots to transmit the received packets to D and E. But with node-disjoint paths, it requires four slots to transport two flows. This example also shows that the intermediate nodes in a wireless network might become bottlenecks for throughput.

Adopting the notation of the one-hop scheduling problem as defined in [19], the channel capacity for a K-MPR receiver is

$$\varphi_v = \varphi\left(\frac{\sum_{i \in S_v} P_{iv}}{\eta}\right),\tag{11}$$

where φ_v is the channel capacity of the receiver v for a given reception power P_v on it. For a general number of transceivers, the sum of transmission rates is within the channel capacity given in (11). Therefore, we have the following inequality:

$$\sum_{i \in S_v} r_{iv} \le \varphi_v\left(\frac{\sum_{i \in S_v} P_{iv}}{\eta}\right),\tag{12}$$

where r_{iv} denotes the transmission rate on i to v.

For M data flows, we denote the source and the destination of mth flow s_m and d_m. The flow rate on a directed link (u, v) is denoted by f_{uv}^m. It is worth noting that this flow rate is an average rate and the transmission rate r_{uv}^m could be much higher for an intermediate receiver. For instance, if node v decodes k packets from different transmitters including u and takes t_r slots to relay the received packets, then the relation between flow rate f_{uv}^m and transmission rate r_{uv}^m can be expressed as

$$\frac{1}{f_{uv}^m} = \frac{t_r + 1}{r_{uv}^m}.\tag{13}$$

4.3.1. Problem Formulation of TMP. We formulate the Throughput Maximizing Problem (TMP) for multi-flow multi-hop communications in [47] as follows.

Definition 1. Maximize the sum of flow rate reaching all destinations:

$$\text{Maximize} \sum_{m=1}^{M} \sum_{i} r_{id_m}^m \tag{14}$$

subject to the following three constraints:

(1) flow conservation constraint:

$$\sum_{i} r_{ij}^m = \sum_{j} r_{ji}^m; \qquad \sum_{i} r_{s_m i}^m = \sum_{i} r_{id_m}^m; \tag{15}$$

(2) receiver constraint:

$$\forall v \in \rho, \quad |S_v| \le K; \tag{16}$$

(3) transmitter constraint:

$$\sum_{i \in S_v} r_{iv} = \varphi\left(\frac{\sum_{i \in S_v} P_{iv}}{\eta}\right).\tag{17}$$

We have adopted the flow conservation constraint (15) from [2]. However, the other two constraints are different.

Receiver Constraint. A receiver v cannot decode more than K packets at the same time, and hence the number of transmitters in S_v should be limited to K for any slot. This constraint covers the receiver's pair-wise interference.

Transmitter Constraint. Each transmitter should operate at sumrate to fully explore the bandwidth of the receiver's multiuser channel, as given in (11).

By resolving TMP as an optimization problem, we can obtain a performance upper bound. Similar problems have been shown to be NP-hard [2, 48]. The size of our optimization problem increases exponentially with the number of routing paths. Let us focus more on the computation of its upper bound with ideal time-space scheduling.

4.3.2. Heuristic Scheme with Distributed Scheduling on k-CDS. A heuristic approach with distributed scheduling based on a k-CDS backbone can approximate the upper bound. The k-CDS (k-connected dominating set) [49] in a network is a set of nodes which is k-dominating and k-connected, meaning that every node in the network is either in the k-CDS or has k neighbors in it. The subgraph of this node set is k-vertex connected. The properties of k-dominating and k-connected are a perfect match for intermediate relay nodes to exploit MPR capability, because each of them is required to collaborate with at least $K + 1$ neighbors for both receptions and transmissions.

(i) If a receiver is a k-dominated node, then the set consisting of all its k-dominating nodes is the schedulable set S.

(ii) If a receiver is a dominating node in k-CDS, then the k-connected property guarantees that it is connected to at least k dominating nodes. These nodes can be selected to form schedulable set S for each reception slot.

(iii) If a transmitter is a k-dominated node, then it could schedule with k dominating nodes to transmit.

(iv) If a transmitter is a dominating node, then it could schedule with k dominating neighbors to transmit.

Based on the k-CDS backbone, only dominating nodes are selected as intermediate relay nodes for multi-hop routing and a dominated node does not participate in the routing unless it is the source or the destination of a flow. This simple rule reduces the complexity of design time-space scheduling in the network.

Many algorithms tend to generate a minimal k-CDS, but the transmission will be too concentrated to this set of nodes. On the other hand, a high cardinality means little reduction from the original network topology, which is not efficient to reduce the complexity of the scheduling based on the $(K + 1)$-CDS. This tradeoff on the cardinality of a $(K + 1)$-CDS can be calculated as follows. Let us assume that the average routing path length is pl. The dominated nodes only participate in the first-hop communications as source nodes or in the last-hop communications as destination nodes, while the dominating nodes can take part in each hop in a

routing path. By assuming the scheduling has a good fairness for all nodes, the amount of flows that the dominated nodes take is approximately

$$T(k - \text{CDS}) = \frac{K + 2}{(K + 1) * (pl - 1)}. \tag{18}$$

To meet the above constraints, we develop a construction algorithm based on a coverage rule [50]. Each node verifies if any pair of its neighbors are k-connected via node-disjoint paths and a higher ID's rule is added to avoid mutual decision blocking. This verification is known as the k-Coverage condition. To realize this algorithm in a distributed and localized manner, nodes exchange their routing tables with their neighbors. The k-Coverage condition is checked via the routing table to count the number of node-disjoint paths from any pair of neighbors.

The $(K + 1)$-CDS construction algorithm results in a backbone for multi-path routing. We present here a transmitter-receiver scheduling to fully exploit K-MPR capability on dominating and dominated nodes, which allows the use of multiple paths for each flow to eliminate bottlenecks on the intermediate nodes.

A potential transmitter i constructs a receiver set ξ_i. The receivers are ordered in each set along with their distances to the final destination d_m in number of hops. If d_m belongs to $N(i)$, the neighbor set of i, then $\{\xi_i\}$ contains only d_m.

With the link scheduling algorithm, a receiver aims to let transmitters operate at a rate based on $(K + 1)$-CDS. It schedules transmitter nodes with the priority pr_i in an arbitrary order. Every node's priority is set to minimal before any transmissions. A transmitter node i is chosen, and checks its possible receivers set ξ_i. If the transmitter finds a receiver v who can receive more flows, then it will be added in the receiver's schedulable set S_v. If the transmitter node cannot find any available receiver, then its priority pr_i will be increased. Hence, during the next time slot, the transmitter i has a higher priority than other transmitters and will be added to the schedulable set sooner.

For each transmitter allowed to transmit, the algorithm selects the corresponding temporary datarate, according to the sum-rate constraint. For a schedulable set $S_v = \{u_1, u_2, \ldots, u_K\}$, the corresponding data-rates are

$$r_1' = \varphi_v\left(\frac{P_1}{\eta}\right); \qquad r_K' = \varphi_v\left(\frac{P_K}{\eta + \sum_{j=0}^{K-1} P_j}\right). \tag{19}$$

The sum of all the data rates is equal to $\varphi_v((\sum_{i \in S_v} P_i)/\eta)$. Those data rates obey the sum-rate constraint, whatever the number of transmitters in schedulable set S_v. The link scheduling algorithm allows the transmitter i an amount of time $t_i = T/K$, where T is the time slot duration. This ensures that all transmitters will have the same time slot fraction to send their data. Since the first temporary data rate is much higher than the others, the channel utilization needs to be respread to the selected transmitters in order to achieve fairness and avoid generating bottlenecks on the low-rate transmitters. As a result, the overall throughput can be improved.

The final data rates also obey the sum-rate constraint. Let $b_i^m(t)$ be the transmitter i's initial amount of data to send during time slot t for the flow m. The amount of effectively transmitted data is $t_i \times r_i$ and hence the remaining amount of data to transmit for the flow m can be represented as $b_i^m(t+1) = b_i^m(t) - t_i \times r_i$. The transmitter i's priority pr_i will be increased, if $b_i^m(t+1)$ is not equal to 0.

4.3.3. Performance Evaluation. We set the channel bandwidth $W = 1\,\mathrm{MHz}$, transmission power $P_0 = 1W$, and path loss exponent $\gamma = 3$. In a square of $300*300$, 50 transmitters are randomly generated. According to low-noise SNR condition ($\mathrm{SNR_{ref}} = 10\,\mathrm{dB}$), $\mathrm{SNR_{ref}} = P_0 d_{\mathrm{ref}}^{-\gamma}/\eta$, and the maximal distance between two nodes $d_{\mathrm{ref}} = 44\,\mathrm{m}$, we can obtain that η is equal to $1,16.10^{-6}\,\mathrm{W}$.

The numerical results on upper bound of TMP are obtained through lpslove [51], a mixed linear programming solver. We simulate our heuristic-based $(K + 1)$-CDS and heuristic based on node-disjoint path [2] in NetLogo4.1 simulator [52]. We performed 100 simulations with a duration of 2000 time slots. For each flow injected in the network, it has fixed source and destination. And it generates one packet per time slot in a saturation condition.

The metrics used are as follows: the throughput represents the number of flows which arrive at destinations during a predefined number of time slots; the average delay represents the difference between the moment the flow was sent and the moment it is received; the average acceptance ratio is the ratio of traffic accepted to the total traffic demand.

The overall throughput results obtained are shown in Figure 9 with a 3D representation. The throughput upper bound describes the maximal amount of occupied reception time slots at all destinations, which is independent of the number of flows. However, it is shown that it increases with MPR capability. Our heuristic based on $(K + 1)$-CDS outperforms the heuristic with node-disjoint paths on almost all simulation settings. The node-disjoint heuristic reaches the limit very quickly with the increase of number of flows, because node-disjoint paths are fewer than the routing paths on k-CDS. Our heuristic has a higher throughput limit, although it decreases when the number of flows is large (15 flows).

We also note that there is a local highest throughput for K-MPR. The throughput of 3-MPR is highest. It is also confirmed in Figure 10. This is a very interesting observation that the throughput decreases when K becomes bigger with both heuristics. One possible explanation is that the 4-MPR capability requires a much higher density to be fully exploited. The increase of node degree results in more links interfering with each other, which could decrease the network throughput. For our heuristic, the decrease of throughput with 4-MPR is also related to our link scheduling algorithm, particularly the way we spread the receiver's channel capacity between its transmitters. Indeed, the increase of channel capacity is not very large with MPR capability, while the amount of data to send is much higher (Figure 11).

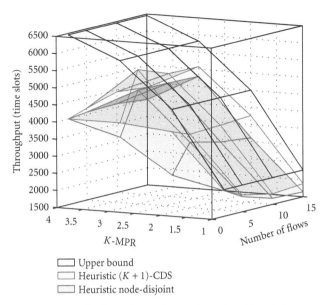

FIGURE 9: The throughput of upper bound and heuristics.

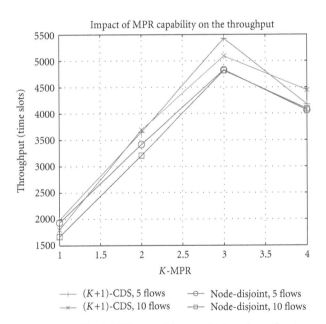

FIGURE 10: The 3-MPR can achieve the highest throughput.

Figure 12 shows that the average delay of a flow increases with the number of flows. Despite that, using MPR can reduce flow delay by around 20% compared to the single reception model. The increase of delay also confirms the presence of bottlenecks, which also cause a degradation of the flow acceptance ratio as indicated in Figure 13. Again, MPR could improve the acceptance ratio by using time-space scheduling to avoid bottleneck generation.

5. Conclusion

The capacity of current wireless random access networks is constrained mainly by concurrent packet transmissions.

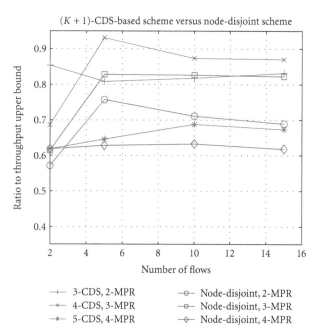

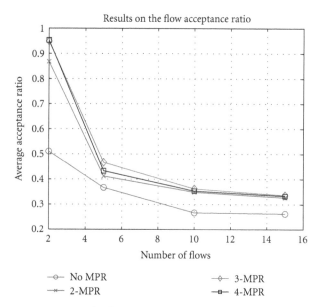

FIGURE 11: The heuristics' efficiency, subject to upper bound.

FIGURE 13: The flow acceptance ratio of K-MPR chutes.

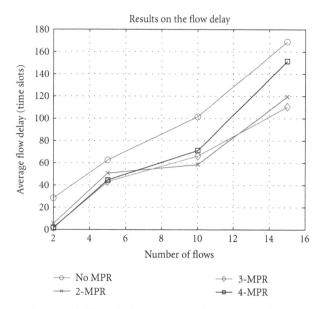

FIGURE 12: The delay increases with the number of flows.

already been applied to telecommunication services, but for wireless networks with typical random access protocols (such as MAC and Network); the protocols should be revised to fully exploit the advantage of MPR. One direction is to jointly consider routing and scheduling. We detailed such work in this paper with extensive performance comparisons. The intent of this paper is to provide a good starting point for future exploration in the area.

Acknowledgments

This research was supported by NSF of China under grant no. 60773091, no. 61100210 and Doctoral Program foundation of Institutions of Higher Education of China under Grant no. 20110073120021.

Multi-access techniques are investigated to avoid concurrent access to the medium. MPR provides another way to shift the responsibility from the transmitters to the receivers. Originally, MPR techniques were proposed for mobile communication systems and then later introduced to wireless random access networks. Therefore, it is important to survey the techniques that enable MPR and in particular those that are applicable for wireless random access networks. This paper provides such a survey.

We also list and compare all the results on the network capacity, throughput, and stability and classify the research efforts on protocol design. Basic MPR techniques have

References

[1] P. X. Zheng, Y. J. Zhang, and S. C. Liew, "Multipacket reception in wireless local area networks," in *Proceedings of the IEEE International Conference on Communications*, vol. 8, pp. 3670–3675, Istanbul, Turkey, June 2006.

[2] X. Wang and J. J. Garcia-Luna-Aceves, "Embracing interference in ad hoc networks using joint routing and scheduling with multiple packet reception," in *Proceedings of the 27th Int'l Conference on Computer Communications (INFOCOM '08)*, pp. 843–851, Phoenix, Ariz, USA, April 2008.

[3] L. Kleinrock and Y. Yemini, "An optimal adaptive scheme for multiple access broadcast communication," in *Proceedings of the Int'l Conference on Communications*, pp. 721–725, Toronto, Canada, 1978.

[4] R. Nelson and L. Kleinrock, "The spatial capacity of a Slotted ALOHA multihop packet radio network with capture," *IEEE Transactions on Communications*, vol. 32, no. 6, pp. 684–694, 1984.

[5] S. Ghez, S. Verdu, and S. C. Schwartz, "Stability properties of slotted Aloha with multipacket receptionca-pability," *IEEE*

Transactions on Automatic Control, vol. 33, no. 7, pp. 640–649, 1988.

[6] S. Ghez, S. Verdu, and S. C. Schwartz, "Optimal decentralized control in the random access multipacket channel," *IEEE Transactions on Automatic Control*, vol. 34, no. 11, pp. 1153–1163, 1989.

[7] I. Chlamtac and A. Farago, "An optimal channel access protocol with multiple reception capacity," *IEEE Transactions on Computers*, vol. 43, no. 4, pp. 480–484, 1994.

[8] G. Mergen and L. Tong, "Receiver controlled medium access in multihop ad hoc networks with multipacket reception," in *Proceedings of the Military Communication Conference (MILCOM '01)*, vol. 2, pp. 1014–1018, Vienna, Austria, October 2001.

[9] M. Coupechoux, T. Lestable, C. Bonnet, and V. Kumar, "Throughput of the multi-hop slotted aloha with multi-packet reception," *Wireless On-Demand Network Systems*, vol. 2928, pp. 239–243, 2004.

[10] J. J. Garcia-Luna-Aceves, H. R. Sadjadpour, and Z. Wang, "Challenges: towards truly scalable ad hoc networks," in *Proceedings of the 13th Annual ACM Int'l Conference on Mobile Computing and Networking (MobiCom)*, pp. 207–214, Montreal, Canada, September 2007.

[11] J. J. Garcia-Luna-Aceves, H. R. Sadjadpour, and Z. Wang, "Extending the capacity of ad hoc networks beyond network coding," in *Proceedings of the Int'l Conference on Wireless Communications and Mobile Computing (IWCMC '07)*, pp. 91–96, Honolulu, Hawaii, USA, August 2007.

[12] Z. Wang, H. R. Sadjadpou, and J. J. Garcia-Luna-Aceves, "The capacity and energy efficiency of wireless Ad Hoc networks with multi-packet reception," in *Proceedings of the 9th ACM International Symposium on Mobile Ad Hoc Networking and Computing*, pp. 179–188, Hong Kong, China, May 2008.

[13] M. F. Guo, X. Wang, and M. Y. Wu, "On the capacity of k-MPR wireless networks," *IEEE Transactions on Wireless Communications*, vol. 8, no. 7, pp. 3878–3886, 2009.

[14] W. Huang, K. Letaief, and Y. Zhang, "Cross-layer multi-packet reception based medium access control and resource allocation for space-time coded MIMO/OFDM," *IEEE Transaction on Wireless Communications*, vol. 7, pp. 3372–3384, 2008.

[15] J. B. Seo and V. C. M. Leung, "Design and analysis of cross-layer contention resolution algorithms for multi-packet reception slotted ALOHA systems," in *Proceedings of the 18th International Conference on Computer Communications and Networks (ICCCN '09)*, pp. 1–6, August 2009.

[16] Q. Zhao and L. Tong, "A multiqueue service room MAC protocol for wireless networks with multipacket reception," *IEEE/ACM Transactions on Networking*, vol. 11, no. 1, pp. 125–137, 2003.

[17] G. D. Celik, G. Zussman, W. F. Khan, and E. Modiano, "MAC for networks with multipacket reception capability and spatially distributed nodes," in *Proceedings of the 27th IEEE Communications Society Conference on Computer Communications*, pp. 1436–1444, Phoenix, Ariz, USA, April 2008.

[18] W. F. Yang, J. Y. Wu, and T. S. Lee, "An enhanced multi-packet reception MAC protocol: cooperative approach," in *Proceedings of the 3rd International Conference on Communications and Networking in China (ChinaCom '08)*, pp. 516–520, August 2008.

[19] J. Crichigno, M. Y. Wu, and W. Shu, "Minimum length scheduling in single-hop multiple access wireless networks," in *Proceedings of the IEEE International Conference on Communications*, Captown, South Africa, May 2010.

[20] J. Jeon and A. Ephremides, "Neighbor discovery in a wireless sensor network: multipacket reception capability and physical-layer signal processing," in *Proceedings of the 48th Annual Allerton Conference on Communication, Control, and Computing*, pp. 310–317, October 2010.

[21] W. Zeng, X. Chen, A. Russell, S. Vasudevan, B. Wang, and W. Wei, "Neighbor discovery in wireless netzorks with multipacket reception," in *Proceedings of the ACM Int'l Symposium on Mobile Ad Hoc Networking and Computing (MobiHoc '11)*, Paris, France, May 2011.

[22] K. Sakakibara, M. Hanaoka, and Y. Yuba, "On the cusp catastrophe of slotted ALOHA systems with capture and multi-packet reception," in *Proceedings of the IEEE Global Telecommunications Conference*, vol. 5, pp. 3093–3098, Sydney, Australia, November 1998.

[23] L. Tong, Q. Zhao, and G. Mergen, "Multipacket reception in random access wireless networks: from signal processing to optimal medium access control," *IEEE Communications Magazine*, vol. 39, no. 11, pp. 108–112, 2001.

[24] M. F. Guo, X. Wang, and M. Y. Wu, "On the capacity of k-MPR wireless networks using multi-channel multi-interface," in *Proceedings of the Int'l Conference on Wireless Communications and Mobile Computing (IWCMC '09)*, pp. 665–669, Leipzig, Germany, June 2009.

[25] Z. Wang, H. R. Sadjadpour, and J. J. Garcia-Luna-Aceves, "Fundamental limits of information dissemination in wireless ad hoc networks-part II: multi-packet reception," *IEEE Transactions on Wireless Communications*, vol. 10, no. 3, pp. 803–813, 2011.

[26] V. Naware, G. Mergen, and L. Tong, "Stability and delay of finite-user slotted ALOHA with multipacket reception," *IEEE Transactions on Information Theory*, vol. 51, no. 7, pp. 2636–2656, 2005.

[27] A. Dua, "Random access with multi-packet reception," *IEEE Transactions on Wireless Communications*, vol. 7, no. 6, pp. 2280–2288, 2008.

[28] N. Pappas, A. Ephremides, and A. Traganitis, "Stability and performance issues of a relay assisted multiple access scheme with MPR capabilities," in *Proceedings of the International Symposium of on Modeling and Optimization of Mobile, Ad Hoc, and Wireless Networks (WiOpt '11)*, pp. 110–116, May 2011.

[29] N. Pappas, A. Ephremides, and A. P. Traganitis, "Relay-Assisted Multiple Access with Multi-Packet Reception Capability and Simultaneous Transmission and Reception," in *Information Theory Workshop (ITW), 2011 IEEE*, pp. 578–582, October 2011.

[30] R. M. D. Moraes, H. R. Sadjadpour, and J. J. Garcia-Luna-Aceves, "Many-to-many communication: a new approach for collaboration in MANETs," in *Proceedings of the 26th IEEE International Conference on Computer Communications (INFOCOM '07)*, pp. 1829–1837, Anchorage, Alaska, USA, May 2007.

[31] A. J. Van der Veen and L. Tong, "Packet separation in wireless ad-hoc networks by know modulus algorithms," in *Proceedings of the IEEE International Conference on Acoustic, Speech, and Signal Processing (ICASSP '02)*, vol. 3, pp. 2149–2152, Orlando, Fla, USA, May 2002.

[32] J. Y. Wu, W. F. Yang, L. C. Wang, and T. S. Lee, "Signal modulus design for blind source separation via algebraic known modulus algorithm: a perturbation perspective," in *Proceedings of the IEEE International Symposium on Circuits and Systems*, pp. 3013–3016, Seattle, Wash, USA, May 2008.

[33] R. Babu and R. Kumar, "Blind equalization using Constant Modulus algorithm and Multi-Modulus Al-gorithm in wireless communication systems," *International Journal of Computer Applications*, vol. 1, no. 3, pp. 40–45, 2010.

[34] A. G. Orozco-Lugo, M. M. Lara, D. C. McLernon, and H. J. Muro-Lemus, "Multiple packet reception in wireless ad hoc networks using polynomial phase-modulating sequences," *IEEE Transactions on Signal Processing*, vol. 51, no. 8, pp. 2093–2110, 2003.

[35] M. K. Tsatsanis, R. Zhang, and S. Banerjee, "Network-assisted diversity for random access wireless networks," *IEEE Transactions on Signal Processing*, vol. 48, no. 3, pp. 702–711, 2000.

[36] X. Wang and J. K. Tugnait, "A bit-map-assisted dynamic queue protocol for multiaccess wireless networks with multiple packet reception," *IEEE Transactions on Signal Processing*, vol. 51, no. 8, pp. 2068–2081, 2003.

[37] S. Verdu, "Minimum probability of error for asynchronous Gaussian multiple access channels," *IEEE Transactions on Information Theory*, vol. 32, no. 1, pp. 85–96, 1986.

[38] A. Li, M. Wang, X. Li, and H. Kayama, "A cross-layer design on the basis of multiple packet reception in asynchronous wireless network," in *Proceedings of the IEEE International Conference on Communications*, pp. 3477–3484, June 2007.

[39] R. Lupas and S. Verdu, "Near-far resistance of multiuser detectors in asynchronous channels," *IEEE Transactions on Communications*, vol. 38, no. 4, pp. 496–508, 1990.

[40] R. M. Buehrer, N. S. Correal, and B. D. Woerner, "A comparison of multiuser receivers for cellular CDMA," in *Proceedings of the Global Telecommunications Conference (Globecom '96)*, pp. 1571–1577, London, UK, November 1996.

[41] Y. J. Zhang, S. C. Liew, and D. R. Chen, "Delay analysis for wireless local area networks with multipacket reception under finite load," in *Proceedings of the IEEE Global Telecommunications Conference (GLOBECOM '08)*, pp. 1–6, New Orleans, La, USA, November 2008.

[42] Y. J. Zhang, P. X. Zheng, and S. C. Liew, "How does multiple-packet reception capability scale the performance of wireless local area networks?" *IEEE Transactions on Mobile Computing*, vol. 8, no. 7, pp. 923–935, 2009.

[43] Y. J. Zhang, S. C. Liew, and D. R. Chen, "Sustainable throughput of wireless lans with multipacket reception capability under bounded delay-moment requirements," *IEEE Transactions on Mobile Computing*, vol. 9, no. 9, pp. 1226–1241, 2010.

[44] Y. J. Zhang, "Multi-round contention in wireless LANs with multipacket reception," *IEEE Transactions on Wireless Communications*, vol. 9, no. 4, pp. 1503–1513, 2010.

[45] Y. Yu and G. B. Giannakis, "SICTA: a 0.693 contention tree algorithm using successive interference cancellation," in *Proceedings of the IEEE International Conference on Computer Communications (INFOCOM '05)*, pp. 1908–1916, March 2005.

[46] G. D. Celik, G. Zussman, W. F. Khan, and E. Modiano, "MAC for networks with multipacket reception capability and spatially distributed nodes," *IEEE Transactions on Mobile Computing*, vol. 9, no. 2, pp. 226–240, 2010.

[47] J. Lu, P. Vandenhove, W. Shu, and M. Wu, "Enhancing throughput in wireless multi-hop network with multiple packet reception," in *Proceedings of the IEEE Int'l Conference on Communications*, pp. 1–5, Kyoto, Japan, 2011.

[48] M. Kodialam and T. Nandagopal, "Characterizing achievable rates in multi-hop wireless networks: the joint routing and scheduling problem," in *Proceedings of the 9th Annual International Conference on Mobile Computing and Networking (MobiCom '03)*, pp. 42–54, San Diego, CA, USA, September 2003.

[49] F. Dai and J. Wu, "On constructing k-connected k-dominating set in wireless ad hoc and sensor networks," *Journal of Parallel and Distributed Computing*, vol. 66, no. 7, pp. 947–958, 2006.

[50] J. Wu and F. Dai, "A generic distributed broadcast scheme in ad hoc wireless networks," *IEEE Transactions on Computers*, vol. 53, no. 10, pp. 1343–1354, 2004.

[51] lp slove 5.5., http://lpsolve.sourceforge.net.

[52] NetLogo, http://ccl.northwestern.edu/netlogo/.

Formal Analysis of SET and NSL Protocols Using the Interpretation Functions-Based Method

Hanane Houmani[1] and Mohamed Mejri[2]

[1]*EAS Group, ENSEM, Hassan II University, Casablanca, Morocco*
[2]*LSFM Group, Laval University, Quebec, QC, Canada*

Correspondence should be addressed to Hanane Houmani, hanane.houmani@ift.ulaval.ca

Academic Editor: Chi-Yao Weng

Most applications in the Internet such as e-banking and e-commerce use the SET and the NSL protocols to protect the communication channel between the client and the server. Then, it is crucial to ensure that these protocols respect some security properties such as confidentiality, authentication, and integrity. In this paper, we analyze the SET and the NSL protocols with respect to the confidentiality (secrecy) property. To perform this analysis, we use the interpretation functions-based method. The main idea behind the interpretation functions-based technique is to give sufficient conditions that allow to guarantee that a cryptographic protocol respects the secrecy property. The flexibility of the proposed conditions allows the verification of daily-life protocols such as SET and NSL. Also, this method could be used under different assumptions such as a variety of intruder abilities including algebraic properties of cryptographic primitives. The NSL protocol, for instance, is analyzed with and without the homomorphism property. We show also, using the SET protocol, the usefulness of this approach to correct weaknesses and problems discovered during the analysis.

1. Motivations and Background

Intuitively, cryptographic protocols are communication protocols that involve cryptography to reach some specific security goals (authentication, secrecy, etc.). Today, these protocols are playing a key role in our daily life. Among others, they protect our banking transactions (e-commerce protocol), our access to private wired and wireless network, and our access to a variety of indispensable services (web, FTP, e-mail, etc.).

Obviously, any flaws in such protocols can have heavy negative consequences on individuals and organizations. It is also a well-known fact that attacks exploiting cryptographic protocols flaws are generally very difficult to detect: tools such as intrusion detections and firewalls are helpless against them since it is difficult (even impossible some-times) to distinguish between legitimate and illegitimate users when the cryptographic protocol is flawed.

Like any sensitive system, cryptographic protocols need to be seriously studied and their correctness should be rigorously analyzed and ideally proved. For that reason, formal specification and verification of security protocols have received much attention in recent years. Some of these works including comparative studies could be found in [1–10].

Today and after more of thirty years of hard work, international community has a better understanding of cryptographic protocols and better support to specify and analyze them. But there remains a lot of work to do in this field. Some of the most important drawbacks of the existing results is that they are limited by either the class of protocols that they can analyze or the context (e.g., limited intruder abilities) in which they can analyze them. For instance, the method described in [11] gives an algorithm that allows to analyze the *pingpong* protocols in a polynomial time but only within the encryption of atomic and closed messages. Others like [12–23] are dedicated to a specific intruder capacity which is usually the standard Dolev and Yao model. These two parameters (the class of the analyzed protocols and the context in which they are analyzed) are generally hard-coded inside the approach making its adaptation to another context or others protocols very difficult. Also, in [24], Paulson has proven that the Bull protocol preserves the secrecy by using an intruder model that does not consider any algebraic property of cryptographic primitives. However, he proved that attacks are possible on this protocol if some algebraic properties of $\oplus$ or of exponentiation are considered in the intruder model. Thereby, the flexibility of an approach to be adapted to different contexts of analysis is helpful to make the conditions of the analysis closer to the reality.

To deal with this problem, we have introduced in [25, 26] a general and flexible approach that allows to analyze a large variety of protocols in different contexts (different intruder capacities including equational theories) based on interpretation functions. The idea is to give some metaresults (independent of a specific context) that give sufficient conditions allowing to guarantee the correctness of a protocol with respect of the secrecy (confidentiality) property.

In this paper, we recall the main results of the approach and we show its efficiency and its flexibility by analyzing some famous cryptographic protocols such as SET protocol [27–29] and NSL protocol [30] under different assumptions. In fact, we first analyze the secrecy property of the NSL protocol in the Dolev and Yao intruder model and after that we consider the homomorphism property of the encryption. This analysis allows us to prove that the NSL protocol is secure in the Dolev and Yao model whereas it is not when considering the homomorphism encryption property and some weaknesses are found. Second, we analyze the secrecy property of SET protocol which could be considered the first analysis until now that concern this protocol and the secrecy property which is very important in such protocols that allow to transmit secret information such as the card credit number.

This paper is organized as follows. Section 2 gives an overview of the interpretation functions-based method. The analysis of the NSL protocol in different contexts is given in Section 3. Section 4 analyzes the SET protocol. Section 5 compares the interpretation functions-based method with some similar works like the rank functions-based method [31, 32] and the typing-based method [33]. Finally, some concluding remarks are given in Section 6.

2. Overview of the Interpretation Functions-Based Method

As stated before, the main idea of our approach is to propose some conditions that are proven (in [25, 26]) sufficient to guarantee the secrecy property of any protocol that respects them. The proposed conditions can be easily verified in PTIME, and they state intuitively that principals involved in the protocol should not decrease the security levels of sent components. The security level of an atomic message is either given within the context of verification (input information) or estimated from received messages. The security levels estimated from received messages is calculated by using some special function called safe interpretation functions.

TABLE 1: Example of increasing protocol.

1. $A \rightarrow B : \{\{A, B, secret\}_{k_b}\}_{k_a^{-1}}$
2. $B \rightarrow A : \{\{A, B, secret\}_{k_a}\}_{k_b^{-1}}$

TABLE 2: Exemple of deacreasing protocol.

1. $A \rightarrow B : \{\{A, B, secret\}_{k_b}\}_{k_a^{-1}}$
2. $B \rightarrow A : \{A, B, secret\}_{k_b^{-1}}$

A brief description about these notions could be found in the next sections. In fact, Section 2.1 gives the intuitive definition and some examples of increasing protocols. Section 2.2 presents the notion of safe interpretation functions. After that Section 2.3 presents the definition of the secrecy property (confidentiality). Finally, Section 2.4 states the main result and show how the interpretation functions-based method could be applied to analyze the secrecy property.

2.1. Increasing Protocols. The sufficient condition to guarantee the secrecy property could be summarized as follows. Principals involved in the protocol should not decrease the security levels of sent components. Protocols that satisfy this condition are called in this work "increasing protocols." For instance, the protocol described by Table 1 is increasing since the security level of the message *secret* in step 1 is the same in step 2. Indeed, in step 1 the message *secret* is encrypted by the secret key of A to say that the message is originated from A and also is encrypted by the public key of B to say that the message *secret* is destined to B, hence the security level of the message *secret* is the security level that allows only B and A to know it. In the same way, we can notice that the security level of the message *secret* in step 2 is the security level that allows B and A to know it and hence, the protocol does not decrease the security level of message *secret* form step to another and so the protocol is increasing.

Let us consider the protocol described by Table 2. This protocol is not increasing since the security level of the message *secret* in step 2 is lower than its security level in step 1. Indeed, in step 1 the message *secret* is encrypted by the secret key of A to say that the message is originated from A and also is encrypted by the public key of B to say that the message *secret* is destined to B, hence the security level of the message *secret* is the security level that allows only B and A to know it. In step 2, the message *secret* is encrypted by the secret key of B, so everybody could decrypt it and hence the security level of the message decreases from step 1 to step 2. The formal definition of decreasing protocol could be found in our previous works [25, 26].

2.2. Safe Interpretation Function. To verify whether a protocol is increasing, we need a safe means to correctly estimate the security levels of received components so that we can appropriately handle them. We called it "safe interpretation function" (The name of the approach (interpretation functions-based approach) come for this notions.). Among the important features of a safe interpretation function is that its results could not be misled by the intruder manipulations. For example, if the interpretation function estimates that the security level of a component α in a set of messages M is top secret, then the intruder can never produce M' from M such that the security level of α in M' is estimated by secret or public. A simple example of a safe interpretation function is the one that attributes a security level for a component α in a message m depending only on the direct keys encrypting α in m. This function, denoted by F_{DEK}, will be referred later by DEK (Direct Encryption Key). Accordingly, $F_{DEK}(N_b, \{S, N_b\}_{k_{ab}})$ calculates the security level of N_b in the message $\{S, N_b\}_{k_{ab}}$, and it is equal to the security level of k_{ab}. For example, if the security level of k_{ab} is $\{A, B\}$ then we have

$$F_{DEK}\left(N_b, \{S, N_b\}_{k_{ab}}\right) = \{A, B\}. \tag{1}$$

Another example of safe interpretation function, used in this paper, is the one that attributes a security level of a component α in a message m depending on both the direct keys encrypting α in m and the neighbors of α in m (the components that can be reached from α without going outside encryptions: usually we consider neighbors that are only identities of agents). This function, denoted by F_{DEKAN}, will be referred later by the DEKAN (direct encryption key and neighbors) function. Accordingly, $F_{DEKAN}(N_b, \{S, N_b\}_{k_{ab}})$ calculates the security level of N_b in the message $\{S, N_b\}_{k_{ab}}$, and it depends on both the security level of k_{ab} and S. For example, if the security level of k_{ab} is $\{A, B\}$ to design that is a shared secret between A and B, then we have

$$F_{DEKAN}\left(N_b, \{S, N_b\}_{k_{ab}}\right) = \{A, B, S\}. \tag{2}$$

The DEK function and the DEKAN function can be used to analyze a large variety of cryptographic protocols. When the analysis fails, we should either adapt the protocol or use another safe function. However, the definition of safe functions is a complicated task. For this reason, we have introduced in [25, 26, 34] a helpful guideline allowing to define a safe interpretation function having the following form:

$$F(\alpha, M) = I \circ S(\alpha, M). \tag{3}$$

The function S selects from M some atomic components on which the security level of α depends. This function is called a *selection function*. The function I interprets what S returns as a security type. This function is called a *rank function*. This type of rank functions has been already introduced and used by Schneider et al. in [31, 32, 35] to attribute to a message a security level (rank).

A simple way to define a selection function is to consider a term (a message in our case) as a tree where its arcs are annotated with real numbers that reflect costs or distances between nodes. After that, it will be easy to define S as a function that selects components that are at some distance from a given component. For instance, let m be the message $\langle B, \{N_b, k_{ab}\}_{k_{as}}\rangle$ then the representation of m can be

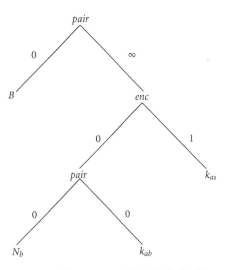

FIGURE 1: The message $(\langle B, \{N_b, k_{ab}\}_{k_{as}}\rangle)$.

described as shown by Figure 1, where the annotations of arcs are explained later.

Recall that the symbol *enc* is the encryption operator and the symbol *pair* is the concatenation operator. Hence, at distance 1, we could select the keys of encryption, and at distance 0 we could select components that are concatenated to some specific components.

Of course, not all the interpretation functions F which are the composition of the selection function S and a rank function I are safe (could not be misled by an intruder). In the sequel, we give some conditions that must be satisfied by the functions S and I so that their composition is safe. Intuitively, the conditions on the selection function S states that at least the direct encryption keys are selected and no components outside direct encryptions could be selected. The idea behind this condition is that only messages encrypted with a secret key could be safe from the intruder manipulations. For example $S(\alpha, \{S, R, \{\alpha, A, N_a, B, C\}_{k_1}\}_{k_2})$ should return k_1 and any subset in $\{A, N_a, B, C\}$. To exclude components outside encryption, we attribute ∞ as a cost between any *enc* node and its father.

In the other side, the conditions on the rank function I state intuitively that the security level of a message, given by this function, should not be greater than its real security level. The idea behind this condition is that the rank function could not give any security level to messages. For instance, if β is a public information (according to the function $\ulcorner \cdot \urcorner$ given within the context of analysis), then I cannot interpret it as secret because elsewhere β could encrypt a secret information whereas β is a public information and so such interpretation functions do give a safe means to estimate the security level. An easy way to construct the rank function is to take it equal to the function $\ulcorner \cdot \urcorner$.

The formal definition of these functions and some sufficient conditions to construct some safe interpretation functions can be found in [25, 26, 34].

As stated in Section 1, there is a large variety of formal methods dedicated to the analysis of cryptographic protocols and particularly with respect to the secrecy property. One of the major differences between them is the assumptions or the restrictions required by each method from the analyzed protocol. They can analyze protocols only under some particular conditions. One of the major drawbacks of these approaches is that the proofs of the their main results are strongly connected to their assumptions making their adaptation to others assumptions a very tedious task.

To overcome this drawback, we introduced in [25, 26] a more general approach that considers the context of verification (some assumptions on protocols, intruder model, etc.) as a parameter of the approach so that it will be clear how it affects any intermediary result. Intuitively, a context of verification contains all the parameters that affect the verification of cryptographic protocols. Among others, a context of verification, denoted by $\mathcal{C}$ in this paper, contains the sorts of messages involved in analyzed protocols, the rules that capturing the intruder capacities, and the algebraic properties of the cryptographic primitives. As we will see later, all the results of our approach consider the context of the verification as a simple input parameter. This great flexibility is useful to change the class of protocols or the intruder capacities and use the approach without any need of reworking the proofs or the conditions. For instance, we can use the approach to analyze protocols that use either symmetric or asymmetric keys. Also, we can employ the approach with or without algebraic properties of cryptographic primitives as it will be shown later within examples.

2.3. Secrecy Property. In this work, the secrecy property is defined in term of information flow security. We adopt also the "no read-up" notion of Bell-La Padula [36] model stating that a subject at a given security level is not allowed to know an information having a higher security level. We suppose, without effective restrictions (notice that it is always possible to define a security lattice that reflects our needs and which is coherent with this hypothesis), that each principal has his security level captured by the highest security level of components in his initial knowledge. In other words, if an agent (including the intruder) knows a message with a security level τ, then he is also eligible to know all messages having a security level lower or equal than τ. Intuitively, we say that a protocol respects the secrecy property if the intruder cannot learn from any valid trace more than what he is eligible to know. For example, if K is the set of the intruder's initial knowledge where α has a security level denoted by $\ulcorner \alpha \urcorner$, then the intruder is illegible to know an information β only if its security level $\ulcorner \beta \urcorner$ is lower or equal to $\ulcorner \alpha \urcorner$.

2.4. Main Result. Now, recall the sufficient conditions allowing to guaranty the correctness of a protocol with respect to the secrecy property. Informally, these conditions state that honest agents should never decrease, according to a safe interpretation function, the security level of any atomic message sent over the network. Protocols that satisfy this function are called increasing protocols. The formalization

of an increasing protocol is as follows. The secrecy property of increasing protocols is guaranteed even for an unbounded number of sessions and in the presence of an active intruder who can use an unbounded number of operations to the messages that he manipulates. Indeed, we proved that, to check if a protocol respects the secrecy property, it is sufficient to verify whether a finite model of the protocol, called in this work a "roles-based specification," is increasing.

The verification process of the interpretation functions-based method can be summarized as described by Figure 2.

Intuitively, if the protocol is increasing according to a specific safe interpretation function, then we can deduce that the protocol respects the secrecy property; otherwise, we cannot make any statement about its correctness. Generally, if the correctness of a protocol cannot be ensured using a given safe interpretation function, it does not mean that a positive result cannot be involved using another one. However, even if the verification is not conclusive, it provides helpful information that can be used either to discover flaws or weaknesses in the analyzed protocol or to deduce another safe interpretation function allowing us to prove the secrecy property of a protocol as it will be illustrated later. Also, this verification is finite since it is conducted on a finite set of generalized roles.

We believe that the sufficient conditions are not very restrictive, that is, for most of secure protocols we can construct a safe interpretation function allowing to prove the secrecy property. As shown later, even when the verification is not conclusive, the effort made to verify if the protocol is increasing could be helpful to discover flaws or weaknesses in the analyzed protocol or sometimes to have an idea about another safe interpretation function allowing to prove that it is increasing one. It is interesting to notice also that, some times, a slight modification on a protocol could make it an increasing one for a given safe interpretation function and allow to conclude that it is correct for secrecy.

2.5. Protocol. This section gives the syntax and semantics of a protocol and how to infer the roles-based specification from the standard description of a given protocol.

2.6. Syntax. Essentially, a protocol is specified by a sequence of communication steps given in the standard notation. Each step has an unique identifier and specifies the sender, the receiver, and the transmitted message. More precisely, a protocol p has to respect the following BNF grammar:

$$p ::= \langle i : A \longrightarrow B : m \rangle \mid p.p. \qquad (4)$$

The statement $\langle i : A \rightarrow B : m \rangle$ denotes the transmission of a message m from the principal A to the principal B in the step i of the protocol.

Table 3 gives an example of a protocol inspired from the Woo and Lam's one [37] and aims to distribute a fresh key that will be shared between two principals A and B.

2.6.1. Roles-Based Specification. To give a semantics to a protocol, we use the notion of generalized roles introduced in [38]. Intuitively, a roles-based specification is a set

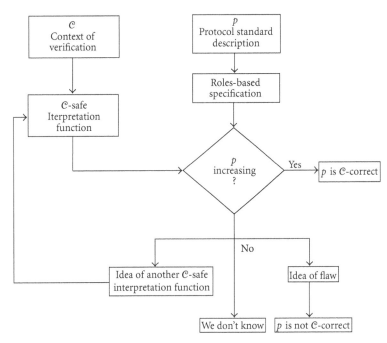

FIGURE 2: Protocol verification process.

containing the prefixes of generalized roles. A generalized role is a protocol abstraction, where the emphasis is put on a particular principal and where all the unknown messages are replaced by variables. Also, an exponent i (the session identifier) is added to each fresh message to emphasize that these components change their values from one run to another. Intuitively, a generalized role reflects how a particular agent perceives the exchanged messages. To a given principal, different generalized roles can be attributed. These generalized roles are not necessarily prefixes of each others and show the different messages that can be accepted by a role to successfully reach a given step in the protocol. More details related to the generalized roles are in [39]. The roles-based specification (the set of generalized roles) of the Woo and Lam protocol is as follow.

(i) The generalized roles of A are $\mathcal{A}_G^1$ and $\mathcal{A}_G^2$ and are as follows:

$$\mathcal{A}_G^1 = \langle i.1, A \longrightarrow I(B) : A \rangle,$$

$$\mathcal{A}_G^2 = \langle i.1, A \longrightarrow I(B) : A \rangle$$
$$\langle i.2, I(B) \longrightarrow A : X \rangle \qquad (5)$$
$$\left\langle i.3, A \longrightarrow I(B) : \left\{ X, k_{ab}^i \right\}_{k_{as}} \right\rangle.$$

If a given role cannot make any verification on a part of the received message, then this part needs to be substituted by a variable. The role of A receives a nonce at step 2 but he cannot make any validation on it (we suppose that there are no different types for different messages). For that reason N_b has been substituted by X.

(ii) The generalized roles of B are $\mathcal{B}_G^1$ and $\mathcal{B}_G^2$ and are as follows:

$$\mathcal{B}_G^1 = \langle i.1, I(A) \longrightarrow B : A \rangle$$
$$\langle i.2, B \longrightarrow I(A) : N_b \rangle,$$

$$\mathcal{B}_G^2 = \langle i.1, I(A) \longrightarrow B : A \rangle$$
$$\langle i.2, B \longrightarrow I(A) : N_b \rangle \qquad (6)$$
$$\langle i.3, I(A) \longrightarrow B : Y \rangle$$
$$\langle i.4, B \longrightarrow I(S) : \{A, Y\}_{k_{bs}} \rangle.$$

The variable Y appears since the principal B receives at the third step the unknown message $\{N_b, k_{ab}\}_{k_{as}}$ and he does not have the key k_{as} to make any verification inside it. For a similar reason, the variable Z appears in the fifth step (the key k_{ab} is initially unknown by B and he could not make any verification on it).

(iii) The generalized role of S is

$$\mathcal{S}_G = \left\langle i.4, I(B) \longrightarrow S : \{A, \{U, V\}_{k_{as}}\}_{k_{bs}} \right\rangle \qquad (7)$$
$$\langle i.5, S \longrightarrow I(B) : \{U, V\}_{k_{bs}} \rangle.$$

Since S does not initially know the value of N_b and k_{ab}, then these messages are, respectively, replaced by the fresh variables U and V.

In the rest of this paper, we denote by $\mathcal{R}_G(p)$ the prefix closed set of generalized roles of the protocol p and if A is an agent, then $\mathcal{R}_G(A)$ denotes the set of its generalized roles.

TABLE 3: Woo and Lam modified protocol.

$$p_{\text{WL}} = \quad \langle 1, A \rightarrow B : A \rangle$$

$$\langle 2, B \rightarrow A : N_b \rangle$$

$$\langle 3, A \rightarrow B : \{N_b, k_{ab}\}_{k_{as}} \rangle$$

$$\langle 4, B \rightarrow S : \{A, \{N_b, k_{ab}\}_{k_{as}}\}_{k_{bs}} \rangle$$

$$\langle 5, S \rightarrow B : \{N_b, k_{ab}\}_{K_{bs}} \rangle$$

TABLE 4: Valid trace for the Woo and Lam modified protocol.

$$\alpha.1.\ A \rightarrow I(B) : A$$
$$\alpha.2.\ I(B) \rightarrow A : N_i^\alpha$$
$$\alpha.3.\ A \rightarrow I(B) : \{N_i^\alpha, k_{ab}^\alpha\}_{k_{as}}$$
$$\quad \beta.4.\ I(B) \rightarrow S : \{A, \{N_i^\alpha, k_{ab}^\alpha\}_{k_{as}}\}_{k_{is}}$$
$$\quad \beta.5.\ S \rightarrow I(B) : \{N_i^\alpha, k_{ab}^\alpha\}_{k_{is}}$$

TABLE 5: Needham schroeder lowe protocol.

$$1.\ A \rightarrow B : \{A, N_a\}_{k_b}$$
$$2.\ B \rightarrow A : \{\langle N_a, N_b \rangle, B\}_{k_a}$$
$$3.\ A \rightarrow B : \{N_b\}_{k_b}$$

TABLE 6

$\mathcal{N}_{\text{NSL}}$	::=	A	(Principal Identifier)
	|	N_a	(Nounce)
	|	k_a^{-1}	(Private key)
	|	k_a	(Public key)

2.6.2. Valid Traces. Based on generalized roles, we define the notion of a *valid trace* of a protocol (an acceptable execution of a protocol). A trace is considered valid if it respects the following tow conditions.

  (i) Any session in the trace is an instance (a substitution) of a prefix of a generalized role.

  (ii) Any message sent by the intruder should be deductible from his previous received messages, his initial knowledge, and his inference rules.

For instance, the trace of Table 4 is valid for the Woo and Lam protocol described by Table 3. This valid trace contains a breach of secrecy since the intruder can obtain the secret k_{ab}^α that should be shared only between A and B.

2.6.3. Semantics. The semantics of a protocol p executed in a context $\mathcal{C}$ is given by the following definition.

Definition 1 (semantics). Let $\mathcal{C}$ be a context of verification and p a protocol. The semantics of p in $\mathcal{C}$, denoted by $[p]_{\mathcal{C}}$, is the set of valid traces of p when executed in $\mathcal{C}$.

3. Analysis of NSL Protocol

This section shows the efficiency and the flexibility of the interpretation functions-based approach when analyzing cryptographic protocols even when taking into consideration cryptographic primitives. We first analyze the NSL-protocol [30] without considering the homomorphism property and we show that it respects the secrecy property. Secondly, we show that if we consider a homomorphism encryption during the analysis, then some weaknesses could appear.

3.1. Analysis of NSL Protocol without the Homomorphism Property. In this section, we consider the NSL-protocol with the standard intruder model of Dolev and Yao (i.e., without algebraic properties).

3.1.1. The NSL-Protocol. The Needham-Schroeder Lowe (NSL) protocol, denoted by p_{NSL} and given in Table 5, is a mutual authentication protocol that uses asymmetric encryption.

The first step of the analysis consists in fixing the context of verification which contains the message algebra, the intruder capabilities, and the security levels of all messages. Second, we define a safe interpretation function

in this context. After that, the role-based specification can be analyzed to verify whether the protocol is increasing by using the defined safe interpretation function. The following paragraphs describe in detail these steps.

3.1.2. NSL Context of Verification in the Dolev-Yao Model. Let $\mathcal{C}_{\text{NSL}} = \langle \mathcal{M}_{\text{NSL}}, \vDash_{\text{NSL}} \mathcal{K}_{\text{NSL}}, \mathcal{L}_{\text{NSL}}^{\sqsupseteq}, \ulcorner \cdot \urcorner_{\text{NSL}} \rangle$ be a context of verification where $\mathcal{M}_{\text{NSL}}$ is $(\mathcal{N}_{\text{NSL}}, \Sigma_{\text{NSL}}, \mathcal{E}_{\text{NSL}})$ such that we have the following.

  (i) $\mathcal{N}_{\text{NSL}}$ is the set of atomic messages given by BNF grammar shown in Table 6.

  (ii) $\Sigma_{\text{NSL}} = \{pair, fst, snd, enc, dec\}$ contains the set of message operators.

  Hence, the set of messages of $\mathcal{M}_{\text{NSL}}$ is defined by BNF rules shown in Table 7.

  (iii) $\mathcal{E}_{\text{NSL}}$ is an equational theory containing the following equations:

$$fst(pair(x, y)) = x,$$
$$snd(pair(x, y)) = y,$$
$$dec(enc(x, k), k^{-1}) = x, \tag{8}$$
$$enc(dec(x, k_a^{-1}), k_a) = x,$$
$$\langle\langle m_1, m_2 \rangle, m_3 \rangle = \langle m_1, \langle m_2, m_3 \rangle \rangle.$$

As usual, we can write $\{m\}_k$ instead of $\text{enc}(m, k)$. Also, we can write m_1, m_2 or $\langle m_1, m_2 \rangle$ instead of $pair(m_1, m_2)$ and $sign(m, k^{-1})$ instead of $dec(m, k^{-1})$ if k^{-1} is a private key.

TABLE 7

m, m_1, m_2	::=	$\mathcal{N}_{NSL}$	
	|	$pair(m_1, m_2)$	(Pair Function)
	|	$enc(m, k_a)$	(Encryption Function)
	|	$dec(m, k_a^{-1})$	(Decryption Function)
	|	$fst(pair(m_1, m_2))$	(First Function)
	|	$snd(pair(m_1, m_2))$	(Second Function)

Given a set of equations $\mathcal{E}_{NSL}$ and a set of signatures Σ_{NSL}, the intruder capacities, denoted by the relation $\vDash_{NSL}$, are defined by the following rules:

$$(\text{knowledge}) \quad \frac{\square}{M \vDash_{NSL} m} \quad [m \in M],$$

$$(\text{construction}) \quad \frac{M \vDash_{NSL} m_1 \cdots M \vDash_{NSL} m_n}{M \vDash_{NSL} f(m_1, \ldots, m_n)} \quad [f \in \Sigma_{NSL}],$$

$$(\mathcal{E}\text{-equality}) \quad \frac{M \vDash_{NSL} m}{M \vDash_{NSL} m'} \quad [m =_{\mathcal{E}_{NSL}} m'].$$

$$(9)$$

The initial knowledge of principals $\mathcal{K}_{NSL}$ can be as follows: each principal knows his identity, the identities of other principals, his public and private key, and all the public keys of the other principals. Also, each principal can generate fresh values.

The security lattice $\mathcal{L}_{NSL}$ is $\mathcal{L}_0 = (2^{\mathit{l}}, \subseteq)$. The security level of a message is the set of principals that are eligible to know its value. Therefore, the supremum of this lattice $\top$ is equal to $\varnothing$ and the infimum $\perp$ is equal to l.

The typing function $\ulcorner . \urcorner_{NSL}$ could be any partial function from $\mathcal{M}_{NSL}$ to $\mathcal{L}_{NSL}$ that reflects the security levels of components exchanged during the protocol. In this example, we choose this function as follows:

$$\ulcorner . \urcorner$$

$$= [N_a \longmapsto \{A, B\}, N_b \longmapsto \{A, B\}, k_a^{-1} \longmapsto \{A\}, k_a \longmapsto \perp],$$

$$(10)$$

where A and B could be substituted by any principal identifier.

3.1.3. NSL Safe Interpretation Function. We use the DEKAN function (that selects the direct encryption keys and neighbors) to analyze the NSL-protocol under the equational theory $\mathcal{E}_{NSL}$. More precisely, the DEKAN function is a composition of a selection function and an interpretation function, that is $F_{NSL} = I_{NSL} \circ S_{NSL}$

(i) The selection function S_{NSL} takes an atomic component α and a message m and returns keys that directly encrypt α in m with principal identities and variables that are neighbors of α in m. The notion of direct encrypting keys and neighbors are formalized using a special labeled tree representing the analyzed message m. More precisely, given a message m, we

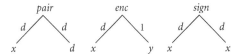

FIGURE 3: Safe costs assignment.

start by annotating the arcs of its corresponding tree according to schema given by Figure 3, where d is defined as follows:

$$d = \begin{cases} \infty & \text{if } x = enc \\ 0 & \text{else.} \end{cases} \quad (11)$$

This means that the distance between a node and his father is 0 if it is not *enc* and its father is either *pair* or *sign*. If the node is *enc*, then the distance that separates it from its father is infinite. Finally, if the node is the encryption key of the function *enc*, then the distance to its father is 1. Using these distances between nodes, we consider two nodes as neighbors if the distance that separates them is equal to 0. Also, we consider a key as a direct encrypting one for α if the distance between them is equal to 1. Using these notions, $S_{NSL}(\alpha, m)$ returns principal identifiers and variables in m having a distance 0 from α (neighbors) with atomic components having a distance 1 from α (direct encrypting keys). For example,

$$S_{NSL}\left(\alpha, \left\{\beta, A, \left\{B, \alpha, \{\alpha, N_a, X\}_{k_3}\right\}_{k_2}\right\}_{k_1}\right) = \{B, X, k_2, k_3\}. \quad (12)$$

(ii) The interpretation function I_{NSL} interprets elements returned by S_{NSL} as follows:

$$I_{NSL}(\varnothing) = \top,$$

$$I_{NSL}(S_1 \cup S_2) = I_{NSL}(S_1) \sqcup I_{NSL}(S_2),$$

$$I_{NSL}(\{\beta\}) = \begin{cases} \{\beta\} & \text{if } \beta \text{ is a principal identifier,} \\ \ulcorner \beta^{-1} \urcorner & \text{if } \beta \text{ is a key,} \\ \tau_\beta & \text{if } \beta \text{ is a variable.} \end{cases} \quad (13)$$

For example, if $\ulcorner k_2^{-1} \urcorner = \{A\}$ and $\ulcorner k_3^{-1} \urcorner = \{S\}$ then,

$$I_{NSL}(\{B, X, k_2, k_3\}) = \tau_X \sqcup \{A, B, S\}. \quad (14)$$

Notice also that, when an equational theory is taken into consideration, a message can have different equivalent forms. In this situation, to be safe, an interpretation function should give to a message the lowest level of the messages of its class. More precisely, if $m_{/\mathcal{E}} = \{m' \in \mathcal{M} \mid m =_{\mathcal{E}} m'\}$, then, for any atomic message α, we have

$$F(\alpha, m) = \prod_{m' \in m_{/\mathcal{E}}} F(\alpha, m'). \quad (15)$$

TABLE 8: Analysis of NSL: role of A.

α	r	$\ulcorner\alpha\urcorner$	$F_{\text{NSL}}(\alpha,r^+)$	$F_{\text{NSL}}(\alpha,r^-)$	$F_{\text{NSL}}(\alpha,r^+)\subseteq\ulcorner\alpha\urcorner\cup F_{\text{NSL}}(\alpha,r^-)$
N_a^i	$\mathcal{A}_G^1$	$\{A,B\}$	$\{B\}$	$\top$	Yes
X	$\mathcal{A}_G^2$	τ_X	$\{B\}$	$\{A,B\}$	Yes (for any $\tau_X\in 2^{\mathit{l}}$)

TABLE 9: Analysis of NSL protocol: role of B.

α	r	$\ulcorner\alpha\urcorner$	$F_{\text{NSL}}(\alpha,r^+)$	$F_{\text{NSL}}(\alpha,r^-)$	$F_{\text{NSL}}(\alpha,r^+)\subseteq\ulcorner\alpha\urcorner\cup F_{\text{NSL}}(\alpha,r^-)$
N_b^i	$\mathcal{B}_G^1$	$\{A,B\}$	$\{A\}$	$\top$	Yes
Y	$\mathcal{B}_G^1$	τ_Y	$\{A,B\}$	$\{A,B\}$	Yes (for any $\tau_Y\in 2^{\mathit{l}}$)

To simplify the computation of F, we usually try to transform the equational theory to a convergent inference system so that the canonical form of a message m, denoted by $m_{\downarrow}$, has always the lowest security level. In other words,

$$F(\alpha,m_{\downarrow})\sqsubseteq\prod_{m'\in m/\varepsilon}F(\alpha,m'). \qquad (16)$$

To reach this goal, we orient the equation so that the right side is greater to the left side according to F and the obtained rewriting system is convergent (the convergence can be proved based on another ordering relation that is independent of F). (Notice that if such orientation is not possible, the approach cannot be applied. However, for all the equational theories that we have already considered till now we didn't find difficulties to orient them.) For our example, it is simple to see that the following rewriting system is convergent and gives the lowest security level:

$$fst(\langle x,y\rangle)\longrightarrow x,$$
$$snd(\langle x,y\rangle)\longrightarrow y,$$
$$dec(enc(x,k),k^{-1})\longrightarrow x, \qquad (17)$$
$$enc\big(dec\big(x,k_y^{-1}\big),k_y\big)\longrightarrow x,$$
$$\langle\langle m_1,m_2\rangle,m_3\rangle\longrightarrow\langle m_1,\langle m_2,m_3\rangle\rangle.$$

3.1.4. NSL Role-Based Specification. The NSL role-based specification is

$$\mathcal{R}_G(p_{\text{NSL}})=\{\mathcal{A}_G^1,\mathcal{A}_G^2,\mathcal{B}_G^1\}, \qquad (18)$$

where the generalized roles $\mathcal{A}_G^1$ and $\mathcal{A}_G^2$ are as follows:

$$\mathcal{A}_G^1=i.1.\ A\longrightarrow I(B):\big\{A,N_a^i\big\}_{k_b}$$
$$i.1.\ A\longrightarrow I(B):\big\{A,N_a^i\big\}_{k_b},$$
$$\mathcal{A}_G^2=i.2.\ I(B)\longrightarrow A:\big\{\big\langle N_a^i,X\big\rangle,B\big\}_{k_a} \qquad (19)$$
$$i.3.\ A\longrightarrow I(B):\{X\}_{k_b},$$

and the generalized role $\mathcal{B}_G^1$ is as follows:

$$\mathcal{B}_G^1=i.1.\ I(A)\longrightarrow B:\{A,Y\}_{k_b}$$
$$i.2.\ B\longrightarrow I(A):\big\{\big\langle Y,N_b^i\big\rangle,B\big\}_{k_a}. \qquad (20)$$

3.1.5. Verifying Whether the NSL Role-Based Specification Is Increasing. Now, we can verify whether the role-based specification of SET is F_{SET}-increasing. More precisely, we need accordingly to verify that principals do not decrease the security level of components from step to another. To that end, we verify this condition on each generalized role of the protocol (i.e., on each point of view of protocol participants). To that end, we should verify whether the security level of sent messages is a subset of the security level of these messages in the received steps, that is,

$$\forall r\quad F_{\text{SET}}(\alpha,r^+)\subseteq\ulcorner\alpha\urcorner\cup F_{\text{SET}}(\alpha,r^-)\quad\forall\alpha. \qquad (21)$$

From the generalized roles of A, we deduce that

$$\mathcal{A}_G^{1^-}=\varnothing,\qquad\mathcal{A}_G^{1^+}=\big\{A,N_a^i\big\}_{k_b},$$
$$\mathcal{A}_G^{2^-}=\big\{\big\langle N_a^i,X\big\rangle,B\big\}_{k_a},\qquad\mathcal{A}_G^{2^+}=\{X\}_{k_b}. \qquad (22)$$

Recall that we are working with the lattice of security $(2^{\mathit{l}},\subseteq)$, so the supremum of this lattice $\top$ is equal to $\varnothing$ and the infimum $\bot$ is equal to l. Then, the security levels of sent and received messages in the generalized roles of A according to F_{NSL} are as shown in Table 8.

Table 8 shows that the generalized roles $\mathcal{A}_G^1$ and $\mathcal{A}_G^2$ are F_{NSL}-increasing.

From the generalized roles of B, we deduce that

$$\mathcal{B}_G^{1^-}=\{A,Y\}_{k_b},\qquad\mathcal{B}_G^{1^+}=\big\{\big\langle Y,N_b^i\big\rangle,B\big\}_{k_a}. \qquad (23)$$

Then, the security levels of sent and received messages in the generalized roles of B according to F_{NSL} are as in Table 9.

Table 9 shows that the generalized role $\mathcal{B}_G^1$ is F_{NSL}-increasing. Since all generalized roles of NSL are F_{NSL}-increasing, then it is an F_{NSL}-increasing protocol. Furthermore, since F_{NSL} is $\mathcal{C}_{\text{NSL}}$-safe interpretation function, we conclude, from our main result, that NSL is $\mathcal{C}_{\text{NSL}}$-correct with respect to secrecy.

3.2. Analysis of the NSL-Protocol with the Homomorphism Property. This section presents the analysis of the Needham-Schroeder Lowe (NSL) protocol with the homomorphism property of encryption:

$$enc(g(x,y))=g'(enc(x),enc(y)), \qquad (24)$$

TABLE 10: Analysis of NSL protocol: role of A.

α	r	$\ulcorner\alpha\urcorner$	$F_{\text{NSL}}(\alpha, r^+)$	$F_{\text{NSL}}(\alpha, r^-)$	$F_{\text{NSL}}(\alpha, r^+) \subseteq \ulcorner\alpha\urcorner \cup F_{\text{NSL}}(\alpha, r^-)$
N_a^i	$\mathcal{A}_G^1$	$\{A, B\}$	$\{B\}$	$\top$	Yes
X	$\mathcal{A}_G^2$	τ_X	$\{B\}$	$\{A\}$	No

where g and g' are any operators (usually the same) from the message algebra. For example, $enc(m_1 \cdot m_2) = enc(m_1) \cdot enc(m_2)$ is satisfied when using block ciphers with Electronic Code Block (ECB) and when m_1 has the same size as requested by the encryption system (64 bits for DES). In fact, the ECB consists of splitting the message into blocks of n-bits and encrypting each of them separately. Many asymmetric systems like RSA, Elgamal, Benaloh, and Paillier are also homomorphic for some algebraic operators.

Related works that take into consideration the homomorphism property in the analysis of cryptographic protocols are rare and most of them do not deal with an unbounded number of sessions. Among the important results obtained in this direction are those described in [40–42] which address the intruder deduction problem and propose a PTIME-decision procedure for it. Despite the importance of the result, the resolution of the intruder deduction problem is not enough to analyze a protocol that can exhibit an infinite number of sessions.

The interpretation functions-based method does not suffer from this problem since it is proved that if the protocol is increasing then it is sufficient to guarantee its correctness for the secrecy property under an unbounded number of sessions. In the sequel, we show how the homomorphism property can affect the analysis of a protocol like NSL.

3.2.1. NSL Context of Verification with the Homomorphism Property.
First, we need to change the context of verification $\mathcal{C}_{\text{NSL}}$ used in the previous section, so that we consider the homomorphism property. Let $\mathcal{C}'_{\text{NSL}}$ be a context of verification such as $\mathcal{C}'_{\text{NSL}} = \langle (\mathcal{N}_{\text{NSL}}, \Sigma_{\text{NSL}}, \mathcal{E}'_{\text{NSL}}), \vDash_{\text{NSL}} \mathcal{K}_{\text{NSL}}, \mathcal{L}^{\sqsupseteq}_{\text{NSL}}, \ulcorner \cdot \urcorner_{\text{NSL}} \rangle$ where all items are the same as those defined in the context $\mathcal{C}_{\text{NSL}}$ except the equational theory $\mathcal{E}'_{\text{NSL}}$ that includes homomorphism of encryption and it is as follows:

$$fst(pair(x, y)) = x,$$

$$snd(pair(x, y)) = y,$$

$$dec(enc(x, k), k^{-1}) = x, \quad (25)$$

$$\langle \langle m_1, m_2 \rangle, m_3 \rangle = \langle m_1, \langle m_2, m_3 \rangle \rangle,$$

$$enc(\langle x, y \rangle, z) = \langle enc(x, z), enc(y, z) \rangle.$$

The last two equations of $\mathcal{E}'_{\text{NSL}}$ reflect the homomorphic property of the encryption enc and the signature $sign$ with respect to the concatenation operator $\langle \cdot \rangle$.

3.2.2. NSL Safe Interpretation Function with the Homomorphism Property.
We use the DEKAN function (that selects the direct encryption keys and neighbors) to analyze the

TABLE 11: Flaw in the NSL-protocol under the homomorphic assumption.

1.1. $A \rightarrow I : \{A, N_a^1\}_{k_i}$
    2.1. $I(A) \rightarrow B : \{A, N_a^1\}_{k_b}$
    2.2. $B \rightarrow I(A) : \{N_a^1, N_b^2, B\}_{k_a}$
1.2. $I \rightarrow A : \{N_a^1, N_b^2, I\}_{k_a}$
1.3. $A \rightarrow I : \{N_b^2\}_{k_i}$
    2.3. $I(A) \rightarrow B : \{N_b^2\}_{k_b}$

Needham-Schroeder Lowe protocol under the equational theory $\mathcal{E}'_{\text{NSL}}$. With the homomorphism property, the DEKAN function becomes equal to the DEK function (that selects direct encryption keys). Indeed, the selection is forbidden beyond encryption and the selection is always calculated on the message $m_\downarrow$ (the canonical form of m according to the rewriting system obtained from the equational theory $\mathcal{E}'_{\text{NSL}}$, when the equality is replaced by $\rightarrow$) instead of m. For example, with the homomorphism property the message $\{\alpha_1, \ldots, \alpha_n\}_k$, where $\alpha_1, \ldots, \alpha_n$ are atomic, is always reduced, by the homomorphism property, to $\{\alpha_1\}_k, \ldots, \{\alpha_n\}_k$. To calculate the security level of a component α_i in the message $\{\alpha_1, \ldots, \alpha_n\}_k$, the DEKAN function is applied on its canonical form that is $\{\alpha_1\}_k, \ldots, \{\alpha_n\}_k$. It follows that the neighbors are never chosen, and we conclude that the DEKAN function behaves as the DEK function.

3.2.3. Verifying Whether the NSL Role-Based Specification Is Increasing.
From the generalized roles of A, we deduce that

$$\mathcal{A}_G^{1^-} = \varnothing, \qquad \mathcal{A}_G^{1^+} = \left\{ A, N_a^i \right\}_{k_b},$$

$$\mathcal{A}_G^{2^-} = \left\{ \langle N_a^i, X \rangle, B \right\}_{k_a}, \qquad \mathcal{A}_G^{2^+} = \{X\}_{k_b}. \quad (26)$$

The security levels of sent and received messages in the generalized roles of A using the DEKAN function F_{NSL} are as shown in Table 10.

Table 10 shows that the generalized role $\mathcal{A}_G^2$ is not increasing. Indeed, the message X is sent with the security level $\{B\}$ which is not always in its security level $\ulcorner X \urcorner \cup \{A\}$ estimated from the received messages. In this case, we can never find a safe interpretation function that guarantees the correctness of the protocol simply because the protocol is flawed and it could be attacked as shown by Table 11. Notice that message of step 1.2 could be generated by the intruder from the message 2.2 using the homomorphic property. In fact, $\{N_a^1, N_b^2, B\}_{k_a} = \{N_a^1, N_b^2\}_{k_a}, \{B\}_{k_a}$ and since the intruder can produce $\{I\}_{k_a}$, then using the homomorphic property he can produce $\{N_a^1, N_b^2, I\}_{k_a}$ by simply concatenating $\{N_a^1, N_b^2\}_{k_a}$ with $\{I\}_{k_a}$.

TABLE 12: Analysis of NSL protocol: role of B.

α	r	$\ulcorner\alpha\urcorner_0$	$F_{NSL}(\alpha, r^+)$	$F_{NSL}(\alpha, r^-)$	$F_{NSL}(\alpha, r^+) \subseteq^? \ulcorner\alpha\urcorner_0 \cup F_{NSL}(\alpha, r^-)$
N_b^i	$\mathcal{B}_G^1$	$\{A, B\}$	$\{A\}$	$\top$	Yes
Y	$\mathcal{B}_G^1$	$\top$	$\{A\}$	$\{B\}$	No

This is because the DEKAN function (that selects direct encryption keys and neighbors) with the homomorphism property acts as the DEK function (that selects the direct encryption keys only) and does not select the neighbors. Therefore, to correct this protocol in the presence of such property, we should find a means (different from the concatenation, such as signatures), allowing A to conclude that N_b is from B. To overcome this problem, we suggest the use of signatures to indicate the correct security level of sent messages. For instance, we can replace the message $\{A, N_a\}_{k_b}$ at step 1 of the NSL-protocol with the message $\{\{N_a\}_{k_a^{-1}}\}_{k_b}$. In this case, signing the message N_a by k_a^{-1} is a safe way to indicate that it comes from the agent A. In the same way, we can replace the message of step 2 of the NSL-protocol by the message $\{\{\langle N_a, N_b\rangle\}_{k_b^{-1}}\}_{k_a}$. Notice that if signature is also homomorphic like encryption, operators like hash functions can be used to forge such type of inseparable links between some elements.

From the generalized roles of B, we deduce that

$$\mathcal{B}_G^{1^-} = \{A, Y\}_{k_b}, \qquad \mathcal{B}_G^{1^+} = \left\{\left\langle Y, N_b^i\right\rangle, B\right\}_{k_a}. \qquad (27)$$

Then, the security level of sent and received messages in the generalized roles of B using the DEKAN function F_{NSL} is as shown in Table 12.

Table 12 shows that the generalized role $\mathcal{B}_G^1$ is not increasing. Indeed, the message Y is sent with the security level $\{A\}$ which is not in its security level $\{B\}$ estimated from the received messages. As for the role of A, we suggest to replace the message $\{A, N_a\}_{k_b}$ of step 1 of the NSL-protocol with the message $\{\{N_a\}_{k_a^{-1}}\}_{k_b}$. In this case, signing the message N_a by k_a^{-1} is a safe way to indicate that it comes from the agent A. In the same way, we can replace the message of step 2 of the NSL-protocol with the message $\{\{\langle N_a, N_b\rangle\}_{k_b^{-1}}\}_{k_a}$.

Therefore, the NSL-protocol is not increasing and, so, we cannot deduce anything about its correctness for the secrecy property. However, the protocol, with the changes suggested above, is increasing and it is therefore correct for the secrecy property even in the presence of the homomorphism property. Table 13 summarizes these changes.

By using the DEK function or the DEKAN function, this new version of the Needham-Schroeder-Lowe protocol is increasing and then respects the secrecy property. Indeed, with this version N_a is received with the security level $\{A, B\}$ and so it could be sent to A. Also, N_b is received with security level $\{A, B\}$ and so it could be sent to B.

4. Analysis of the SET Protocol

Electronic commerce, commonly denoted by e-commerce, or eCommerce, consists in buying and selling goods or

TABLE 13: Needham schroeder lowe protocol: corrected version.

1. $A \rightarrow B: \{\{N_a\}_{k_a^{-1}}\}_{k_b}$
2. $B \rightarrow A: \{\{\langle N_a, N_b\rangle\}_{k_b^{-1}}\}_{k_a}$
3. $A \rightarrow B: \{N_b\}_{k_b}$

TABLE 14: SET protocol.

1. $C \rightarrow M: C, N_c$
2. $M \rightarrow C: \{M, C, XID, N_c, N_M, CA(G)\}_{k_M^{-1}}$
3. $C \rightarrow M: OI, DualSign, \{PI\}_{k_G}$
4. $M \rightarrow G: \{\{AuthReqData, LinkOIPI\}_{k_M^{-1}}\}_{k_G}, DualSign, \{PI\}_{k_G}$
5. $G \rightarrow M: \{\{M, C, XID, AuthRRTags, PurchAmt, AuthCode\}_{k_G^{-1}}\}_{k_M}$
6. $M \rightarrow C: \{M, C, XID, N_C, AuthCode\}_{k_M^{-1}}$

services over the Internet. To make a purchase, a customer usually submits his credit card number to a merchant protected according to a specific cryptographic protocol such as SET and SSL.

Many researchers have addressed the problem of analyzing the SET protocol during the last years. For example, Paulson et al. tried in [43, 44] to prove some security properties (authentication and repudiation properties) during the purchase phase as well as during the cardholder registration one by using the inductive approach and the theorem prover "Isabelle." However, the analysis was very difficult and could not be achieved because of the complexity of the exchanged messages and the complexity of targeted properties. However, they discovered some flaws related to repudiation and authentication properties. In [45], the authors present some weaknesses in the purchase phase of the SET protocol and propose their correct version. The weaknesses concern the repudiation property. However, no results concerning the secrecy property have been given till now. In the following, we show the efficiency of the interpretation function-based method when analyzing such difficult protocol and how it could be used to give a correct version of this protocol.

The SET protocol [27–29] has been proposed by a consortium of credit card and software companies. It aims to protect sensitive cardholder information, to ensure payment integrity, and confidentiality, and to authenticate merchants and cardholders. It contains five subprotocols: cardholder registration; merchant and payment gateway registration; purchase request; payment authorization and transaction payment. We focus here on the analysis of the purchase phase which involves three parties: the cardholder (C); the merchant (M) and a payment gateway (G). The formal description of the purchase phase of SET, denoted in the sequel by p_{SET}, is defined by Table 14.

The *OI*, *PI*, *DualSign*, and *Link OIPI* are as follows:

$$OI := OIData, H(PIData),$$

$$OIData := M, C, XID, N_M, N_C, HOD,$$

$$HOD := H(OrderDesc, PurchAmt),$$

$$PIData := PIHead, PANData,$$

$$PIHead := M, C, XID, HOD, PurchAmt,$$

$$MerID, H(XID, CardSecret),$$

$$PANData := PAN, PANSecret,$$

$$PI := PIHead, H(OIData), PANData,$$

$$DualSign := \{H(PIData), H(OIData)\}_{k_c^{-1}},$$

$$LinkOIPI := H(AuthReqData, DualSign, \{PI\}_{K_G}),$$

$$AuthReqData := H(OIData), HOD,$$

$$M, C, XID, AuthRRTags.$$

$$(28)$$

PAN is the cardholder's primary account number, and *PANSecret* is a secret number known by the cardholder and used to prove his identity when making purchases. The *OrderDesc* is the description of the customer's detailed order and *PurchAmt* is the total amount of the purchase order. The intuitive meaning of each step is as follows.

(i) Initialization request (step 1): before starting the purchase, the cardholder and the merchant agree upon the order description and its price. This shopping step is out of the SET protocol. The cardholder then sends to the merchant his local ID (C) and a fresh random challenge N_c.

(ii) Initialization response (step 2): The merchant M generates a transaction ID (XID) and sends it to the costumer with the gateway's public encryption key certificate ($CA(G)$).

(iii) Order request (step 3): after validating the signature of the merchant and the certificates of the gateway, the cardholder sends an order request which contains the payment instruction (PI), the order information (OI), and the dual signature ($DualSign$) to the merchant.

(iv) Authorization request (step 4): the message sent during this step contains PI and $DualSign$ sent by the cardholder, the hash codes $H(OIData)$ and HOD. This information enables the gateway to verify the dual signature, the different IDs involved in the transaction, and the authorization request/response tags ($authRRTags$) that should be returned in the authorization response. The purpose of $AuthRRTags$ is to match the request/response paired messages; it contains the merchant's financial ID and some

TABLE 15

n	::=	A	(Principal Identifier)
	|	N_a	(Nounce)
	|	k_a^{-1}	(Private key)
	|	k_a	(Public key)

TABLE 16

m, m_1, m_2	::=	n	
	|	$enc(m, k_a)$	(Encryption Function)
	|	$dec(m, k_a^{-1})$	(Signature Function)
	|	$pair(m_1, m_2)$	(Pair Function)
	|	$fst(pair(m_1, m_2))$	(First Function)
	|	$snd(pair(m_1, m_2))$	(Second Function)
	|	$H(m)$	(Hash Function)

optional data that are used by the merchant's bank to authorize the transaction.

(v) Authorization response (step 5): if both PI and OI agree, the gateway proceeds to the transaction authorization using the existing financial networks. If the authorization is allowed, the gateway sends the authorization response containing $authRRTags$ copied from step 4, the purchase amount, and the transaction status (a boolean value).

(vi) Purchase response (step 6): the merchant verifies the gateway's signature and whether the IDs and the $authRRTags$ in the response match with those sent in his request message. Then, he forwards to the cardholder the authorization status combined with IDs and challenges involved in the transaction.

In the following, we focus on verifying the secrecy property of this protocol by using the interpretation functions-based method. To that end, we follow the steps described by Figure 2. First, we define the context of verification and a safe interpretation function for it. After that, the role-based specification is generated to verify whether this protocol is increasing.

4.1. SET Context of Verification in the Dolev-Yao Model. Let $\mathcal{C}_{SET} = \langle (\mathcal{N}_{SET}, \Sigma_{SET}), F_0, \mathcal{K}_{SET}, \mathcal{L}_{SET}^{\sqsubseteq}, \ulcorner \cdot \urcorner_{SET} \rangle$ be a context of verification where $\mathcal{N}_{SET}$ is the set of atomic messages given by BNF grammar shown in Table 15 and $\Sigma_{SET} = \{enc, dec, pair, fst, snd, hash\}$.

As usual, we write $\{m\}_k$ instead of $enc(m, k)$ or $sign(m, k)$. Also, we write m_1, m_2 instead of $pair(m_1, m_2)$, $H(m)$ instead of $hash(m)$ and $sign(m, k^{-1})$ instead of $dec(m, k^{-1})$ if k^{-1} is a private key. Hence, the set of messages $\mathcal{M}_{SET}$ is the set of messages that respect BNF rules shown in Table 16.

Let $\mathcal{E}_{SET}$ be the equational theory containing the following equations:

$$fst(\langle x, y \rangle) = x,$$

$$snd(\langle x, y \rangle) = y,$$

$$dec(enc(x, k), k^{-1}) = x,$$

$$enc(dec(x, k^{-1}), k) = x, \qquad (29)$$

$$check(sign(m, k_a^{-1}), k_a) = ok,$$

$$\langle \langle m_1, m_2 \rangle, m_3 \rangle = \langle m_1, \langle m_2, m_3 \rangle \rangle.$$

The intruder model $\vDash_{SET}$ is the famous Dolev-Yao model for asymmetric key given as follows:

$$(\text{knowledge}) \quad \frac{\square}{M \vDash_{SET} m} \quad [m \in M],$$

$$(\text{construction}) \quad \frac{M \vDash_{SET} m_1 \cdots M \vDash_{SET} m_n}{M \vDash_{SET} f(m_1, \ldots, m_n)} \quad [f \in \Sigma_{SET}],$$

$$(\mathcal{E}\text{-equality}) \quad \frac{M \vDash_{SET} m}{M \vDash_{SET} m'} \quad [m =_{\mathcal{E}_{SET}} m'].$$

$$(30)$$

The initial knowledge of principals $\mathcal{K}_{SET}$ is as follows. Each principal knows his identity, the identities of other principals, his public and private key, all the public keys of the other principals and his card numbers (its *PAN* and its *PANSecret*). Also, each principal can generate fresh values.

The security lattice $\mathcal{L}_{SET}$ is the same as the one defined in the NSL-example, that is, $\mathcal{L}_{SET} = \mathcal{L}_0 = (2^I, \subseteq)$. The security level of a message is simply the set of principals that are eligible to know its value. Therefore, the supremum of this lattice $\top$ is equal to $\varnothing$ and the infimum $\bot$ is equal to I.

The typing relation $\ulcorner \cdot \urcorner_{SET}$ (or shortly denoted by $\ulcorner \cdot \urcorner$ if there is no confusion) is a partial function from $\mathcal{M}_{SET}$ to $\mathcal{L}_{SET}$ defined as follows:

$$[N_c \longmapsto \bot, PurchAmt \longmapsto \bot, MerID \longmapsto \bot,$$

$$CardSecret \longmapsto \{C, G\},$$

$$PANSecret \longmapsto \{C, G\}, PAN \longmapsto \{C, G\}, XID \longmapsto \bot,$$

$$N_M \longmapsto \bot, CA(G) \longmapsto \bot,$$

$$AuthRRTags \longmapsto \{M, G\}, AuthCode \longmapsto \bot]. \qquad (31)$$

4.2. SET Safe Interpretation Function in the Dolev-Yao Model. We use an extended version of the DEKAN function to deal with hash functions. To that end, we follow the guideline defined in Section 2.2. In fact, the guideline states that we have to consider the interpretation function as a composition of a selection and rank function (i.e., $F_{SET} = I_{SET} \circ S_{SET}$). In this example, we consider the selection function S_{SET} that allows to select principal identifiers that are at distance 0

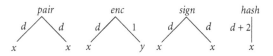

FIGURE 4: Safe costs assignment.

(neighbors) and component at distance 1 (encryption keys). A hashed message is considered in this example as a black box for the selection function. This means that selection function could not select components from a hashed message and this done by making the hashed components at distance strictly greater than 1 (the maximum distance that the selection function can reach to select components). Also, to have a safe function, we forbid the selection of components that are beyond an encryption operator. To that end, we set distances so that any two components separated by an encryption are at distance equal to ∞. More precisely, the selection function S_{SET} could be defined by considering the costs between nodes in messages as described by Figure 4, where d is as follows:

$$d = \begin{cases} \infty & \text{if } x \in \{enc, hash\} \\ 0 & \text{else.} \end{cases} \qquad (32)$$

The DEKAN function F_{SET}, used to analyze the SET protocol, could be built by composing the selection function and the rank function as follows:

$$F_{SET} = I_{SET} \circ S_{SET}, \qquad (33)$$

where I_{SET} gives the rank$\{A\}$ to any principal identity A that is selected as a neighbor and the rank $\ulcorner k^{-1} \urcorner$ to the keys k which are selected as direct keys of encryption.

4.3. SET Roles-Based Specification. For more details about how we compute a roles-based specification from a protocol and a context of verification, we refer the reader to Section 2.6.1. Following the steps described in Section 2.6.1, the SET roles-based specification is

$$\mathcal{R}_G(p_{SET}) = \left\{ \mathcal{C}_G^1, \mathcal{C}_G^2, \mathcal{C}_G^3, \mathcal{M}_G^1, \mathcal{M}_G^2, \mathcal{M}_G^3, \mathcal{G}_G^1 \right\}, \qquad (34)$$

where $\mathcal{C}_G^1$, $\mathcal{C}_G^2$, and $\mathcal{C}_G^3$ (the generalized roles of C) are as follows:

$$\mathcal{C}_G^1 = i.1. \ C \longrightarrow I(M) : C, N_c^i,$$

$$\mathcal{C}_G^2 = \begin{cases} i.1. \ C \longrightarrow I(M) : C, N_c^i, \\ i.2. \ I(M) \longrightarrow C : \{M, C, X_1, N_c^i, X_2, CA(G)\}_{k_M^{-1}}, \\ i.3. \ C \longrightarrow I(M) : IO_G^C, DualSign_G^C, \{PI_G^C\}_{k_G}, \end{cases}$$

$$\mathcal{C}_G^3 = \begin{cases} i.1. \ C \longrightarrow I(M) : C, N_c^i, \\ i.2. \ I(M) \longrightarrow C : \{M, C, X_1, N_c^i, X_2, CA(G)\}_{k_M^{-1}}, \\ i.3. \ C \longrightarrow I(M) : IO_G^C, DualSign_G^C, \{PI_G^C\}_{k_G}, \\ i.6. \ I(M) \longrightarrow C : \{M, C, X_1, N_C^i, X_3\}_{k_M^{-1}}. \end{cases}$$

$$(35)$$

The OI_G^C, $DualSign_G^C$, and PI_G^C are, respectively, OI, $DualSign$, and PI in which XID, N_M and N_c are, respectively, replaced by X_1, X_2, and N_c^i. The generalized roles of M ($\mathcal{M}_G^1$, $\mathcal{M}_G^2$, and $\mathcal{M}_G^3$) are as follows:

$$\mathcal{M}_G^1 = \begin{cases} i.1. \ I(C) \longrightarrow M : C, Y_1, \\ i.2. \ M \longrightarrow I(C) : \\ \quad \left\{ M, C, XID^i, Y_1, N_M^i, CA(G) \right\}_{k_M^{-1}}, \end{cases}$$

$$\mathcal{M}_G^2 = \begin{cases} i.1. \ I(C) \longrightarrow M : C, Y_1, \\ i.2. \ M \longrightarrow I(C) : \\ \quad \left\{ M, C, XID^i, Y_1, N_M^i, CA(G) \right\}_{k_M^{-1}}, \\ i.3. \ I(C) \longrightarrow M : OIData_G^M, Y_7, DualSign_G^M, Y_8, \\ i.4. \ M \longrightarrow I(G) : \\ \quad \left\{ \{AuthReqData, LinkOIPI\}_{k_M^{-1}} \right\}_{k_G}, \\ \quad DualSign_G^M, Y_8, \end{cases}$$

$$\mathcal{M}_G^3 = \begin{cases} i.1. \ I(C) \longrightarrow M : C, Y_1, \\ i.2. \ M \longrightarrow I(C) : \\ \quad \left\{ M, C, XID^i, Y_1, N_M^i, CA(G) \right\}_{k_M^{-1}}, \\ i.3. \ I(C) \longrightarrow M : OIData_G^M, Y_7, DualSign_G^M, Y_8, \\ i.4. \ M \longrightarrow I(G) : \\ \quad \left\{ \left\{ AuthReqData_G^M, LinkOIPI_G^M \right\}_{k_M^{-1}} \right\}_{k_G}, \\ \quad DualSign_G^M, Y_8, \\ i.5. \ I(G) \longrightarrow M : \\ \quad \left\{ \{M, C, XID^i, authRRTags, Y_3, Y_9\}_{k_G^{-1}} \right\}_{k_M}, \\ i.6. \ M \longrightarrow I(C) : \{M, C, XID^i, Y_1, Y_9\}_{k_M^{-1}}. \end{cases}$$

$$(36)$$

The $OIData_G^M$, $DualSign_G^M$, $AuthReqData_G^M$ and $LinkOIPI_G^M$ are as follows:

$$OIData_G^M := M, C, XID^i, N_M^i, Y_1, Y_2,$$

$$DualSign_G^M := \left\{ Y_7, H\left(OIData_G^M\right) \right\}_{k_c^{-1}},$$

$$LinkOIPI_G^M := H\left(AuthReqData, DualSign_G^M, Y_8\right),$$

$$AuthReqData_G^M := H\left(OIData_G^M\right), Y_2, M, C, XID^i,$$

$$AuthRRTags.$$

$$(37)$$

The generalized role of G ($\mathcal{G}_G^1$) is as follows:

$$\mathcal{G}_G^1 = \begin{cases} i.4. \ I(M) \longrightarrow G : \\ \quad \left\{ \left\{ AuthReqData_G^G, LinkOIPI_G^G \right\}_{k_M^{-1}} \right\}_{k_G}, \\ \quad DualSign_G^G, \left\{ PI_G^G \right\}_{k_G}, \\ i.5. \ G \longrightarrow I(M) : \\ \quad \left\{ \{M, C, Z_1, Z_{11}, Z_6, AuthCode\}_{k_G^{-1}} \right\}_{k_M}. \end{cases}$$

$$(38)$$

The PI_G^G, $DualSign_G^G$, $AuthReqData_G^G$, and $LinkOIPI_G^G$ are as follows:

$$PIData_G^G := PIHead_G^G, PANData_G^G$$

$$PIHead_G^G := M, C, Z_1, Z_4, Z_6, MerID, Z_8$$

$$PANData_G^G := Z_9, Z_{10}$$

$$PI_G^G := PIHead_G^G, Z_{12}, PANData_G^G$$

$$DualSign_G^G := \left\{ H\left(PIData_G^G\right), Z_{12} \right\}_{k_c^{-1}}$$

$$LinkOIPI_G^G := H\left(AuthReqData_G^G, DualSign_G^G, \{PI\}_{K_G}\right)$$

$$AuthReqData_G^G := Z_{12}, Z_4, M, C, Z_1, Z_{11}.$$

$$(39)$$

4.4. Verifying Whether the SET Role-Based Specification is Increasing. Now, we can verify whether the role-based specification of SET is F_{SET}-increasing. More precisely, we need accordingly to verify that principals do not decrease the security level of components from step to another. To that end, we verify this condition on the each generalized role of the protocol (i.e., on each point of view of protocol participants). To that end, we should verify whether the security level of sent messages is a subset of the security level of these messages in the receieved steps that is,

$$\forall r \cdot \mathsf{F}_{SET}(\alpha, r^+) \subseteq \ulcorner \alpha \urcorner \cup \mathsf{F}_{SET}(\alpha, r^-). \quad (40)$$

(i) Let us start with the generalized roles of C. According to the definition of r^+ and r^-, we have

$$\begin{aligned} \mathcal{C}_G^{1^-} &= \varnothing, \\ \mathcal{C}_G^{1^+} &= C, N_c^i, \\ \mathcal{C}_G^{2^-} &= \left\{ M, C, X_1, N_c^i, X_2, CA(G) \right\}_{k_M^{-1}}, \\ \mathcal{C}_G^{2^+} &= IO_G^C, DualSign_G^C, \left\{ PI_G^C \right\}_{k_G}. \end{aligned} \quad (41)$$

From the definition of F_{SET} and $\mathcal{C}_G^{2^+}$, it follows that, for all atomic message α, we have that

$$\mathsf{F}_{SET}\left(\alpha, \mathcal{C}_G^{2^+}\right) = \mathsf{F}_{SET}\left(\alpha, IOData_G^C, \{PIHead, PANData\}_{k_G}\right). \quad (42)$$

Now, the security levels of sent and received messages in the generalized roles of C using the F_{SET} function are as shown in Table 17.

From the analysis of the role of C shown in Table 17, we deduce that its generalized roles are not increasing. This is due to the fact that an unknown message X_1 is put beside the secret components *CardSecret*, *PAN*, and *PANSecret* and this lowers their security level. Moreover, putting the identity

TABLE 17: SET analysis: role of C.

α	r	$\ulcorner \alpha \urcorner$	$F_{SET}(\alpha, r^+)$	$F_{SET}(\alpha, r^-)$	$F_{SET}(\alpha, r^+) \subseteq \ulcorner \alpha \urcorner \cup F_{SET}(\alpha, r^-)$
N_c^i	$\mathcal{C}_G^1$	$\perp$	$\perp$	$\top$	Yes
N_c^i	$\mathcal{C}_G^2$	$\perp$	$\perp$	$\top$	Yes
X_1	$\mathcal{C}_G^2$	τ_{X_1}	$\perp$	$\perp$	Yes
X_2	$\mathcal{C}_G^2$	τ_{X_2}	$\perp$	$\perp$	Yes
$PurchAmt$	$\mathcal{C}_G^2$	$\perp$	$\{C, G\} \cup \tau_{X_1}$	$\top$	Yes
$MerID$	$\mathcal{C}_G^2$	$\perp$	$\perp$	$\top$	Yes
$CardSecret$	$\mathcal{C}_G^2$	$\{C, G\}$	$\{C, M, G\} \cup \tau_{X_1}$	$\top$	No
PAN	$\mathcal{C}_G^2$	$\{C, G\}$	$\{C, M, G\} \cup \tau_{X_1}$	$\top$	No
$PANSecret$	$\mathcal{C}_G^2$	$\{C, G\}$	$\{C, M, G\} \cup \tau_{X_1}$	$\top$	No

TABLE 18: SET analysis: role of M.

α	r	$\ulcorner \alpha \urcorner$	$F_{SET}(\alpha, r^+)$	$F_{SET}(\alpha, r^-)$	$F_{SET}(\alpha, r^+) \subseteq \ulcorner \alpha \urcorner \cup F_{SET}(\alpha, r^-)$
Y_1	$\mathcal{M}_G^1$	τ_{Y_1}	$\perp$	$\perp$	Yes
XID^i	$\mathcal{M}_G^1$	$\perp$	$\perp$	$\top$	Yes
N_M^i	$\mathcal{M}_G^1$	$\perp$	$\perp$	$\top$	Yes
$CA(G)$	$\mathcal{M}_G^1$	$\perp$	$\perp$	$\top$	Yes
Y_2	$\mathcal{M}_G^2$	τ_{Y_2}	$\perp$	$\perp$	Yes
XID^i	$\mathcal{M}_G^2$	$\perp$	$\perp$	$\perp$	Yes
$AuthRRTags$	$\mathcal{M}_G^2$	$\{M, G\}$	$\perp$	$\top$	No

M beside $CardSecret$, PAN, and $PANSecret$ means that these messages could be known by M according to our interpretation function. Therefore, if X_1 (XID in the description of the protocol step 3) and M are hashed in $PIHead$, then this role can be proved increasing. More precisely, we redefine $PIHead$ as follows:

$$PIHead = C, HOD, PurchAmt, MerID,$$
$$H(M, XID), H(CardSecret). \tag{43}$$

(ii) From the generalized roles of M, we deduce that

$$\mathcal{M}_G^{1-} = C, Y_1,$$

$$\mathcal{M}_G^{1+} = \left\{ M, C, XID^i, Y_1, N_M^i, CA(G) \right\}_{k_M^{-1}},$$

$$\mathcal{M}_G^{2-} = \mathcal{M}_G^{1-} \cup \left\{ OIData_G^M, Y_7, DualSign_G^M, Y_8 \right\},$$

$$\mathcal{M}_G^{2+} = \left\{ \{ AuthReqData, LinkOIPI \}_{k_M^{-1}} \right\}_{k_G},$$
$$DualSign_G^M, Y_8,$$

$$\mathcal{M}_G^{3-} = \mathcal{M}_G^{2-}$$
$$\cup \left\{ \left\{ \{ M, C, XID^i, AuthRRTags, Y_3, Y_9 \}_{k_G^{-1}} \right\}_{k_M} \right\},$$

$$\mathcal{M}_G^{3+} = \left\{ M, C, XID^i, Y_1, Y_9 \right\}_{k_M^{-1}}. \tag{44}$$

The security levels of sent and received messages in the generalized roles of M using the DEKAN function are as shown in (Table 18).

From Table 19, we can deduce that the generalized roles of M are not increasing. This is because the message $AuthRRTags$ is sent at step 4 of the generalized role $\mathcal{M}_G^2$, with the security level $\{C, M, G\}$, which is not greater than its real security level ($\{M, G\}$). This is since the identity C is beside $AuthRRTags$ and that means that this message is for C which also lowers the security level of $AuthRRTags$. One way to make this role increasing is as follows. We remove (or put it beyond the encryption) the identity C from the message $AuthReqData$ of step 4 of the generalized role. More precisely, we redefine $AuthReqData$ as follows:

$$AuthReqData = H(OIData), HOD, M, XID, AuthRRTags. \tag{45}$$

(iii) From the generalized roles of G, we deduce that

$$\mathcal{G}_G^{1-} = \left\{ \left\{ AuthReqData_G^G, LinkOIPI_G^G \right\}_{k_M^{-1}} \right\}_{k_G},$$
$$DualSign_G^G, \left\{ PI_G^G \right\}_{k_G} \tag{46}$$

$$\mathcal{G}_G^{1+} = \left\{ \{ M, C, Z_1, Z_{11}, Z_6, AuthCode \}_{k_G^{-1}} \right\}_{k_M}.$$

Then, the security levels of sent and received messages in the generalized roles of M using the DEKAN function are as in Table 20.

TABLE 19: SET analysis: role of M.

α	r	$\ulcorner\alpha\urcorner$	$F_{SET}(\alpha, r^+)$	$F_{SET}(\alpha, r^-)$	$F_{SET}(\alpha, r^+) \subseteq \ulcorner\alpha\urcorner \cup F_{SET}(\alpha, r^-)$
Y_8	$\mathcal{M}_G^2$	τ_{Y_8}	$\bot$	$\bot$	Yes
XID^i	$\mathcal{M}_G^3$	$\bot$	$\{M, C, G\} \cup \tau_{Y_2}$	$\{M, C, Y_3\} \cup \tau_{Y_9}$	Yes
Y_1	$\mathcal{M}_G^3$	τ_{Y_1}	$\bot$	$\bot$	Yes
Y_9	$\mathcal{M}_G^3$	τ_{Y_9}	$\bot$	$\bot$	Yes

TABLE 20: SET analysis: role of G WLMV:prot.

α	r	$\ulcorner\alpha\urcorner$	$F_{SET}(\alpha, r^+)$	$F_{SET}(\alpha, r^-)$	$F_{SET}(\alpha, r^+) \subseteq \ulcorner\alpha\urcorner \cup F_{SET}(\alpha, r^-)$
Z_1	$\mathcal{G}_G^1$	τ_{Z_1}	$\{M, C, G\} \cup \tau_{Z_6} \cup \tau_{Z_{11}}$	$\{M, C, G, \tau_{Z_4}\} \cup \tau_{Z_6} \cup \tau_{Z_8} \cup \tau_{Z_{11}} \cup \tau_{Z_{12}}$	Yes
Z_6	$\mathcal{G}_G^1$	τ_{Z_6}	$\{M, C, G\} \cup \tau_{Z_1} \cup \tau_{Z_{11}}$	$\{M, C, G\} \cup \tau_{Z_1} \cup \tau_{Z_4} \cup \tau_{Z_8} \cup \tau_{Z_{11}} \cup \tau_{Z_{12}}$	Yes
Z_{11}	$\mathcal{G}_G^1$	$\tau_{Z_{11}}$	$\{M, C, G\} \cup \tau_{Z_1} \cup \tau_{Z_6}$	$\{M, C, G\} \cup \tau_{Z_1} \cup \tau_{Z_4} \cup \tau_{Z_{12}}$	No
$AuthCode$	$\mathcal{G}_G^1$	$\bot$	$\{M, C, G\} \cup \tau_{Z_1} \cup \tau_{Z_4} \cup \tau_{Z_6}$	$\top$	Yes

TABLE 21: A Secure version of the SET protocol.

1. $C \rightarrow M : C, N_c$
2. $M \rightarrow C : \{M, C, XID, N_c, N_M, CA(G)\}_{k_M^{-1}}$
3. $C \rightarrow M : OI, DualSign, \{PI\}_{k_G}$
4. $M \rightarrow G : \{\{AuthReqData, LinkOIPI\}_{k_M^{-1}}\}_{k_G}, DualSign,$
   $\quad \{PI\}_{k_G}$
5. $G \rightarrow M : \{\{M, C, XID, AuthRRTags, PurchAmt,$
   $\quad AuthCode\}_{k_G^{-1}}\}_{k_M}$
5′. $G \rightarrow M : \{\{M, XID, AuthRRTags, AuthCode\}_{k_G^{-1}}\}_{k_M},$
   $\{\{M, C, XID, PurchAmt, AuthCode\}_{k_G^{-1}}\}_{k_M}$
6. $M \rightarrow C : \{M, C, XID, N_C, AuthCode\}_{k_M^{-1}}$

From Table 20, we can deduce that the generalized roles of G are not increasing. This is since the messages Z_{11} (*AuthRRTags*) and Z_6 (*PurchAmt*) are neighbors in step five while it is not the case in the step four. So, to make this role increasing we should put Z_6 (*PurchAmt*) beyond the encryption that contains *AuthRRTags* in step five. For instance, we replace the message of step five as follows:

5. $G \longrightarrow M:$

$$\left\{\{M, C, XID, AuthRRTags, AuthCode\}_{k_G^{-1}}\right\}_{k_M}, \quad (47)$$

$$\left\{\{M, C, XID, PurchAmt, AuthCode\}_{k_G^{-1}}\right\}_{k_M}.$$

To sum up, we propose hereafter a secure version of the SET protocol for the secrecy property. It replaces the message of step 5 by message 5′ in Table 21.

Also, the *OI*, *PI*, *DualSign*, and *LinkOIPI* messages are as follows:

$$OI := OIData, H(PIData),$$

$$OIData := M, C, XID, N_M, N_C, HOD,$$

$$HOD := H(OrderDesc, PurchAmt),$$

$$PIData := PIHead, PANData,$$

$$PIHead(oldversion) := C, HOD, PurchAmt,$$

$$MerID, M, XID,$$

$$H(XID, CardSecret),$$

$$\textbf{PIHead} := C, HOD, PurchAmt, MerID,$$

$$\textbf{H(M, XID), H(CardSecret)},$$

$$PANData := PAN, PANSecret,$$

$$PI := PIHead, H(OIData), PANData,$$

$$DualSign := \{H(PIData), H(OIData)\}_{k_C^{-1}},$$

$$LinkOIPI := H(AuthReqData, DualSign,$$

$$\{PI\}_{K_G}),$$

$$AuthReqData := H(OIData), HOD,$$

$$M, \mathcal{C}, XID, AuthRRTags.$$

$$(48)$$

Such modifications allow to prove, by using the DEKAN function, that the new version is increasing and therefore respects the secrecy property.

5. Comparison with Related Works

The interpretation functions-based method is flexible framework allowing to verify different classes of protocols against a variety of intruder models. This flexibility gives to it a great advantage when compared to the related works where almost all the approaches can deal only with a specific class of protocols and under some specific assumptions. When using the interpretation functions-based method, we do not have any restriction neither on the class of protocols that we can analyze nor on the intruder model and the algebraic properties. We are limited only by our capacity to find a suitable and safe interpretation function for the protocol that we want to analyze under a selected intruder model (context of verification).

Also, the analysis of protocols using the interpretation function-based method can help to discover the algebraic properties that should not be satisfied by an operator of encryption to guarantee the correctness of the analyzed protocol. This information is useful for the implementation of the protocol when time comes to select a specific encryption system. For instance, the commutativity property of the "exclusive or" and the "nilpotence" property should not be combined since they allow to decrypt a message without knowing the key.

Moreover, the interpretation function-based method has the significant advantage to ensure the correctness of cryptographic protocols for unbound number of sessions without any restriction neither on the number of principals nor on the size of exchanged messages. In fact, may existing approaches restrict their results by either limiting the number of sessions, the sizes of messages, or/and the number of involved principals to be able to overcome infinite number of traces that can be exhibited by a protocol. Other works tried to find a finite number of traces that are representative for all the others, that is, the analysis of the selected traces is enough to conclude about the correctness of the protocol. However, finding this representative and finite set of traces, if it exists, can be as complicated as the original problem even for some particular class of protocols. There are, however, some tentatives to analyze protocols without restriction on their traces, but they still suffer from some heavy restrictions both on the class of protocols that they can analyze and on the intruder model that they use.

In the remaining part of this section, we focus on the typing-based method [33] and the rank function-based method [32] which have some similarities with the interpretation functions-based method.

5.1. Typing-Based Method. In 1997, Abadi introduced in [33] a typing system to verify the secrecy property. This system uses three types {*secret, public, any*} as security levels and verifies whether the sent messages during the protocol are appropriately protected, that is, according to their security levels. The approach uses the Spi-calculus as a formal language to specify the analyzed protocol. Then, a typing system is applied on the protocol: if it typechecks we conclude that it ensures the secrecy property.

Compared to interpretation functions-based method, the secrecy by typing approach has the following restrictions.

(i) The exchanged messages have to respect some particular form. They must always be composed of four separated parts having the following type {*secret, public, any, confounder*}. This restriction helps to recognize the parts that are "secret," "public," and "any" (component with unknown security level) of messages. But, this involves that this approach cannot be applied to analyze existing protocols which have not been developed with this restriction in mind. The interpretation functions-based method, on the other side, does not require any particular form related to the exchanged messages during a protocol.

(ii) The secrecy by typing approach uses only the the Dolev and Yao model for the intruder, while interpretation functions-based method can deal with different intruder models.

5.2. Rank Functions-Based Method. In 1997, Schneider suggested, in [31, 32], an interesting approach to verify the cryptographic protocols, specified as a process in CSP [46]. A protocol is considered as correct for the secrecy property if all its exchanged messages have a suitable rank according to a well-designed rank function. A message is either secret or public and the result returned by the ranking function should be in harmony with these security levels, that is, it assigns ranks (negative value) to secret messages different from the ones (positive value) assigned to public messages.

The main ideas behind the typing system, the interpretation function, and the rand function approach are the same, that is, find someway to evaluate the security levels of exchanged messages and then evaluate if they are appropriately protected to guaranty the correctness of the protocol for the secrecy property. However, there are some fundamental differences between them. Hereafter, we focus on the difference between the approach presented in this paper and the rank function.

(i) For each protocol, we need to define a suitable rank function which is a complicated task. There are no universal functions, like DEK or DEKAN for the interpretation function approach, that are independent of the analyzed protocols. A rank function is extracted from the analyzed protocol itself and should respect some specific conditions (like safe condition for the interpretation function). Though the author makes a great effort, in [35, 47], to help find rank functions, the task remains complicated. On the other hand, in [25], the interpretation functions-based method gives a guideline which helps to define in an easier way safe interpretation functions.

(ii) The results given within the rank function approach are linked to a specific intruder ability. The approach based on interpretation function, on the other hand, is more flexible since it can handle a large variety of intruder abilities without reworking proofs.

(iii) When using a given interpretation function to analyze a protocol, even if we are unable to ensure its correctness the result is generally very helpful to either adapt the protocol or to build another interpretation function. This is not generally the case with the rank function approach.

6. Conclusion

By analyzing the SET and the NSL protocols, this paper is an attempt to show that the interpretation functions-based method is an efficient technique to analyze and to ensure the correctness of cryptographic protocols for the secrecy property. Based on some special functions called "Interpretation Functions," this technique allows to guarantee the secrecy property under an unbound number of sessions and without any restriction on the size of messages sent by the intruder. To verify the secrecy property, it is sufficient to check whether a finite specification of the protocol, called generalized roles, respects some precise conditions. Intuitively, these conditions state that involved principals could not decrease, for a safe interpretation function, the security levels of exchanged messages. Another interesting feature of this approach is that it can handle different verification contexts with different intruder abilities including algebraic properties.

As future works, we want to implement the approach, extend it to authentication property, and propose more safe interpretation functions.

References

[1] M. J. Banks and J. L. Jacob, "Unifying theories of confidentiality," in *Proceedings of the International Symposium on Unifying Theories of Programming (UTP '10)*, vol. 6445 of *Lecture Notes in Computer Science*, pp. 120–136, 2010.

[2] V. Cortier, S. Delaune, and P. Lafourcade, "A survey of algebraic properties used in cryptographic protocols," *Journal of Computer Security*, vol. 14, no. 1, pp. 1–43, 2006.

[3] V. Cortier, S. Kremer, and B. Warinschi, "A survey of symbolic methods in computational analysis of cryptographic systems," *Journal of Automated Reasoning*, vol. 46, no. 3-4, pp. 225–259, 2011.

[4] S. Escobar, C. Meadows, and J. Meseguer, "A rewriting-based inference system for the NRL protocol analyzer: grammar generation," in *Proceedings of the ACM Workshop on Formal Methods in Security Engineering (FMSE '05)*, pp. 1–12, ACM, New York, NY, USA, November 2005.

[5] J. Feigenbaum, A. Johnson, and P. Syverson, "Probabilistic analysis of onion routing in a black-box model," in *Proceedings of the 6th ACM Workshop on Privacy in the Electronic Society (WPES '07)*, pp. 1–10, October 2007.

[6] P. Lafourcade, V. Terrade, and S. Vigier, "Comparison of cryptographic verification tools dealing with algebraic properties," in *Proceedings of the 6th international conference on Formal Aspects in Security and Trust (FAST '09)*, pp. 173–185, Springer, Berlin, Germany, 2010.

[7] C. Meadows, "What makes a cryptographic protocol secure?" in *Proceedings of the European Symposium on Programming (ESOP '03)*, Springer, April 2003.

[8] "Security and trust management," in *Proceedings of the 7th International Workshop (STM '11)*, C. Meadows, M. Carmen, and F. Gago, Eds., vol. 7170 of *Lecture Notes in Computer Science*, Springer, Copenhagen, Denmark, June 2011.

[9] A. Sabelfeld and A. C. Myers, "Language-based information-flow security," *IEEE Journal on Selected Areas in Communications*, vol. 21, no. 1, pp. 5–19, 2003.

[10] A. Sinha, "A survey of system security in contactless electronic passports," *Journal of Computer Security*, vol. 19, no. 1, pp. 203–206, 2011.

[11] D. Dolev, S. Even, and R. M. Karp, "On the security of ping-pong protocols," *Information and Control*, vol. 55, no. 1–3, pp. 57–68, 1982.

[12] R. M. Amadio, D. Lugiez, and V. Vanackère, "On the symbolic reduction of processes with cryptographic functions," *Theoretical Computer Science*, vol. 290, no. 1, pp. 695–740, 2003.

[13] B. Blanchet, "An efficient cryptographic protocol verifier based on prolog rules," in *Proceedings of the 14th IEEE Workshop on Computer Security Foundations (CSFW '01)*, pp. 82–96, Novia Scotia, Canada, June 2001.

[14] H. Comon-Lundh, F. Jacquemard, and N. Perrin, "Tree automata with one memory, set constraints, and ping-pong protocols," in *Proceedings of the 8th International Conference on Automata, Languages and Programming (ICALP '07)*, vol. 2076 of *Lecture Notes in Computer Science*, pp. 682–695, 2007.

[15] H. Comon-Lundh and V. Shmatikov, "Intruder deductions, constraint solving and insecurity decision in presence of exclusive or," in *Proceedings of the 18th Annual IEEE Symposium on Logic in Computer Science (LICS '03)*, pp. 271–280, June 2003.

[16] N. Durgin, P. Lincoln, J. Mitchell, and A. Scedrov, "Undecidability of bounded security protocols," in *Proceedings of the Workshop on Formal Methods and Security Protocols (FMSP '99)*, N. Heintze and E. Clarke, Eds., Trento, Italy, July 1999.

[17] M. Fiore and M. Abadi, "Computing symbolic models for verifying cryptographic protocols," in *Proceedings of the 14th IEEE Computer Security Foundations Workshop (CSFW '14)*, pp. 160–173, June 2001.

[18] D. Kindred, Theory generation for security protocols, 1999.

[19] G. Lowe, "Towards a completeness result for model checking of security protocols," in *Proceedings of the 11th IEEE Computer Security Foundations Workshop (CSFW '98)*, pp. 96–105, June 1998.

[20] J. Millen and V. Shmatikov, "Constraint solving for bounded-process cryptographic protocol analysis," in *Proceedings of the 8th ACM Conference on Computer and Communications Security (CCS '01)*, pp. 166–175, November 2001.

[21] M. Rusinowitch and M. Turuani, "Protocol insecurity with a finite number of sessions and composed keys is NP-complete," *Theoretical Computer Science*, vol. 299, no. 1–3, pp. 451–475, 2003.

[22] S. D. Stoller, "A bound on attacks on payment protocols," in *Proceedings of the 16th Annual IEEE Symposium on Logic in Computer Science (LICS '01)*, pp. 61–70, June 2001.

[23] Y. Chevalier, R. Küsters, M. Rusinowitch, M. Turuani, and L. Vigneron, "Extending the Dolev-Yao intruder for analyzing an unbounded number of sessions," vol. 2803, pp. 128–141.

[24] L. C. Paulson, "Mechanized proofs for a recursive authentication protocol," in *Proceedings of the 10th IEEE Computr Security Foundations Workshop (CSFW '97)*, pp. 84–94, June 1997.

[25] H. Houmani and M. Mejri, "Analysis of some famous cryptographic protocols using the interpretation-function-based method," *International Journal of Security and Its Applications*, vol. 2, no. 4, pp. 99–116, 2008.

[26] H. Houmani and M. Mejri, "Ensuring the correctness of cryptographic protocols with respect to secrecy," in *Proceedings of the International Conference on Security and Cryptography*

(SECRYPT '08), pp. 184–189, INSTICC Press, Porto, Portugal, July 2008.

[27] SetCo., "Set secure electronic transaction Specification: business description," Tech. Rep., 1997.

[28] SetCo, "Set secure electronic transaction specification: formal protocol definition," Tech. Rep., 1997.

[29] SetCo, "Set secure electronic transaction specification: programmer's guide," Tech. Rep., 1997.

[30] R. M. Needham and M. D. Schroeder, "Using encryption for authentication in large networks of computers," *Communications of the ACM*, vol. 21, no. 12, pp. 993–999, 1978.

[31] R. Delicata and S. Schneider, "Temporal rank functions for forward secrecy," in *Proceedings of the 18th IEEE Computer Security Foundations Workshop (CSFW '05)*, pp. 126–139, Washington, DC, USA, June 2005.

[32] S. Schneider, "Verifying authentication protocols in CSP," *IEEE Transactions on Software Engineering*, vol. 24, no. 9, pp. 741–758, 1998.

[33] M. Abadi, "Secrecy by typing in security protocols," *Journal of the ACM*, vol. 46, no. 5, pp. 749–786, 1999.

[34] H. Houmani and M. Mejri, "Secrecy by interpretation functions," *Knowledge-Based Systems*, vol. 20, no. 7, pp. 617–635, 2007.

[35] B. Dutertre and S. Schneider, "Using a pvs embedding of csp to verify authentication protocols," in *Proceedings of the Theorem Proving in Higher Order Logics (TPHOL's '97)*, pp. 121–136, Springer, 1997.

[36] D. E. Bell and L. J. La Padula, *Secure Computer Systems: Mathematical Foundations*, vol. I, The MITRE Corporation, 1973.

[37] T. Y. C. Woo and S. S. Lam, "A lesson on authentication protocol design," *Operating Systems Review*, pp. 24–37, 1994.

[38] M. Debbabi, M. Mejri, N. Tawbi, and I. Yahmadi, "From protocol specifications to flaws and attack scenarios: an automatic and formal algorithm," in *Proceedings of the 2nd International Workshop on Enterprise Security*, Massachusetts Institute of Technology (MIT), IEEE Press, Cambridge, Mass, USA, June 1997.

[39] M. Debbabi, N. A. Durgin, M. Mejri, and J. C. Mitchell, "Security by typing," *International Journal on Software Tools for Technology Transfer*, vol. 4, no. 4, pp. 472–495, 2003.

[40] H. Comon-Lundh and R. Treinen, "Easy intruder deductions," in *Verification: Theory and Practice*, vol. 2772/2004 of *Lecture Notes in Computer Science*, pp. 182–184, Springer, Berlin, Germany, 2004.

[41] S. Delaune, "Easy intruder deduction problems with homomorphisms," *Information Processing Letters*, vol. 97, no. 6, pp. 213–218, 2006.

[42] P. Lafourcade, D. Lugiez, and R. Treinen, "Intruder deduction for the equational theory of Abelian groups with distributive encryption," *Information and Computation*, vol. 205, no. 4, pp. 581–623, 2007.

[43] G. Bella, F. Massacci, and L. C. Paulson, "Verifying the SET registration protocols," *IEEE Journal on Selected Areas in Communications*, vol. 21, no. 1, pp. 77–87, 2003.

[44] L. C. Paulson, "Verifying the SET protocol: overview," in *Proceedings of the International Conference on Formal Aspects of Security (FASec '03)*, vol. 2629 of *Lecture Notes in Computer Science*, pp. 4–14, 2003.

[45] S. Brlek, S. Hamadou, and J. Mullins, "A flaw in the electronic commerce protocol SET," *Information Processing Letters*, vol. 97, no. 3, pp. 104–108, 2006.

[46] S. Schneider, "An operational semantics for timed CSP," in *Proceedings of the Chalmers Workshop on Concurrency*, Report PMGR63, pp. 428–456, Chalmers University of Technology and University of Göteborg, 1992.

[47] J. W. Bryans and S. Schneider, "Mechanical verification of the full needhamschroeder public key protocol," Tech. Rep. CSD-TR-97-11, University of London, 1997.

3

Learning-Based Spectrum Sensing for Cognitive Radio Systems

Yasmin Hassan, Mohamed El-Tarhuni, and Khaled Assaleh

Department of Electrical Engineering, American University of Sharjah, P.O. Box 26666, Sharjah, UAE

Correspondence should be addressed to Mohamed El-Tarhuni, mtarhuni@aus.edu

Academic Editor: Lixin Gao

This paper presents a novel pattern recognition approach to spectrum sensing in collaborative cognitive radio systems. In the proposed scheme, discriminative features from the received signal are extracted at each node and used by a classifier at a central node to make a global decision about the availability of spectrum holes for use by the cognitive radio network. Specifically, linear and polynomial classifiers are proposed with energy, cyclostationary, or coherent features. Simulation results in terms of detection and false alarm probabilities of all proposed schemes are presented. It is concluded that cyclostationary-based schemes are the most reliable in terms of detecting primary users in the spectrum, however, at the expense of a longer sensing time compared to coherent based schemes. Results show that the performance is improved by having more users collaborating in providing features to the classifier. It is also shown that, in this spectrum sensing application, a linear classifier has a comparable performance to a second-order polynomial classifier and hence provides a better choice due to its simplicity. Finally, the impact of the observation window on the detection performance is presented.

1. Introduction

In the past few years, there have been remarkable developments in wireless communications technology leading to a rapid growth in wireless applications. However, this dramatic increase in wireless applications is severely limited by bandwidth scarcity. Traditionally, fixed spectrum assignments, in which frequency bands are statically assigned to licensed users are employed. The static spectrum allocation prevents from assigning vacant spectrum bands to new users and services. Further, spectrum occupancy measurements have shown that some licensed bands are significantly underutilized. For example, the Spectral Policy Task Force reported that radio channels are typically occupied 15% of the time [1]. Hence, the limitation in the available spectrum bands occurs mainly due the underutilization of available spectrum resulting from the inefficient static allocation techniques. This underutilization of available spectrum resources has led regulatory bodies to urge the development of dynamic spectrum allocation paradigms, called cognitive radio (CR) networks.

A CR network senses the operating environment for vacant spectrum opportunities and dynamically utilize the available radio resources [2, 3]. In CR technology, unlicensed (secondary) users are allowed to share the spectrum originally assigned to licensed (primary) users. Hence, frequency bands that are legally assigned to primary users are exploited by secondary users when primary users are idle. However, primary users have the right to occupy their assigned bands whenever needed. Consequently, secondary users should be aware of the variations in the surrounding environment and should be ready to adjust their operating parameters accordingly in order to make a productive usage of the spectrum [4].

Secondary users in CR networks are restrained by the condition of providing adequate protection to primary users. Hence, secondary users need to employ efficient spectrum sensing techniques that ensure the quality of service for primary users and exploit all dynamic spectrum sharing chances. That is to say, in order to facilitate dynamic spectrum access in licensed bands, effective spectrum sensing algorithms need to be developed whereby high reliability along with efficient utilization is achieved.

Spectrum sensing approaches that are commonly considered in CR applications include energy detection, cyclostationary feature detection, and coherent detection [2, 4–6]. Based on the prior knowledge a secondary user has about primary users, a specific technique would be more appropriate. For instance, if a priori information about a primary user signal is known by secondary users, coherent detection can be utilized. Coherent detection uses features such as synchronization messages, pilots, preambles, midambles, and spectrum spreading sequences. When these patterns are known at the CR network, sensing is performed by correlating the incoming signal with the known patterns [6]. Coherent sensing based on pilot detection was implemented experimentally in [7]. On the other hand, when CRs have very limited information about the primary signal, energy detection is used. Another reason for using energy detection in spectrum sensing applications is the low complexity involved. However, the performance of energy detection in terms of the ability to detect primary signals is degraded, especially in low signal-to-noise ratio (SNR) conditions.

Another approach to spectrum sensing is based on cyclostationary detection to sense the presence of a primary user by exploiting cyclostationary features exhibited by the statistics of the primary signal [8]. In cyclostationary detection, the spectral correlation function (SCF) of a modulated signal is analyzed to decide on the presence of primary signal in the target spectrum. Cyclostationary feature detection based on multicycle detection has been proposed in [9, 10], where the cyclostationarity is detected at multiples of the cycle frequency. In orthogonal frequency division multiplexing (OFDM) systems, a cyclic prefix is intentionally inserted as a guard interval, which could be used to detect cyclostationarity of incumbent primary signals [11, 12]. Furthermore, the OFDM waveform could be modified in order to generate specific signatures at certain frequencies [13] such that the cyclic features created by these signatures are then extracted via cyclostationary detection to achieve an effective signal identification mechanism.

In order to preserve the quality of service for primary users, the interference caused by secondary users needs to be maintained below an acceptable level. Hence, reliable spectrum sensing needs to be performed by secondary users to detect the presence of a primary user, especially under shadowing and fading effects. Collaboration among spatially displaced secondary users is, hence, required to mitigate such effects without requiring excessively long detection times. In this case, several CR nodes utilize the spatial diversity gain provided by cooperative spectrum sensing to achieve better performance in fading environments [4, 9, 10, 14, 15].

In this work, we propose a collaborative spectrum sensing approach in CR applications. Specifically, we utilize classification techniques used in pattern recognition applications to identify the available and busy bands in the radio spectrum. Previously, pattern recognition techniques were used mainly in signal classification for determining type of modulation rather than spectrum sensing [16–18]. The proposed pattern recognition scheme represents a centralized cooperative CR network, whereby the decision of spectrum availability is made at a central node after collecting spectral sensing information from all collaborating users. Sensing information is subjected to a classifier model that outputs a global decision regarding the availability of the target spectrum band. Polynomial classifiers are

proposed in this work as classifier models, in which first- and second-order expansions are investigated. Three spectrum sensing techniques are implemented to provide informative features to the classifier about the surrounding environment. Spectrum sensing techniques used for feature extraction can be classified into parametric and nonparametric. Nonparametric detection includes energy detection where the cognitive network does not have a priori knowledge on the primary users' signals. On the other hand, in parametric detection, cyclic features characterizing primary signals and prior knowledge of synchronizing preamble patterns are utilized. The parametric detection schemes include coherent detection and cyclostationary feature detection.

Many of the collaboration techniques in the prior work implement maximum ratio combining, likelihood ratio test, or hard decision rules, such as AND logic operation and one-out-of-n rule [4, 5, 19, 20]. Cooperative sensing based on energy detection has been proposed in [4], in which linear combination of local test statistics from multiple users is utilized in the decision making. The performance of a cyclostationary-based spectrum sensing cooperative CR system was considered in [20, 21], where binary decisions with different fusion rules of the secondary user's decisions using cyclic detectors were compared. Moreover, multiple user single-cycle detectors are proposed to accommodate secondary user collaboration [9], where different cyclic frequencies are utilized by different users and combined to make a global decision. In [10], the summation of local tests statistics of secondary users is employed as the fusion rule when multicycle detection is performed by CRs. Finally, cooperation based on hard decision rules was investigated with coherent detection in [7].

The contributions of this paper are as follows. The problem of collaborative spectrum sensing in CR networks is investigated from a new perspective based on a pattern recognition approach. More specifically, polynomial classifiers are used in this work. The design, validation and evaluation of first- and second-order polynomial classifiers are presented. The parameters of these classifiers are optimized based on the signal strength of the individual secondary users in a collaborative manner. The performance in terms of false alarm rate and detection probability under low SNR conditions has been thoroughly examined and analyzed. Comprehensive performance evaluation of energy-based detection is provided. Finally, extensive simulations are performed to evaluate the performance of the proposed classifiers with parametric spectrum sensing schemes, where carrier frequency and synchronization preamble patterns are assumed to be known at the CR network. The results of this investigation were partially presented in [22, 23].

The rest of the paper is organized as follows: in Section 2, we introduce the signal model and the proposed cooperative spectrum sensing scheme. In Section 3, different feature extracting techniques are presented. The polynomial classifier structure is developed in Section 4. Simulation results and discussions are given in Section 5. Finally, Section 6 concludes the paper. All notations and symbols used in this paper are explained in Table 1.

TABLE 1: List of notations.

Notation/symbol	Explanation
$r_j[n]$	Received signal by user j
$x[n]$	Transmitted primary signal
g_j	Channel gain coefficients
$\eta_j[n]$	Zero-mean additive white Gaussian noise (AWGN) at user j's end
N	Number of users in cognitive network
$\mathbf{d}$	N-dimensional feature vector consisting of features extracted from different CRs
M	Number of samples observed to make a decision (observation window size)
$R_x^\alpha(\tau)$	Cyclic autocorrelation function
$S_x^\alpha[k]$	Spectral correlation density function
$R_{jc}[k]$	Cross-correlation between the received signal and the preamble sequence
$\boldsymbol{\varphi}(\mathbf{d})$	l-dimensional vector consisting of the monomials of a another vector $\mathbf{d}$
$\mathbf{w}_i$	The classifier model parameters for class i
$\mathbf{D}_{\text{train}}$	$K \times N$ matrix, where N is the dimensionality of the input feature vectors (provided by N CR users) and K is the number of feature vectors used in the training process
$\mathbf{M}$	A $(K \times l)$ matrix representing the polynomial expansion of elements in training data set $\mathbf{D}_{\text{train}}$
$\mathbf{t}_i$	An ideal target vector representing the ideal channel state (ON or OFF)
Y_d	Binary global decision on channel availability

2. Signal Model and System Description

We consider dynamic spectrum allocation in a collaborative CR network with the structure illustrated in Figure 1. The primary user and CR network are assumed to coexist within the same geographical area. The CR network consists of N users with a central node that detects the presence of primary signals and decides on the channel availability. CRs temporarily access the underutilized licensed frequency bands, without conflict with primary spectrum holders' usage.

The binary hypothesis test for spectrum sensing is formulated as

$$r_j[n] = \begin{cases} g_j x[n] + \eta_j[n] : & H_1 \\ \eta_j[n] : & H_0 \end{cases} \quad \text{for } j = 1, 2, \ldots, N, \quad (1)$$

where $r_j[n]$ represents the received signal by the jth CR user at the nth instant of time, and $x[n]$ denotes the primary user transmitted signal. H_1 represents the hypothesis of an occupied spectrum, while H_0 corresponds to an idle spectrum. The received signal at the jth user is corrupted by a zero-mean additive white Gaussian noise (AWGN), $\eta_j[n]$ with variance σ_j^2. The primary signal passes through a wireless channel to reach the jth CR user with a channel gain g_j. The wireless channel is modeled as a flat channel with slow fading. Each channel has a complex valued coefficient with Rayleigh distributed magnitude and uniformly distributed phase over the range $[0, 2\pi)$. The channel coefficients of different CRs in the network are assumed to be constant over a number of received signal symbols, that is, slow fading, and are also assumed to be independent and identically distributed.

In this paper, spectrum sensing in CR networks is formulated as a pattern recognition problem. Generally speaking, pattern recognition is used to classify a given set of data into several different categories. A pattern recognition system assigns an input signal to one of a number of known categories based on features derived to emphasize commonalities between those signals. A generic term that is used to describe input signals that need to be classified in a recognition system is *patterns*. Usually, patterns may not be useful for classification, and hence they need to be processed to acquire more useful input to the classifier [24, 25]. This processed information is called *features*. In supervised learning, a labeled training set of feature vectors is processed through the classification algorithm to determine the classifier model parameters. These parameters are used in predicting the class of new data that have not been seen during the learning phase. In this paper, supervised pattern recognition is utilized at the CR base station (CRBS) to classify available spectrum holes such that maximum detection is achieved with a desired false alarm rate.

In the proposed system, secondary users are constantly sensing the target spectrum band for primary signal presence. Within a secondary user receiver, discriminative features are extracted from the sensed signal. The extracted features from the difference secondary users are transmitted to the CRBS through a relatively low data rate control channel. This control channel is used for exchanging information between CRs and CRBS. At the CRBS, a decision about the spectrum availability is made based on a pattern recognition classifier that is previously trained. The block diagram of the proposed system is depicted in Figure 2 showing the signal flow of the CR inputs through feature extraction

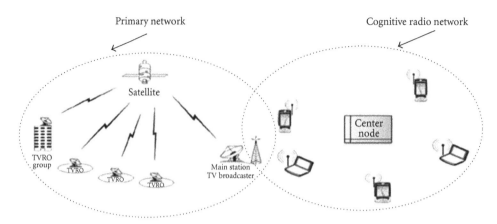

FIGURE 1: An example of a centralized CR network.

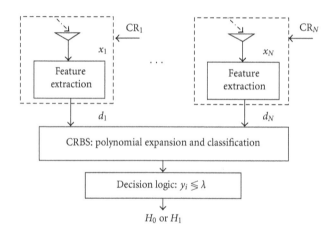

FIGURE 2: Pattern recognition CR system model.

and classification leading to a decision about the spectrum availability at the CRBS.

The first step is spectrum sensing which involves input data acquisition by processing the signals received by antennas at different CR receivers. The received signal of the jth user is assumed to follow the mathematical model described in (1). These signals are transformed into multidimensional feature vectors that compactly characterize the sensed signals.

When secondary users in a CR network have no prior information about the transmitted primary signal, the energy of the received signal is used at the feature extraction stage and utilized by the classifier to discriminate between the noise only and primary signal present cases. On the other hand, if prior information, such as carrier frequency and synchronizing patterns, is known about the primary user's signal, feature extraction will be achieved by either exploiting cyclic features present in the signal or through coherent detection. Features extracted by any of the mentioned detection schemes will exhibit certain patterns when the spectrum is occupied by a primary user that are different from the patterns extracted when only noise is present in the spectrum. The difference between these patterns will be exploited as discriminative input data to

the pretrained classifier for decision making. The following section discusses the different feature extraction schemes used in this paper.

3. Feature Extraction Techniques

In this work, three different feature extraction schemes have been used, namely, noncoherent energy-based features, cyclostationary-based features, and coherent detection-based features.

3.1. Energy-Based Feature Extraction. Energy detection is one of the most commonly used techniques in spectrum sensing due to its low computational complexity and simple implementation. It does not require any prior knowledge of the primary users' signal; hence, it is considered as a nonparametric detection scheme. The classification system identifies spectrum availability relying on the energy of the received signal over an observation period. However, the task of detecting the signal becomes very challenging under low SNR levels and fading channels [5, 14]. As a preprocessing step, the received signal by the jth secondary user, $r_j(t)$, which follows the model specified in (1), is filtered according to the desired frequency band to obtain $y_j(t)$. The sampled

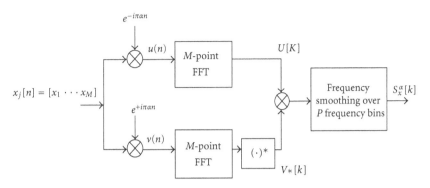

FIGURE 3: Cyclostationary feature detection estimator.

version of the signal is used to extract one representative energy feature d_j defined as

$$d_j = \frac{1}{M} \sum_{n=1}^{M} \left| y_j[n] \right|^2, \qquad (2)$$

where M is the length of the observation period in samples. Accordingly, a feature vector for this observation period is constructed from the N users' signals such as $\mathbf{d} = [d_1 \cdots d_N]^T$, where T is the vector transpose operation. This feature vector will be presented to the classifier in the classification stage. A new set of energy features is obtained every observation window.

3.2. Cyclostationary-Based Feature Extraction.

Most communication signals can be modeled as cyclostationary random processes, as they are usually characterized by built-in periodicities in their mean and autocorrelation. These underlying periodicities arise from the use of sinusoidal carriers, repeating spreading codes, pulse trains, or cyclic prefixes in signal transmission. On the other hand, noise signals do not exhibit such periodicity characteristics. Hence, the sensing of the spectrum availability can be based on the detection of the signal periodicity.

A binary phase shift keying (BPSK) that digitally modulated signal $x(t)$ with symbol duration T_0 has a cyclic autocorrelation function (CAF) defined as

$$R_x^\alpha(\tau) \triangleq \frac{1}{T_0} \int_{-T_0/2}^{T_0/2} \left(x\left(t + \frac{\tau}{2}\right) x^*\left(t - \frac{\tau}{2}\right) e^{-j2\pi\alpha t} \right) dt, \quad (3)$$

where τ is a nonzero delay, and $\alpha \in \{0, \pm 1/T_0, \pm 2/T_0, \dots\}$. $R_x^\alpha(\tau)$ represents the Fourier transform of the delay product $x(t + \tau/2)x^*(t - \tau/2)$ evaluated at the frequencies in α. The signal $x(t)$ is said to contain second order periodicity if and only if the Fourier transform of $R_x^\alpha(\tau)$ has discrete spectral lines at nonzero frequencies $\alpha \neq 0$ [26, 27].

Cyclostationarity of a signal leads to the presence of specific patterns in the spectrum of the signal, which can be examined using the so-called spectral correlation density function (SCD) [27, 28] defined as the Fourier transform of its CAF as

$$S_x^\alpha(f; \alpha) = \int_{-\infty}^{\infty} R_x^\alpha(\tau) e^{-j2\pi f \tau} d\tau. \qquad (4)$$

The SCD is the cross-correlation function between the spectral translates of the signal at $f \pm \alpha/2$, for some cyclic frequency α. This function is smoothed using a frequency smoothing vector (window) W with P frequency bins. Since discrete-time samples of the received are used in estimating the SCD, it is possible to show that the SCD is given by

$$S_x^\alpha[k] = \frac{1}{P} \sum_{v=-(P-1)/2}^{(P-1)/2} X\left[k + \frac{\alpha}{2} + v\right] X^*\left[k - \frac{\alpha}{2} + v\right] W(v), \qquad (5)$$

with

$$X[k] = \sum_{n=0}^{M-1} x[n] e^{-j2\pi kn/M}, \qquad (6)$$

where $k = 0, 1, \dots, M - 1$, and M is the number of samples over which the spectrum of the received signal is calculated (FFT length). The SCD estimation is implemented to obtain the cyclic feature extraction receiver structure as shown in Figure 3. The SCD of the received signal will depend on the presence or absence of the primary transmitted signal according to the following:

$$S_{r_j}^{\alpha_0}[k] = \begin{cases} \left| g_j \right|^2 S_x^{\alpha_0}[k] + S_{\eta_j}^{\alpha_0}[k] : & H_1, \\ S_{\eta_j}^{\alpha_0}[k] : & H_0, \end{cases} \qquad (7)$$

where $S_{\eta_j}^{\alpha_0}[k]$ is the SCD of the AWGN only at the jth CR user, and $S_x^{\alpha_0}[k]$ is the SCD of the transmitted primary signal at some cyclic frequency $\alpha = \alpha_0$. Since the AWGN is a wide sense stationary process and does not possess second-order cyclostationarity, it will not have a peak at any cyclic frequency. On the other hand, the band-pass BPSK signal exhibits second-order cycle frequencies at $\alpha_0/2 = f_c + m/T_0$ [2, 9], for some integer m. Since the strongest spectral lines of a BPSK signal appear at $= f_c$, the strongest cyclic components are observed at $\alpha_0/2 = f_c$ [9]. Therefore, the local decision variable for cyclostationary detection from jth CR user is chosen to be the value of the SCD in (7) evaluated at $k = 0$. This value is used as the jth element in the feature vector $\mathbf{d} = [d_1 \cdots d_N]^T$ that will be presented to the classifier in the classification stage, where $d_j = S_{r_j}^{\alpha_0}[k]$ with $k = 0$.

3.3. Coherent Based Feature Extraction. Another sensing scheme investigated in this work is feature extraction using coherent detection. Coherent detection is performed by demodulating the primary user's signal, which requires a priori information of the primary signal such as packet format, control, or synchronization sequences. [6]. If the synchronizing preamble patterns are known at the CR network end, coherent sensing can be exploited by correlating the incoming signal with the known patterns. This is effectively correlating the signal with itself resulting in an autocorrelation function that peaks at zero delay when the primary user is present. Primary users are assumed to use a frame size of M bits with an L-bit synchronization preamble referred to as $x_p[n]$. Accordingly, the cognitive users will be acquiring data during the preamble period (i.e., L bits every M bits). The received signal from jth CR user, $r_j(t)$, is cross-correlated with the preamble sequence over the preamble length to obtain

$$R_{jc}[k] = \begin{cases} |g_j|^2 \sum_{n=1}^{L} |x_p[n]|^2 + \mathrm{Re}\left\{\sum_{n=1}^{L} x_p[n]\eta_j^*[n]\right\} & : \quad H_1 \\ \mathrm{Re}\left\{\sum_{n=1}^{L} x_p[n]\eta_j^*[n]\right\} & H_0. \end{cases}$$
(8)

Under hypothesis H_1, $R_{jc}[k]$ becomes an autocorrelation of the transmitted preamble having a strong peak at $k = 0$. However, under H_0, $R_{jc}[k]$ will not exhibit strong peaks. The peak value of $R_{jc}[k]$ is used as the jth element in the feature vector $\mathbf{d} = [d_1 \cdots d_N]^T$ that will be presented to the classifier in the classification stage, where $d_j = \max\{|R_{jc}[k]|\}$.

4. Polynomial Classifiers

In this paper, we use polynomial classifiers (PCs) as the classification models to decide on the spectrum availability. Polynomial classifiers have shown improved recognition performance with lower computational complexity as compared to other recognitions methods, such as neural networks and hidden Markov models [25, 29]. Furthermore, polynomial classifiers deal with simple mathematical operations such as multiplication and summation, which makes them suitable for practical implementation in digital signal processing algorithms. The principle of a polynomial classifier is the expansion of the input feature space into a higher dimensional space that is linearly separable [30].

Consider an input pattern $\mathbf{d} = [d_1 \cdots d_N]^T$, where N is the number of features and T represents the transpose operation. The rth order polynomial classifier first performs a vectorial mapping of the N-dimensional feature vector, $\mathbf{d}$,

into an l-dimensional vector $\boldsymbol{\varphi}(\mathbf{d})$. The elements of $\boldsymbol{\varphi}(\mathbf{d})$ are monomials of the form [24, 25]

$$\begin{aligned} \boldsymbol{\varphi}(\mathbf{d}) = \Big[&1, d_1, d_2, \ldots d_N, d_1^2, d_1 d_2, d_1 d_3, \ldots, d_1 d_N, d_1^3, d_1^2 d_2, \\ &\ldots d_1^2 d_N, \ldots, d_1^r, d_1^r d_2, \ldots d_1^r d_N, \\ &d_2^2, d_2 d_3, \ldots, d_2 d_N, d_2^3, d_2^2 d_1, d_2^2 d_3, \ldots d_2^2 d_N, \\ &\ldots, d_2^r, d_2^r d_1, \ldots, d_2^r d_N, \ldots \Big]^T. \end{aligned}$$
(9)

Then, the output scorer y_i is obtained at the output layer after linearly combining the expansion terms $\boldsymbol{\varphi}(\mathbf{d})$ using

$$y_i = \mathbf{w}_i^T \boldsymbol{\varphi}(\mathbf{d}),$$
(10)

where $\mathbf{w}_i$ is the model (weights) of class i. The dimensionality of the expanded vector $\boldsymbol{\varphi}(\mathbf{d})$ can be expressed in terms of the polynomial order and the dimensionality of the input vector $\mathbf{d}$. The design of the classifier comprises of two stages, namely, training and testing.

4.1. Training. The training process involves finding the optimal model parameters that best map a multidimensional input sequence to a corresponding one-dimensional target sequence. The model is designed to classify between two different classes, H_i for $i = \{0, 1\}$, corresponding to the binary hypotheses in (1). The multidimensional input sequence $\mathbf{D}_{\mathrm{train}}$ is a $K \times N$ matrix, where N is the dimensionality of the input feature vectors (provided by N CR users) and K is the number of feature vectors used in the training process. The training matrix $\mathbf{D}_{\mathrm{train}}$ is given by

$$\mathbf{D}_{\mathrm{train}} = \begin{bmatrix} d_{11} & d_{12} & \cdots & d_{1N} \\ \vdots & & \ddots & \vdots \\ d_{K1} & d_{K2} & \cdots & d_{KN} \end{bmatrix}.$$
(11)

The one-dimensional target vector $\mathbf{t}_i = [t_{i_1} \ t_{i_2} \cdots t_{i_K}]^T$ for $i = \{0, 1\}$ consists of K elements where $t_{i_z} = 1$ if the corresponding zth feature vector belongs to class i, and $t_{i_z} = 0$ if the corresponding zth feature vector does not belong to class i, for $z = 1, 2, \ldots, K$.

The training vectors are expanded into their polynomial terms as defined in (9) resulting in a model training $\mathbf{M}$ data set of size $(K \times l)$ that is defined by

$$\mathbf{M} = \begin{bmatrix} \boldsymbol{\varphi}(\mathbf{d}_1) & \boldsymbol{\varphi}(\mathbf{d}_2) & \cdots & \boldsymbol{\varphi}(\mathbf{d}_K) \end{bmatrix}^T.$$
(12)

Once training feature vectors are expanded into their polynomial basis terms, the polynomial classifier is trained to find an optimum set of weights, $\mathbf{w}_i^{\mathrm{opt}}$, that minimizes the Euclidian distance between the ideal target vector $\mathbf{t}_i$ and the corresponding outputs of the classifier using the mean-squared error criterion to get

$$\mathbf{w}_i^{\mathrm{opt}} = \arg\{\min_{\mathbf{w}} \|\mathbf{M}\mathbf{w} - \mathbf{t}_i\|_2\}.$$
(13)

The problem of (13) can be solved using the method of normal equation to explicitly obtain the optimal model for the two-class spectrum sensing problem as [25, 29]

$$\mathbf{w}_i^{\text{opt}} = \left(\mathbf{M}^T\mathbf{M}\right)^{-1}\mathbf{M}^T\mathbf{t}_i. \qquad (14)$$

4.2. Testing. In the testing stage, novel feature vectors $\mathbf{d}_{\text{test}}$ are used to represent the testing data set. The features are initially expanded into their basis terms $\boldsymbol{\varphi}(\mathbf{d}_{\text{test}})$ and then presented to the trained models $\{\mathbf{w}_0^{\text{opt}}, \mathbf{w}_1^{\text{opt}}\}$ to obtain the corresponding set of scores $\{y_i\}$ as

$$\{y_i\} = \boldsymbol{\varphi}(\mathbf{d}_{\text{test}})\,\mathbf{w}_i^{\text{opt}} \quad \text{for } i = 0, 1. \qquad (15)$$

Accordingly, we assign the testing feature vector to hypothesis H_i that satisfies [25]

$$Y_d = \arg_i\{\max\{y_i\}\}. \qquad (16)$$

Ideally, the output from the classifier model, for a certain input feature vector, should be one when the spectrum is occupied and zero when the spectrum is idle as we apply it to the corresponding model $\mathbf{w}_i^{\text{opt}}$. However, when new input data are fed to the classifier, the output has values varying around one for hypothesis H_1 and values varying around zero for H_0 and vice versa. In order to achieve a desired level of constant false alarm rate, a threshold needs to be defined to separate the two classes instead of just comparing different models output scores.

An iterative algorithm is applied at the training stage to search for the threshold for different signal levels that achieves a specific false alarm rate as follows. First, the output score is computed by subjecting a validation data set (with known class labels) to the model $\mathbf{w}_1^{\text{opt}}$. The threshold is initialized to $\lambda = 0.5$, such that the global decision variable $Y_d = 1$ if $y_1 > \lambda$ and $Y_d = 0$ otherwise. The false alarm rate is then estimated by comparing the output decisions of all validation feature vectors to the ideal output $\mathbf{t}_1$. A false alarm will be declared when the output decision is one indicating that the spectrum is busy while the ideal output $\mathbf{t}_1$ is zero indicating that the actual spectrum is available. The threshold λ is incremented or decremented with a small value such that the desired false alarm rate is achieved with a specified accuracy, for example, a mean-squared error of less than 1%. The above steps are repeated for the validation data with different received SNR levels to form a lookup table that could be used when new test data is received. Note that the threshold setting operation, in addition to the training process, is performed offline. The training and validation data sequences are retrieved from a database that is maintained at the CRBS for offline training and validation.

5. Simulation Results

In this section, the performance of a first-order polynomial classifier (known also as linear classifier (LC)) and second-order polynomial classifiers (PCs) using the previously discussed feature extraction methods is evaluated. A band pass BPSK primary signal is used when cyclostationary feature detection is utilized, while antipodal baseband signaling with $S(k) = \pm 1$ in the case of coherent detection. To emulate a more challenging and practical situation, we assume the distance between the CR network and the primary transmitter is relatively large; hence, the average received SNR_{avg} is in the low SNR range, that is, $\text{SNR}_{\text{avg}} \leq 0\,\text{dB}$. In addition, the jth CR receives a signal with a signal-to-noise ratio SNR_j that depends on the ith CR's proximity from the primary user. To account for signal shadowing, SNR_j follows a log-normal distribution with a variance $\sigma^2 = 4\,\text{dB}$ and a mean equivalent to SNR_{avg}. The small-scale channel variations follow a flat Rayleigh fading model. It is also assumed that the channel variation is relatively slow compared to the bit duration (slow fading model). We remark that the simulation parameters were used for illustrative purposes, and other values could be used without loss of generality.

5.1. Energy-Based Feature Extraction. Energy detection is performed at the various secondary users, and the extracted decision variables are provided to the recognition model at the CRBS. The probability of detection achieved by the LC and PC at different average received signals levels is presented in Figure 4. The results are obtained for a window size of 200 bits and a target false alarm (P_f) of 10%. The value of the false alarm rate was chosen to be consistent with the IEEE 802.22 requirements for CR networks [3]. It is interesting to notice that although the PC requires more memory and computational complexity to perform the expansion operation, it does not improve the detection probability performance compared to the LC. Hence, it is recommended to use an LC since it provides good performance with less required memory space and computational cost resulting in making faster decisions about the availability of the spectrum. Moreover, the advantage of cooperative sensing compared to single-radio-based sensing is demonstrated by the improvement in the detection performance as the number of secondary users contributing to signal classification is increased. For instance, a received SNR of around $-9\,\text{dB}$ is appropriate to reach a detection probability of 90% with three CRs, while a received signal with an average SNR of around $-6.5\,\text{dB}$ is required to achieve the same detection rate with one CR, resulting in a 2.5 dB gain which improves the ability to avoid interfering with weak primary users. It is notable from Figure 4 that the enhancement in performance diminishes as the number of receivers collaborating in global decision increases.

The probability of detection results of the energy detector for a received signal with $\text{SNR}_{\text{avg}} = -5\,\text{dB}$, $N = 3$ users, and $P_f = 10\%$ is depicted in Figure 5 for both the LC and PC as a function of the observation window size. It is evident that the detection performance is highly affected by the window size over which the local decision variables are estimated. As the window size increases, the data used for training and testing becomes more representative to the present signal in the spectrum, and hence the classifier's output score is more accurate. However, the larger the window size is, the longer

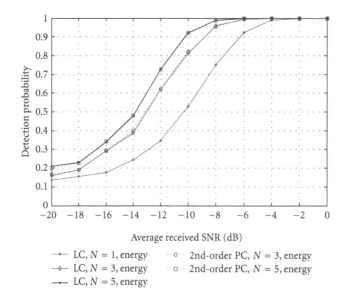

FIGURE 4: Detection performance for cooperative LC and PC with energy-based feature extraction.

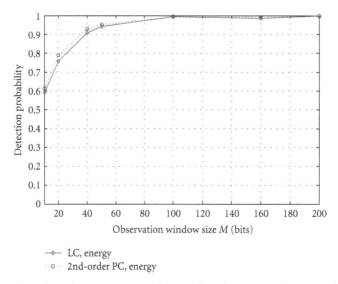

FIGURE 5: Impact of the window size on detection performance of energy-based schemes: $SNR_{avg} = -5\,dB$, $N = 3$ users, and $P_f = 10\%$.

it takes for decision making of spectrum availability by the classifier at the base station. This yields a delay in spectral allocation when the spectrum is available, hence, resulting in lower spectral utilization.

A useful performance measure is the receiver operational characteristic (ROC) that represents the variation of the probability of detection with the false alarm probability at certain operational parameters. Since the LC provided a better choice with energy detection, its ROC is obtained as shown in Figure 6 when the primary signal is received at an $SNR_{avg} = -14\,dB$ and observation window size of $M = 200$ bits. It is observed that the detection probability deteriorates for low false alarm rates and improves when higher false alarm probability is tolerable. This behavior is expected since in order to achieve a low false alarm rate, the threshold level needs to be raised. Raising the

threshold level above classifier's output score, corresponding to occupied spectrum class, may lead to miss detecting primary signal's presence, and consequently causing more interference to the primary network's users. It can be noted that higher detection is accomplished with higher number of cooperating CRs.

5.2. *Cyclostationary Based Feature Extraction.* Simulation results for the proposed classification system when cyclostationary features are fed to the CRBS for spectrum sensing are presented in Figure 7. It is shown that cyclostationary feature detection can achieve very high detection probability even with low SNR values by using more cooperating CRs. For instance, a detection probability of about 90% is achieved with an average SNR of $-18\,dB$ when five CRs are used.

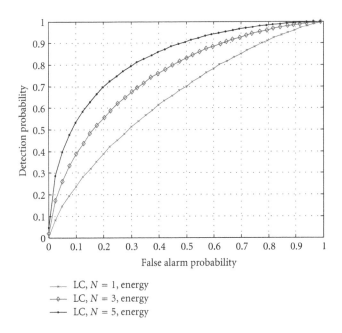

FIGURE 6: ROC curves of energy-based linear classifier scheme: SNR$_{avg}$ = −14 dB and M = 200 bits.

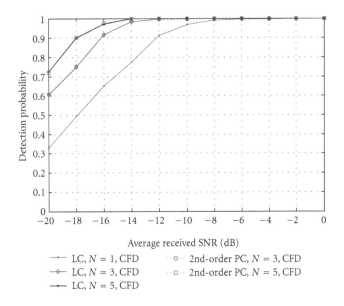

FIGURE 7: Detection performance for cooperative LC and PC with cyclostationary-based feature extraction: P_f = 10% and M = 200 bits.

The results demonstrate improved performance compared to the energy-based detector. For instance, a gain of about 4 dB is observed when the number of CRs cooperating in making the decision increases from one to three at P_d = 90%. As in the case of energy detection, it is observed that there is no significant performance improvement as the order of the classifier is increased from first order to second order. Furthermore, performance improvements due to increasing cooperative CRs saturate for higher number of users.

The detection performance of the cyclostationary detection scheme is improved by increasing the observation window size as illustrated in Figure 8. The detection results

for the LC and PC are presented at SNR$_{avg}$ = −14 dB, N = 3 users, and P_f = 10%. Increasing the observation window size from 20 to 200 bits results in improving the probability of detecting from about 70% to 98%, at a SNR$_{avg}$ of −14 dB. The ROC curve is shown in Figure 9 for a SNR$_{avg}$ = −14 dB and observation window of 200 bits indicating that using more cooperating radios results in better detection performance.

5.3. Coherent-Based Feature Extraction. For the coherent-based scheme, Figure 10 shows the detection probability as the received primary signal's level is varied. Coherent

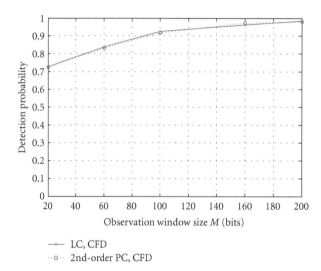

FIGURE 8: Impact of the window size on detection performance of cyclostationary-based schemes: $SNR_{avg} = -14\,dB$, $N = 3$ users, and $P_f = 10\%$.

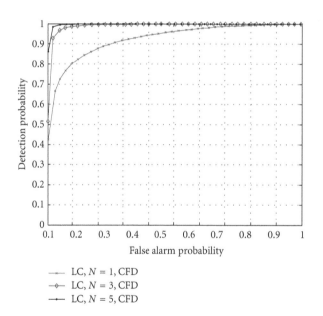

FIGURE 9: ROC curves of cyclostationary-based linear classifier scheme: $SNR_{avg} = -14\,dB$ and $M = 200\,bits$.

detection was simulated for a primary signal with a preamble size of $L = 16\,bits$ and a frame length of $M = 200\,bits$. It is noticed that a gain of about 6 dB is achieved as the number of collaborating radios N increases from one to three, at a detection probability of 90%. The achieved gain, however, reduces to around 1.5 dB as N increases from three to five. Coherent detection provides reliable signal identification with $P_d > 98\%$, when the received signal level is above $-10\,dB$ and $N = 5$. We notice that the LC and PC perform comparably when coherent detection is utilized in feature extraction.

The ROC curve for coherent-detection-based sensing for various numbers of cooperative CRs is demonstrated in Figure 11. It is apparent that there is a performance variation as the different number of CRs collaborates in making the

decision. The performance gap between various numbers of CRs shrinks as the false alarm probability increases.

Finally, Figure 12 shows the performance gain achieved using coherent detection LC scheme as the length of preamble sequence increases. The figure presents the SNR_{avg} required to obtain a specific detection probability and false alarm rate, as the preamble length increases. Longer preamble sequences result in lower values of the required SNR_{avg} indicating that a lower level of received primary signal is sufficient to achieve a certain detection rate as preamble length is increased.

5.4. Discussion. Among the three considered schemes, cyclostationary feature detection provides the best performance

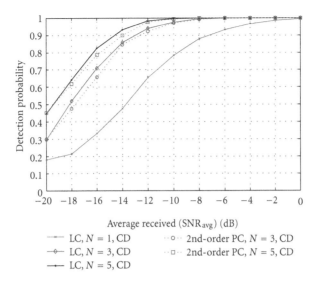

FIGURE 10: Detection performance for cooperative LC and PC with coherent-based feature extraction: $P_f = 10\%$ and preamble length $L = 16$ bits.

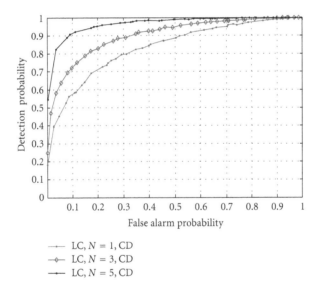

FIGURE 11: ROC curves of coherent-based linear classifier scheme: $SNR_{avg} = -14$ dB and $L = 16$ bits.

in terms of both detection and false alarm rates, while energy detection results in the poorest performer. The implementation of cyclostationary feature detection relies on the knowledge of carrier frequency and modulation type of the primary signal. The obvious drawback of cyclostationary detection is the high computational complexity required to extract cyclic features at CRs, as compared to other techniques. On the other hand, it provides high reliability to the CR network under low SNR conditions.

It has been shown that a longer sensing time can improve the detection performance considerably. However, detection improvement due to increasing sensing time is achieved at the expense of lowering the network's agility, since longer time is required to decide on the vacancy of the spectrum. This comment is very important when comparing

the performance of the cyclostationary scheme over coherent scheme. Specifically, the cyclostationary-based scheme achieves a better detection performance when compared to the coherent detection scheme. This is so because the former uses the entire frame in the process of decision making. On the other hand, the coherent-based scheme uses a shorter observation window (preamble) leading to a more timely decision making. Increasing the preamble length will improve the performance for the coherent-based scheme but at the expense of a reduction in the spectral efficiency of the primary user, while the cyclostationary-based scheme does not suffer from this drawback.

Finally, although energy detection represents the feature extraction scheme with least detection capability under low SNR conditions, representing severe fading and shadowing,

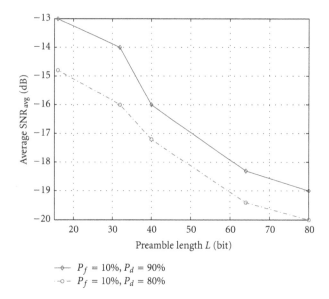

FIGURE 12: Impact of the preamble length on detection performance of coherent-based linear classifier scheme.

it is still an attractive technique under high SNR regimes due to its simplicity and minimum prior information requirements.

6. Conclusion

In this paper, pattern recognition models were proposed to tackle the problem of spectrum sensing in CR networks. The proposed classifier model is based on collaborative sensing, in which secondary users monitor channel usage in a given area and cooperate through a centralized node to provide the spectrum occupancy information. The cooperation between secondary users was achieved through first- and second-order polynomial classifiers that were modeled, trained, validated, and evaluated. Results indicate that both the linear and the polynomial classifiers provide high detection rates of primary signal over wireless fading channel and very small signal to noise ratios. Moreover, simulation results show that both classifiers perform comparably; consequently, the linear classifier is chosen as the best model for cooperative CR networks due to its lower complexity. Energy-, cyclostationary-, and coherent-based feature extraction techniques were compared. Simulation results demonstrated that cyclostationary detection constitutes the best candidate for feature extraction when information on primary signal is available, since it outperforms energy and coherent detection substantially. However, the remarkable detection capability of cyclostationary detection is achieved at the expense of higher implementation complexity.

References

[1] M. Naraghi and T. Ikuma, "Autocorrelation-based spectrum sensing for cognitive radios," *IEEE Transactions on Vehicular Technology*, vol. 59, pp. 718–733, 2010.

[2] E. Hossain and V. Bhrgava, *Cognitive Wireless Communication Network*, Springer, 1st edition, 2007.

[3] C. Cordeiro, K. Challpali, and D. Birru, "IEEE 802.22: an introduction to the first wireless standard based on cognitive radios," *Journal of Communications*, vol. 1, pp. 38–47, 2006.

[4] Z. Quan, S. Cui, and A. H. Sayed, "Optimal linear cooperation for spectrum sensing in cognitive radio networks," *IEEE Journal on Selected Topics in Signal Processing*, vol. 2, no. 1, pp. 28–40, 2008.

[5] T. Yücek and H. Arslan, "A survey of spectrum sensing algorithms for cognitive radio applications," *IEEE Communications Surveys and Tutorials*, vol. 11, no. 1, pp. 116–130, 2009.

[6] D. Cabric, S. M. Mishra, and R. W. Brodersen, "Implementation issues in spectrum sensing for cognitive radios," in *Proceedings of the 38th Asilomar Conference on Signals, Systems and Computers*, vol. 1, pp. 772–776, November 2004.

[7] D. Cabric, A. Tkachenko, and R. W. Brodersen, "Spectrum sensing measurements of pilot, energy, and collaborative detection," in *Proceedings of the Military Communications Conference (MILCOM '06)*, pp. 1–7, October 2006.

[8] P. Wang, J. Fang, N. Han, and H. Li, "Multiantenna-assisted spectrum sensing for cognitive radio," *IEEE Transactions on Vehicular Technology*, vol. 59, no. 4, pp. 1791–1800, 2010.

[9] M. Derakhshani, M. Nasiri-Kenari, and T. Le-Ngoc, "Cooperative cyclostationary spectrum sensing in cognitive radios at low SNR regimes," in *Proceedings of the IEEE International Conference on Communications (ICC '10)*, pp. 604–608, May 2010.

[10] J. Lundén, V. Koivunen, A. Huttunen, and H. V. Poor, "Collaborative cyclostationary spectrum sensing for cognitive radio systems," *IEEE Transactions on Signal Processing*, vol. 57, no. 11, pp. 4182–4195, 2009.

[11] N. Khambekar, C. Spooner, and V. Chaudhary, "Listen-while-talking: a technique for primary user protection," in *Proceedings of the IEEE Wireless Communications and Networking Conference (WCNC '09)*, pp. 1–5, April 2009.

[12] N. Khambekar, D. Liang, and V. Chaudhary, "Utilizing OFDM guard interval for spectrum sensing," in *Proceedings of the IEEE*

Wireless Communications and Networking Conference (WCNC '07), pp. 38–42, March 2007.

[13] P. D. Sutton, K. E. Nolan, and L. E. Doyle, "Cyclostationary signatures in practical cognitive radio applications," *IEEE Journal on Selected Areas in Communications*, vol. 26, no. 1, pp. 13–24, 2008.

[14] D. Cabric, A. Tkachneko, and R. Brodersen, "Experimental study of spectrum sensing based on energy detection and network cooperation," Tech. Rep., Berkeley Wireless Research Center, Berkeley, Calif, USA, 1997.

[15] N. S. Shankar, C. Cordeiro, and K. Challapali, "Spectrum agile radios: utilization and sensing architectures," in *Proceedings of the 1st IEEE International Symposium on New Frontiers in Dynamic Spectrum Access Networks (DySPAN '05)*, pp. 160–169, November 2005.

[16] K. Kim, I. A. Akbar, K. K. Bae, J. S. Um, C. M. Spooner, and J. H. Reed, "Cyclostationary approaches to signal detection and classification in cognitive radio," in *Proceedings of the 2nd IEEE International Symposium on New Frontiers in Dynamic Spectrum Access Networks*, pp. 212–215, April 2007.

[17] K. Assaleh, K. Farrel, and R. Mammone, "A new method of modulation classification for digitally modulated signals," in *Proceedings of the IEEE Military Communications Conference*, vol. 2, pp. 712–716, 1992.

[18] A. F. Cattoni, M. Ottonello, M. Raffetto, and C. S. Regazzoni, "Neural networks Mode classification based on frequency distribution features," in *Proceedings of the 2nd International Conference on Cognitive Radio Oriented Wireless Networks and Communications, CrownCom*, pp. 251–257, August 2007.

[19] T. Y. Yücek and H. Arslan, "Spectrum characterization for opportunistic cognitive radio systems," in *Proceedings of the IEEE Military Communications Conference*, pp. 1–6, 2006.

[20] B. Wang, *Dynamic spectrum allocation and sharing in cognitive cooperative networks [Ph.D. thesis]*, University of Maryland, 2009.

[21] T. Zhang, G. Yu, and C. Sun, "Performance of cyclostationary features based spectrum sensing method in a multiple antenna cognitive radio system," in *Proceedings of the IEEE Wireless Communications and Networking Conference (WCNC '09)*, pp. 1–5, April 2009.

[22] Y. Hassan, M. El-Tarhuni, and K. Assaleh, "Comparison of linear and polynomial classifiers for co-operative cognitive radio networks," in *Proceedings of the IEEE 21st International Symposium on Personal Indoor and Mobile Radio Communications (PIMRC '10)*, pp. 797–802, Istanbul, Turkey, September 2010.

[23] Y. Hassan, M. El-Tarhuni, and K. Assaleh, "Knowledge based cooperative spectrum sensing using polynomial classifiers in cognitive radio networks," in *Proceedings of the 4th International Conference on Signal Processing and Communication Systems (ICSPCS '10)*, Sydney, Australia, December 2010.

[24] S. Theodoridis and K. Koutroumbas, *Pattern Recognition*, Academic Press, San Diego, Calif, USA, 3rd edition, 2006.

[25] W. M. Campbell, K. T. Assaleh, and C. C. Broun, "Speaker recognition with polynomial classifiers," *IEEE Transactions on Speech and Audio Processing*, vol. 10, no. 4, pp. 205–212, 2002.

[26] W. Gardner, *Cyclostationarity in Communications and Signal Processing*, IEEE Press, 1st edition, 1994.

[27] W. A. Gardner, "Exploitation of spectral redundancy in cyclostationary signals," *IEEE Signal Processing Magazine*, vol. 8, no. 2, pp. 14–36, 1991.

[28] Y. Lin and C. He, "Subsection-average cyclostationary feature detection in cognitive radio," in *Proceedings of the IEEE International Conference on Neural Networks & Signal Processing*, pp. 604–608, 2008.

[29] T. Shanableh, K. Assaleh, and M. Al-Rousan, "Spatio-temporal feature-extraction techniques for isolated gesture recognition in arabic sign language," *IEEE Transactions on Systems, Man, and Cybernetics B*, vol. 37, no. 3, pp. 641–650, 2007.

[30] D. Specht, "Generation of polynomial discriminant functions for pattern recognition," *IEEE Transactions on Electronic Computers*, vol. 16, no. 3, pp. 308–319, 1967.

4

Optimizing Cooperative Cognitive Radio Networks with Opportunistic Access

Ammar Zafar,[1] Mohamed-Slim Alouini,[1] Yunfei Chen,[2] and Redha M. Radaydeh[3, 4]

[1] Electrical Engineering Program, KAUST, Al Khawarizmi Applied Mathematics Building 1, Mail Box 2675, Makkah Province, Thuwal 23955-6900, Saudi Arabia
[2] School of Engineering, University of Warwick, Coventry, CV4 7AL, UK
[3] Electrical Engineering Department, KAUST, Thuwal 23955-6900, Saudi Arabia
[4] Department of Electrical and Computer Engineering, Texas A&M University, Texas A&M Engineering Building, Education City, Doha, Qatar

Correspondence should be addressed to Ammar Zafar, ammar.zafar@kaust.edu.sa

Academic Editor: Enrico Del Re

Optimal resource allocation for cooperative cognitive radio networks with opportunistic access to the licensed spectrum is studied. Resource allocation is based on minimizing the symbol error rate at the receiver. Both the cases of all-participate relaying and selective relaying are considered. The objective function is derived and the constraints are detailed for both scenarios. It is then shown that the objective functions and the constraints are nonlinear and nonconvex functions of the parameters of interest, that is, source and relay powers, symbol time, and sensing time. Therefore, it is difficult to obtain closed-form solutions for the optimal resource allocation. The optimization problem is then solved using numerical techniques. Numerical results show that the all-participate system provides better performance than its selection counterpart, at the cost of greater resources.

1. Introduction

The ever increasing wireless communication networks have put great stress on the already limited spectrum. Due to the fixed spectrum allocation policy, only the licensed users, otherwise known as primary users, are able to access the licensed spectrum. Additionally, the Federal Communications Commission (FCC) task force highlighted in their report the fact that at any given time only 2% of the spectrum is being used [1]. Therefore, ensuring better spectrum usage is of paramount importance.

Cognitive radios have been proposed to resolve this issue [2]. In cognitive radio, the unlicensed users, otherwise known as secondary users, first sense the licensed bands for spectrum holes (parts of the licensed spectrum which are not being employed by the primary users at some time in certain geographical location) [3]. Then, if a spectrum hole is found, the secondary users transmit data to the intended destination. However, the secondary user has to be careful

so as not to cause interference to the primary user. The two stages of spectrum sensing and data transmission are related and for optimal performance must be optimized jointly. This is due to the probability of detection, P_d, and probability of false alarm, P_f, associated with spectrum sensing. If the secondary user with probability P_f misses a spectrum hole, then it will keep silent and miss an opportunity to transmit, reducing throughput. However, if a transmission from the primary is missed, with probability $1 - P_d$, then the secondary user transmits and causes interference to the primary user. Moreover, due to interference, the signal-to-noise-ratio (SNR) of the secondary user also decreases, decreasing the throughput and the symbol error rate (SER). Resource allocation that optimizes this sensing-throughput tradeoff has been discussed in [4]. Other optimal resource allocation algorithms for cognitive radio networks have been discussed in [5]. More specifically, in [5], the authors considered a multiband system and considered the two cases of sensing-based spectrum sharing and opportunistic spectrum access. However, both the above-mentioned works maximize the throughput.

In this paper, optimal resource allocation is discussed to minimize the SER. In order to achieve minimum SER, cooperation is introduced into the system as it decreases the SER due to diversity [6]. Hence, the transmitting secondary user now, upon sensing a spectrum hole, transmits to the relays as well as the destination. Power allocation for relay-assisted cognitive radio networks has been discussed in [7–15]. These works proposed strategies to maximize the throughput for a cognitive relay network that is allowed to share the frequency band with the primary user. Thus, they did not consider spectrum sensing for opportunistic access. Here, we consider an opportunistic system with amplify-and-forward (AF) relays. Full channel state information is assumed at the central controller which performs the resource allocation. Firstly, an all-participate (AP) system is discussed and it is shown that the optimization problem is nonconvex and hence cannot be solved using analytical means. It is then noted that the AP system is limited due to the systems resources being orthogonally distributed. To rectify this, a selection scheme is proposed and the optimal resource allocation, in this case, is discussed.

The rest of the paper is organized as follows. Section 2 gives the system model. The AP system is considered in Section 3. Section 4 details selective relaying. Numerical results are discussed in Section 5. Finally, Section 6 concludes the paper.

2. System Model

Consider a cognitive radio network in which the secondary source utilizes m relays to send data to the secondary destination as shown in Figure 1. The secondary network only has opportunistic access to the licensed spectrum. Therefore, it needs to perform spectrum sensing. The source performs the spectrum sensing and then transmits information to the relays and destination if it finds a "spectral hole" in the first time slot. The relays then forward the received signal to the destination after amplification. In this paper narrowband channel is assumed. The source and the relays can use frequency orthogonal channels to avoid causing interference to each other in wideband channels. For ease of analysis, we consider time orthogonal channels here. Hence, a total of $m + 1$ time slots are used.

2.1. Received Signal Model. Based on the spectrum sensing result, there are two possible received signal models.

2.1.1. Without Interference from the Primary User. In this scenario, with probability $1 - P_f$, where P_f is the probability of false alarm, the source correctly detects the presence of a "spectral hole" and transmits. The signals received at the destination and the relays are

$$
\begin{aligned}
y_{r_t} &= \sqrt{E_{ST}} h_{r_t} s + n_{r_t}, \\
y_{i_t} &= \sqrt{E_{ST}} h_{i_t} s + n_{i_t},
\end{aligned}
\tag{1}
$$

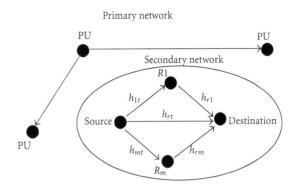

FIGURE 1: Primary and secondary networks.

where s is the zero-mean and unit-energy transmitted symbol, E_{ST} is the source energy, h_{r_t} is the channel response between the source and the destination, h_{i_t} is the channel response between the ith relay and the source, and $n_{r_t} \sim CN(0, \sigma_{n_{r_t}}^2)$ and $n_{i_t} \sim CN(0, \sigma_{n_{i_t}}^2)$ are the complex Gaussian noise samples. The relay, after normalization and amplification, forwards the received signal to the destination. The signal after normalization becomes

$$
s_i = \sqrt{\frac{E_{ST}}{E_{ST} |h_{i_t}|^2 + \sigma_{n_{i_t}}^2}} h_{i_t} s + \sqrt{\frac{1}{E_{ST} |h_{i_t}|^2 + \sigma_{n_{i_t}}^2}} n_{i_t}.
\tag{2}
$$

Therefore, the received signal at the destination from the ith relay is

$$
y_{r_i} = \sqrt{E_i} h_{r_i} s_i + n_{r_i},
\tag{3}
$$

where h_{r_i} is the known channel response between the receiver and the ith relay, E_i is the ith relay's energy, and $n_{r_i} \sim CN(0, \sigma_{n_{r_i}}^2)$ is the complex Gaussian noise. Substituting s_i in (3) gives

$$
y_{r_i} = \sqrt{\frac{E_{ST} E_i}{E_{ST} |h_{i_t}|^2 + \sigma_{n_{i_t}}^2}} h_{r_i} h_{i_t} s + \tilde{n}_{r_i},
\tag{4}
$$

where $\tilde{n}_{r_i} \sim CN(0, \tilde{\sigma}_{n_{r_i}}^2)$ and

$$
\tilde{\sigma}_{n_{r_i}}^2 = \frac{E_i |h_{r_i}|^2 \sigma_{n_{i_t}}^2}{E_{ST} |h_{i_t}|^2 + \sigma_{n_{i_t}}^2} + \sigma_{n_{r_i}}^2.
\tag{5}
$$

Writing the $m + 1$ received signals in matrix form, one has

$$
\mathbf{y} = \mathbf{h}s + \mathbf{n},
\tag{6}
$$

where

$$\mathbf{y} = \left[\frac{1}{\sigma_{n_{r_t}}} y_{r_t} \frac{1}{\tilde{\sigma}_{n_{r_1}}} y_{r_1} \cdots \frac{1}{\tilde{\sigma}_{n_{r_m}}} y_{r_m} \right]^T,$$

$$\mathbf{h} = \left[\sqrt{\frac{E_{ST}}{\sigma_{n_{r_t}}^2}} h_{r_t} \sqrt{\frac{E_{ST}E_1}{\tilde{\sigma}_{n_{r_1}}^2 \left(E_{ST} |h_{1_t}|^2 + \sigma_{n_{1_t}}^2 \right)}} \right.$$
$$\times h_{r_1} h_{1_t} \cdots \sqrt{\frac{E_{ST}E_m}{\tilde{\sigma}_{n_{r_m}}^2 \left(E_{ST} |h_{m_t}|^2 + \sigma_{n_{m_t}}^2 \right)}}$$
$$\left. \times h_{r_m} h_{m_t} \right]^T, \tag{7}$$

and $\mathbf{n}$ is a $(m+1)$ dimensional vector whose components are zero mean and unit variance complex Gaussian random variables. Therefore $\mathbf{n}$ is also complex Gaussian with mean vector of all zeros and covariance matrix being the identity matrix, $\mathbf{I}_{(m+1)\times(m+1)}$, that is $\mathbf{n} \sim \mathrm{CN}(\mathbf{0}, \mathbf{I})$.

2.1.2. With Interference from the Primary User.

In this case, with probability $1 - P_d$ where P_d is the probability of detection, the source misses the transmission from the primary user and transmits, which causes interference. The signals at the destination from both the source and the relays now also include an interfering signal due to primary user activity is

$$y_{r_t} = \sqrt{E_{ST}} h_{r_t} s + n_{r_t} + y_{I_{r_t}},$$
$$y_{i_t} = \sqrt{E_{ST}} h_{i_t} s + n_{i_t} + y_{I_{i_t}}, \tag{8}$$

where $y_{I_{r_t}}$ and $y_{I_{i_t}}$ are the interference signals.

Taking into account the fact that the source and relays have no knowledge of the interfering signal and adopting the same approach as previously, one can write

$$y_{r_i} = \sqrt{\frac{E_{ST}E_i}{E_{ST}|h_{i_t}|^2 + \sigma_{n_{i_t}}^2}} h_{r_i} h_{i_t} s + \hat{n}_{r_i} + \hat{y}_{I_{r_i}}, \tag{9}$$

where $\hat{n}_{r_i} \sim \mathrm{CN}(0, \hat{\sigma}_{n_{r_i}}^2)$ and

$$\hat{\sigma}_{n_{r_i}}^2 = \frac{E_i |h_{r_i}|^2 \sigma_{n_{i_t}}^2}{E_{ST}|h_{i_t}|^2 + \sigma_{n_{i_t}}^2} + \sigma_{n_{r_i}}^2,$$
$$\hat{y}_{I_i} = y_{I_{r_i}} + \sqrt{\frac{E_i}{E_{ST}|h_{i_t}|^2 + \sigma_{n_{i_t}}^2}} h_{r_i} y_{I_{i_t}}. \tag{10}$$

Again in matrix form one has

$$\mathbf{y}_I = \mathbf{h}_I s + \mathbf{n}_I + \mathbf{Y}_I, \tag{11}$$

where

$$\mathbf{y}_I = \left[\frac{1}{\sigma_{n_{r_t}}} y_{r_t} \frac{1}{\hat{\sigma}_{n_{r_1}}} y_{r_1} \cdots \frac{1}{\hat{\sigma}_{n_{r_m}}} y_{r_m} \right]^T,$$

$$\mathbf{h}_I = \left[\sqrt{\frac{E_{ST}}{\sigma_{n_{r_t}}^2}} h_{r_t} \sqrt{\frac{E_{ST}E_1}{\hat{\sigma}_{n_{r_1}}^2 \left(E_{ST}|h_{1_t}|^2 + \sigma_{n_{1_t}}^2 \right)}} \right.$$
$$\times h_{r_1} h_{1_t} \cdots \sqrt{\frac{E_{ST}E_m}{\hat{\sigma}_{n_{r_m}}^2 \left(E_{ST}|h_{m_t}|^2 + \sigma_{n_{m_t}}^2 \right)}}$$
$$\left. \times h_{r_m} h_{m_t} \right]^T, \tag{12}$$

$$\mathbf{Y}_I = \left[\frac{1}{\sigma_{n_{r_t}}} y_{I_{r_t}} \frac{1}{\hat{\sigma}_{n_{r_1}}} \hat{y}_{I_1} \cdots \frac{1}{\hat{\sigma}_{n_{r_m}}} \hat{y}_{I_m} \right]^T,$$

and $\mathbf{n}_I \sim \mathrm{CN}(\mathbf{0}, \mathbf{I})$.

2.2. Spectrum Sensing.

Spectrum sensing is performed, by means of an energy detector, for the first t_s seconds out of total time slot duration of T seconds at the source node only. The remaining $T - t_s$ is used for transmission, after detecting a "spectral hole". The probabilities of detection and false alarm, according to [16], are given by

$$P_d = Q\left(\frac{\lambda - N - \gamma_d}{\sqrt{2(N + 2\gamma_d)}} \right),$$
$$P_f = Q\left(\frac{\lambda - N}{\sqrt{2N}} \right), \tag{13}$$

respectively, where λ is the threshold of the energy detector, $N = t_s f_s$ is the number of samples, f_s is the sampling frequency, γ_d equals N times the SNR at the output of the detector and $Q(\cdots)$ is the Gaussian Q-function.

3. All Participate System

In this section, an all-participate (AP) system is discussed. In such a system, all the relays forward the signal to the destination. Firstly, the optimization problem is formulated. Then the constraints on the objective function are derived. The SER at the destination is given by

$$\mathrm{SER} = P(H_0)\left(Q\left(\sqrt{k\gamma_0} \right) \right)\left(1 - P_f \right)$$
$$+ P(H_1)\left(Q\left(\sqrt{k\gamma_I} \right) \right)(1 - P_d), \tag{14}$$

where γ_0 is the SNR after combining, γ_I is the signal-to-interference-plus-noise-ratio (SINR) after combining, k is a constant which depends on the modulation scheme used, $P(H_0)$ is the probability of no primary user transmission, and $P(H_1) = 1 - P(H_0)$ is the probability of a primary user transmission. The SNR γ_0 can be found, assuming maximal ratio combining (MRC), as

$$\gamma_0 = \alpha + \sum_{i=1}^{m} \frac{\beta_i}{\widehat{\sigma}_{n_{r_i}}^2}, \qquad (15)$$

where

$$\alpha = \frac{p_{ST} T_s |h_{r_t}|^2}{\sigma_{n_{r_t}}^2}, \qquad \beta_i = \frac{p_{ST} p_i T_s^2 |h_{r_i}|^2 |h_{i_t}|^2}{p_{ST} T_s |h_{i_t}|^2 + \sigma_{n_{i_t}}^2}, \qquad (16)$$

where the source and relay energies have been replaced by

$$E_{ST} = p_{ST} T_s, \qquad E_i = p_i T_S, \qquad (17)$$

where p_{ST} and p_is are the source and relay powers, respectively, and T_s is the symbol time. Similarly, γ_I can be expressed as

$$\gamma_I = \frac{\left(\alpha + \sum_{i=1}^{m}\left(\beta_i/\widehat{\sigma}_{n_{r_i}}^2\right)\right)^2}{\alpha + \sum_{i=1}^{m}\left(\beta_i/\widehat{\sigma}_{n_{r_i}}^2\right) + \left(\alpha c/\sigma_{n_{r_t}}^2\right) + \sum_{i=1}^{m}\left(d_i/\widehat{\sigma}_{n_{r_i}}^2\right)\left(\beta_i/\widehat{\sigma}_{n_{r_i}}^2\right)}, \qquad (18)$$

where

$$c = E\left[|y_{I_{r_t}}|^2\right], \qquad (19)$$

$$d_i = E\left[|\widehat{y}_{I_i}|^2\right], \qquad (20)$$

$$E\left[|\widehat{y}_{I_i}|^2\right] = E\left[|y_{I_{r_i}}|^2\right] + E\left[|y_{I_{i_t}}|^2\right]\left(\frac{E_i}{E_{ST}|h_{i_t}|^2 + \sigma_{n_{i_t}}^2}|h_{r_i}|^2\right). \qquad (21)$$

After substituting (15) and (18) in (14), the SER can be obtained as

$$\mathrm{SER} = P(H_0)Q\left(\sqrt{k\left(\alpha + \sum_{i=1}^{m}\frac{\beta_i}{\widehat{\sigma}_{n_{r_i}}^2}\right)}\right)$$

$$\times \left(1 - Q\left(\frac{\lambda - N}{\sqrt{2N}}\right)\right)$$

$$+ P(H_1)\left(1 - Q\left(\frac{\lambda - N - \gamma_d}{\sqrt{2(N + 2\gamma_d)}}\right)\right)Q$$

$$\times \left(\sqrt{\frac{k\left(\alpha + \sum_{i=1}^{m}\left(\beta_i/\widehat{\sigma}_{n_{r_i}}^2\right)\right)^2}{\alpha + \sum_{i=1}^{m}\left(\beta_i/\widehat{\sigma}_{n_{r_i}}^2\right) + \left(\alpha c/\sigma_{n_{r_t}}^2\right) + \sum_{i=1}^{m}\left(d_i/\widehat{\sigma}_{n_{r_i}}^2\right)\left(\beta_i/\widehat{\sigma}_{n_{r_i}}^2\right)}}\right). \qquad (22)$$

Now we form the different constraints on the problem. First, we consider both individual power constraints at the source and the relay and a global power constraint on the whole system. Therefore, the constraints are given by

$$0 \le p_{ST} \le p_T, \quad 0 \le p_i \le p_i^{max}, \quad P_f \le P_f^{th},$$

$$p_{ST} + \sum_{i=1}^{m} p_i \le p_{total}, \quad RT_s + t_s \le T, \qquad (23)$$

where p_{ST} is the power available at the source, p_i^{max} is the power available at each relay, p_{total} is the power available to the whole system, and P_f^{th} specifies the constraint on the probability of false alarm. The constraints on P_f, T_s, and t_s are introduced to maintain an acceptable throughput. Next the two cases of global power constraint only and individual power constraints only are considered. For the case of global power constraint only, the constraints will be

$$P_f \le P_f^{th}, \quad p_{ST} + \sum_{i=1}^{m} p_i \le p_{total}, \quad RT_s + t_s \le T. \qquad (24)$$

In the other scenario, the constraints are given by

$$0 \le p_{ST} \le p_T, \quad 0 \le p_i \le p_i^{max}, \quad P_f \le P_f^{th},$$

$$RT_s + t_s \le T. \qquad (25)$$

The individual power constraints are set to limit the interference suffered by the primary user in the case of missed detection. As there is no individual power constraint, the interference caused to the user in the global power constraint only case, where the primary user is only protected by spectrum sensing, is greater.

The problem with optimizing (22) is that it is a nonlinear and nonconvex function due to the Gaussian Q-function being nonlinear and, in general, nonconvex. Thus, the Lagrangian multiplier method [17] cannot be applied here to obtain closed form expressions of the optimal resource allocation. One has to resort to numerical techniques to obtain the optimal solution.

A special case of importance is the absence of the direct link between source and destination, because the relays take on a more prominent role in the presence of no direct link. In this case, the SER is can be obtained by setting $\alpha = 0$ in (22).

4. Selective Relaying

The drawback of the all-participate (AP) scheme discussed in the previous section is that to avoid causing interference, the source and the relay transmit on orthogonal channels. Hence, consuming a considerable amount of resources. In our discussion of a time orthogonal systems, $m + 1$ time slots are utilized for the transmission of one data frame. Additionally, as no sensing is performed at the relays, the primary may become active over any one of the m time slots and cause interference.

To overcome these problems, a selection scheme is proposed in this section in which only one relay is selected to take part in forwarding the signal from the source. Now only 2 time slots are used in transmitting one frame of data and thus decreasing the likelihood of primary becoming active again during relay transmission. In the selection case, the SER is

$$\mathrm{SER} = P(H_0)Q\left(\sqrt{k\left(\alpha + \frac{\beta_j}{\widehat{\sigma}_{n_{r_j}}^2}\right)}\right)\left(1 - Q\left(\frac{\lambda - N}{\sqrt{2N}}\right)\right)$$

$$+ P(H_1)Q$$

$$\times \left(\sqrt{\frac{k\left(\alpha + \left(\beta_j/\hat{\sigma}_{n_{r_j}}^2\right)\right)^2}{\alpha + \left(\beta_j/\hat{\sigma}_{n_{r_j}}^2\right) + \left(\alpha c/\sigma_{n_{r_t}}^2\right) + \left(d_j/\hat{\sigma}_{n_{r_j}}^2\right)\left(\beta_j/\hat{\sigma}_{n_{r_j}}^2\right)}} \right)$$

$$\times \left(1 - Q\left(\frac{\lambda - N - \gamma}{\sqrt{2(N + 2\gamma)}} \right) \right),$$

$$(26)$$

where b_j, d_j, and $\sigma_{n_{r_j}}^2$ correspond to the jth relay that is selected. The SER in (26) is first optimized for all the relays and the relay which gives the minimum optimum SER is selected. Again, all three cases given in (23), (24) and (25) of both global and individual constraints, global constraint only and individual constraint only are considered. The selection criteria of minimizing SER adds complexity. However, such a criteria provides results which can serve as a benchmark as minimizing SER is the optimal selection criteria.

It is again evident that, even in the selection case, the SER is still a nonlinear and nonconvex function. Therefore, one has to resort to numerical techniques to find the optimal solution. The special case of no direct link is again of particular interest and considered separately.

5. Numerical Results

In this section, numerical results are provided for the optimization problems discussed. First, the proposed AP system with optimal resource allocation is discussed and it is shown that the proposed AP schemes give better performance than the uniform power allocation (UPA) scheme. In UPA, the power is uniformly distributed among the source and the relays and the sensing time and the symbol time are set so that the inequality $RT_s + t_s \leq T$ is satisfied. The selection scheme is discussed next and its performance is compared with selection with UPA. To make it easy for the reader to follow the discussion, a glossary is included in Table 1.

An interior-point algorithm was used to perform the optimization. The MATLAB function *fmincon*, which performs constrained optimization, is used to run the interior-point algorithm. To ensure that the algorithm converged to the optimal solution, the algorithm was run for a large number of initial values. All the variances are set as equal, $\sigma_{n_{r_t}}^2 = \sigma_{n_{i_t}}^2 = \sigma_{n_{r_j}}^2 = \sigma^2$. The constraint of P_f is set at $P_f^{\text{th}} = 0.1$. The total time duration is taken to be 100 ms. Binary phase shift keying (BPSK) is the modulation scheme employed. Due to the the number of samples and the sensing time being linearly related, the results are plotted against the number of samples.

The relationship between the number of samples (N) and SER is shown in Figure 2. As one can clearly observe from Figure 2, there is an optimal value of the number of samples, hence for the sensing time, which minimizes the SER. This is because of the tradeoff between symbol time, T_s and sensing time, t_s. Increasing sensing time means higher probability of detection which leads to a lower SER. However, an increase in sensing time comes at the cost of a decrease in symbol time which leads to lower γ_0 and γ_I. Therefore, the SER

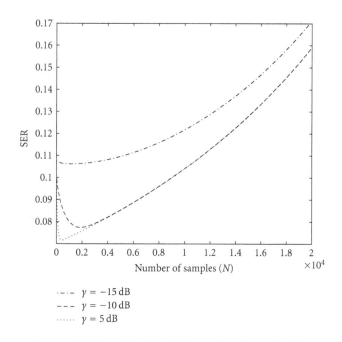

$$\cdot\!-\!\cdot\!- \quad \gamma = -15\,\text{dB}$$
$$-\!-\!- \quad \gamma = -10\,\text{dB}$$
$$\cdots\cdots \quad \gamma = 5\,\text{dB}$$

FIGURE 2: SER as a function of the number of samples (N).

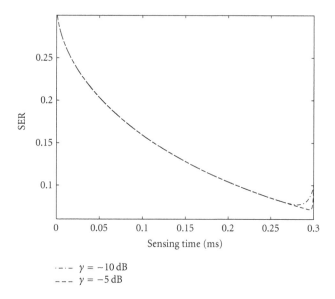

$$\cdot\!-\!\cdot\!- \quad \gamma = -10\,\text{dB}$$
$$-\!-\!- \quad \gamma = -5\,\text{dB}$$

FIGURE 3: SER as a function of the symbol time (T_s).

increases. Similarly, decreasing sensing time implies a lower probability of detection and, in turn, higher SER. However, it also means high values of γ_0 and γ_I due to increase in symbol time, which in turn leads to lower SER. Hence, there exists an optimal value. This optimal value is affected by the primary user's SNR. The higher the primary user's SNR, the lower the optimal value of the sensing time will be as it takes shorter time to reach the same value of P_d as it would take for a lower SNR of the primary user.

Figure 3 shows the relationship between the symbol time, T_s, and the SER. The relationship follows the opposite pattern as the sensing time. This is due to the constraint relating sensing time and the symbol time. Therefore, when

TABLE 1: Glossary.

Acronym	Full name
AP-ORA	All-participate with optimal resource allocation
AP-ORA-GL	All-participate optimal resource allocation with global constraint only
AP-ORA-Ind	All-participate optimal resource allocation with individual constraints only
UPA	uniform power allocation
AP-ORA-NDL	All-participate optimal resource allocation with no direct link
AP-ORA-GL-NDL	All-participate optimal resource allocation with global constraint only and no direct link
AP-ORA-Ind-NDL	All-participate optimal resource allocation with individual constraints only and no direct link
UPA-NDL	uniform power allocation with no direct link
Sel-ORA	selection with optimal resource allocation
Sel-ORA-GL	selection optimal resource allocation with global constraint only
Sel-ORA-Ind	selection optimal resource allocation with individual constraints only
Sel-UPA	selection with uniform power allocation
Sel-ORA-NDL	selection optimal resource allocation with no direct link
Sel-ORA-GL-NDL	selection optimal resource allocation with global constraint only and no direct link
Sel-ORA-Ind-NDL	selection optimal resource allocation with individual constraints only and no direct link
Sel-UPA-NDL	selection uniform power allocation with no direct link

the optimal value of the sensing time is low, the optimal value of the symbol time is high.

Figure 4 shows the SER performance of the different AP schemes plotted against γ_s, where $\gamma_s = 1/\sigma^2$. As expected, for the case with a direct link, the three optimal resource allocation (ORA) scenarios, global constraint only (GL), individual constraints only (Ind), and both global and individual constraints, outperform the uniform power allocation (UPA) and the direct link only for all values of γ_s and the gap in performance becomes wider with increasing γ_s.

In Figure 4, in the case where there is no direct link (NDL) between source and destination, the performance is a little different. In this case, all three ORA schemes, AP-ORA-NDL, AP-ORA-GL-NDL, and AP-ORA-Ind-NDL, outperform the uniform power allocation scheme (UPA-NDL). However, for γ_s less than 0 dB, the direct link only case provides better SER performance than the three ORA cases with no direct link. The three ORA schemes with no direct link start to catch up to the direct link only scenario after 0 dB and completely outperform it after 5 dB. This phenomena coupled with the fact that AP-ORA-NDL, AP-ORA-GL-NDL, and AP-ORA-Ind-NDL, are handily outperformed by AP-ORA, AP-ORA-GL, and AP-ORA-Ind, respectively, demonstrate the significance of the presence of a link between the source and destination.

Comparing the different constraints, AP-ORA gives the worst performance in both scenarios of direct and no direct link. This is due to the fact that AP-ORA is constrained both globally and individually. Thus, even if one relay has more favourable conditions, the power allocated to it cannot exceed $p_i^{\max}$ which is not the case in global constraint only case. In global constraint only case more power can be allocated to the source and relay which has more favourable conditions. The comparison between global constraint only and individual constraints only requires further elaboration.

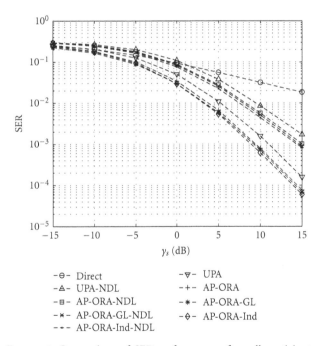

FIGURE 4: Comparison of SER performance of an all-participate under different schemes and constraints with $m = 3$.

First, the global constraints only and individual only scenarios are compared in the no direct link case. Here, AP-ORA-Ind-NDL provides lower SER than AP-ORA-GL-Ind for all values of γ_s. AP-ORA-GL-NDL has the advantage of allocating more power to relays with better channel conditions. However, AP-ORA-Ind-NDL makes up for this advantage by having more total power in the system as it is not constrained by a total power constraint.

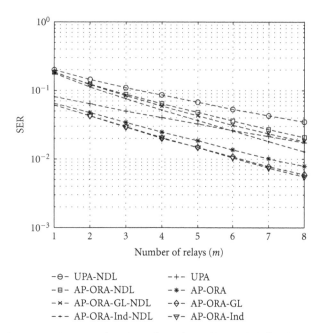

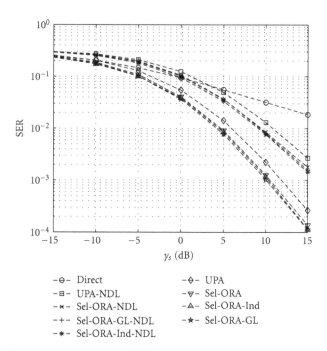

FIGURE 5: SER as a function of number of layers (m) for the AP system.

FIGURE 6: Comparison of SER performance of a selection system under different schemes and constraints with $m = 3$.

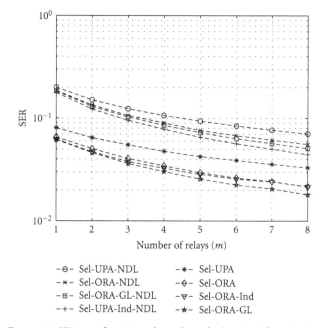

FIGURE 7: SER as a function of number of relays (m) for selective relaying.

Now consider the direct link case. Here, AP-ORA-GL outperforms AP-ORA-Ind at low values of γ_s due to the presence of the direct link. As discussed before, the direct link is quite important, hence, as AP-ORA-GL is not limited by individual constraints, more power can be allocated to the direct link. This is not the case for AP-ORA-Ind. Therefore, AP-ORA-GL gives lower SER. However, with an increase in γ_s, the noise decreases and the greater total power in the case of AP-ORA-Ind comes more into play. Thus, AP-ORA-Ind starts to outperform AP-ORA-GL at higher values of γ_s. However, we must keep in mind that in the global power constraint only case, the interference to the primary is greater than those in the other two cases. Hence, the advantage in performance at low γ_s comes at the cost of greater interference to the primary.

Figure 5 shows the SER performance of the AP system as a function of the number of relays, m. A similar pattern to Figure 4 is observed. The ORA schemes outperform the UPA schemes in both cases of direct and no direct link. Among the proposed ORA schemes, AP-ORA-Ind-NDL provides lower SER than AP-ORA-NDL and AP-ORA-GL-NDL in the no direct link scenario while in the direct link scenario AP-ORA is outperformed by both AP-ORA-Ind and AP-ORA-GL. In addition, AP-ORA-GL has better performance than AP-ORA-Ind for a small number of relays. However, as the number of relays increases AP-ORA-Ind surpasses AP-ORA-GL in terms of performance due to greater total power. Moreover, AP-ORA-NDL, AP-ORA-GL-NDL, and AP-ORA-Ind-NDL even start to outperform UPA for a large number of relays which shows the gain in performance due to ORA.

Figure 6 shows the performance of the various selection schemes as a function of γ_s. The comparison in performance follows a similar pattern as in the AP case with the proposed

selection ORA schemes outperforming their UPA counterparts and direct link only scenario. However, there is one major difference. In the presence of a direct link, Sel-ORA-Ind gives poorer performance than Sel-ORA-GL even for high values of γ_s. Only at around 15 dB does Sel-ORA-Ind starts to catch up to Sel-ORA-GL. This is due to the fact that as pointed out in the AP system, in the case of global constraints only more power can be allocated to the

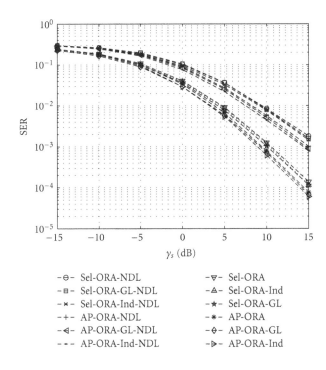

-⊖- Sel-ORA-NDL   -▽- Sel-ORA
-⊟- Sel-ORA-GL-NDL   -△- Sel-ORA-Ind
-✕- Sel-ORA-Ind-NDL   -★- Sel-ORA-GL
-+- AP-ORA-NDL   -✳- AP-ORA
-◁- AP-ORA-GL-NDL   -◇- AP-ORA-GL
-•- AP-ORA-Ind-NDL   -▷- AP-ORA-Ind

FIGURE 8: Comparison of AP vs Sel with $m = 3$.

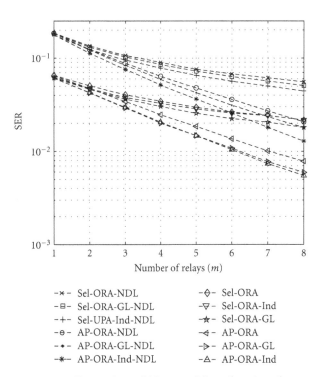

-✕- Sel-ORA-NDL   -◇- Sel-ORA
-⊟- Sel-ORA-GL-NDL   -▽- Sel-ORA-Ind
-+- Sel-UPA-Ind-NDL   -★- Sel-ORA-GL
-⊖- AP-ORA-NDL   -◁- AP-ORA
-•- AP-ORA-GL-NDL   -▷- AP-ORA-GL
-✳- AP-ORA-Ind-NDL   -△- AP-ORA-Ind

FIGURE 9: Comparison of AP versus Sel as a function of m.

source. However, unlike AP, in Sel there is only one additional relay which implies less total power for Sel-ORA-Ind and, therefore, requires a high value of γ_s to make the difference in total power count.

SER performance for selective relaying as a function of the number of relays is shown in Figure 7. Again, the main difference from the AP case is that Sel-ORA-GL outperforms Sel-ORA-Ind even for a large number of relays. This is due to the fact that even though the number of relays increase, the total power for Sel-ORA-Ind remains constant as only one relay in addition to the source takes part in data transmission. An interesting point to note here is that the there seems to be a minimum threshold for the SER for the selective system.

Figures 8 and 9 show the performance comparison between the AP and Sel system as a function of γ_s and m, respectively. The comparison is presented separately for clarity, as if it was included in the previous figures, they would have become cluttered. From Figure 8, one can see that AP scheme outperforms the selection scheme in all scenarios, however, the gap in performance is not too big. This is due to the fact that the total number of relays is 3. If m is increased, the performance gap will also increase. Still, one has to keep in mind the extra cost and spectral inefficiency associated with the AP scheme. This becomes more clear when the Figure 9 is examined.

As one can see, the difference in performance between the respective AP schemes and Sel schemes increases with increase in number of relays. As discussed earlier, the Sel schemes look to be bounded by a minimum threshold. Due to this, Sel with direct link scenarios even fall below the AP with no direct link scenarios for a large number of relays.

6. Conclusions

In this paper, ORA for a cognitive relay network has been discussed. It has been shown that for an AP system that ORA improves SER performance and the discussed schemes outperform the UPA schemes. The importance of the direct link between the source and the destination has also been demonstrated. Among the different constraints on the system, the case of both individual and global constraints gives the worst performance while global constraints only is the best for low γ_s. However, this comes at the cost of greater interference to the primary user. The individual constraints only case takes over as the best scheme as γ_s increases.

It was then noted that the AP scheme consumes considerable resources and is spectrally inefficient. Therefore, a simple relay selection scheme has been proposed. Optimal resource allocation was then discussed for the selection scheme. The performance comparison of the AP and Sel shows that while AP provides better SER performance, it comes at the cost of considerable resources.

Acknowledgment

This work was supported by King Abdullah University of Science and technology (KAUST).

References

[1] "Federal communications comission (fcc), et docket no 03-322 notice of proposed rule making and order," 2003.

[2] J. Mitola and G. Maguire Jr., "Cognitive radio: making software radios more personal," *IEEE Personal Communications*, vol. 6, no. 4, pp. 13–18, 1999.

[3] S. Haykin, "Cognitive radio: brain-empowered wireless communications," *IEEE Journal on Selected Areas in Communications*, vol. 23, no. 2, pp. 201–220, 2005.

[4] Y. Liang, Y. Zeng, E. C. Y. Peh, and A. T. Hoang, "Sensing-throughput tradeoff for cognitive radio networks," *IEEE Transactions on Wireless Communications*, vol. 7, no. 4, pp. 1326–1337, 2008.

[5] S. Stotas and A. Nallanathan, "Optimal sensing time and power allocation in multiband cognitive radio networks," *IEEE Transactions on Communications*, vol. 59, no. 1, pp. 226–235, 2011.

[6] J. Laneman, D. Tse, and G. Wornell, "Cooperative diversity in wireless networks: efficient protocols and outage behavior," *IEEE Transactions on Information Theory*, vol. 50, no. 12, pp. 3062–3080, 2004.

[7] W. Yue, B. Zheng, and Q. Meng, "Optimal power allocation for cognitive relay networks," in *Proceedings of the International Conference on Wireless Communications and Signal Processing (WCSP '09)*, pp. 1–5, Nanjing, China, November 2009.

[8] L. Li, X. Zhou, H. Xu, G. Y. Li, D. Wang, and A. Soong, "Simplified relay selection and power allocation in cooperative cognitive radio systems," *IEEE Transactions on Wireless Communications*, vol. 10, no. 1, pp. 33–36, 2011.

[9] J. Mietzner, L. Lampe, and R. Schober, "Distributed transmit power allocation for multihop cognitive-radio systems," *IEEE Transactions on Wireless Communications*, vol. 8, no. 10, pp. 5187–5201, 2009.

[10] Z. Liu, Y. Xu, D. Zhang, and S. Guan, "An efficient power allocation algorithm for relay assisted cognitive radio network," in *Proceedings of the International Conference on Wireless Communications and Signal Processing (WCSP '10)*, pp. 1–5, Suzhou, China, October 2010.

[11] X. Liu, B. Zheng, J. Cui, and W. Ji, "A new scheme for power allocation in cognitive radio networks based on cooperative relay," in *Proceedings of the 12th IEEE International Conference on Communication Technology (ICCT '10)*, pp. 861–864, Tsukuba Science City, Novmber 2010.

[12] X. Qiao, Z. Tan, S. Xu, and J. Li, "Combined power allocation in cognitive radio-based relay-assisted networks," in *Proceedings of the IEEE International Conference on Communications Workshops (ICC '10)*, pp. 1–5, Cape Town, South Africa, May 2010.

[13] X. Liu, B. Zheng, and W. Ji, "Cooperative relay with power control in cognitive radio networks," in *Proceedings of the 6th International Conference on Wireless Communications, Networking and Mobile Computing (WiCOM '10)*, pp. 1–5, Chengdu, China, September 2010.

[14] L. Jayasinghe and N. Rajatheva, "Optimal power allocation for relay assisted cognitive radio networks," in *Proceedings of the IEEE 72nd Vehicular Technology Conference Fall (VTC2010-Fall '10)*, pp. 1–5, Ottawa, Canada, September 2010.

[15] Z. Shu and W. Chen, "Optimal power allocation in cognitive relay networks under different power constraints," in *Proceedings of the IEEE International Conference on Wireless Communications, Networking and Information Security (WCNIS '10)*, pp. 647–652, Beijing, China, June 2010.

[16] H. Urkowitz, "Energy detection of unknown deterministic signals," *Proceedings of the IEEE*, vol. 55, no. 4, pp. 523–531, 1967.

[17] S. Boyd and L. Vandenberghe, *Convex Optimization*, Cambridge University Press, 2004.

5

Self-Optimization of Pilot Power in Enterprise Femtocells Using Multi objective Heuristic

**Lina S. Mohjazi,[1] Mahmoud A. Al-Qutayri,[1] Hassan R. Barada,[1]
Kin F. Poon,[2] and Raed M. Shubair[1]**

[1] *College of Engineering, Khalifa University of Science, Technology and Research, UAE*
[2] *Etisalat-BT Innovation Centre (EBTIC), UAE*

Correspondence should be addressed to Lina S. Mohjazi, lina.mohjazi@kustar.ac.ae

Academic Editor: Youyun Xu

Deployment of a large number of femtocells to jointly provide coverage in an enterprise environment raises critical challenges especially in future self-organizing networks which rely on plug-and-play techniques for configuration. This paper proposes a multi-objective heuristic based on a genetic algorithm for a centralized self-optimizing network containing a group of UMTS femtocells. In order to optimize the network coverage in terms of handled load, coverage gaps, and overlaps, the algorithm provides a dynamic update of the downlink pilot powers of the deployed femtocells. The results demonstrate that the algorithm can effectively optimize the coverage based on the current statistics of the global traffic distribution and the levels of interference between neighboring femtocells. The algorithm was also compared with the fixed pilot power scheme. The results show over fifty percent reduction in pilot power pollution and a significant enhancement in network performance. Finally, for a given traffic distribution, the solution quality and the efficiency of the described algorithm were evaluated by comparing the results generated by an exhaustive search with the same pilot power configuration.

1. Introduction

Coverage and capacity are two major aspects which operators have to address while offering new mobile multimedia services to their customers such as video on demand, web 2.0 services, and social networking. At the same time, indoor coverage presents many challenges in the current 3rd generation (3G) (e.g., UMTS) and future 4th generation (4G) (e.g., LTE) cellular networks. Those networks operate at higher frequencies in comparison with the conventional 2nd generation (2G) (e.g., GSM) networks [1]. Consequently, signal penetration through building walls becomes a complex process. This fact creates a real challenge, especially that studies on wireless usage show that more than 50% of voice calls and more than 70% of data traffic are generated indoors [2]. Therefore, proposing data intensive services in conjunction with the presence of the indoor coverage challenges are the main drives for deploying specific devices such as femtocells to complement the traditional outdoor base stations.

A femtocell is a short-range (up to 40 m) low-cost low-power base station (BS) installed by end users indoors to enhance voice and data receptions. Femtocells make use of the broadband connections such as digital subscriber line (DSL), cable modem, or a separate radio frequency (RF) backhaul channel to communicate with the cellular network [3] as shown in Figure 1.

Unlike other wireless indoor solutions, such as relays and picocells, femtocells are connected to the cellular operator via internet. Therefore, they do not need to be planned carefully and maintained by cellular operators. Both capital expenditures (CAPEXs) and operational expenditures (OPEXs) are expected to be remarkably lowered and therefore, femtocells will increasingly attain a strong appeal by operators. According to the market analysis carried out in [4], about 23 million femtocell devices are expected to be sold worldwide within

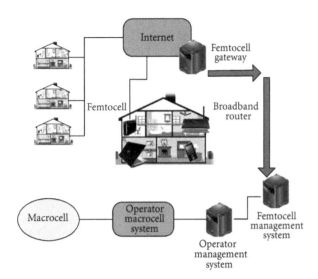

FIGURE 1: Basic femtocell network.

the next few years for a total market of over one billion dollars.

The major benefits of femtocells to both operators and end users are summarized below.

(a) Femtocell benefits for operators [1] are as follows.

(i) *Increased network capacity*: indoor traffic will be offloaded to femtocells and operators will relieve stress on macrocell networks which in turn increase the network capacity.

(ii) *Lower capital costs*: deploying femtocells will reduce the cost required on extending the macrocell layer as the number of subscribers in a mobile operator's network increases.

(iii) *Expanded revenue opportunities*: the average revenue per user (ARPU) will be raised due to the increase in using mobile multimedia services when the provided coverage is excellent and superior broadband wireless performance is available.

(iv) *Lower backhaul costs*: the cost of backhauling traffic to the operator's core network will not be handled by the operator anymore. Instead, it will be handled by the user via DSL, cable, or fiber access lines.

(v) *Increased customer stickiness and conversion*: more users will be attracted to the operators family plans when they experience high quality in-home coverage and home zone calling plans

(b) Femtocell benefits for end users [5] are as follows.

(i) *Better coverage*: users will experience better signal quality and higher communication reliabilities and throughputs because they operate on short transmit-receive distance

(ii) *Faster access*: due to the availability of high performance mobile data, faster access to mobile

services and multimedia content will be available.

(iii) *Easier bill tracking*: femtocells enable a converged billing infrastructure allowing a subscriber to receive a single bill providing itemized information on all communications services consumed by a subscriber. Subscribers also benefit from unlimited calling instead of perminute charges.

(iv) *Prolonged mobile battery life*: mobile terminals transmit at significantly less powers due to the short distance separation from the femtocell.

Femtocells can be deployed in three different scenarios; home, enterprise, and hotspots. According to Informa Telecoms & Media, the number of femtocell customer premises equipment vendors is expanding at an accelerated base [6]. These vendors are also starting to expand their product lines to enterprise and larger area femtocells.

This paper focuses on enterprise environment where femtocells are deployed in companies and thus, no concrete planning is needed and only rudimentary settings are required. However, in contrast with the residential deployment where interference between femtocells is not a major concern, the interference between femtocells in enterprise environment has to be eliminated. As a result, when dense femtocell deployment takes place to jointly provide seamless coverage in a large area, it forms a real challenge. Therefore, self-organizing network (SON) capabilities have to be embedded in the physical device of a femtocell for instant downlink power control. Adaptive downlink power control is required to reduce the overlaps between cells while maintaining a good coverage at the same time depending on the load and locations of the users [7].

Another important aspect that is stated in [8] and needed to be addressed in the SON capabilities of a femtocell is load balancing. The arrival of mobile users and the resulting traffic generated by the users are random, time varying, and often unbalanced. This eventually leads the cells in the network to handle unequal amounts of load. In this situation, some cells will be overloaded and the resources of others might not be fully utilized.

The load balancing problem becomes even more crucial when Long Term Evolution (LTE) networks are deployed. This could be anticipated by the following two situations. First, due to the rapid development of network applications and services, the resources of a particular femtocell will soon be running out if they are not well balanced. Second, traffic patterns are time varying and unpredictable. In that event, the network has to dynamically adapt its resources in a timely fashion according to the varying load. Obviously, this could not be achieved by static and prefixed network planning. Therefore, SON capabilities are essential in the femtocell operation to address a large-scale femtocell deployment. In order to successfully execute the process of self-organization, three main functions have to be performed as described in [9]: self-configuration, self-optimization, and self-healing. Figure 2 illustrates the life cycle of a self-organizing network.

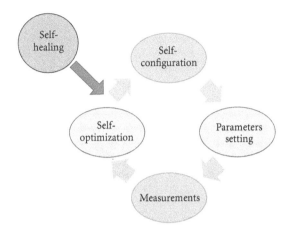

Figure 2: Life cycle of a self-organizing network.

The three processes of a self-organizing network are described as follows.

(a) *Self-configuration*: this process is a preoperational state and is done each time a new femtocell is deployed in the network. It has to configure its initial settings including IP address, association with a gate way, neighbor list, radiated power, channels, and handover parameters.

(b) *Self-optimization*: in this process, with the help of an external optimization tool, the femtocell tunes its parameters to optimize the network according to the varying conditions of the surrounding environment such as traffic demands and users locations. This process takes place in the operational state and depends on measurements taken from user equipment (UE) as well as from femtocells.

(c) *Self-healing*: in contrast with microcells and picocells, femtocells are not maintained by the operator. Therefore, femtocells should be able to automatically detect and localize then heal failures of the network such as reducing the output power in case of temperature failure.

As described in the SOCRATES (Self-Optimisation and self-ConfiguRATion in wirelEss networks project) framework for future wireless networks [10], SON can be implemented in three different approaches: distributed, centralized, and hybrid.

(a) *Distributed SON*: the functionalities of an SON reside in each evolved NodeB (eNB) and self-optimization algorithms are executed on a local basis inside the eNB itself.

(b) *Centralized SON*: all optimization algorithms are executed only in a central node. In most cases, it is performed in the Operations, Administrations, and Maintenance (OAM) system. Individual eNBs have no role in carrying out independent actions.

(c) *Hybrid SON*: depending on the network requirements, self-organization tasks are divided between individual eNBs and a central node.

In a distributed SON, the adjustment of parameters will have a local scope and is difficult to support complex optimization schemes. They generally require the coordination of numerous eNBs whereas a centralized SON has the ability to control the parameters of an entire network. Furthermore, the centralized SON could be best fit in situations where there is a need to manage the interaction between different cells.

Accordingly, the optimization algorithm proposed in this paper is dedicated to the centralized approach. The objective is to centrally and dynamically optimize the coverage of a group of femtocell base station (FBSs) based on a multi objective function. The algorithm simultaneously minimizes the interference, reduces the coverage gaps, and balances the load of all FBSs in the network deployed in an enterprise scenario.

The remainder of the paper is organized as follows: related work is presented in Section 2. Section 3 defines the problem statement and addresses the proposed system architecture. The application of the GA to the self-optimization of enterprise femtocell pilot powers is described in Section 4. Section 5 presents the simulation parameters and the results achieved. Finally, the conclusions and future work are presented in Section 6.

2. Related Work

Most of the published literature concentrate on optimizing the locations of base stations to achieve certain requirements such as coverage and capacity targets, minimizing average bit error rate (BER), and so forth, as in [11–15]. However, although this kind of optimization is applicable to theoretical networks, it has some limitations in practical networks where several aspects restrict the operation of base stations including zoning and power emissions. Therefore, since the introduction of new and complex cellular technologies, the recent trend in research is converging towards employing optimization techniques that assume fixed base station locations and optimize their settings instead. Those settings basically characterize the network performance and usually include pilot channel power, antenna tilt, and azimuth. This can be evidenced by the research carried out by Siomina et al. [16] and Ho et al. in [17].

As discussed in the previous section, dynamic optimization of the femtocell parameters is essential for its successful deployment in current and future cellular networks. One of those parameters is Common Pilot Channel (CPICH) as in Universal Mobile Telecommunications System (UMTS) and High Speed Downlink Packet Access (HSDPA) networks. The CPICH power is usually set to a fixed value between 10 and 20 percent of maximum transmit power in conventional macrocell networks. The CPICH signal is used by mobile terminals to estimate channel quality, cell selection/reselection, and handover evaluation. CPICH power also determines the cell coverage. In other words, higher CPICH power leads to larger cell coverage area. The maximum downlink transmit power of a base station is constant, and hence, the amount of CPICH affects the cell performance. Lower

CPICH power means more power is left for traffic and cell overlaps are reduced. However, higher CPICH power increases the downlink interference due to the increased cell overlaps. As a result, a tradeoff has to be done between coverage and pilot pollution when implementing pilot power adaptation schemes.

A number of studies investigated the effect of pilot power in scenarios where femtocells are deployed. The work in [18] proposed a power control scheme to uniformly configure a constant 10-meter cell radius. The main purpose of the study was to reduce the interference levels of residential femtocells to the macrocell users. In addition, the work done in [19] demonstrated that when femtocells are deployed, the call dropping probability experienced by macrocell users is potentially minimized when power adaptation techniques are implemented. Several studies in the literature address the topic of self-organization of home femtocells [20–22] where femtocells are in the presence of neighboring macrocells and femtocells.

In the literature to date, only a few studies deal with self-organization of enterprise or a group of femtocells. The aim of coverage optimization differs amongst the network requirements and constraints of the three femtocell types. For example, in a home femtocell deployment, the key objective of coverage optimization is to minimize leakage of coverage by a single femtocell to public areas as in [19, 23].

On the contrary, when a number of femtocells are densely deployed such as in an enterprise environment, the aim would be to jointly provide seamless coverage throughout the whole area. Previous work related to optimizing the downlink pilot power of a group of femtocells through an autonomous central control unit mainly focuses on maximizing the cell coverage while mitigating the interference between user-deployed femtocells [24, 25]. In [26] Zhang et al. address power management. They present an algorithm based on linear programming to minimize pilot power in dense residential HSDPA femtocells deployment. On the other hand, the research carried out in [27, 28] proposes a distributed radio coverage optimization in enterprise femtocells. In [29], Wei et al. use the Voronoi diagram to control the coverage area of each femtocell in a public area.

3. Proposed Centralized Self-Optimization of Pilot Power

This paper expands on the work highlighted in [3]. The objective of the proposed algorithm is to centrally and dynamically optimize the coverage of a group of femtocell base station (FBSs) based on a multi objective function that would simultaneously minimize the interference, reduce the coverage gaps, and balance the load of all FBSs in the network. This paper presents the implementation of a heuristic approach based on the genetic algorithm (GA) for coverage optimization in an enterprise femtocell network.

Due to the plug-and-play manner by which femtocells are deployed, autonomous power control is required to achieve the objectives described in Section 3.2 below. In order to achieve that, the proposed algorithm is run by the OAM

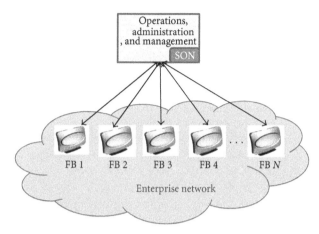

FIGURE 3: Centralized self-optimizing enterprise femtocell network.

after collecting the required statistics from the femtocells through the broadband link such as DSL, TV Cable, or others. As a result, the downlink pilot power of the group of femtocells is adaptively changing according to the global traffic distribution in the network. Our optimization model autonomously finds the best pilot power configuration for N user-deployed femtocells provided that the OAM is aware of local knowledge available for all femtocells. The effectiveness of the proposed approach was evaluated by simulating a real enterprise environment that incorporates a comprehensive indoor channel model.

3.1. System Architecture. This section provides an overview of the centralized self-optimizing cellular network. Figure 3 shows the basic elements that make up the architecture of such a network.

The network operator deploys the macrocellular infrastructure to provide endusers with public telephone and low-rate data access. Within this infrastructure, the femtocells are deployed by endusers in an enterprise in an unstructured fashion. Although the distribution of these small cells could be significantly irregular in geography, the network operator still has to manage the whole cellular interference by employing the OAM. The proposed optimizer is supposed to be executed within the OAM after receiving the required measurement reports from all FBSs deployed in the network. Depending on those measurements, the algorithm compares the current network behavior with the desired one, then determines the optimal or near optimal pilot power configurations of the FBSs. At the end of the process, the OAM sends the new pilot power settings to the connected FBSs. This process resembles a centralized SON as described in Section 1. The block diagram of the process is illustrated in Figure 4.

The following is a general description of the major components for an enterprise network deploying *N* femtocells.

(1) Small base station/femtocell: a small device that is solely deployed and maintained by the user in a plug-and-play manner. Interference management is fully optimized by the OAM.

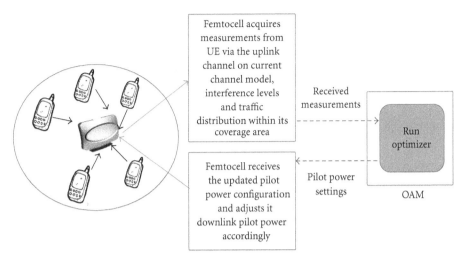

FIGURE 4: Self-optimization of pilot power diagram.

(2) Operations, Administration, and Management (OAM): a smart part of the architecture introduced for autonomous spectrum management and dynamic resource allocation through SON capabilities. When traffic distribution changes, the OAM can adaptively configure the femtocell's radio parameters and optimize its resource allocation through executing SON functionalities.

(3) User Equipment (UE): a mobile device that has spectrum sensing and access capabilities. Major features of future UE terminals will more likely incorporate cognitive radio- and software-defined radio capabilities.

3.2. Problem Description. The objective is to provide end-users with cellular services in an intended area, such as a large enterprise. Therefore, a group of N femtocells are deployed without careful cell planning to jointly achieve this requirement. The coverage area of a FB is the region where its downlink transmitted pilot signal is the strongest signal received by mobile terminals and its value is greater than a predefined threshold ε. Therefore, the number of terminals connected to a certain FB depends on the received pilot power received from that FB. In the presented optimization, the role of the OAM is to adjust the pilot power and thus the coverage of the femtocells in order to fulfill the following objectives.

(i) Minimize the coverage overlaps between neighboring femtocells. The objective is to reduce the interference levels caused by adjacent femtocells as much as possible. In addition, minimize pilot pollution level.

(ii) Minimize the coverage gaps within the specified area where femtocells are to be deployed. By doing this, the total coverage area is maximized and more traffic is offloaded from the outdoor macrocell. Moreover, the amount of signaling due to the femto-macro or macro-femto handovers is substantially reduced.

(iii) Balance the load handled amongst all femtocells in the covered area. The aim here is to abstain overloading or underutilization which affect the call dropping/blocking probability.

Depending on the operator's requirements, weighting factors are introduced in order to emphasize on different objectives as some of them conflict with each other. For example, minimizing the overlaps would subsequently increase the coverage, which may cause some of the femtocells to be underutilized.

4. GA Optimization Model for Femtocell Pilot Power Adjustment

The purpose of formulating the optimization problem is to find the optimal or near-optimal downlink pilot power configuration of N deployed femtocells to fulfill the three previously presented requirements. Since multiple solutions (i.e., multiple CPICH configurations) can be considered as candidate solutions to this particular problem, GA has the potential advantage as a multipoint search engine for optimization problems with multiple objectives. The number of possible CPICH configurations is massive, and this number grows as the number of femtocells in the network increases. As a result, it would be almost impossible to find an optimum solution within a reasonable amount of computing time without employing any optimization techniques, specifically when having to deal with several variables and constraints. In order to perform such optimization, the radio propagation characteristics of a given area need to be included in the objective function. Another issue in the design is the existence of conflicting objectives. For example, increasing the CPICH of a FB would increase the coverage, but doing so might also increase the load that the FB is handling, and eventually cause an increase in the overlaps with neighboring FBSs. This kind of problem does not have a closed form solution and therefore, is a nonconvex optimization problem with numerous local optima. Moreover, it can be shown that it is an NP-hard and could not be solved in polynomial time. The only way to find a global optimal solution is through a computationally intensive, exhaustive analysis, in which all possible inputs are tested. However, it can only be achievable for a very small number of femtocells. Therefore, a heuristic technique is applied to solve such a problem. Heuristics represent a family of approximate optimization techniques that have gained a lot of popularity over the years. They are considered to be the most promising and successful techniques. Moreover, they provide acceptable solutions in a reasonable time for solving hard and complex problems in science and engineering [30]. One of the most well-known and commonly used heuristics is GA. GA belongs to the evolutionary algorithm family that mimics the process of natural evolution. This algorithm has several advantages over other optimization techniques including parallelism, robustness to dynamic changes, and can be hybridized with other methods.

Given the above stated advantages, GA has been chosen to be applied in this research in order to adjust the coverage of a group of femtocells periodically. In addition, GA has proven to have a fast convergence time [31], and that is necessary for the dynamic environment where the femtocell is to be deployed. It is assumed that the GA is periodically executed by the OAM embedded processor to modify the pilot power of the femtocells after performing the process of data acquisition from the network.

4.1. Overview of Genetic Algorithm.
GA is a method that uses genetics as its archetype for problem solving. GA is based on the survival of the best individual in a population [31]. Each individual or solution represents a chromosome in a population. Based on a specific fitness function, all individuals undergo a test to measure their fitness. For each population and depending on the selection rate and method, individuals having the highest fitness are more likely to be selected as parents to go through the reproduction process. The effect of reproduction is very important as it produces children that inherit a combination of good characteristics from two different parents. Finally, mutation is done for the children before including them in the new population.

The following steps should be performed to solve a problem using GA.

(1) *Fitness evaluation function*: a fitness or an objective function is defined according to the parameters and constraints of the problem to be solved.

(2) *Encoding style*: the way a solution to be represented as a chromosome in the algorithm is selected through the different encoding styles that exist (binary, octal, permutation, value, etc.)

(3) *Initialization*: the first population is generated where each bit of the chromosome is randomly generated depending on the encoding style.

(4) *Evaluation*: the fitness of each chromosome is calculated according to the objective function.

(5) *Selection*: this step is done randomly with a probability depending on the relative fitness of the

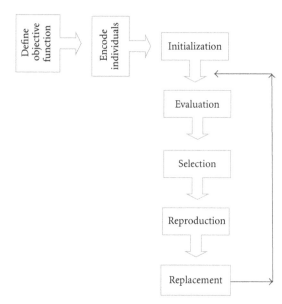

FIGURE 5: Process of a genetic algorithm.

chromosome; the higher the fitness, the higher the chance of being chosen for reproduction.

(6) *Reproduction*: genetic operators such as crossover and mutation on selected chromosomes are executed to produce children.

(7) *Replacement*: this is the last step where chromosomes from the old population are replaced by the generated children.

(8) Steps 4 through 7 are repeated until a predefined number of iterations is reached or no further improvement can be observed within a defined period. Figure 5 demonstrates an overview of the GA process described above.

4.2. GA Setup for Coverage Optimization

4.2.1. Presentation of Population.
In order to formulate the problem, it was assumed that N user-deployed FBSs are connected to a centralized self-optimizing management system such as the OAM. The locations of the FBSs are fixed by the enterprise owner with no precise cell planning but with some elementary arrangements. Therefore, it is intended to find a vector $\mathbf{P} = (\mathcal{P}_1, \mathcal{P}_2, \mathcal{P}_3, \ldots, \mathcal{P}_N)$ where each element in the vector denotes the downlink pilot power strength for a specific FB i such that $i \in N$. This is done by the OAM on a continuous basis. This means that the OAM periodically collects measurements from all FBSs in the network about the surrounding environment (i.e., traffic distribution, power levels received at mobile users, etc.) and then sends the updated pilot power level to each FB accordingly.

Therefore, each vector $\mathbf{P}$ is considered as a possible solution in the population and affects the three objectives defined in the objective function. Population **K** is represented as follows:

$$K = \begin{bmatrix} \mathscr{P}_{11} & \mathscr{P}_{12} & \cdots & & & \cdots & \cdots & \mathscr{P}_{1N} \\ \mathscr{P}_{21} & \mathscr{P}_{22} & \cdots & & \cdots & \cdots & \cdots & \mathscr{P}_{2N} \\ \mathscr{P}_{31} & \mathscr{P}_{32} & \cdots & & & \cdots & \cdots & \mathscr{P}_{3N} \\ & \vdots & & \vdots & & \vdots & & \\ \mathscr{P}_{S1} & \cdots & \cdots & \cdots & \cdots & \cdots & \cdots & \mathscr{P}_{SN} \end{bmatrix}, \tag{1}$$

where S is the population size. The pilot power of each cell is randomly generated. The elements of **P** are constrained such that $\min power < \mathscr{P}_{si}[mW] < \max power$, where $s \in S$. Consequently, the value encoding style was used to enumerate the possible solution into chromosomes.

4.2.2. Objective Function. The algorithm presented adjusts the FB's pilot power channel and eventually its coverage area depending on the collected measurements and statistics from the N FBSs in the network. The objective function used in this paper is similar to the one utilized in the research carried out in [28]. However, in this method, fitness is centrally computed and is based on the global knowledge of the network conditions.

Formulation of the objective function that takes into account the three objectives described in Section 3.2 is one of the most important tasks to be performed in order to evaluate the fitness of each individual in the population **K**. Several methods such as finding a Pareto-optimal set, weighted sum, or hierarchical optimization are often applied to solve a multi objective problem. The weighted sum is the most widely used approach and is employed in this research. This method allows the scores of all objectives to be summed up into an aggregate fitness value. This is done by multiplying each objective function by a weighting factor and summing up all weighted objective functions. Therefore, when GA is applied to this 3-objective optimization problem, the values of the three objective functions for each individual have to be estimated. Then, according to these values the overall fitness value of each individual could be calculated. As a consequence, GA searches for an individual (s) with a better fitness as in the normal case of a single-objective optimization problem. In order to transform the values of the three objectives into one single value, the three objectives are combined to produce one scalar function.

The three objective functions used to formulate the main objective function are described below. Three types of statistics are required from each FB in order to process the GA.

(1) The first function $f_L(s)$ is used to maximize the load experienced by all FBS in the network. The load that a femtocell can handle at any time, L_i, is subject to an upper bound L_{th}: the purpose here is to balance the load handled by the FBSs across the network and block overloading. Therefore, each femtocell reports back to the OAM the load of voice traffic in Erlangs that it is handling. In order to capture the load of

the whole network, the mean value of all FBSs load is calculated as follows:

$$f_L(s) = \begin{cases} \dfrac{1}{N} \sum_{i=1}^{N} \dfrac{L_i}{L_{th}} & \text{if } L_i \le L_{th}, \\ 0, & \text{otherwise} \end{cases} \tag{2}$$

here a femtocell i estimates the load that it is handling L_i for all its covered users U by

$$L_i = \sum_{j=1}^{U} L_j \qquad \text{if } Pr_{ji} = Pt_{si} - PL_{ij} \ge \varepsilon, \tag{3}$$

where Pr_{ji} is power received by user terminal j from FB i, Pt_{si} is CPICH transmitted from FB i in individual s, and PL_{ij} is path loss between FB i and user terminal j.

It can be observed that whenever the load of femtocell i does not exceed L_{th}, the value of f_L increases. This allows the femtocells to take more load as long as their load is less than L_{th}. The path loss $PL(dB)$ model used to approximate the path loss between a FB and a mobile terminal is

$$PL(dB) = 38.5 + \eta x\, 10 \log_{10}(d) + \sum_{f=1}^{F} a_f W_f, \tag{4}$$

where η is the distance power decay factor, d is the direct transmitter-receiver distance in meters, α_f is the number of penetrated walls of type f, W_f is the attenuation due to the wall of type f, $f = 1, 2,\ldots, F$. In our simulations, $\eta = 2$. Moreover, correlated shadow fading with a standard deviation of 8 dB was considered to reflect the effect of obstacles such as furniture.

(2) The second objective function $f_G(s)$ is used to minimize the probability of users in coverage gaps. A coverage gap is part of the total area intended to be covered where a mobile terminal does not receive any pilot power from any of the FBSs that is above ε. This is calculated by each FB i and can be achieved by measuring the number of handovers that occurred between the FB i and the underlay macrocell. The probability of users entering a femtocell coverage gap G_i should not exceed an upper bound G_{th}. The mean value of the coverage gaps of the whole network is computed using

$$f_G(s) = \frac{1}{N} \sum_{i=1}^{N} G_i, \tag{5}$$

where

$$G_i = \frac{u_G}{u_G + u_i}, \tag{6}$$

where u_G is the number of users handed over from femtocell i to the macrocell, and u_i is the number of users handed over from femtocell i to a neighboring femtocell.

(3) The third objective function $f_V(s)$ is employed to minimize the coverage overlaps in the network: an overlap V_i represents a fraction of the coverage area of a FB i intersecting with the coverage area of neighboring femtocells. In order to perform the process of overlap estimation as in (7), a femtocell i keeps record of the received measurement reports gathered from mobile terminals u_V where more than one pilot power measured by a mobile terminal is higher than ε. Therefore, V_i is calculated as the ratio of u_V to the total number of pilot power measurements sent back by all users, U, in FB i. The algorithm restricts V_i from surpassing an upper bound V_{th}. Then $f_V(s)$ for the whole network is approximated as in (8)

$$V_i = \frac{u_V}{U}, \tag{7}$$

$$f_V(s) = \frac{1}{N} \sum_{i=1}^{N} V_i, \tag{8}$$

where

$$u_V = \sum_{b=1}^{B} \sum_{j=1}^{U} u_{bj}, \tag{9}$$

where B is the number of neighboring femtocells of femtocell i. Here, u_{bi} is the number of users who's both Pr_{ji} and at least one Pr_{jb} are greater than ε.

The GA is executed in the OAM to maximize the overall objective function $f(s)$ defined in (10). In this case, evaluation of how good the whole network performance is would be performed for each individual (s) in the population **K**.

$$f(s) = \frac{\omega_L \cdot f_L(s) + \omega_G \cdot (1 - f_G(s)) + \omega_V \cdot (1 - f_V(s))}{\omega_L + \omega_G + \omega_V}, \tag{10}$$

where $f_L(s)$, $f_G(s)$, and $f_V(s)$ are normalized between 0 and 1. Moreover, as stated earlier, depending on the requirements of the operator more emphasis can be put on one objective over the others through the weighting factors ω_L, ω_V, and ω_G which can take values between 0 and 1.

According to the previous mathematical formulation, L_{th}, G_{th}, and V_{th} are the required upper bound for femtocell coverage load, gap, and overlap, respectively, and L_i, G_i, and V_i are the current coverage performance observations. $f(s)$ is a function with L_{th}, G_{th}, V_{th}, L_i, G_i, and V_i as input parameters. The output parameter is the optimized CPICH configuration **P** which enables the N FBSs to achieve the expected performance.

4.2.3. Genetic Operators. Genetic operators such as crossover and mutation are used to reproduce children from the selected parents. Double point crossover was used in the simulation. Mutation is performed by randomly selecting one of the genes of the chromosome (i.e., pilot power of one

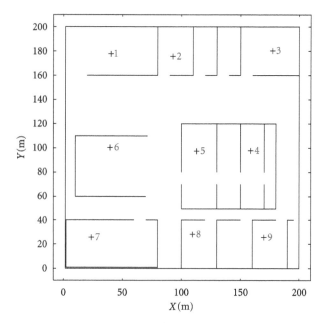

FIGURE 6: Layout of the simulated area.

of the femtocells) then either decrease or increases it by a step size equal to Δm. The decision to increase or decrease the selected femtocell pilot power depends on another random value n, that is, if n = 0 then this would increase $\mathcal{P}_{li}$ by Δm, otherwise if n = 1 then $\mathcal{P}_{li}$ is decreased by Δm.

5. Simulation Results

In order to evaluate the effectiveness of the described algorithm, MATLAB was used to simulate the enterprise environment. The simulation scenario is a large typical business area of 200 m × 200 m, it consists of partitioned offices as well as meeting rooms as shown in Figure 6. The partitions are made up of light walls and all other walls are heavy walls. The positions of 9 UMTS femtocells of the 21 dBm class (125 mW) were assumed to be placed by the enterprise owner without any detailed planning. Their locations can also be found in Figure 6. A number of 400 mobile terminals are uniformly scattered across the entire area. Voice traffic is randomly distributed amongst those mobile terminals such that each of them can generate traffic between 0.2 and 0.5 Erlangs. The value of ε that is the minimum required signal level for a FB user equipment (UE) to maintain a 12.2 kb/s voice call is assumed to be −104.18 dBm considering a chip rate equal to 3.84 Mb/s, a UE noise floor of −87.50 dBm, and a Eb/No requirement equal to 8.3 dB for a voice call as recommended in [32] for additive white Gaussian noise AWGN channel. The path loss model in (4) is used to generate a path loss map for the 200 m × 200 m.

In UMTS systems CPICH is usually set to 10% of the maximum downlink transmit power. It was found that if the initial pilot power of the FBSs was set to 6 mW (7.78 dBm) which is half of the maximum pilot power, it would speed up the process. This was done by setting

TABLE 1: Simulation parameters.

Simulation parameter	Value
Population size (S)	30
Maximum number of generations	300
Mutation rate	0.1
Selection rate	1
Min femtocell coverage pilot power	1 mW
Max femtocell coverage pilot power	12 mW
W_1 (Attenuation due to light wall)	3.8 dB
W_2 (Attenuation due to heavy wall)	2.7 dB
L_{th}	8 Erlangs
G_{th}	0.1
V_{th}	0.3
Δm	1 mW

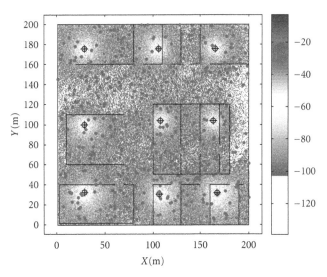

FIGURE 7: Optimized femtocells coverage when highest weight is given to balance the load, colorbar shows received pilot powers in dBm.

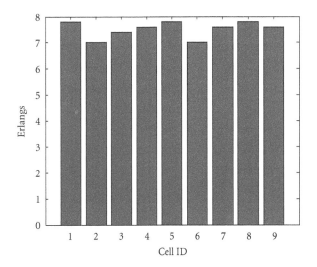

FIGURE 8: Final load handled by the femtocells (no. of FBSs = 9).

20% of the population of the first GA generation to this value and the rest was randomly generated. A roulette wheel selection was performed to select parent solutions for reproduction. Therefore, in this process a parent is selected with a probability that is proportional to its fitness. In order to show the effect of the weighting factor, the weights were changed each time after the entire simulation was executed and then the result was recorded. Other simulation parameters are displayed in Table 1.

Figure 7 illustrates the optimized pilot power coverage when $\omega_L = 1$, $\omega_V = 0.5$, and $\omega_G = 0.5$. The blue dots represent the scattered mobile terminals. Moreover, Figure 8 shows the load handled by the 9 FBSs. Although the areas covered by the FBS are not equal, yet they are handling very close amount of loads as shown in Figure 6. This is significant in cells 7 and 8 that have the minimum pilot power channel of all other femtocells as in Figure 9 but still handles as much load as the other cells. The fitness for this scenario is 0.8727. It can also be observed in Figure 7 that some areas are not fully covered. This is due to the fact that emphasis has been given to balance the load (i.e., $\omega_L = 1$) for the entire network. Therefore, the OAM does not impose high pilot power for FBS to ensure that the load they are handling does not remarkably deviate from the average.

In the next scenario, the maximum weight is given to minimize the coverage gaps (i.e., maximize the total coverage area). The weights are modified such that $\omega_L = 0.5$, $\omega_V = 0.5$, and $\omega_G = 1$. The optimized pilot power coverage is presented in Figure 10.

It can be observed that most of the cells in this case increased their pilot power to cover more mobile terminals as illustrated in Figure 12. With those modified weights, it is clear that the overlaps have increased and the load has become unbalanced and some cells become overloaded as shown in Figure 11.

In the third case, the weights have been set as $\omega_L = 0.5$, $\omega_V = 1$, and $\omega_G = 0.5$. Figure 13 demonstrates the optimized cell coverage where more emphasis is given to minimizing the overlaps. It can be observed that the overlaps have not totally disappeared but instead are minimized as much as possible. This can be seen especially between

cells 2 and 3, and cells 1 and 6. Controlling the weight given to minimizing the overlaps is important especially in systems that require a certain amount of overlap to perform soft handover from one cell to the other as in CDMA (Code Division Multiple Access). It can also be noticed from Figure 14 that the load distribution across FBSs is not balanced compared to the first case. During the simulation, it was realized that the algorithm decreased the coverage whenever the overlaps increased.

Compared with the simulation results presented in [24] which implements linear programming to minimize the interference and maximize the smallest cell size for femtocells, the proposed algorithm considers load balancing in addition to their objectives. In addition, it performs autonomous optimization of the cell size of a group of femtocells in a more realistic environment where the effect of walls and other obstacles is taken into account when

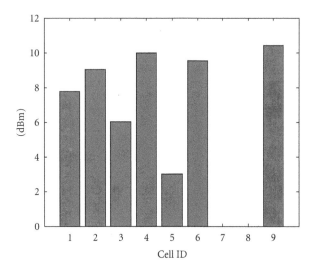

FIGURE 9: Converged pilot power setting of the femtocells (no. of FBSs = 9).

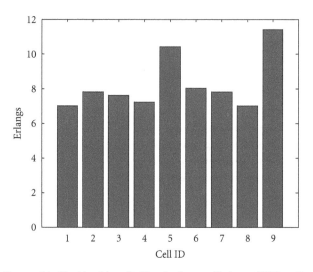

FIGURE 11: Final load handled by the femtocells (no. of FBSs = 9).

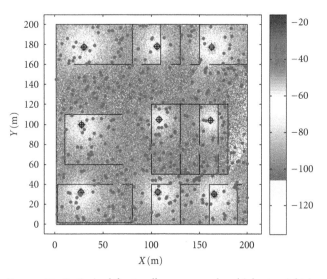

FIGURE 10: Optimized femtocells coverage when highest weight is given to minimize coverage gaps.

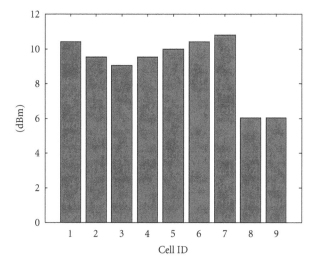

FIGURE 12: Converged pilot power setting of the femtocells (no. of FBSs = 9).

estimating the coverage area of the cell. The effect of balancing the load by adjusting the pilot power according to the relative traffic intensity handled in each cell was also considered. Furthermore, unlike the research done in [26], we were able to control the amount of pilot power leakage by altering the weight given to minimizing the overlaps depending on the current traffic distribution.

The results also demonstrated the ability of our centralized algorithm to achieve comparable results to the ones presented in [28] which is based on decentralized genetic programming approach. In addition, it was illustrated that our proposed algorithm is robust to the dynamic changes of the network. That can be evidenced by the short convergence time which is due to the parallelism of the GA. With the roulette wheel selection and reproduction operations, more time will be spent on finding good solutions than moderate ones. Being one of the population-based techniques, GA

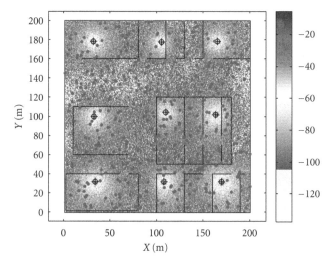

FIGURE 13: Optimized femtocells coverage when highest weight is given to minimize overlaps.

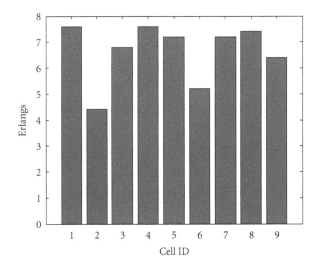

FIGURE 14: Final load handled by the femtocells (no. of FBSs = 9).

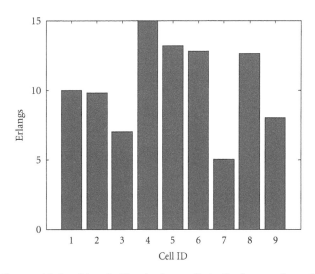

FIGURE 15: Load handled by the femtocells in fixed power (no. of FBSs = 9).

TABLE 2: Fixed and optimized power network performance.

Mean value	Load	Gaps	Overlaps
Fixed power	0.1667	0.2302	0.4037
Optimized power	0.8694	0.2749	0.1656

provides an opportunity to choose good nonlocal moves from the large space of possibilities.

With the same objective function applied in [28] to a whole network, the authors in [28] presented their results of one scenario with all the weights of (5) set to one whilst our algorithm was evaluated in three different scenarios. A different set of weights was used to emphasize a particular objective. The results were represented in Figures 7, 10, and 13.

The presented approach was also employed to compare with the fixed pilot power scheme mentioned in [18]. In order to do that, the GA was run with ω_V, ω_L, and ω_G set to 1. For the fixed power approach, the pilot power was set to 11 dBm (typically around 1/10th of the total power. Figures 15 and 16 show the load distribution across FBSs when fixed pilot power and optimized pilot power schemes were employed respectively. It can be noticed from Figure 15 that some FBSs are underutilized while others are overloaded. This increases in turn the numbers of dropped and blocked calls. Table 2 demonstrates the differences of network mean load, gaps, and overlaps between the two schemes. The values illustrate the effectiveness of the proposed algorithm to balance the three objectives and to significantly improve the whole network performance.

Table 2 shows that although the mean gaps have increased due to the decreased overlaps, the load is more balanced and pilot power pollution is minimized.

Figure 17 illustrates the final optimized pilot power in this scenario. Compared with the fixed power of 11 dBm, the optimized pilot power configuration indicates a 57% reduction in the total power pollution.

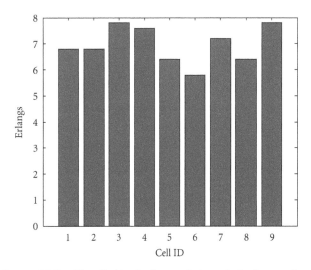

FIGURE 16: Load handled by the femtocells in optimized power (no. of FBSs = 9).

Finally, an exhaustive search was performed in order to assess the solution quality of the presented algorithm. In this case, a simplified scenario was considered where only 5 femtocells are deployed. The locations of the FBSs and the UE are identical in both cases in order to precisely compare the performance of GA. Again all weights of the objectives in the fitness function were set to 1. Figures 18 and 19 demonstrate the final load distribution when executing the exhaustive and the GA, respectively. Similarly, Figures 20 and 21 show the best pilot power configuration as generated from the exhaustive search and the GA, respectively.

It can be seen that the GA is able to produce the optimal pilot power configuration as generated by the exhaustive search. Figure 22 demonstrates the fitness of the solution obtained by the exhaustive search and the converged fitness of the GA. It took 2769 s for the exhaustive search to find the solution with the highest fitness (0.8797 in this scenario),

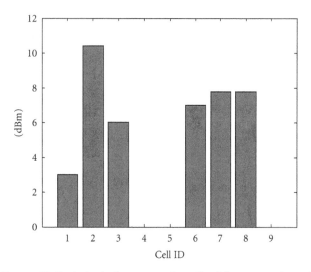

FIGURE 17: Optimized pilot power when all weights set to 1 (no. of FBSs = 9).

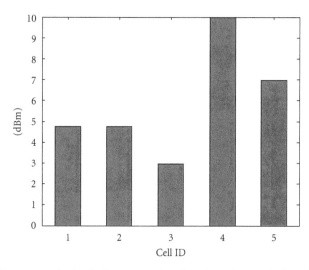

FIGURE 20: Optimal pilot power given by exhaustive search (no. of FBSs = 5).

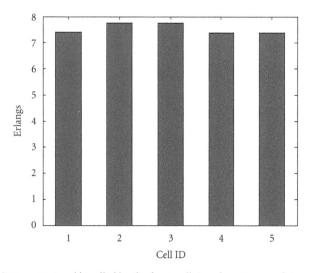

FIGURE 18: Load handled by the femtocells in exhaustive search (no. of FBSs = 5).

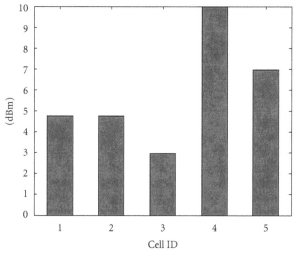

FIGURE 21: Optimized pilot power given by GA (no. of FBSs = 5).

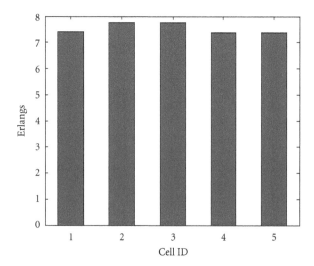

FIGURE 19: Load handled by the femtocells in GA (no. of FBSs = 5).

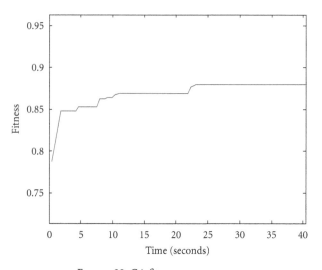

FIGURE 22: GA fitness convergence.

while it took the GA only 23 s to produce the same optimal solution. Those results assure that the proposed algorithm can produce a very high quality solution in a fraction of time.

6. Conclusions & Future Work

Self-optimizing capabilities for future mobile network are driven by both the market perspective and the technological potentials. At the same time, femtocells are expected to be widely deployed to enhance indoor radio coverage and system capacity. Their deployment is extending to cover the enterprise area. An approach based on genetic algorithm was presented in this paper to automatically optimize the coverage of a group of femtocells in an enterprise environment. The results demonstrated the ability of the algorithm to dynamically update the pilot powers of the femtocells as per the time varying global traffic distribution and interference levels.

The algorithm was evaluated on UMTS femtocells, but it can work with any air interface by introducing minor modifications. It was also compared with the fixed pilot power scheme and results illustrate a notable network performance and reduction in pilot power pollution. Finally, in comparison with the exhaustive search, the presented algorithm provides an optimal or near optimal solution with significant time reduction.

Future work will include evaluating the effectiveness of the algorithm in a decentralized femtocell deployment. The algorithm will be extended such that it automatically tunes the weights of the objectives of the fitness function depending on the current network requirements. Furthermore, the performance of other optimization methods will be compared to the one proposed in this paper.

References

[1] Airvana, "Femtocells: transforming the indoor experience," White paper, 2007.

[2] V. Chandrasekhar, J. G. Andrews, and A. Gatherer, "Femtocell networks: a survey," *IEEE Communications Magazine*, vol. 46, no. 9, pp. 59–67, 2008.

[3] L. Mohjazi, M. Al-Qutayri, H. Barada, K. Poon, and R. Shubair, "Deployment challenges of femtocells in future indoor wireless networks," in *Proceedings of the IEEE GCC Conference and Exhibition (GCC '11)*, pp. 405–408, Dubai, UAE, 2011.

[4] IDATE, "Femtocell worldwide market, Rep," 2010, http://www.idate.org/en/News/Femtocell_650.html.

[5] FemtoForum, http://www.femtoforum.org/femto/.

[6] Informa Telecoms & Media, "Femtocell Market Status, Rep," 2011, http://www.femtoforum.org/femto/.

[7] G. De La Roche and J. Zhang, "Femtocell networks: perspectives before wide deployments," E-Letter IEEE, 2010.

[8] H. Hu, J. Zhang, X. Zheng, Y. Yang, and P. Wu, "Self-configuration and self-optimization for LTE networks," *IEEE Communications Magazine*, vol. 48, no. 2, pp. 94–100, 2010.

[9] S. Feng and E. Seidel, "Self-organizing networks (SON) in 3GPP long term evolution," Nomor Research GmbH, White Paper, May 2008.

[10] SOCRATES, "Framework for the development of self-organization methods," 2008.

[11] I. Vilovic, N. Burum, and Z. Sipus, "Ant colony approach in optimization of base station position," in *Proceedings of the European Conference on Antennas and Propagation (EuCAP '09)*, pp. 2882–2886, Berlin, Germany, March 2009.

[12] M. Kobayashi, S. Haruyama, R. Kohno, and M. Nakagawa, "Optimal access point placement in simultaneous broadcast system using OFDM for indoor wireless LAN," in *Proceedings of the 11th IEEE International Symposium on Personal, Indoor and Mobile Radio Communications (PIMRC '00)*, pp. 200–204, London, UK, September 2000.

[13] J. Munyaneza, "Optimization of antenna placement in 3G networks using genetic algorithm," in *Proceedings of the 3rd International Conference on Broadband Communications, Information Technology and Biomedical Applications*, Gauteng, South Africa, 2008.

[14] H. R. Anderson and J. P. McGeehan, "Optimizing microcell base station locations using simulated annealing techniques," in *Proceedings of the IEEE 44th Vehicular Technology Conference*, pp. 858–862, Stockholm, Sweden, June 1994.

[15] A. Molina, G. E. Athanasiadou, and A. R. Nix, "Automatic location of base-stations for optimized cellular coverage: a new combinatorial approach," in *Proceedings of the IEEE 49th Vehicular Technology Conference*, pp. 606–610, Houston, Tex, USA, May 1999.

[16] D. Fagen, P. A. Vicharelli, and J. Weitzen, "Automated wireless coverage optimization with controlled overlap," *IEEE Transactions on Vehicular Technology*, vol. 57, no. 4, pp. 2395–2403, 2008.

[17] I. Siomina et al., "Automated optimization of service coverage and base station antenna configuration in UMTS networks," *IEEE Wireless Communications*, vol. 13, no. 6, pp. 16–25, 2006.

[18] L. Ho, "Performance of macro- and co-channel femtocells in a hierarchical cell structure," in *Proceedings of the 18th Annual IEEE International Symposium on Personal, Indoor and Mobile Radio Communications (PIMRC '07)*, Athens, Greece, September 2007.

[19] L. T. W. Ho and H. Claussen, "Effects of user-deployed, co-channel femtocells on the call drop probability in a residential scenario," in *Proceedings of the 18th Annual IEEE International Symposium on Personal, Indoor and Mobile Radio Communications (PIMRC '07)*, pp. 1–5, Athens, Greece, September 2007.

[20] H. Claussen, L. T. W. Ho, and L. G. Samuel, "Self-optimization of coverage for femtocell deployments," in *Proceedings of the 7th Annual Wireless Telecommunications Symposium (WTS '08)*, pp. 278–285, Pomona, Calif, USA, April 2008.

[21] D. Lopez-Perez et al., "Intracell handover for interference and handover mitigation in OFDMA two-tier macrocell-femtocell networks," *Eurasip Journal on Wireless Communications and Networking*, vol. 2010, Article ID 142629, 15 pages, 2010.

[22] G. Guvenc, M.-R. Jeong, F. Watanabe, and H. Inamura, "A hybrid frequency assignment for femtocells and coverage area analysis for co-channel operation," *IEEE Communications Letters*, vol. 12, no. 12, pp. 880–882, 2008.

[23] V. Chandrasekhar, J. G. Andrews, T. Muharemovic, Z. Shen, and A. Gatherer, "Power control in two-tier femtocell networks," *IEEE Transactions on Wireless Communications*, vol. 8, no. 8, Article ID 5200991, pp. 4316–4328, 2009.

[24] Y. Y. Li and E. S. Sousa, "Base station pilot management for user-deployed cellular networks," in *Proceedings of the IEEE International Conference on Communications (ICC '09)*, pp. 1–5, Dresden, Germany, June 2009.

[25] K. Han et al., "Optimization of femtocell network configuration under interference constraints," in *Proceedings of the IEEE 7th International Symposium on Modeling and Optimization in Mobile, Ad Hoc, and Wireless Networks*, pp. 1–7, Seol, South Korea, 2009.

[26] Y. Zhang et al., "Pilot power minimization in HSDPA femtocells," in *Proceedings of the IEEE Global Telecommunications Conference*, Miami, Fla, USA, 2011.

[27] I. Ashraf, H. Claussen, and L. T. W. Ho, "Distributed radio coverage optimization in enterprise femtocell networks," in *2010 IEEE International Conference on Communications (ICC '10)*, Cape Town, South Africa, May 2010.

[28] L. T. W. Ho, I. Ashraf, and H. Claussen, "Evolving femtocell coverage optimization algorithms using genetic programming," in *Proceedings of the IEEE 20th Personal, Indoor and Mobile Radio Communications Symposium (PIMRC '09)*, pp. 2132–2136, Tokyo, Japan, September 2009.

[29] Z. Wei, Z. Feng, Y. Li, and Q. Zhang, "Voronoi-based coverage optimization for multi-femtocells," in *Proceedings of the IEEE International Conference on Wireless Information Technology and Systems (ICWITS '10)*, Honolulu, Hawaii, USA, September 2010.

[30] S. M. Sait and H. Youssef, *Iterative Computer Algorithms with Applications in Engineering*, IEEE Computer Society, Calif, USA, 1999.

[31] S. N. Sivanandam and S. N. Deepa, *Introduction to Genetic Algorithms*, Springer, Berlin, Germany, 2008.

[32] 3GPP Technical Specification 25.104 v.7.9.0, "Base Station (BS) radio transmission and reception (FDD)," 2008, http://3gpp.org/.

6

Peer-to-Peer Multicasting Inspired by Huffman Coding

Bartosz Polaczyk, Piotr Chołda, and Andrzej Jajszczyk

AGH University of Science and Technology, Department of Telecommunications, Al. Mickiewicza 30, 30-059 Kraków, Poland

Correspondence should be addressed to Piotr Chołda; piotr.cholda@agh.edu.pl

Academic Editor: Zhiyong Xu

Stringent QoS requirements of video streaming are not addressed by the delay characteristics of highly dynamic peer-to-peer (P2P) networks. To solve this problem, a novel locality-aware method for choosing optimal neighbors in live streaming multicast P2P overlays is presented in this paper. To create the appropriate multicast tree topology, a round-trip-time (RTT) value is used as a parameter distinguishing peers capabilities. The multicast tree construction is based on the Huffman source coding algorithm. First, a centrally managed version is presented, and then an effective use of a distributed paradigm is shown. Performance evaluation results prove that the proposed approach considerably improves the overlay efficiency from the viewpoint of end-users and content providers. Moreover, the proposed technique ensures a high level of resilience against gateway-link failures and adaptively reorganizes the overlay topology in case of dynamic, transient network fluctuations.

1. Introduction

For previous few years peer-to-peer (P2P) related flows (overlay traffic) have represented a vast majority of the whole Internet traffic. Thus, P2P networking has become an important branch of today's telecommunications. It involves not only file-sharing (BitTorrent, Ares Galaxy, Gnutella), but also multimedia streaming (PPLive, SopCast), Internet telephony (Skype), anonymous routing (Tor), and many aspects of content distribution networks or cloud networking.

With the increased interest in quality-requiring applications, the problem of the quality of service (QoS) assurance is a real challenge in P2P-based streaming. Live streaming transfers based on the P2P paradigm impose strict constraints on latency between a video server and peers (end-users). Since the requirements are not fully addressed by the characteristics of P2P networking, a considerable attention has been put on the overcoming techniques. One of the most basic parameters that highly influence the quality experienced by end-users is the effective downloading speed and its stability over time. A buffering process, observed by end-users as a transient interruption of content delivery, can be minimized, or even avoided, when oscillations of the downloading speed are small. To accomplish the gapless

playback, the P2P application-layer links should be set over short distances with additional care about the available capacity. This task is a nontrivial problem as P2P systems were invented to be underlay-agnostic. In practice, they have not usually recognized proximity between the candidate peers nor estimate attainable bandwidth. This situation has changed and the focus has been brought to the so-called localization-aware overlays.

Here, we elaborate on the localization-aware P2P overlays: an organization of the transmission tree is not spontaneous (following the flowing process of the peers to the overlay), but instead it uses the underlying information on the Internet paths. In effect, the video quality is improved. Our method is called "Huffmies" due to its inspiration by the Huffman source coding. The Huffman algorithm constructs a tree representing a code of the shortest average codeword length, calculated as the sum of the paths from the root to the leaves (messages). The elements of the sum are weighted by the probabilities associated with the leaves. In Huffmies, a similar mechanism is used to create a multicast streaming tree, where the root is a video server and leaves represent the peers. We aim at generating the shortest average path from the root to a leaf, while the weight of a leaf is related to a measure based on the underlay-related knowledge, namely, round-trip-time, RTT. With the relationship of our algorithm to the Huffman method providing the optimal tree, we are able to show the optimality of Huffmies.

The remainder of this paper is organized as follows: Section 2 overviews the context and the related literature on the covered topic. Section 3 refreshes Huffman coding definitions and notations necessary to understand the proposed solution. Section 4, the main part of this paper, describes our novel approach in detail. Section 5 analyzes simulation results, verifying that the proposed approach is a promising alternative. Finally, the paper is summarized, and a few challenges of the proposed method are discussed.

2. Background and Previous Works

With regard to the routing topology, there are the following three types of P2P streaming systems used in practice:

(a) push: structured, based mainly on multicasting tree(s);

(b) pull: unstructured, similar to the mesh-based file-sharing BitTorrent system;

(c) hybrid: combined push-pull, based on a two-layer or two-phased mesh-tree architecture.

Currently, the majority of existing implementations and methods are related to the second type [1–4]. This stems from their flexibility and the high fault tolerance. However, we focus on the tree-based multicasting. It has also received strong research attention [5–8] due to its control potential. Additionally, by the usage of the tree-like approach, we are able to prove the bound optimality with the inspiration of the Huffman source-coding algorithm. Additionally, we study the reliability performance of our method to prove its usefulness in the case of random failures.

The challenge related to P2P networks is to find the optimal topology able to satisfy each of the three entities involved in the overlay content delivery: (a) peers, (b) the Internet service providers (ISPs), and (c) content providers. Each of them has its own requirements and prominent objectives. A peer requires the high streaming rate of the content, short start-up times, and lack of prefetching. In particular, in live video transmissions, small delays between the content source and end-users are of vital importance. While interdomain traffic load is essential to ISPs, a reduction of that load should not affect the quality experienced by customers. Finally, goals of a content provider are in-between the end-users and ISPs' needs. The content provider appreciates a high customer satisfaction (enhanced video quality) and favorable network resource utilization, as it enables a successful cooperation with operators. Our method pays to the end-user QoS satisfaction; however it reconciles also other entities' matters which are respected and considered in the simulation study.

A lot of effort has been put to improve the operation of P2P systems by taking into account the network constraints; for review see [9, 10]. Sometimes, even a strong cooperation between an overlay operator and a network carrier is assumed. The topic has been recognized as an important issue for the Internet community [11]. The research was mainly focused on file-sharing with introduction of methods like the so-called biased neighbor selection in the BitTorrent context. They rely on centrally managed devices impeding dynamic and quick decisions in case of nodes departure or network partitions. Therefore, their application prospects in video multicast networks are limited, especially when failures are considered.

A classification of approaches using locality awareness in P2P overlays can be found in [12] (a) awareness of the ISPs network, to which a peer is assigned to; (b) storage of some additional information on other peers, for example, when they serve as supernodes; (c) delay assessments; (d) geolocation information as a base for the peer node selection. Our research follows the third avenue; that is, we base on the latency measured by RTT. This group of approach is quite well represented. The streaming tree construction idea presented in [6] involved just a delay-aware technique to build a network friendly tree (NFT). In this scheme, an arriving peer contacts and requests a streaming flow from the node that has the smallest RTT among all peers in the overlay swarm. In contrast to our approach, the tree is constructed in a receiver-centric way and it does not adapt to transient network conditions. A similar concept of grouping peers into clustered trees, based on RTT, was presented in [7]. However, this method assumes evaluating RTT between an end-user and static landmarks (like DNS servers), instead of ordinary overlay peers. Our approach is based on the RTT between peers.

On the other hand, a proposal of Kovačević et al. [13] was based on the geolocation system, introducing zones and a two-layered, distance-aware system to accomplish strict QoS requirements. We do not assume such a sophisticated method, but base on the "application-layer ping," which is very simple to implement. The authors of [14] proposed to construct an optimized multicasting P2P tree, assuming that the coordination data is given in advance. Again, we decided to use a much easier method.

3. Overview of Huffman Coding

A Huffman code [15] is the minimum redundancy source code, where each message (out of N messages) is represented as a prefix-free *codeword* (a "message code"). $l(i)$, a codeword length, equal to the number of symbols in codeword i, depends on an occurrence probability $p(i)$ of the ith message generation, so that the average message length

$$\overline{L} = \sum_{i \in N} p(i) \, l(i) \qquad (1)$$

is minimized. Each codeword is constructed using symbols from an alphabet of t letters (the t-ary alphabet). We skip the details of the code construction, but we remind that the ultimate idea is based on the fact that messages with higher $p(i)$ are represented with shorter codewords. A Huffman *ensemble code* (see Figure 1), that is an agreement between the source encoder and the decoder about corresponding messages and codewords, can be presented in the tree form. Thus, an ensemble code and its tree are equivalent. In such

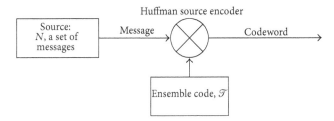

<FIGURE>Figure 1: The Huffman coding concept.</FIGURE>

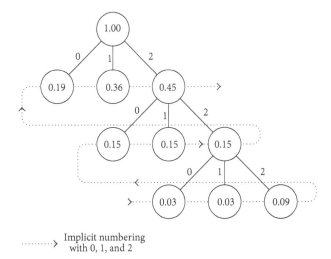

Figure 2: Example of a ternary *Huffman tree* $\mathcal{T}$. Numbers in ovals represent probabilities.

a labeled tree $\mathcal{T}$, called here a *Huffman tree* (an example is presented in Figure 2), the internal and leaf nodes have different meanings. The leaf corresponds to a single message, labeled with its occurrence probability $p(i)$. The internal node is just an auxiliary vertex with labels equal to the sum of its children's label values. In tree $\mathcal{T}$, the edges are also uniquely labeled with one of t symbols. Edge labels over a path from the tree root to a given leaf define a codeword representing the respective message. Such a definition of tree $\mathcal{T}$ is used also in [16, 17] to create an adaptive Huffman algorithm. The original static (two-pass) and newer adaptive (one-pass) Huffman algorithms differ in the ensemble code construction method and its exchange between the encoder and decoder. However, both ensemble codes have the same structure and the $\overline{L}$ value. Therefore, for the sake of interpretation purposes, we can use the static and adaptive algorithms interchangeably, since results for those approaches are the same.

4. Huffmies Design

Below, we present "Huffmies," the centralized and distributed approaches that create a streaming topology for a multicast tree-enabled P2P overlay network. Both approaches are inspired by the Huffman algorithm. The summary of the notation related to the Huffman coding and Huffmies is given in Table 1.

4.1. Centralized Huffmies. Each P2P streaming network uses a content server s, which can upload to only a limited number of nodes simultaneously due to the bandwidth and computing resource limits. Among all the active peers subscribed to the stream, the server has to choose at most t peers that will receive the data directly from it. The centralized Huffmies algorithm uses a single device managing all connections between the peer nodes in the entire overlay swarm. For the rest of this subsection we assume that server s, which is a reliable, rich in resources, and credible node, can take responsibility of the overlay network construction and control. Hence, the terms "centralized device" and "server" will be used interchangeably here.

The Huffmies method introduces $p(i)$ value, namely, *peer i aggravation*. It forms a concise representation of peer i's network resources in such a way that higher values indicate inferior resources due to a tight bandwidth limit or high latency of the network access. Finding strict and accurate value of $p(i)$ is not a trivial problem, since it is influenced by many unpredictable parameters (the location, available capacity, congestion). We simply use the round-trip-time metric (RTT) between a peer and the server or between a peer and another peer. The high value suggests that the given peer has considerably limited network resources or can be located in a long distance from the source node (or another peer). Nonetheless, more complex and sophisticated metrics can be involved here as well. Furthermore, as a peer receives data using a multiple-hop path, the sum of all $p(i)$ values over this path emphasizes *service aggravation* of the connection.

In the centralized scheme, only the streaming server gathers all individual $p(i)$ values, independently measured by the peers and sent to the server. The final value of $p(i)$ is defined as an aggregated sum of RTTs between peer i and all other peers in the swarm, including the server:

$$p(i) = \sum_{j \in (N \setminus \{i\}) \cup \{s\}} RTT_{ij}, \qquad (2)$$

where RTT_{ij} represents the evaluated RTT to node j observed from the peer i's point of view (we set $p(s) \equiv 0$). All probing packets are analyzed individually by each node in a swarm and the computed result of $p(i)$ is forwarded to the server. As the central device has the entire $p(i)$ map, it builds a *Huffman tree*, analogously to the Huffman coding with Vitter's algorithm Λ extension [18], in a manner that $p(i)$ is treated like a probability of message i generation. In a *transmission tree* T we are constructing, a codeword length $l(i)$ is defined as a path length from the root (the streaming server s) to leaf i:

$$l(i) = d_{\mathcal{T}}(s, i). \qquad (3)$$

Let us remind that the *Huffman tree* $\mathcal{T}$ is a form, where only leaves represent something real (i.e., the messages). Therefore, in order to transform a *Huffman tree* to a *transmission tree* T, a process called *climbing* is introduced (see Figure 3). It consists in using the internal vertices as something of real meaning, that is, as the peers that are indeed present in the multicast tree to both download the data and simultaneously upload it to other peers. The climbing starts from the most

TABLE 1: The relation of the basic notions for the Huffman coding and the Huffmies concept.

Not.	Huffman	Huffmies
s	Root node	Streaming server
$\mathcal{T}$	Ensemble code (Huffman tree)	—
T	—	Transmission tree
i	Message i	Peer i
N	Set of all messages	Set of all peers in the overlay swarm
$p(i)$	Probability of message i generation	Probability of peer i being a bad relay (peer i aggravation)
t	Number of the source alphabet symbols	Maximum number of simultaneous upload connections (slots)
—	Codeword	A route from the root server s to a leaf in a transmission tree
$l(i)$	Length of a codeword representing message i	Peer i level in a transmission tree, $l(i) = d_{\mathcal{T}}(s, i)$ (hop distance between s and i in the tree)
—	Leaf: a message; internal vertex: auxiliary	Leaf: a downloading peer; internal vertex: a downloading and uploading peer
O_i	—	Peers downloading from peer i, the offspring of i

bottom layer where each internal node, noted as "X" in Figures 3(b)-3(c), is replaced by the node with the lowest $p(i)$ value beneath this auxiliary node. While going upward, it can happen that the minimum value of $p(j)$ characterizes a node j that already has downstream nodes (a node with $p(j) = 1$ in Figure 3(c)). In such a case, peer j's child with a minimum peer *aggravation* has to take its place (a peer with $p(i) = 2$ in Figures 3(c)-3(d)) and the node j is free to jump into an upper layer. Such a process creates a *transmission tree T* with a bounding number of children equal to t. Hence, parameter t is considered as a maximum number of simultaneous unicast connections that a given peer can serve simultaneously. To simplify, we assume the same value for all peers. However, a dynamic adjustment of this value, for instance depending on the swarm size, streaming ratio, or peer's resources, is also possible.

4.2. Optimality of the Centralized Huffmies. In general, P2P tree-based streaming dissemination has to cope with conflicting objectives to design either a narrow or a short transmission tree. A wide tree, where each peer has to send data to numerous neighbors, divides the peer's upload capacity among all children. This can inflict the degradation of quality of experience (QoE), that is, the perceived quality, for the downstream peers. On the other hand, a high tree involves long paths between the streaming source and the peers. Such a tree should be averted since it imposes additional delays and decreases the system reliability in case of an intermediate node fault or departure. Thus, a convenient trade-off between the width and height should be found. The Huffmies method involves optimization of the worst-case *peer aggravation* suffered by an entire overlay swarm. We prove this fact below.

In general, each peer that arises on a path from the streaming server to a single destination node introduces bandwidth and delay limits that inflict a higher probability of service quality degradation for downstream nodes. Sum of all intermediate nodes' $p(i)$ on a path from the server

to a destination node is called a *service aggravation s(i)*. We model a deteriorated QoE caused by a multihop overlay path and observed by peer i, as $s(i)$, where

$$s(i) \overset{\text{def}}{=} p(i) + \sum_{j \in d_T(s,i)} p(j), \qquad (4)$$

where $d_T(s, i)$ is a path from the server to the destination peer i in a *transmission tree T*. The main goal of the Huffmies method is to minimize this parameter for the entire overlay swarm.

We can note the two following fundamental facts.

Theorem 1. *The Huffmies algorithm presented in Section 4.1 ensures that each peer receives the data from a node that has a smaller or equal peer aggravation $p(i)$ value.*

Proof. We show it by a contradiction. Assuming that peer k receives data from node j such that $p(j) > p(k)$, leads to a contradictory statement, since peer k, as a peer with smaller $p(k)$ value among other siblings, would be elected for *climbing* instead of j. □

Theorem 2. *An upper bound for service aggravation $s(i)$ suffered by peer i in the centralized Huffmies is $p(i)l(i)$.*

Proof. From the fact that the *climbing* process performed on the Huffman tree $\mathcal{T}$, as described in Section 4.1, only uplifts some nodes into higher layers, then $l(i)$ is an upper bound for the length of the transmission path from the server to the peer i, $d_T(s, i)$. On the basis of Theorem 1 we also state that $p(i)$ bounds the maximum *peer aggravation* of nodes that can occur over this path. That provides the upper bound $s(i) \leq p(i)l(i)$. □

According to the Huffman coding algorithm, which minimizes average message length $\overline{L}$ (given in (1)), and Theorem 2 we can see that the centralized Huffmies algorithm minimizes

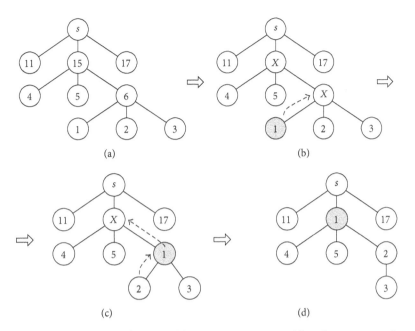

FIGURE 3: A *climbing* process: evolution from a *Huffman tree* (a) to a *transmission tree* (d) with two intermediate steps: (b) and (c). $t = 3$, numbers labeling vertices denote peers' aggravation $p(i)$.

the *service aggravation* bound for all nodes in the overlay swarm.

4.3. Distributed Huffmies. Application of Huffmies in a huge swarm inflicts a `ping` packet flood, since each peer has to evaluate RTT between all other network members. Indeed, a number of such probes at the order of $\mathcal{O}(N^2)$ limit the practicality of the centralized scheme. Overview of the consecutive stages in the distributed Huffmies algorithm is presented in Figure 4. The principal difference between the distributed and centralized version consists in a subjective estimation of the $p(i)$ value accomplished by a single node in a P2P network. In the first step, the server estimates RTT to each member in a swarm, which is assumed as its $p(i)$. Then, on the basis of peers' $p(i)$ values, the server forms t disjoint groups of peers. Among all the members of each group, the server elects a single peer to which it will upload the stream directly. Such a peer is called the group *leader* and it has to replicate the data towards the rest of the group nodes called an *offspring* of a given *leader*. The decision criteria used by the *leaders* to disseminate the data are completely independent and the server does not have any influence or authority regarding this issue. Practically, a *leader* performs the same steps as those of the server in the first step; that is, it selects the best *leaders* among its *offspring* and assigns them a next-level *offspring* (i.e., offspring of those nodes). A *leader* bases its decision on independently obtained $p(i)$ values. In the next steps, such a procedure is consecutively repeated until a pool of all peers in the overlay network is exhausted.

The key point, where the Huffman algorithm is engaged, concerns the selection of the *leader* nodes and assigning them appropriate peers to disseminate data downstream. To accomplish this task, each *leader* k assigns a codeword for all of peers of its *offspring* O_k, analogously to the centralized

approach. Thus, it is necessary to calculate the Huffman tree in each group. Note that in this case, contrary to the centralized Huffmies, $p(i)$ is assessed only from a group leader (or the server) to each peer, but not between all pairs of peers. The corresponding probabilities $p(i)$, $i \in O_k$, are equal to RTT evaluated over the individual probe between the *leader* k and peer i. After applying a codeword for each peer in O_k, all peers whose first digit is the same constitute one group, obviously disjoint with other groups. Among all members of a group, a peer with the lowest value $p(i)$ is selected as a group *leader*. Now, this leader is fully responsible for dissemination of data towards other members of its group. Looking at this issue from the *Huffman tree* viewpoint, a group is constituted by all peers, whose corresponding leaves belong to the same root's subtree. Figure 5 presents two *Huffman trees* (with omitted edge labels) for $t = 2$ (binary tree) and $t = 3$ (ternary tree) with group borders for the same set of peers and the same RTT measurements.

Such a distributed algorithm significantly diminishes aggregated number of links that are engaged in the RTT probing process. While the streaming server has to evaluate all N `pings` to all nodes in the swarm, other peers in lower *transmission tree* layers make a decision about much smaller groups, whose cardinality deteriorates at the order of $\mathcal{O}(t^{-l_i})$, where l_i is a peer's layer index in a *transmission tree*.

The Huffmies method clusters peers into groups, so that the sum of members' *aggravation* is almost equal for all groups. That means that peers with large values of $p(i)$ will be present in groups of smaller number of members. This is a very advantageous and practical property. Let us remind that a low $p(i)$ value for a given peer means that it inflicts a small negative effect on other children. We argue that it is highly recommended to create groups with a comparable sum of *aggravation* indicators. For instance, one group consisting

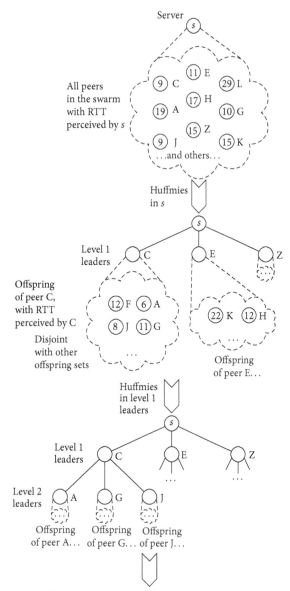

Figure 4: Overview of the consecutive stages in the fully distributed Huffmies approach. Values in circles denote $p(i)$.

of peers that are fast, reliable, and localized in a short distance from the source (all those parameters result in low $p(i)$) can aggregate a higher number of peers and the transmission quality will not be reduced. On the contrary, a high $p(i)$ value of a member in a group prevents from accepting too many other peers. It prevents from low QoS parameters (like high delay and low streaming rate), experienced by many peers, when peer i (with poor resources) becomes a relay point. In particular, when a peer has a notably higher $p(i)$ (with comparison to the values of $p(i)$ for other peers), caused by low-quality transmission (e.g., wireless access), it will constitute an independent group receiving data directly from the server to alleviate the negative effects related to this peer's poor resources.

4.4. Churn Effect. The considerations presented above assume the static environment: all peers are permanently on-line. However, in a real overlay, peers can freely join and depart the P2P network. In result, the population of the swarm and the connections within it often change, what is known as the *churn* effect. To avoid frequent chaotic rearrangements of connections in case of every peer joining or departure, we assume that the overlay members apply the Huffmies algorithm only in a specified point of time, called *reorganization*. In the interim, every new peer is temporarily serviced by a random node. On the other hand, for each *leader* of a group, a *backup leader* is defined. It is selected as a peer with the second lowest $p(i)$ value in the group. The *backup leader* takes care of a group in case of the *leader* departure. Therefore, a single peer departure does not destroy the existing multicast tree.

5. Numerical Results: Simulations

To evaluate benefits of the Huffmies concept in a video streaming network, we carried out simulations, obtained using a C# simulator developed by us. Two scenarios for performance investigation and one scenario for fault resilience were examined. For all simulations, a core network has been randomly constructed according to the model presented in [19], with symmetric 100 Mbit/s links between selected routers. Peers were grouped into five ISP networks (ISP A–E), where each ISP was connected to one of the backbone routers with a symmetric speed of 10 Mbit/s. To mimic a real-world environment, a number of customers and their access bandwidths were generated taking into account statistics offered by a connection speed estimation web service (http://www.netmeter.eu/). An interdomain network topology contains nine domains connected via fourteen links. A network topology, used for simulations, is presented in Figure 6. The content server (located in the biggest ISP A) had 2 Mbit/s uplink and 4 Mbit/s downlink bitrates. Moreover, each peer could handle at most four simultaneous upload connections ($t = 4$). To limit frequent reorganization of the network transmission tree, due to the churn effect, Huffmies *reorganization*s were separated with 5 minutes long space. All results are presented with 95% confidence intervals.

To investigate the overlay streaming efficiency and exhibit the Huffmies features, we exploited various overlay creation concepts, such as

  (i) Huffmies (H),

  (ii) centralized Huffmies (H-C),

  (iii) random (R),

  (iv) Network Friendly Tree (NFT),

  (v) minimum *RTT* tree (M).

The distributed Huffmies algorithm, described in Section 4.3, is denoted as the Huffmies (H) concept to distinguish it from the centralized Huffmies (H-C). The simplest random (R) method assumes that an entering peer connects to one of the randomly selected peers. It also pays attention to the maximum number of the upload connections to be handled.

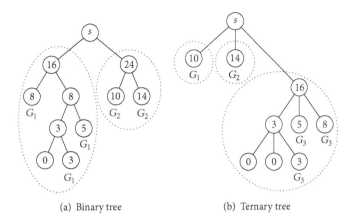

(a) Binary tree   (b) Ternary tree

FIGURE 5: Example of binary and ternary *Huffman trees*. Labels G_i given beneath nodes indicate to which group a given peer should belong. The dotted circles indicate group borders. The values in circles denote $p(i)$.

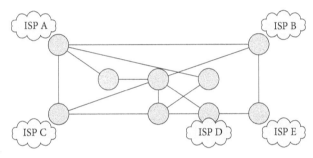

FIGURE 6: The interdomain network topology used in the simulations.

t. The R concept can be treated as a reference idea due to its underlay agnostic principle. In the NFT, the receiver-centric algorithm chooses a neighbor achieving the minimum value of RTT across all peers in the swarm. The minimum tree (M) is similar to the Huffmies concept; however, it differs with the grouping scheme: the peers sorted according to $p(i)$ in the decreasing order are consecutively pooled (with the round-robin technique) into t groups. Similarly to the Huffmies, a peer with the lowest $p(i)$ value in a group is selected as a group *leader*. The data is always transferred to t peers with the lowest RTT value. Figure 7 gives examples with (i) a *Huffman tree* and (ii) a minimum tree for the same RTT values.

We analyze four types of relative metrics which span requirements of all entities involved in the P2P transfer:

(i) *speed*: average end-user download speed,

(ii) *delay*: average delay of the content playback,

(iii) *network efficiency*: the ratio between the total load received by all peers to the total inter-ISP traffic,

(iv) *fault immunity*: the percentage volume of peers that suffer data loss in case of a failure of a gateway (intradomain) ISP link.

All the aforementioned parameters, except for the *network efficiency*, are relevant for an end-user, since they influence QoE. The *network efficiency* shows how efficient the overlay network is in utilizing expensive inter-ISP links and,

therefore, this factor is related to the ISP objective. The last interested player, a content/streaming provider, wishes to provide a streaming service with a high reliability and high quality for an end-user, while optimal utilization of network devices is also prominent. Therefore, the content provider is interested in all the studied metrics.

5.1. Scenario I: Basic Performance Evaluation. In Scenario I, we compared the Huffmies approaches, both centralized and distributed, with NFT and underlay oblivious R concepts. Live streaming content uses 256 kbit/s rate. Peers' lifetimes follow a normal distribution with mean equal to 30 and standard deviation equal to 10 minutes, while their offline times follow a normal distribution with mean equal to 10 and standard deviation equal to 3 minutes. Each simulation took 90 minutes and was repeated 24 times to accomplish credible and representative results. The warm-up period, determined according to a standard method presented by Tyszer [20, Chapter 7.3.1], oscillated in vicinity of 30 minutes.

Figure 8 presents the average download *speed* with various numbers of peers in a swarm. The centralized Huffmies (H-C) achieves the best result for small swarms and with increasing number of peers the downloading *speed* drastically deteriorates. Most likely it is caused by ping packets flood in case of a new peer joining, which has to estimate $RTTs$ to all on-line nodes in a swarm. The churn effect does not inflict such degradation in case of the distributed Huffmies (H) method. Its results are slightly worse for small swarms; nonetheless it copes with scaling problems and the churn effect much better than the centralized algorithm. The NFT and R concepts achieve lower downloading *speeds* for all inspected swarms. It is also interesting to note that the R approach also suffers from the churn effect in a bigger swarm, like the centralized Huffmies (H-C). Figure 9 shows the *speed* fluctuations. The large disadvantage of NFT can be especially observed with this plot.

The *network efficiency* results are plotted in Figure 10, where NFT significantly outperforms other considered schemes. This is caused by a high clusterization of peers within each ISP network as a consequence of a mere delay-aware neighbor selection process. Other approaches obtain

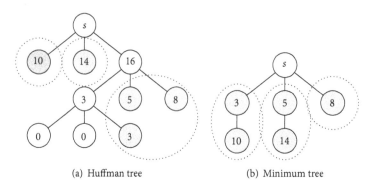

(a) Huffman tree   (b) Minimum tree

FIGURE 7: Huffman and Minimum trees for the same peers with selected *RTT*s (values 3, 5, 8, 10, and 14). Members of each group are placed within dotted circles. *t* = 3.

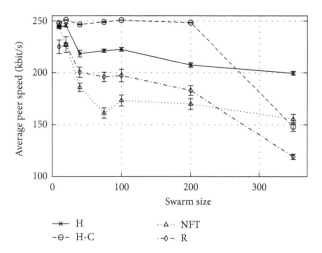

FIGURE 8: Average peer *speed* in Scenario I.

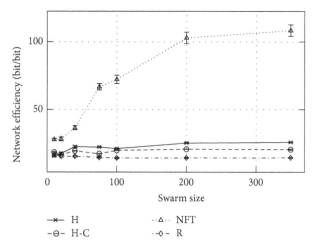

FIGURE 10: Average *network efficiency* in Scenario I.

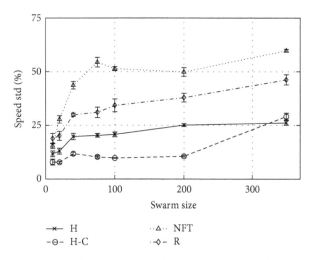

FIGURE 9: Average peer *speed* fluctuations in Scenario I.

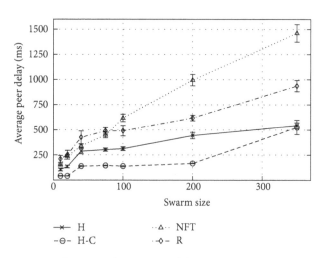

FIGURE 11: Average peer *delay* in Scenario I.

stable results along various swarm sizes. Altogether, both Huffmies algorithms inflict a lower inter-ISP load than a simple R approach. The *network efficiency* for the distributed Huffmies is almost doubled in comparison to the R case. The *delay* between the server and end-users is relevant for

multimedia streaming, in particular when live content is involved. Figure 11 shows that the Huffmies approach keeps low delay for various swarm sizes, contrary to other concepts that notably increase the content lag as a swarm size increases. A considerable growth of the *delay* for NFT, which we observe

TABLE 2: Parameters of the performance evaluation cases in Scenario II.

Case	Switch on time	Lifetime	Offline time
NC (no churn)	0–20 minutes	Infinite	—
C (churn)	0–20 minutes	0–120 minutes	0–20 minutes

between networks with 100 and 350 nodes (although in the case of file-sharing, such a size is very large, for live streaming such an extension of the peer set is quite real or even quite small, e.g., football league match), is caused by a long average path from the server to a peer. For other concepts, a mean number of overlay hops is smaller than three, but NFT creates a topology where the data has to be relayed to reach a destination by more than five other peers on average. Every overlay hop introduces additional delay, that is, why NFT achieves high values. Based on the previous results we noticed that the centralized Huffmies provides better results for small swarms. However when the number of nodes in the overlay exceeds a threshold level, its efficiency deteriorates drastically. On the other hand, NFT gracefully utilizes inter-ISP links, but it introduces a huge delay between the server and peers and this method achieves low streaming rates. Thus, for Scenario II investigating head-to-head comparison with the reference R approach and involving bigger swarms, we decided to omit the centralized Huffmies (H-C) and NFT schemes as evidently inferior.

5.2. Scenario II: Extensive Performance Evaluation. In Scenario II, each simulation took 5 hours. The streaming content rate was equal to 128 kbit/s. To explore the churn effect impact, we exploited two cases. The first case dealt with all peers joining the overlay according to the uniform distribution during first 20 minutes and are kept on until the end of the simulation (no departures). In the second case, the peer's lifetime and offline time were obtained from a uniform distribution between 0 to 120 minutes and 0 to 20 minutes, respectively. The parameters of those cases are presented in Table 2.

An improvement, against the reference R concept, of the *speed* (Figure 12(a)) and the *network efficiency* (Figure 12(b)) is presented. We can see that the both *speed* and *network efficiency* results are better for the Huffmies approach (compared to the R and M concepts). The difference is greater when the swarm becomes larger, due to the fact that the Huffmies approach serves more traffic inside one operator domain; thus inter-ISP links (which become bottlenecks) are not heavily occupied. From Figure 13, where the *speed* for all approaches is presented, we can observe that for swarms larger than 200 peers average *speed* significantly decreases for the R and M methods. At the same time, the Huffmies approach still achieves a very good transfer speed. A relatively stable streaming rate among various swarm sizes proves that the distributed Huffmies has good scalability abilities since a bigger swarm does not result in the downloading speed degradation. Although the minimum (M) alternative is characterized by a higher network efficiency in comparison to the reference R scheme (Figure 12(b)), the average *speed*

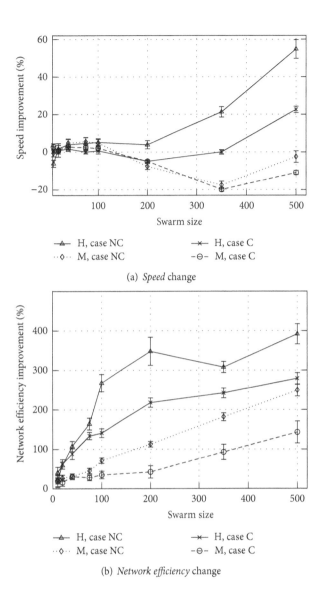

(a) *Speed* change

(b) *Network efficiency* change

FIGURE 12: Scenario II: improvement against the reference R tree creation scheme.

received by peers is often lower than that in the case of the simple R method (Figure 12(a)).

One of the main challenges the Huffmies concept still has to cope with its resilience against the churn effect. Figure 12 illustrates that the improvement of both the *speed* and *network efficiency* decreases when peers join or depart the overlay network at will (case C). Note that in spite of that decrease, the Huffmies approach immensely outperforms other methods from the viewpoint of those two metrics.

5.3. Scenario III: Fault Resilience. The Huffmies approach is characterized by a decreased number of backbone links involved in the transmission. Keep in mind that the usage of additional network nodes (i.e., routers in the IP multicast applications) when the data unnecessarily traverses several times over the same link leads to single points of failure that can noticeably affect the system reliability. Here, in Scenario III, we also investigate the number of nodes that

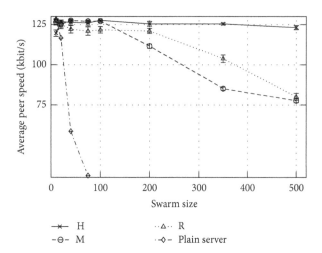

FIGURE 13: Scenario II: average peer *speed* depending on a swarm size.

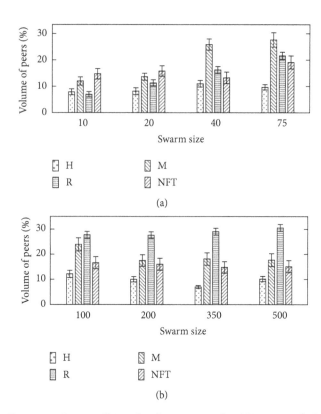

FIGURE 14: Peers suffering data loss in case of an ISP gateway-link fault.

suffer data loss when a (randomly selected) ISP gateway-link fault occurs. The results presented in Figure 14 are obtained from simulations, where suddenly all peers from one of the five ISP networks are pulled apart from the rest of the overlay network, resulting in the tree decay. To prevent the overlay network from the content server isolation (in case of ISP A fault), the server is located in a separate network which permanently services the content streaming. In case of the Huffmies algorithm, the percentage of suffering peers was usually 10–20% less than that in the M and R approaches, respectively. We envisioned that the NFT concept, characterized with a good clusterization observed in Scenario I, will achieve low number of decoupled nodes in case of an ISP break. However, it achieved values higher by only 5–10% than the proposed approach and oscillated in vicinity of 15%. The reason for it can arise from a long average path from the server to a peer as we observed in Section 5.1. The accomplished results show that when using the Huffmies method, connections are densely and efficiently clustered within ISP networks. Thus, isolating one region from the entire community has a smaller impact on the rest of overlay nodes, proving that network resilience against ISP gateway-link faults, using Huffmies, is higher than that in the other considered concepts.

6. Summary

We present a novel method, "Huffmies," to be used in P2P video live streaming networks. It leverages the Huffman coding method to create a connection graph fitted to the underlay network properties and peers heterogeneous network access. First we show the optimal centralized algorithm, difficult to implement in a real world due to the scalability problems and intricate probing process. Then, the distributed algorithm, a main contribution of this work, is elaborated as a practical application. The Huffmies concept emphasizes the following three issues: (a) minimizing delays between the content server and end-users, (b) maximizing the transmission speed, and (c) enhancing ISP gateway-link fault immunity. Based on

the presented simulations, we illustrated that the proposed distributed Huffmies approach achieves better results than other concepts, especially when a swarm aggregates more peers and the ISP networks become congested. Since the approach is beneficial for end-users, content providers and also ISPs, we can argue that the usage of Huffmies is fit for all entities involved in the overlay video multicast.

The properties of our approach are based on its similarity to the Huffman source coding providing the optimal *t*-ary tree. Likewise, we provide the optimal transmission tree for the P2P video streaming basing on the *RTT* measurements. There are two main challenges related to such an approach.

(1) The node aggravation, that is, the counterpart of the probability in the Huffman algorithm, calculated on the basis of the *RTT* measurements, might change in time due to the well-known measurement problems (e.g., the results are unstable). We counteract the negative consequences by repeating the measurements and rebuilding the tree. Additionally, the nodes are grouped in the distributed version of Hummies in such a way that the delay measurements are more precise, since they are related to peers located close to each other.

(2) The Huffman coding assumes that each intermediate node should have *t* children to attain the optimality, but in the case of some peers in the Huffmies tree, the assumed number of the attached children might harm

the performance due to lack of resources. This problem can be dealt with by letting the nodes "cheat" if they have insufficient resources. The cheating consists in informing that some of their t transmission slots are used, while in fact they are not.

Acknowledgment

This paper is an extended version of [21]. The work is supported by the Polish National Science Centre under Grant N N517 555239.

References

[1] S. Tang, Y. Lu, J. M. Hernández, F. Kuipers, and P. van Mieghem, "Topology dynamics in a P2PTV network," in *Proceedings of the IFIP-TC6 International Conference on Networking (NETWORKING '09)*, Aachen, Germany, May 2009.

[2] R. J. Lobb, A. P. Couto da Silva, E. Leonardi, M. Mellia, and M. Meo, "Adaptive overlay topology for mesh-based P2P-TV systems," in *Proceedings of the 19th International Workshop on Network and Operating Systems Support for Digital Audio and Video (NOSSDAV '09)*, pp. 31–36, Williamsburg, Va, USA, June 2009.

[3] F. Picconi and L. Massoulié, "ISP-friend or foe? Making P2P live streaming ISP-aware," in *Proceedings of the 29th IEEE International Conference on Distributed Computing Systems (ICDCS '09)*, Montreal, Canada, June 2009.

[4] W. Liang, J. Bi, R. Wu, Z. Li, and C. Li, "On characterizing PPStream: measurement and analysis of P2P IPTV under large-scale broadcasting," in *Proceedings of the IEEE Global Telecommunications Conference (GLOBECOM '09)*, Honlulu, Hawaii, USA, November-December 2009.

[5] E. K. Lua, X. Zhou, J. Crowcroft, and P. van Mieghem, "Scalable multicasting with network-aware geometric overlay," *Computer Communications*, vol. 31, no. 3, pp. 464–488, 2008.

[6] T. Peng, Q. Zheng, W. Lv, S. Jiang, and J. Gao, "Network friendly tree for peer-to-peer streaming," in *Proceedings of the 12th International Conference on Computer Supported Cooperative Work in Design (CSCWD '08)*, pp. 1024–1028, Xi'an, China, April 2008.

[7] R. Besharati, M. Bag-Mohammadi, and M. A. Dezfouli, "A topology-aware application layer multicast protocol," in *Proceedings of the 7th IEEE Consumer Communications and Networking Conference (CCNC '10)*, Las Vegas, Nev, USA, January 2010.

[8] T. Kikkawa, T. Miyata, and K. Yamaoka, "Maximum-bandwidth ALM tree on tree network," in *Proceedings of the 7th IEEE Consumer Communications and Networking Conference (CCNC '10)*, Las Vegas, Nev, USA, January 2010.

[9] I. Rimac, V. Hilt, M. Tomsu, V. Gurbani, and E. Marocco, "A Survey on Research on the Application-Layer Traffic Optimization (ALTO) Problem," IETF RFC 6029, October 2010.

[10] G. Dán, T. Hoßfeld, S. Oechsner et al., "Interaction patterns between P2P content distribution systems and ISPs," *IEEE Communications Magazine*, vol. 42, no. 5, pp. 222–230, 2011.

[11] J. Seedorf and E. W. Burger, "Application-Layer Traffic Optimization (ALTO) Problem Statement," IETF RFC 5693, October 2009.

[12] O. Abboud, A. Kovačević, K. Graffi, K. Pussep, and R. Steinmetz, "Underlay awareness in P2P systems: techniques and challenges," in *Proceedings of the 23rd IEEE International Parallel and Distributed Processing Symposium (IPDPS '09)*, Rome, Italy, May 2009.

[13] A. Kovačević, O. Heckmann, N. C. Liebau, and R. Steinmetz, "Location awareness-improving distributed multimedia communication," *Proceedings of the IEEE*, vol. 96, no. 1, pp. 131–142, 2008.

[14] X. Tu, H. Jin, X. Liao, and J. Cao, "Nearcast: a locality-aware P2P live streaming approach for distance education," *ACM Transactions on Internet Technology*, vol. 8, no. 2, 2008.

[15] D. A. Huffman, "A method for the construction of minimum-redundancy codes," *Proceedings of the IRE*, vol. 40, no. 9, pp. 1098–1101, 1952.

[16] R. Gallager, "Variations on a theme by Huffman," *IEEE Transactions on Information Theory*, vol. 24, no. 6, pp. 668–674, 1978.

[17] D. E. Knuth, "Dynamic Huffman coding," *Journal of Algorithms*, vol. 6, no. 2, pp. 163–180, 1985.

[18] J. S. Vitter, "Design and analysis of dynamic Huffman codes," *Journal of the ACM*, vol. 34, no. 4, pp. 825–845, 1987.

[19] E. W. Zegura, K. L. Calvert, and S. Bhattacharjee, "How to model an internetwork," in *Proceedings of the 15th Annual Joint Conference of the IEEE Computer and Communications Societies (INFOCOM '96)*, San Francisco, Calif, USA, March 1996.

[20] J. Tyszer, *Object-Oriented Computer Simulation of Discrete-Event Systems*, Kluwer Academic Publishers, Dordrecht, The Netherlands, 1999.

[21] B. Polaczyk, P. Chołda, and A. Jajszczyk, "Huffman coding inspired peer-to-peer multicasting," in *Proceedings of the 10th International Symposium on Electronics and Telecommunications (ISETC '12)*, Timisoara, Romania, November 2012.

7

Routing in IPv6 over Low-Power Wireless Personal Area Networks (6LoWPAN): A Survey

Vinay Kumar and Sudarshan Tiwari

Department of Electronics and Communication Engineering, Motilal Nehru National Institute of Technology, Allahabad 211004, India

Correspondence should be addressed to Vinay Kumar, vinay2008el03mnnit@gmail.com

Academic Editor: Yang Yang

6LoWPANs (IPv6-based Low-Power Personal Area Networks) are formulated by devices that are compatible with the IEEE 802.15.4 standard. To moderate the effects of network mobility, the Internet Protocol (IP) does not calculate routes; it is left to a routing protocol, which maintains routing tables in the routers. 6LowPAN uses an adaptation layer between the network (IPv6) and data link layer (IEEE802.15.4 MAC) to fragment and reassemble IPv6 packets. The routing in 6LoWPAN is primarily divided on the basis of routing decision taken on adaptation or network layer. The objective of this paper is to present a state-of-the-art survey of existing routing protocols: LOAD, M-LOAD, DYMO-Low, Hi-Low, Extended Hi-Low, and S-AODV. These routing protocols have compared on the basis of different metric like energy consumption, memory uses, mobility, scalability, routing delay, an RERR message, a Hello message, and local repair. We have also presented the taxonomy of routing requirement; parameter for evaluating routing algorithm, and it was found that the routing protocol has its own advantages depending upon the application where it is used.

1. Introduction

6LoWPANs are formed by devices that are compatible with the IEEE 802.15.4. However, ZigBee uses the IEEE 802.15.4 standard as its communication protocol for Medium Access Control (MAC) layer and Physical (PHY) layer. IEEE 802.15.4 devices are characterized by low computational power, scarce memory capacity, lower bit rate, short range, and low cost [1]. LoWPAN have devices that work together and connect the physical working environment to real-world applications like sensors with wireless application. Some protocols exist in sensor networks that have a non-IP network layer protocol such as ZigBee, where the TCP/IP protocol is not used. As node density in sensor networks increases and these networks required connection with other networks via internet, then Internet Engineering Task Force (IETF) [2] defines IPv6 over LoWPAN as techniques to implement the TCP/IP protocol in WSNs [3]. 6LoWPAN provides a WSN node with IP communication capabilities by putting an adaptation layer above the IEEE 802.15.4 link layer

for the packet fragmentation and reassembly purpose [4–6]. IP routing protocols are used to maintain routing tables on IP routers which indicates on which next-hop forwarding decision should be made for the destination of an IP packet. In this paper, we have surveyed a number of existing routing protocols in 6LoWPAN like: LOAD (6LoWPAN Ad-hoc On-Demand Distance Vector), MLOAD (Multipath-based 6LoWPAN Ad-hoc On-Demand Distance Vector), DYMO-Low (Dynamic MANET On-demand for 6LoWPAN Routing), Hi-Low (Hierarchical Routing), Extended Hi-Low, and S-AODV (Sink-Ad-hoc on demand Distance Vector Routing). IP networks are packet switched, in which forwarding decisions are made hop-by-hop, based on the destination address in a packet. IP addresses are structured, and this structure is used to group addresses together under a single route entry. In IPv6, an address prefix is used, hence this routing is called prefixed-based routing. We have compared the different routing protocols in 6LoWPAN on the basis of energy consumption, memory usage, scalability, routing delay, and so forth. The rest of the paper is organized as follows: Section 2 presents 6LoWPAN architecture. Section 3 presents the basic requirement of routing in 6LoWPAN. Section 4 presents a survey on state-of-art of different routing in 6LoWPAN reported in the literature till date. The final paper is concluded in Section 5.

2. 6LoWPAN Architecture

There are three types of LoWPANs [7–9]: Ad-Hoc LoW-PANs, Simple LoWPANs, and Extended LoWPANs. Ad-hoc LoWPANs are infrastructure less and not connected to the internet, a Simple LoWPANs is connected through one LoWPANs edge router to another Internet Protocol (IP) network. Extended LoWPANs have the LoWPANs consisting of multiple edge routers along with a backbone link in order to interconnect them. The role of edge router is as it routes traffic data or video in and out of the LoWPANs. Figure 1 shows the architecture of 6LoWPAN. A LoWPAN consists of a number of nodes, which can play the role of a router or host, along with one or multiple edge routers. One important term used with 6LoWPAN is the Neighbor discovery (ND), which facilitates the nodes to register with the edge router in order to provide efficient network operation. ND is the basic mechanism in 6LoWPAN and defines how routers and hosts communicate with each other on the same link. Nodes in the LoWPAN are free to move throughout the LoWPAN, between edge routers, and even between LoW-PANs. Protocol stacks of 6LoWPAN are shown in Figure 2 compared to TCP/IP and ISO/OSI Layer. 6LoWPAN standards enable the efficient use of IPv6 over low-rate, low-power wireless networks of simple embedded devices through an optimization of related protocols and adaptation layer.

3. Routing in 6LoWPAN

There are four basic requirements for routing in 6Lowpan [10]:

(i) the node should support sleep mode for considering battery saving;

(ii) generated overhead on data packets should be low;

(iii) routing overhead should be lower;

(iv) minimal computation and memory requirements.

3.1. 6LoWPAN Routing Requirements. Figure 3 shows the taxonomy of routing requirement in 6LoWPAN [10].

3.1.1. Devices Properties

Low Routing State. 6LoWPAN routing protocols must allow implementation with small code size and require low routing state to fit the typical 6LoWPAN node capacity. Due to these hardware constraints, size of code not more than (48–128 KB) flash memory ranges. 6LoWPAN technology reduces power consumption and improves robustness and easy to analyze because of low complexity.

Minimal Power Consumption. 6LoWPAN technology has the ability to efficiently use available resources, because of this routing protocol should cause minimal power consumption. One way of battery lifetime optimization is by achieving a reducible control message overhead.

3.1.2. Link Properties

Minimal Routing Overhead. For energy conservation, routing overhead should be minimized to fragmentation of the frames. The size of the control packet frame should not cross the IEEE 802.15.4 standard frame size. This provides a reduction in the power consumption for transmission of packet frame, avoids unnecessary usage of bandwidth, and stops the requirement for packet reassembly.

Successful Packet Delivery. The design of routing protocol must consider about the probability of successfully delivering of packet frames and all of this is done according to the requirement of applications. The requirement of a successful end-to-end packet delivery ratio may be varied according to different application.

Link Latency Characteristics. Depending upon the types of application, the range of link latency characteristics vary from a few hundred milliseconds to minutes.

Robust to Dynamic Loss. 6LoWPAN routing protocols should be robust to dynamic loss caused by link failure or device enriched ability, operating system misbehavior, hardware problem, and power consumption by source. The link failure condition occurs in harsh environments, but in few condition, user desires the feedback after carrying out actions, routing protocols must cover within 2 seconds if the destination node of the packet has moved and must cover within 0.5 seconds if only the sender has moved, such as for home applications.

Designed to Successfully Operate. Link asymmetry occurs when the probabilities of successful transmission between two nodes is significantly higher in one direction than in the other one. In case of link asymmetry, 6LoWPAN routing protocols should be designed to successfully function.

3.1.3. Network Characteristics

Periodically Hibernate. Some node in the network does not respond during certain time duration due to periodic hibernation. In 6LoWPAN condition, the nodes may be hibernating periodically because of saving power consumption. After the successful transmission of packets, nodes frequently shut off their radio transmission.

Flexibility, Energy Balance, and Link Qualities. The metrics used in 6LoWPAN are flexible as well as others to optimize the route selection after considering the energy balance and link qualities. Simple hop-count-only mechanism may be

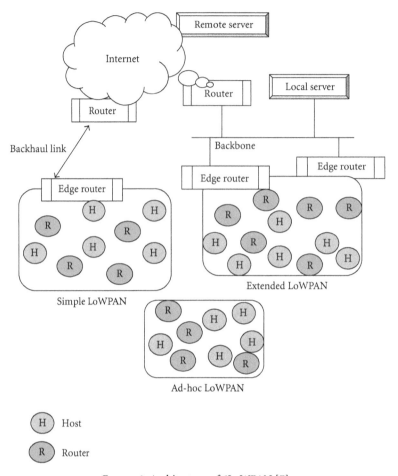

FIGURE 1: Architecture of 6LoWPAN [7].

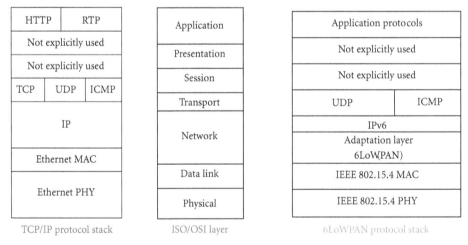

FIGURE 2: Protocol Stack of TCP/IP, ISO/OSI, and 6LoWPAN.

inefficient in 6LoWPANs. There is a Link Quality Indication (LQI), or/and RSSI from IEEE 802.15.4 that may be taken into account for better metrics.

Scalability and Minimality. In 6LoWPAN, scalability of nodes ranges from few to millions of nodes and minimality

should be designed in order to get the maximum utilization of the resources. For home automation application, it is envisioned that the routing protocol must support 250 devices in the network while the routing protocol for metropolitan-scale sensor networks must be capable of clustering a large number of sensing nodes into regions containing the order of 10^2 to 10^4 sensing nodes each.

Route Repair. 6LoWPAN routing protocols should be designed to achieve route repair and should not disturb power saving from routing protocols. Local repair improves throughput and end-to-end latency, especially in large networks. Since routes are repaired quickly, fewer data packets are lossy, and a smaller number of routing protocol packet transmissions are needed.

Dynamic Adaptive Topology. Dynamic adaptive topology is used in the 6LoWPAN routing protocol and mobile nodes. This supports the minimal routing state and routing protocol message overhead. Physical mobility of nodes making the change in radio environment, because of this topology and routing protocols, is changed. Some nodes may move from one 6LoWPAN to another 6LoWPAN and are expected to become functional members of the latter 6LoWPAN in a limited amount of time.

Multicast Traffic Pattern. 6LoWPAN routing protocol supports multicast traffic pattern, that is, point-to-point, point-to-multipoint, or vice-versa. 6LoWPAN routing protocols should be designed with the consideration of forwarding packets from/to multiple sources/destinations.

3.1.4. Security

Confidentiality and Authentication. 6LoWPAN supports secure delivery of control messages or packets, among others. Security of documents is very important to prevent the misuse of confidential information and also important for designing robust routing protocols. 6LoWPAN poses unique challenges to which traditional security techniques cannot be applied directly. For example, public key cryptography primitives are typically avoided as are relatively heavyweight conventional encryption methods.

3.1.5. Mesh under Forwarding

MAC Addresses. 6LoWPAN routing protocols must support 16-bit short and 64-bit extended MAC addresses.

Neighbor Discovery. In neighbor discovery, ND-style performs the operation to the discovery and maintenance of neighbor. 6LoWPAN nodes should avoid sensing separate "Hello" messages because of link-layer mechanisms. IP Multicast: 6LoWPAN routing protocol supports functionality included.

IP Multicast. It may employ structure in the network for efficient distribution in order to minimize link layer broadcast.

3.2. Parameters for Evaluating the Routing Protocols. 6LoWPAN technology is a very hot field for the researchers. Research in the area of sensor networks has various routing protocols that may be used. Taxonomy of parameters for evaluating the routing protocols is shown in Figure 4. We have evaluated the parameters for the routing protocols, such as [10] the following.

3.2.1. Network Properties

Number of Devices and Network Parameters. These parameters directly change the routing state, routing table, or neighbor list.

Connectivity. 6LoWPAN devices have several states of connectivity, ranging from "always connected" to "rarely connect."

Mobility. Mobility of nodes in a LoWPANs directly affects the routing state and influencing radio propagation change.

Deployment. In 6LoWPAN, nodes can be placed either in the controlled or random manner. Once the nodes deployed in the network, they affect the routing state.

Spatial Distribution of Nodes and Gateways. Connectivity of the network is related to the spatial distribution of the nodes and other parameters. Nodes can be deployed any of the manner, but here we assume random spatial distribution where an average of 7 neighbors per node are required for approximately 95% network connectivity.

Traffic Pattern, Topology, and Application. 6LoWPAN devices use the efficient routing protocols. For various traffic patterns and network architectures, various routing mechanisms have been deployed.

Classes of Service. These various protocols support multiple classes of service and required resource—constrained in LoWPAN.

Security. This technology carries various confidential data with a high level of security and affects the power consumption.

3.2.2. Node Parameters

Processing Speed and Memory Size. These fundamental parameters explore the maximum size of the routing state and the maximum complexity of its process.

Power Consumption and Power Source. The nodes position in the topology created by the routing protocol affected the power consumption.

Transmission Range. Routing protocol directly affects the transmission range in 6LoWPAN.

Traffic Pattern. Traffic pattern affects the routing protocol since highly loaded nodes may distribute to higher delivery delays and may consume more energy than lightly loaded nodes.

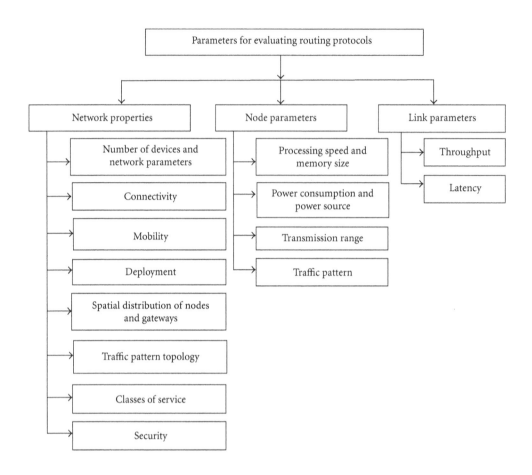

FIGURE 3: Taxonomy of parameters for evaluating routing.

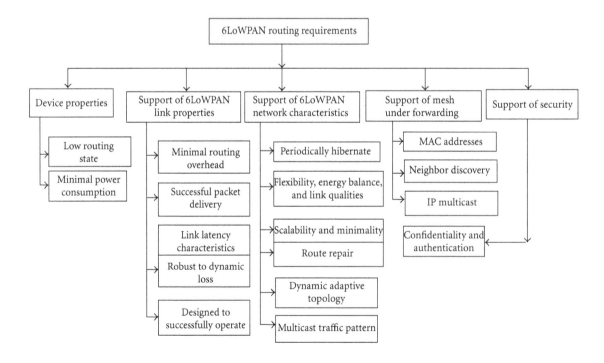

FIGURE 4: Taxonomy of routing requirement in 6LoWPAN.

3.2.3. Link Parameters

Throughput. The user data throughput of loaded data transmission is between a single sender and a single receiver through an unslotted IEEE 802.15.4 2.4 GHz channel in ideal conditions such as 16-bit MAC addresses.

Latency. Payload size fixed the range of latencies of a frame transmission between a single sender and a single receiver through an unslotted IEEE 802.15.4 2.4 GHz channel in ideal condition such as 16-bit MAC addresses.

4. Routing Protocols in 6LoWPAN

The routing protocol in 6LoWPAN is very sensitive due to limited node's capabilities in terms of power, transmission range, and so forth. Routing in 6LoWPAN is divided on the basis of layering decision [11], application-based, and other parameter bases. On the bases of layering, decision the routings are of two types: mesh-under routing and route-over routing. In mesh routing, routing decision is taken on adaptation layer and in route-over routing, routing decision taking is on the network layer. Based on application requirements, the routing in 6LoWPAN can be divided as data-aware routing, probabilistic routing, geographic routing, event-driven, query-based routing, and hierarchical routing. The different routing protocols in 6LoWPAN are LOAD, MLOAD, DYMO-Low, Hi-Low, Extended Hi-Low, S-AODV, and so forth.

Mesh-Under Routing. Figure 5 shows the mesh-under and route-over routing. In this, the adaptation layer performs the mesh routing and forwards packets to the destination over multiple hops in mesh-under the scheme. The network layer does not involve performing the routing inside a LoWPAN. In mesh-under routing, routing and forwarding are performed at data link layer based on 6LoWPAN header or IEEE 802.15.4 frame. An IP packet is fragmented by the adaptation layer to a number of fragments. These fragments are transferred to the next hop by mesh routing.

Route-Over Routing. In route-over routing scheme, all routing decisions are taken in the network layer where each node acts as an IP router. Each link layer hop is an IP hop in the route over the scheme. The IP routing supports the forwarding of packets between these links. In this adaptation, layer of 6LoWPAN establishes a direct connection between the frame and the IP headers.

4.1. Discussion of Routing Protocol in 6LoWPAN

4.1.1. Hierarchical Routing (Hi-Low). In order to increase the network scalability, Hi-Low [12] is proposed for 6LoWPAN. Unlike AODV and LOAD that use IEEE 64-bit identifier, Hi-Low use 16-bit unique short address as an interface identifier for memory saving and larger scalability. In Hi-Low, routing protocol address assigned to the nodes is totally dependent upon the existence of 6LoWPAN in the area of

POS (Personal Operating Space), when the nodes entering, existing 6LoWPAN. If they found that, 6LoWPAN exists in their POS, which is an area within the reception range of the wireless transmission. If there is not any 6LoWPAN in their POS, they become the coordinator of a new 6LoWPAN and assign the short address by 0. If in POS, they become the member of an existing parent node and are assigned 16 bit short address of a parent node. Maximum number of child nodes that a parent can have is called Maximum number of Child (MC). If a parent node does have child nodes, the new child node becomes a First Child node (FC) and receives a short address which is determined by (1) from a parent of the current node. A Second Child node is assigned a short address like FC. It means that the N in (1) is the nth child node. An address allocation of (1) is as follows:

$$FC = AP * MC + N, \quad 0 < N \le MC, \quad (1)$$

for Figure 6, $MC = 4$.

4.1.2. 6LoWPAN Ad-Hoc On-Demand Distance Vector Routing (LOAD). A LOAD routing protocol is a simplified version of an on-demand routing protocol based on AODV [13]. It should be only run on FFDs. LOAD does not use the destination sequence number just like AODV in MANETs. For ensuring loop freedom, only the destination of a route should generate a Route Reply (RREP) in the reply. A route will be preferred by LOAD if the number of Weak links along the way is smaller and less hops from the source to the destination. In case of link break, the nodes of link break try to repair locally broadcasted Route Request (RREQ) and unicast RREP message. If the repairing node unable to repair to link, it unicasts an RERR with an error code that indicate the reason of the repair failure to the originator of the failed data message only. It does not require any precursor list as used in AODV for forwarding the RERR messages. It requests MAC layer acknowledgement for every sent data message and is termed as Link Layer Notification (LLN) acknowledgements. LOAD does not use destination sequence number. Figure 7 shows the message exchange in LOAD protocol. The message exchange in DYMO-Low protocol can be described by Figure 8.

4.1.3. Dynamic MANET On-Demand for 6LoWPAN Routing (DYMO-Low). In DYMO-Low [14] routing protocol, DYMO packets should not be fragmented because RREQ messages are transmitted as IEEE 802.15.4 standard broadcast messages to reach all the next hop neighbors. In this Link quality (LQI) of IEEE 802.15.4 standard in addition to the route, cost is utilized for selecting the best route to the destination. Only the final destination should respond to an RREQ by replying with an RREP. Hello messages are not used by this protocol. All of the features that discussed in LOAD above are used in DYMO-low except that the 16-bit sequence numbers are used in DYMO-low to ensure loop freedom. Beside that, local repair and route cost accumulation that used in LOAD are now used as well in DYMO-Low. DYMO-Low uses 16-bit destination sequence number and does not use local repair, and route cost accumulation is not used.

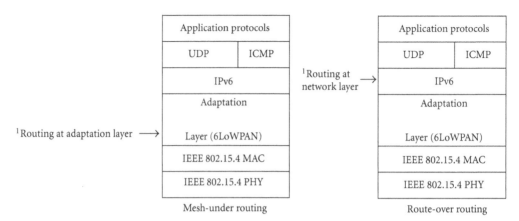

FIGURE 5: Mesh-under and route-over routing. [1]Routing is not equivalent to IP routing, but includes the functionalities of path computation and forwarding under the IP layer. The term routing is used in the figure in order to illustrate which layer handles path computation and packet forwarding in mesh under compared to route over.

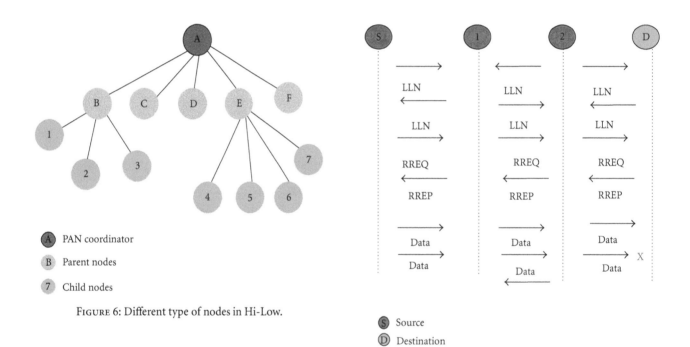

FIGURE 6: Different type of nodes in Hi-Low.

FIGURE 7: Message exchange in LOAD protocol [13].

4.1.4. Extended Hi-Low [15].

4.1.4. Extended Hi-Low [15]. In Hierarchical routing, if any node failure occurs, it does not support path recovery. Extended Hi-Low routing protocol provides path recovery techniques for Hi-Low routing. If any node parent or child is a failure due to hardware or software problem which can be seen below the given figure, it is not suitable for maintaining the routing tree. Extended Hi-Low routing protocol provides recovery of a hierarchical routing path when a parent node is a failure. This mechanism uses NAC (Neighbor Added Child) and NRP (Neighbor Replace Parent) with existing routing table for recovery path. Figure 9 shows the route recovery mechanism in which if Node B is failure, the child nodes of node B cannot transmit the packet to parent node or upstream node. In Extended Hi-Low, the child node 3 has new NRP as node E. So Node-3 can appoint a new upstream node or parent node to Node E after it did not receive a reply of its parent for a while. After the child node's NRP is set to the new parent node and new parent node's NAC is set to the child, the process of packet delivery is as follows. For example, when node-8 (source node) transmits a packet to Node-3 (the destination node), Node-8 sends a packet through Node-D to Node-A which is the coordinator. When the node-A asks the Node-3 passway to parent nodes, if one of them had Node-3 as a new NAC address at that time, the parent node, which has it, would give an answer to Node-A. Then, the packet can be sent from source node (Node-8) to the destination node (Node-3). The recovery path would be completed using this mechanism.

4.1.5. Sink Routing Table over AODV. S-AODV [16] provided benefits in terms of traffic reduction, power consumption, and network lifetime extension for 6LoWPAN. In S-AODV,

TABLE 1: Comparisons of different routing protocols in 6LoWPAN.

Parameters	Hi-Low	LOAD	DYMO-Low	Extended Hi-Low	S-AODV	MLOAD
Energy consumption	Low	Low	Low	Low	Low	Low
Memory usage	Low	Medium	Medium	Low	Medium	Medium
Mobility	Static	Mobile	Mobile	Static	Static	Mobile
Scalability	High	Low	Low	High	Low	Low
Routing delay	Low	Low	High	Low	Low	Low
RERR message	No Use	Use	Use	No Use	Use	Use
Hello message	No Use	No Use	Use	No Use	Use	No Use
Local repair	No Use	Use	No Use	Use	No Use	Use
Layer for routing	Network layer	Network layer	Network layer	Network layer	Adaptation layer	Network layer
Route discovery count	No Use	High	High	No Use	High	Less
Type of routing protocol	Route-over	Route-over	Route-over	Route-over	Mesh-under	Route-over
Year of publication	June 2007	June 2007	June 2007	Sept. 2008	June 2010	Aug. 2010

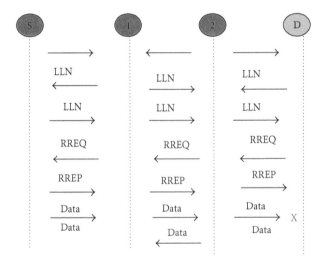

FIGURE 8: Message exchange in DYMO-Low protocol [14].

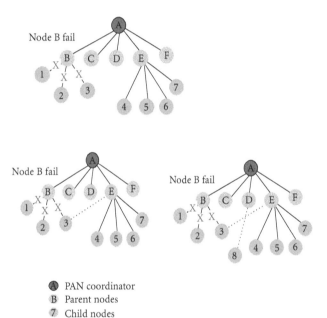

- (A) PAN coordinator
- (B) Parent nodes
- (7) Child nodes

FIGURE 9: Route recovery mechanism.

traffic of route discovery in original AODV is reduced by using SRT (Sink Routing Table). By the new mechanism, the delay and energy consumption of the connection between each internal common node and the sink are reduced. More importantly, the new mechanism in the S-AODV optimizes the routing performance, but it does not ask the 6LoWPAN to provide more powerful hardware. The SRT would not shut down the routing capability of original AODV routing between internal nodes at all. On the whole SRT and AODV are able to work well together. Figure 10 shows the S-AODV routing.

4.1.6. MLOAD (Multipath 6LoWPAN Ad-Hoc On-Demand Distance Vector Routing). In LOAD routing protocol, every route discovery will broadcast RREQ over the 6LoWPAN. MLOAD [17] reduces the network overhead of route discovery by using multipath techniques. During route discovery, the MLOAD will find the multipath, when the main route fails, then it uses the alternate route for transmission data. MLOAD uses multipath link-disjoint path during route

discovery. The route discovery has two phases, which route request and route reply. If the node in 6LoWPAN needs a route to transmit data, the node will broadcast a route request. When the destination node received the request, it will reply a packet to the source node. MLOAD improved the LOAD routing technique by reducing the route discovery count, power consumption in 6LoWPAN mesh network. Multipath techniques used by M-LOAD is shown in Figure 11.

4.2. Comparisons of Different Routing Protocols in 6LoWPAN. Table 1 shows the timeline comparison of routing protocols on the basis of different performance metric like energy consumption, memory uses, mobility, scalability, routing delay, an RERR message, a Hello message, and Local repair. In this table, we can see that some routing protocols belong to

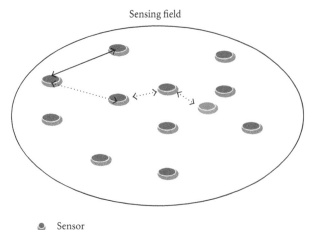

Sensing field

🔘 Sensor
🔘 Sink
⟵⟶ AODV routing
⟨···⟩ SRT routing

FIGURE 10: S-AODV routing.

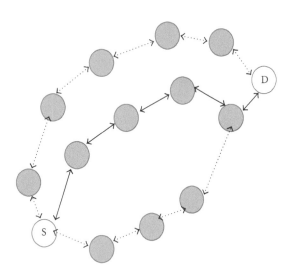

⟵⟶ Main route
⟨······⟩ Alternate route
🔘 Intermediate nodes
Ⓓ Destination
Ⓢ Source

FIGURE 11: Multipath techniques used by MLOAD.

route-over routing and some belong to mesh-under routing protocol. It is confirmed from Table 1 that the routing protocols have their own advantages depending upon the application where it they are used.

5. Conclusion

In this paper, survey was done on the different routing algorithm and IP mobility in 6LoWPAN. The existing routing algorithms in 6LoWPAN like LOAD, M-LOAD, DYMO-Low, Hi-Low, Extended Hi-Low, and S-AODV compared

on the basis of different metric like energy consumption, memory uses, mobility, scalability, and so forth. We have also presented the taxonomy of routing requirement, parameter for evaluating routing algorithm and mobility, and so forth. It was found that the routing protocols have their own advantages depending upon the application where they are used. There exists some trade-off in the respective routing protocols such as routing protocol that uses Hello message that may provide more reliable but have higher end-to-end delay in the packet routing. Hi-Low routing protocol provides an advantage of memory saving by which the networks become more scalable. Hi-Low provides low memory usage and higher scalability compared to LOAD, DYMO-Low, and S-AODV. DYMO-Low provides more routing delay compared to other routing protocols. S-AODV provides benefits in terms of traffic reduction, power consumption, and network lifetime extension, for 6LoWPAN.

References

[1] 802.15.4-2003 IEEE standard, "Part 15.4: Wireless Medium Access Control (MAC) and Physical Layer (PHY) Specifications for Low-Rate Wireless Personal Area Networks (LR-WPANs)," IEEE Computer Society Sponsored by the LAN/MAN Standards Committee, October 2003.

[2] N. Kushalnagaret, G. Montenegro, and C. Schumacher, "IPv6 over Low-Power Wireless Personal Area Networks (6LoW-PANs): overview, assumptions, problem statement, and goals," IETF RFC 4919, August 2007.

[3] D. Singh and K. Daeyeoul, "Performance analysis of gateway discovery techniques: IPv6-based wireless sensor networks," in *Proceedings of the 2nd International Conference on Evolving Internet (INTERNET '10)*, pp. 142–146, Seoul, South Korea, November 2010.

[4] N. Kushalnagar, G. Montenegro, J. Hui, and D. Culler, "Transmission of IPv6 Packets over IEEE 802.15.4 Networks," IETF RFC 4944, September 2007.

[5] X. Ma and W. Luo, "The analysis of 6LowPAN technology," in *Proceedings of the Pacific-Asia Workshop on Computational Intelligence and Industrial Application (PACIIA '08)*, pp. 963–966, Wuhan, China, December 2008.

[6] C. Yibo, K. Hou, H. Zhou et al., "6LowPAN stacks: a survey," in *Proceedings of the 7th International Conference on Wireless Communications, Networking and Mobile Computing (WiCOM '07)*, pp. 1–4, Wuhan, China, October 2011.

[7] Z. Shelby and C. Bormann, *6LoWPAN: The Wireless Embedded Internet*, John Wiley & Sons, Chichester, UK, 2009.

[8] L. Atzori, A. Iera, and G. Morabito, "The internet of things: a survey," *Computer Networks*, vol. 54, no. 15, pp. 2787–2805, 2010.

[9] G. Mulligan, "The 6LoWPAN architecture," in *Proceedings of the 4th Workshop on Embedded Networked Sensors (EmNets '07)*, pp. 78–82, June 2007.

[10] E. Kim, D. Kaspar, C. Gomez, and C. Bormann, "Problem Statement and Requirements for 6LoWPAN Routing," draft-ietf-6lowpan-routing-requirements-10, November 2011.

[11] A. H. Chowdhury, M. Ikram, H. S. Cha et al., "Route-over vs mesh-under routing in 6LoWPAN," in *Proceedings of the ACM*

International Wireless Communications and Mobile Computing Conference (IWCMC '09), pp. 1208–1212, March 2009.

[12] K. Kim, S. Yoo, J. Park, S. Daniel Park, and J. Lee, "Hierarchical Routing over 6LoWPAN (HiLow)," draft-deniel-6lowpan-hilow- hierarchical-routing-01, June 2007.

[13] K. Kim, S. Daniel Park, G. Montenegro, S. Yoo, and N. Kushalnagar, "6LoWPAN Ad Hoc On-Demand Distance Vector Routing (LOAD)," draft-daniel-6lowpan-load-adhoc-routing-03, June 2007.

[14] K. Kim, S. Park, S. I. Chakeres, and C. Perkins, "Dynamic MANET On-demand for 6LoWPAN (DYMO-low) Routing," draft-montenegro- 6lowpan-dymo-low-routing-03, June 2007.

[15] C. S. Nam, H. J. Jeong, and D. R. Shin, "Extended hierarchicalrouting over 6LoWPAN," in *Proceedings of the 4th International Conference on Networked Computing and Advanced Information Management (NCM '08)*, pp. 403–405, Gyeongju, Korea, September 2008.

[16] Z. Cao and G. Lu, "S-AODV: Sink routing table over AODV routing protocol for 6LoWPAN," in *Proceedings of the 2nd International Conference on Networks Security, Wireless Communications and Trusted Computing (NSWCTC '10)*, vol. 2, pp. 340–343, June 2010.

[17] J. Chang, T. Chi, H. Yang, and H. Chao, "The 6LoWPAN Ad-hoc on demand distance vector routing with multi-path scheme," in *Proceedings of the IET International Conference on Frontier Computing. Theory, Technologies and Applications*, pp. 204–209, August 2010.

8

Estimation of Modelling Parameters for H.263-Quantized Video Traces

A. Drigas and S. Kouremenos

National Center for Scientific Research "DEMOKRITOS", Institute of Informatics and Telecommunications, Agia Paraskevi, Attici, 15310 Athens, Greece

Correspondence should be addressed to A. Drigas; dr@iit.demokritos.gr

Academic Editor: Rui Zhang

We propose methods for selecting the modelling parameters of H.263-quantized video traffic under two different encoding scenarios. For videos encoded with a constant quantization step (unconstrained), we conclude that a two-parameter power relation holds between the exhibited video bit rate and the quantizer value and that the autocorrelation decay rate remains constant for all cases. On the basis of these results, we propose a generic method for estimating the modelling parameters of unconstrained traffic by means of measuring the statistics of the single "raw" video trace. For rate-controlled video (constrained), we propose an approximate method based on the adjustment of the "shape" parameter of the counterpart—with respect to rate—unconstrained video trace. The convergence of the constructed models is assessed via *q*-*q* plots and queuing simulations. On the assumption that the popular MPEG-4 encoders like XVID, DIVX usually employ identical H.263 quantization and rate control schemes, it is expected that the results of this paper also hold for the MPEG-4 part 2 family.

1. Introduction

With the rapid spread of multimedia applications and the great progress of video streaming technologies such as the MPEG-4 and H.26x standards, network-based multimedia applications, for example, IPTV, VoD, and videoconference, have become increasingly popular services. Video traffic, which is going to be streamed by these services, is expected to account for large portions of the multimedia traffic in future heterogeneous networks (wireline, wireless, and satellite). Despite the high data rates of the contemporary network settings, there is still a need for quality assurance for the above services especially when a real-time session has to be established (e.g., videoconference or video streaming without buffering options, e-collaboration, remote control, etc.). Since such services rely on the exchange of bandwidth demanding video information, with the MPEG-4 and H.263 encoders being the most commonly used standards for the moment, extensive deployment of these services calls for careful modelling of the associated network traffic, so that the appropriate amount of resources may be anticipated by the network. The video traffic models for these networks must cover a wide range of traffic types and characteristics because the type of the terminals will range from a single home or mobile user (low video bit rate), where rate-constrained (or rate-controlled) video traffic is mainly produced, to a terminal connected to a backbone network (high video bit rate), where the traffic is presented to be out of the loop, that is, the encoder is not forced to conform to a certain video bit rate. Furthermore, successful video traffic modelling can lead to a more economical network usage (improved traffic policing schemes), leading to lower communication costs and a more affordable and higher quality service to the end-users.

Partly due to the above reasons, the modelling and performance evaluation of video traffic have been extensively studied in the literature, and a wide range of modelling methods exist. The results of relevant early studies [1–10] concerning the statistical analysis of variable bit rate videoconference streams being multiplexed in ATM and IP networks indicate that the histogram of the videoconference frame-size sequence exhibits an asymmetric bell shape and that the autocorrelation function decays approximately exponentially to zero. An important body of knowledge, in videoconference traffic modelling, is the approach in [5] where the DAR(1)

[11] model was proposed. More explicitly, in this study, the authors noted that AR models of at least order two are required for a satisfactory modelling of the examined H.261-encoded traffic patterns. However, in the same study, the authors observed that a simple DAR(1) model, based on a discrete-time, discrete state Markov Chain performs better—with respect to queueing—than a simple AR(2) model. The results of this study are further verified by similar studies of videoconference traffic modelling and VBR video performance and simulation [6, 12]. The above studies certainly constitute a valuable body of knowledge. However, most of the above studies examine video traffic traces compressed by encoders like MPEG-2, MPEG-4, H.261, and H.263 that were operating in an unconstrained mode and as a result produced traffic with similar characteristics. As denoted in [13], for active sequences, that is, movies, which is the subject of the current study, the use of a single model, for example, DAR [5], based on a few meaningful parameters and applicable to large number of sequences does not appear to be possible. On this basis, complicated scene-based models have been proposed. Furthermore, most of the above studies examined MPEG encoding schemes which were implemented with B-frames encoding. However, for real-time streaming applications, which is the interest of this paper, only I- and P-frames usually appear in the generated traffic patterns.

Our modelling approach, in this study, is based on the recommendations towards a good traffic model that were proposed in [14]. According to them, a model must be realistic, reusable, and computationally efficient. In order not to decline from the above requirements, we used realistic experimental data, movies, and concerts and worked on the modelling parameters of well-established and simple models proposed in the literature. More explicitly, we provide methods for calculating the parameters of the simple DAR model. Taking into account the reasonable assumption that the statistical characteristics of the same video compressed with different encoding schemes are similar, we use the modelling parameters of a raw unconstrained offline video trace as a basis and adjust it to the traffic traces under different encoding sets, that is, different quantization levels, mean video bit rate. The q-q plots of the sample versus the model data show that the adjusted models provide accurate fits.

The rest of the paper is structured as follows: Section 2 presents the state of the art in H.263-quantized video compression and traffic modelling. Section 3 discusses the measurement procedure and the statistical analysis of H.263-quantized video traffic, unconstrained and constrained. Section 4 analyses the appropriate methods for selecting the parameters of the autoregressive video traffic models. Finally, Section 5 culminates with conclusions and pointers to further research.

2. State of the ART: Video Traffic Modelling

Today, a large number of video systems exist using practical implementations of the MPEG-4-ISO/IEC open standard for video encoding developed by MPEG (Moving Picture Experts Group) [15]. The MPEG-4 standard is characterized by a small output video file size and quite good picture quality even when a relatively low bit rate is used. It is coded with XviD, DivX, 3ivx, Nero Digital, and other video codecs. Moreover the H.263 (H.263+ included) codec [16] is a widely adopted standard for videoconference communication as well as for video streaming via mp4 encapsulation. Both of the above standards use the H.263 quantization scheme and employ the same rate control algorithms. In addition, they are capable of working in both unconstrained and constrained modes of operation. In unconstrained VBR mode, the video system operates independently of the network (i.e., using a constant quantization scale throughout transmission). This type of quantization/compression is usually applied in high capacity networks. In the constrained mode, the encoder has knowledge of the networking constraints (either imposed offline by the user) and modulate its output in order to achieve the maximum video quality for the given content (by changing the quantization step). This is the typical encoding scenario in low capacity networks where a QoS algorithm has to be implemented.

MPEG-4-H.263-quantized videoconference traffic, thanks to its widely used compression algorithms which result in lower bandwidth requirements, accounts for large portions of the multimedia traffic in today's heterogeneous networks (wireline, wireless, and satellite), with the ADSL network being the most notable one. Under the above expectation, it is evident that a statistical model for this type of traffic would be very useful to predict network usage and estimate resources. For this reason, a lot of traffic models exist mainly as autoregressive (see [17] for a review of such models). Newer studies of video traffic modelling, for example, [18–20] reinforce the general conclusions obtained by the above earlier studies by evaluating and extending the existing models and also proposing new methods for successful and accurate modelling. An extensive public available library of frame-size traces of unconstrained and constrained MPEG-4, H.263, and H.263+ off-line encoded video was presented in [21] along with a detailed statistical analysis of the generated traces. In the same study, the use of movies, as visual content, led to frames generation with a Gamma-like frame-size sequence histogram (more complex when a target rate was imposed) and an autocorrelation function that quickly decayed to zero (a traffic model was not proposed though in the certain study). Of particular relevance to our work is the approach in [22], where an extensive study on multipoint videoconference traffic (H.261-encoded) modelling techniques was presented. In this study, the authors discussed methods for correctly matching the parameters of the modelling components to the measured H.261-encoded data derived from realistic multipoint conferences (in "continuous presence" mode). In [23, 24], the authors propose an accurate DAR model based on the Pearson V distribution which on the basis of their statistical tests provides the best fit. Moreover, in [25], the authors use wavelets to model the distribution of I-frames and a simple time-domain model for P/B frames and present a novel method to capture the correlation properties of vbr traffic using group of pictures analysis. Finally, in [26], traffic modeling of M2M mobile video services is studied via several distributions with heavy tail. According to the authors results, the Lognormal distribution was able to represent more accurately the video traffic.

Aiming at a realistic, reusable, and simple video traffic model, accurate enough for queueing analysis and network estimation, this study discusses methods for calculating the appropriate model parameters from the observed traffic data and proposes methods for correctly estimating the parameters of the DAR model on different compression and network scenarios. This is addressed by improving the models presented in [22] by means of importing the compression parameters, that is, the quantizer value for the case of unconstrained traffic and the mean video bit rate for constrained traffic.

3. Video Traces: Measurement and Processing of Video Data

The data we are modelling were gathered off-line using the ffmpeg libavcodec suite [27]. The off-line mode assured that no packet losses exist during the trace collection process and that the traffic model will always represent the best quality of the encoded video. On this basis, it is stressed that, in the current study, there was no point in investigating an online environment. It is evident that the proposed model is applicable in any network environment as it represents source-faithful video traffic encoded during UDP communication of video terminals. Movies scenes of at least 20 minutes were selected among popular commercial DVDs, for example, Aviator, Jethro Tull concert, Lord of War, and were encoded (in fact transcoded from the common MPEG-2 DVD format) using the libavcodec H.263 codec. We used as raw video some popular movies scenes from the DVD-Video movies Aviator (VTS, 22 min), Jethro Tull concert (VTS, 30,55 min), Lord of War (VTS, 15,20 min), and Million Dollar Hotel (VTS, 27,05 min). All video files were stored in a common DVD-Video format MPEG-2 at a high resolution 720×576, 25 frames/sec with average rate (approximately for all video files) of 5500 Kbps. There were two encoding scenarios: the first one was designed to contribute results for traffic which is quantized with a constant quantization scale (step) and as a result is presented to be out of the loop or unconstrained, in a sense that no rate limitations are imposed. The second one gave results for the counterpart in the loop cases; that is, no quantization scale was selected, and instead a rate control was imposed, at a certain target rate. An encoder's conformation to the rate control of the system is commonly performed by reducing the video quality (and consequently the frame-size quantity) through the dynamic modulation of the quantization step. These operation modes were presented in [13] where Variable Bit Rate (VBR) video is thoroughly examined and categorized according to encoding and networking parameters (From now on, U-VBR will stand for unconstrained video and C-VBR for constrained video.).

In both scenarios, the following parameters of the ffmpeg command were set: -vcodec: h263, -r: 25, -g: 250, and -s: qcif where -vcodec is the encoder used, -r is the video frame rate, -g is the number of P-frames before and I-frame appearing

and -s is the video size. B-frame encoding was not employed as it is not recommended for real-time streaming. As a consequence, the resulting video sequence is consisted of I- and P-frames. An .mp4 encapsulation enables this type of traffic to be streamed at an RTP level via a common streaming server, for example, the Darwin Streaming Server [28]. However, in this paper, we examined the video source in an off-line mode, and no network feedbacks were included, for example, F-VBR traffic as explained in [13]. To implement the above encoding scenarios we added an appropriate parameter correspondingly, that is, -qscale set from 2 to 15 for U-VBR traffic and -b set to a certain rate (100, 200, and 400 kbps) for C-VBR traffic.

In all cases the video statistics at a frame level were collected using the -vstatsfile parameter and were processed for further analysis. We must note here, that I-frames are excluded from the analysis to follow as it was found that they have a minimal impact with respect to queueing performance. However, a uniform I-frame generator could be also integrated so as to ensure the conservativeness of the proposed model.

4. Estimation of Modelling Parameters

4.1. The Discrete Autoregressive Model. The DAR model that was proposed and used analytically in [5] can be directly applied for full modelling and analytical treatment of video traffic presented in this context. This model is defined as a discrete state Markov chain with a transition rate matrix P of the form

$$P = \rho I + (1 - \rho) A, \qquad (1)$$

where ρ is the autocorrelation decay rate of the n length frame-size sequence X_n (always of type p), I is the identity matrix, and A is a rank-one stochastic matrix with all rows equal to the probabilities resulting from the fit of the frequency histogram of X_n. The DAR model demands the representation of X_n with a constant number of states, whose probabilities values will fill the rows of the stochastic matrix A. These states can be easily chosen by dividing the interval between the maximum and the minimum frame sizes of the sequence into M frame-size states. So, if $X_{\min}$ is the minimum and $X_{\max}$ the maximum frame-size value, then a reasonable state step s is $s = (X_{\max} - X_{\min})/M$, with s rounded to the nearest integer. The rate of each state can be easily calculated by the relative mean rate of a histogram window as follows: if $\mathbb{P}_i$ is the probability mass of frame size X_i (derived from the corresponding density), then the rate value of the state value is equal to $f \sum_{i=1}^{n} \mathbb{P}_i X_i / \sum_{i=1}^{n} \mathbb{P}_i$, with f being the frame rate of the traffic.

The DAR model has an exponentially matching autocorrelation and so matches the autocorrelation of the data over approximately hundred frame lags. This match is more than enough for real-time streaming of video traffic engineering. When using the DAR model, it is sufficient to know the mean, variance, and autocorrelation decay rate of sequence X_n. These parameters can be calculated using a commonly wide approach in this area, proven to be efficient in a variety of

TABLE 1: Statistics for Aviator (22 min) and Jethro Tull (30,55 min) in unconstrained mode, constant quantizer Q.

| Q | Aviator | | | | | Jethro | | | | |
	Rate	Mean	Variance	α	β	Rate	Mean	Variance	α	β
2	677	3385	5900630	1.94	1743.29	700	3817	6338374	2.30	1660.74
3	430	2153	2788937	1.66	1295.12	456	2488	3088517	2.00	1241.17
4	317	1585	1618647	1.55	1021.52	341	1860	1845143	1.88	991.76
5	240	1201	999173	1.44	832.02	262	1429	1173983	1.74	821.52
6	192	963	669046	1.39	694.59	212	1156	807965	1.66	698.66
7	158	792	470254	1.34	593.49	175	957	580782	1.58	606.70
8	134	672	344746	1.31	512.65	149	816	436341	1.53	534.90
9	114	574	255208	1.29	444.90	127	697	329451	1.48	472.46
10	99	499	195853	1.27	392.65	111	606	257134	1.43	424.27
11	83	430	152470	1.21	354.34	101	525	206670	1.33	393.50
12	74	384	122190	1.21	318.42	90	467	167740	1.30	359.02
13	66	345	98506	1.21	285.53	81	419	137440	1.28	328.06
14	60	313	81893	1.20	261.46	73	379	115710	1.24	305.20
15	55	287	69001	1.19	240.66	67	345	98748	1.21	285.88

studies, for example, [5, 21], that is, using the Gamma density for modelling the frequency histogram and an exponential model for fitting the autocorrelation function, for instance, the compound exponential model proposed in [22]:

$$f(x) = \frac{1}{\beta\Gamma(\alpha)}\left(\frac{x}{\beta}\right)^{\alpha-1}e^{-x/\beta}, \qquad (2)$$

where $\Gamma(\alpha) = \int_0^\infty u^{\alpha-1}e^{-u}du$

$$\rho_k = w\lambda_1^k + (1-w)\lambda_2^k. \qquad (3)$$

4.2. Estimation of the DAR Parameters for U-VBR Traffic. Under the context of encoding video with a constant quantizer, that is, none rate control scheme is employed, we statistically analysed the resulting U-VBR video data for a quantizer q range between 2 and 15 (for values of $q > 15$ video quality was suppressed for the selected video size). We present here results for the video data of Aviator and Jethro Tull concert in Table 1. With reference to this table, it is easily observed that, in all cases, the mean bit rate of the video streams is decaying along with the increase of the quantizer value. This is normal as for higher quantization values compensation criteria are adjusted in order to achieve lower frame sizes and as a consequence lower quality video. Although this appear to be a trivial result, to the best knowledge of these authors, not an analytical function has been proposed in the literature to express the relation of these two parameters. Given the above and the results of Table 1, the following questions arose naturally (and their answers were pursued) during data analysis.

(i) What is the form of the frequency histogram and of the autocorrelation function of the frame-size sequence for all quantization values? Could a common model be applied for all cases?

(ii) Is the DAR model applicable to the measured data? If, yes; are the modelling parameters (mean, variance,

and decay rate) related somehow to the quantization value?

(iii) What is the type of the function that relates bit rate with quantization value?

In brief, the answers to these questions, as supported by consistence evidence from the experiments' results, are as follows: the sequence of frame sizes for all cases $q = 2$–15 exhibits an autocorrelation function that decays exponentially to zero with approximately the same autocorrelation decay rate value as calculated via (3) and a frequency histogram that can be fitted successfully by a Gamma density from (2) using the method of moments: if m is the mean and v the variance of the sample sequence X_n, then $\alpha = m^2/v$, $\beta = v/m$. In Figure 3, the autocorrelation graphs are plotted for indicative quantization values for Aviator ($q = 2, 5, 8, 11$) where it is noticed that all graphs present similar decay rates, a claim that was further verified by applying a least squares fit to the model of (3) where the critical parameter *rho* was found to be equal to 0.9981 for all cases. Concerning the frequency frame-size histograms, the moments matching method gave satisfactory fitting results (we show indicative q-q plot results for Aviator and Jethro Tull ($q = 5, 8$ in Figure 2). The corresponding α and β parameters of the Gamma density (2) are presented in Table 1.

What is of great importance, at this moment, is to find a simple rule that relates the estimation of the modelling parameters to the quantization value. A first step towards this direction is to try to model the empirical data of Table 1.

Consider,

$$R_q = \widehat{R}(q-1)^{-z_1}, \qquad q = 2, 3, \ldots, 31, \qquad (4)$$

where z_1 was found to be approximately equal to 0.81 for all cases and $\widehat{R} = R_2$ is the rate of the *raw* video, that is, the video with the higher quality under the given encoding scenario. The above equation also holds for the mean frame size of the sequence m, that is, $m_q = \widehat{m}(q-1)^{-z}$. Equation (4) is a

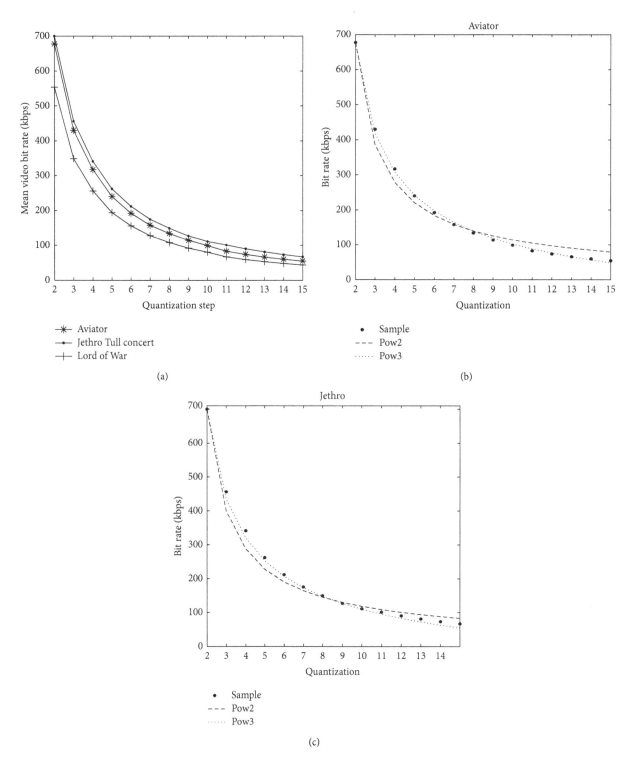

FIGURE 1: Mean video bit rate and quantization.

two-parameter power function that provides a satisfactory fit as shown in Figure 1 for both samples (Aviator and Jethro Tull). However, towards a more accurate representation of the sample data a three-parameter power equation was also tested, with a least square fit, as follows:

$$R_q = \left(\widehat{R} + \varepsilon\right)\left(q - 1\right)^{-z_2} - \varepsilon, \quad q = 2, 3, \ldots, 31, \qquad (5)$$

where ε values were found to be in the area $[140, 150]$ and $z_2 = 0.54$ for all cases. With $\varepsilon = 150$, a fit via (5) is presented in Figure 1 for Aviator and Jethro Tull. However, for simplicity reasons, in the analysis to follow, we will use the two-parameter model since it is simpler (a more careful analysis upon the ε has to be conducted before adoption of the "pow3" model).

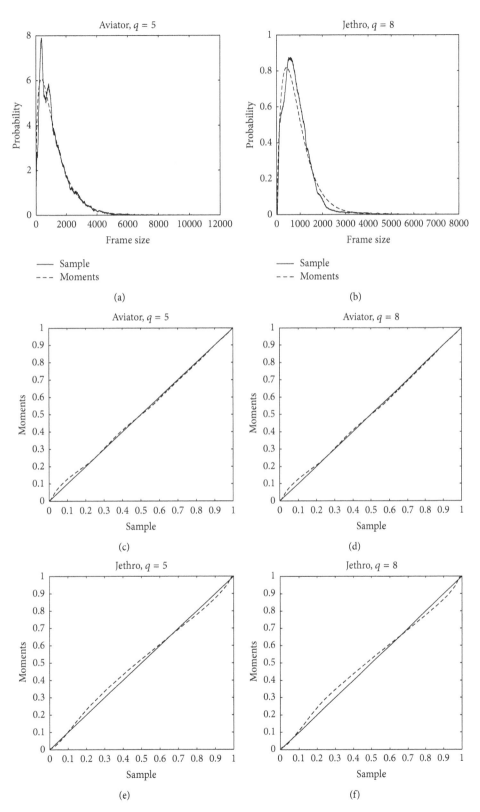

FIGURE 2: Frequency histograms, moments fit, and q-q plots.

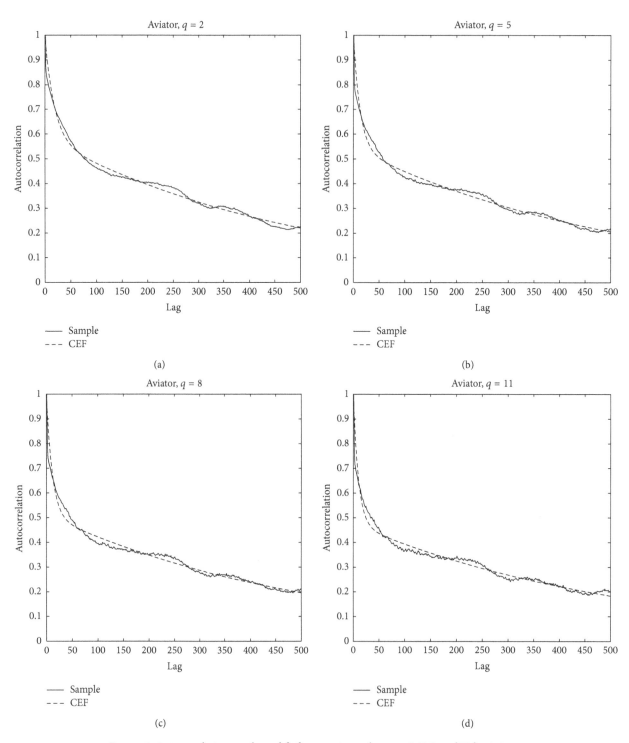

FIGURE 3: Autocorrelation graphs and fit for quantizer values $q = 2, 5, 8$, and 11 for Aviator.

On the basis of the model "pow2" (4), as an analytical function that relates the mean frame size of the sequence to the quantization value, and taking into account the property of the Gamma density $m = \alpha\beta$, similarly we have

$$\alpha_q = \widehat{\alpha}(q-1)^{-z_\alpha}, \qquad \beta_q = \widehat{\beta}(q-1)^{-z_\beta},$$
$$q = 2, 3, \ldots, 31, \tag{6}$$

where $\widehat{\alpha} = \alpha_2$, $\widehat{\beta} = \beta_2$, $z_\alpha = 0.21$, and $z_\beta = 0.6$. Since $m = \alpha\beta$, it is expected to hold $z = z_\alpha + z_\beta$.

On the basis of (4) and (6), a relation between the Gamma modelling parameters and the quantizer has been established, with an a priori knowledge of the maximum rate $\widehat{R}$. Hence, only an off-line measurement of the video at $q = 2$ is adequate in order to estimate some few meaningful parameters for all traces encoded with a constant quantizer $q = i$ with $i =$

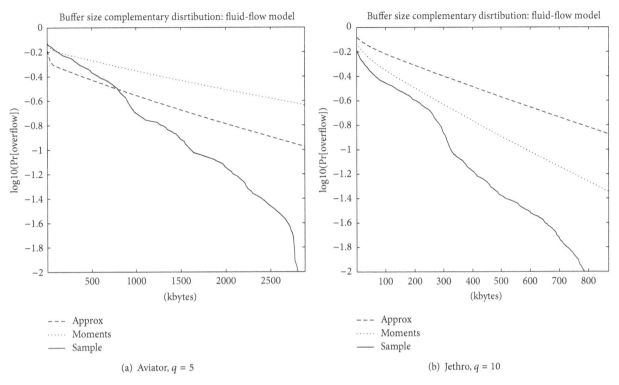

FIGURE 4: (a) Complementary buffer size distribution; fluid-flow model for Aviator $q = 5$ (b) complementary buffer size distribution; fluid flow-model for Jethro $q = 10$.

$3, 4, \ldots, 31$. These are the mean bit rate (or mean frame size) given by (4) and the autocorrelation decay rate which has equal values for all values of q.

Towards a validation of the above method, we examine two simple scenarios. Given the statistics of the trace *Aviator*, $q = 2$, acquired by an off-line measurement, we estimate the DAR modelling parameters of the video trace with $q = 5$, that is, α_5, β_5, and ρ. From (6), we have $\alpha_5 = 1.45$, $\beta_5 = 758.81$, and $\rho = 0.981$ as calculated for all cases via (3). As can be concluded from Table 1, the values of α_5 and β_5 are approximately close to the actual ones. With the same analysis for movie Jethro, we have, for $q = 10$ trace, $\alpha_{10} = 1.4499$, $\beta_{10} = 444.3817$, and $\rho = 0.9939$. The above parameters fed the DAR model (1) for each trace separately. The resulting model is called "Approx." Another model was created, too, where the α and β parameters were calculated via the moment matching method by means of the actual trace (see Table 1, $\alpha_5 = 1.44$, $\beta_5 = 832.02$ for Aviator, $q = 5$ and $\alpha_{10} = 1.43$, $\beta_{10} = 424.27$ for Jethro, $q = 10$), to be referenced as the "Moments" model. Then, following the fluid-flow approach via the Continuous Markov Chain model C-DAR model [29, 30], we calculated the buffer size distribution in a single-server queueing scenario with a common traffic intensity equal to 0.85. This method is analytically described in a previous study [31] (see Section 3.3) where the important literature references are also presented. More explicitly, we consider a single-server queueing system fed by video traffic as a Markov modulated rate process with a finite number of states and transition rate matrix from the

C-DAR model using the infinite buffer assumption. A trace-driven simulation—under an identical queuing testbed—was also conducted for both traces (sample). The complementary buffer size distributions are plotted in Figure 4 ((a): Aviator, (b): Jethro). With reference to these figures, it is seen that the "Approx" and "Moments" graphs deviate at a small percentage in both cases. This was expected since their mean rates differ as a property of the difference of the α and β parameters ($m = \alpha\beta$). With respect to queueing, both models are conservative—in terms of convergence to the sample—as a consequence of the choice of ρ based on the slow decay of the autocorrelation function of the sample. However, if an upper target bound is a priori given, that is, a worst case scenario (usually the case of the section to follow) for single source video traffic, for example, R_w, the "Approx" model could be adjusted to the certain mean rate by means of multiplying the DAR rate states with the factor R_w / R_q.

4.3. Estimation of the DAR Parameters for C-VBR Traffic.

We present here the results for the constrained counterpart traffic; see Table 2 for Aviator and Jethro Tull concert movies encoded under a rate control scheme (variable quantization) with certain rate constraints at 100, 200, and 400 kbps. A similar analysis to that of the previous subsection leads to some first conclusions concerning the statistical characteristics of constrained vbr traffic. Briefly, the autocorrelation function appeared to decay faster (compare to the u-vbr case) to zero for the first 200 lags. In low bit rate cases, for example,

TABLE 2: Statistics for Aviator (22 min) and Jethro Tull (30,55 min) in rate control mode.

Movie	Aviator			Jethro		
Target rate	100	200	400	100	200	400
Mean rate	96	196	397	96	197	399
Mean	484	984	1988	481	981	1984
Variance	74471	220500	1064400	122710	365535	1253100
Moments						
α	3.15	4.39	3.71	1.89	2.63	3.14
β	153.76	224.06	535.48	255.00	372.58	631.72
C-LVMAX						
α	8.73	8.55	5.16	8.74	8.41	7.27
β	55.92	117.63	382.39	54.84	118.53	283.47

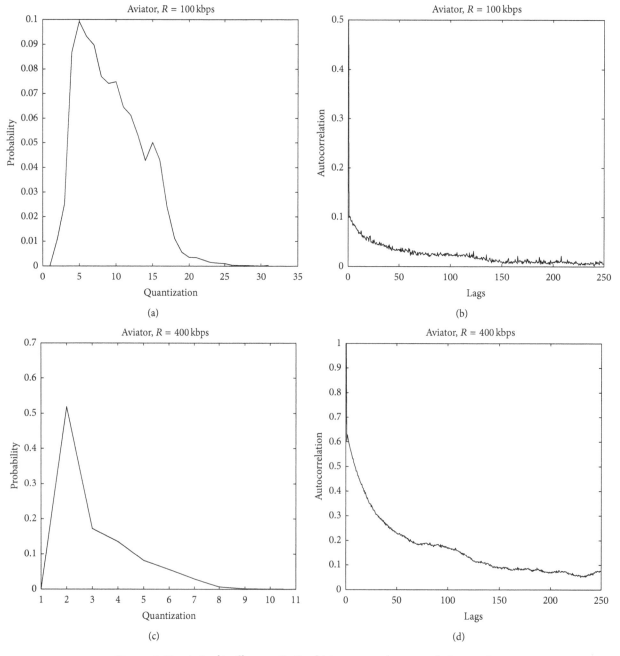

FIGURE 5: Constrained traffic, quantization histograms, and autocorrelation graphs.

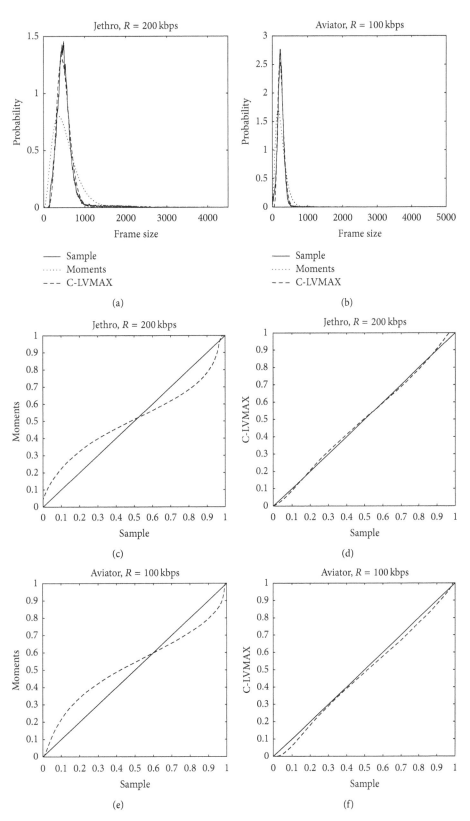

FIGURE 6: Constrained traffic, frame-size histograms, and q-q plots of moments matching method.

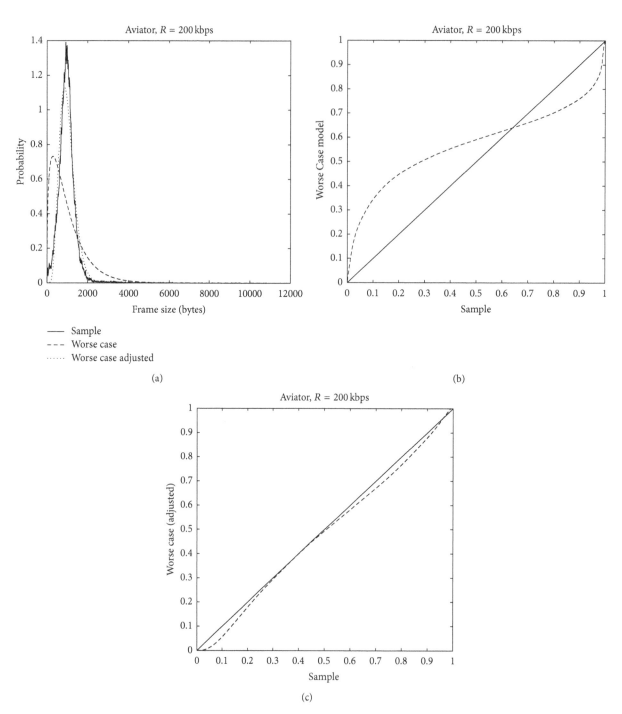

FIGURE 7: Constrained traffic, Worse Case model.

encoding at a target rate of 100 or 200 kbps, this property was even stronger giving rough indications of uncorrelated traffic (calling for an $M/G/\infty$ model to be applied). However, in the 400 kbps encoding case, frame correlation values were higher and a least squares fit to (3) gave autocorrelation decay rate values approximately equal to 0.9951. To find a reasonable explanation for the above, the sequence of the quantization values was also examined for each case, and the corresponding quantization histograms were plotted (see Figure 5). In the case of $R = 100$ kbps, the quantization values followed

a Gaussian (bell-shaped) histogram whereas in the case of $R = 400$ kbps an asymmetrical (more narrow) histogram is exhibited; that is, the majority of q-values are between 2 and 5. Hence, the variance of the quantization sequence is a measure of the correlation of the frame sequence. However, since an a priori knowledge of the quantization sequence is not given, for our analysis in this paper, and taking into account that with respect to queueing what matters the most is the long-term trend of the autocorrelation function; its conservative approach to consider correlated models for all cases by selecting the autocorrelation decay rare value from the analysis of the unconstrained counterpart $q = 2$ trace.

The frequency histograms for c-vbr traffic have Gamma form more narrow and tall compared to the counterpart cases of u-vbr traffic, that is, the traffic is mostly concentrated around the target mean rate (see Figure 6 for the case of Aviator with a target rate of 100 kbps). With reference to this figure, it is observed that the moments matching method fails to meet the characteristics of the sample's histogram (approximately divergent results hold for the other movies too in c-vbr mode). This phenomenon was also presented in [22, 31] where H.261 and H.263 videoconference traffic in multipoint sessions was analysed. In both studies, due to rate constraints imposed by a video server (multipoint control units/gatekeepers), the video traffic exhibited similar characteristics. In order to overcome the fitting problems of the moments method, the authors estimated different parameters of the Gamma family. The C-LVMAX model, presented in both studies, appeared to have a stable behaviour in cases of c-vbr traffic. This method relates the peak of the histogram's convolution to the location at which the Gamma density achieves its maximum and to the value of this maximum. The values of the shape and scale parameters of the Gamma density are derived from $\alpha = (2\pi\hat{x}^2\hat{f}^2 + 1)/2$ and $\beta = 1/(2\pi\hat{x}\hat{f}^2)$, where $\hat{f}$ is the unique maximum of the histogram's convolution density at $\hat{x}$. Numerical values for this fit appear also in Table 2, and the corresponding q-q plots, demonstrating the dominance of the model, are shown in Figure 6. From the values of the C-LVMAX Gamma parameters, it is also observed that the shape parameter α has larger values compared to the ones of the "moments" model. This explains in an analytical way the narrowness of the frame-size histogram property we have already noted. The specific model, though demands the full-histogram information (i.e., the actual trace), hence, separates measurements for each constraint scenario of mean rate R. In the paragraph to follow, we propose a simple method towards an approximate estimation of the Gamma parameters of c-vbr video traffic.

Within the context of the dominance of the C-LVMAX model for c-vbr traffic, we adopt in this paper—for this type of traffic—the idea in [13] (Section 6.3.2, p. 40). According to this paper, an approach towards modelling contrained video traces is to "assume worst case sources, operating close to the maximum capacity and then characterize these sources." Based on this idea, we considered as a "worst case" source at a constrain rare R_w the counterpart u-vbr trace with mean rate close to R_w. From (4) and (6) it is simple to calculate α and β for a certain trace of rate $R_w \neq R_q$.

Consider,

$$\alpha_{R_w} = \hat{\alpha}\left(\frac{R_w}{\hat{R}}\right)^{-z_\alpha/z}, \qquad \beta_{R_w} = \hat{\beta}\left(\frac{R_w}{\hat{R}}\right)^{-z_\beta/z}, \tag{7}$$

$$q = 2, 3, \ldots, 31.$$

However, the values of the above parameters correspond to unconstrained video traces which—as described in the corresponding section—exhibit frequency histograms of small shape α values ($\alpha < 2$, see Table 1) while for the constrained

traces the shape values where found to be larger ($\alpha > 5$, as given by C-LVMAX; see Table 2). Based on that, the fit of the sample c-vbr histogram via the parameters of (7) would be divergent, as shown in Figure 7. To overcome this problem, we adjust the above parameters so as to increase shape and reduce scale by a factor equal to 5, that is, adjusted shape $5\alpha_{R_w}$ and adjusted scale $\beta_{R_w}/5$. The improved fitting results appear in Figure 7 (where $\alpha_{R_w} = 1.4142$ and $\beta_{R_w} = 706.4866$ for the Worse Case model and $\alpha_{R_w} = 7.0710$ and $\beta_{R_w} = 141.2973$).

5. Conclusions

In this paper, we proposed methods for selecting the modelling parameters of H.263-quantized video traffic under two different encoding scenarios. For videos encoded with a constant quantization step (unconstrained), we conclude that a two-parameter power relation holds between the exhibited video bit rate and the quantizer value and that the autocorrelation decay rate remains constant for all cases. On the basis of these results, we propose a generic method for estimating the modelling parameters of unconstrained traffic by means of measuring the statistics of the single "raw" video trace. For rate-controlled video (constrained), we propose an approximate method based on the adjustment of the "shape" parameter of the counterpart—with respect to rate—unconstrained video trace. The convergence of the constructed models is assessed via queuing simulations. On the assumption that the popular MPEG-4 encoders like XVID, DIVX usually employ identical H.263 quantization and rate control schemes, it is expected that the results of this paper also hold for the MPEG-4 part 2 family.

References

[1] B. Maglaris, D. Anastassiou, P. Sen, G. Karlsson, and J. D. Robbins, "Performance models of statistical multiplexing in packet video communications," *IEEE Transactions on Communications*, vol. 36, no. 7, pp. 834–844, 1988.

[2] R. Kishimoto, Y. Ogata, and F. Inumara, "Generation interval distribution characteristics of packetized variable rate video coding data streams in an ATM network," *IEEE Journal on Selected Areas in Communications*, vol. 7, no. 5, pp. 833–841, 1989.

[3] H. S. Chin, J. W. Goodge, R. Griffiths, and D. J. Parish, "Statistics of video signals for viewphone-type pictures," *IEEE Journal on Selected Areas in Communications*, vol. 7, no. 5, pp. 826–832, 1989.

[4] M. Nomura, T. Fujii, and N. Ohta, "Basic characteristics of variable rate video coding in ATM environment," *IEEE Journal on Selected Areas in Communications*, vol. 7, no. 5, pp. 752–760, 1989.

[5] D. P. Heyman, A. Tabatabai, and T. V. Lakshman, "Statistical analysis and simulation study of video teleconference traffic in ATM networks," *IEEE Transactions on Circuits and Systems for Video Technology*, vol. 2, no. 1, pp. 49–59, 1992.

[6] D. M. Cohen and D. P. Heyman, "Performance modeling of video teleconferencing in ATM networks," *IEEE Transactions on Circuits and Systems for Video Technology*, vol. 3, no. 6, pp. 408–420, 1993.

[7] D. M. Lucantoni, M. F. Neuts, and A. R. Reibman, "Methods for performance evaluation of VBR video traffic models," *IEEE/ACM Transactions on Networking*, vol. 2, no. 2, pp. 176–180, 1994.

[8] M. Law and W. D. Kelton, *Simulation Modelling and Analysis*, McGraw-Hill Higher Education, 3nd edition, 1999.

[9] G. Sisodia, L. Guan, M. Hedley, and S. De, "A new modeling approach of H.263+ VBR coded video sources in ATM networks," *Real-Time Imaging*, vol. 6, no. 5, pp. 347–357, 2000.

[10] S. Domoxoudis, S. Kouremenos, V. Loumos, and A. Drigas, "Modelling and simulation of videoconference traffic from VBR video encoders," in *Proceedings of the Performance Modeling and Evaluation of Heterogeneous Networks (HET-NETs '04)*, 2004, http://www.comp.brad.ac.uk/het-net/HET-NETs04/papers .html.

[11] P. A. Jacosb and P. A. W. Lewis, "Time series generated by mixtures," *Journal of Time Series Analysis*, vol. 4, no. 1, pp. 19–36, 1983.

[12] A. Elwalid, D. Heyman, T. V. Lakshman, D. Mitra, and A. Weiss, "Fundamental bounds and approximations for ATM multiplexers with applications to video teleconferencing," *IEEE Journal on Selected Areas in Communications*, vol. 13, no. 6, pp. 1004–1016, 1995.

[13] T. V. Lakshman, A. Ortega, and A. R. Reibman, "VBR Video: tradeoffs and potentials," *Proceedings of the IEEE*, vol. 86, no. 5, pp. 952–972, 1998.

[14] R. Bo, "Modeling and simulation of broadband satellite networks—part II: traffic modeling," *IEEE Communications Magazine*, vol. 37, no. 7, pp. 48–56, 1999.

[15] MPEG-4 Overview, http://www.m4if.org//resources/Overview .pdf.

[16] ITU Recommendation (01/05). H.263: Video coding for low bit rate communication, http://www.itu.int/rec/T-REC-H .263-200501-I/en.

[17] A. Alheraish, "Autoregressive video conference models," *International Journal of Network Management*, vol. 14, no. 5, pp. 329–337, 2004.

[18] J. Shahbazian and K. J. Christensen, "TSGen: a tool for modeling of frame loss in streaming video," *International Journal of Network Management*, vol. 14, no. 5, pp. 315–327, 2004.

[19] A. Abdennour, "Short-term MPEG-4 video traffic prediction using ANFIS," *International Journal of Network Management*, vol. 15, no. 6, pp. 377–392, 2005.

[20] A. Abdennour, "VBR video traffic modeling and synthetic data generation using GA-optimized Volterra filters," *International Journal of Network Management*, vol. 17, no. 3, pp. 231–241, 2007.

[21] F. H. P. Fitzek and M. Reisslein, "MPEG-4 and H.263 video traces for network performance evaluation," *IEEE Network*, vol. 15, no. 6, pp. 40–54, 2001.

[22] C. Skianis, K. Kontovasilis, A. Drigas, and M. Moatsos, "Measurement and statistical analysis of asymmetric multipoint videoconference traffic in IP networks," *Telecommunication Systems*, vol. 23, no. 1-2, pp. 95–122, 2003.

[23] A. Lazaris, P. Koutsakis, and M. Paterakis, "A new model for video traffic originating from multiplexed MPEG-4 videoconference streams," *Performance Evaluation*, vol. 65, no. 1, pp. 51–70, 2008.

[24] P. Koutsakis, "On modeling multiplexed VBR videoconference traffic from H.263 video coders," *Computer Communications*, vol. 31, no. 1, pp. 1–4, 2008.

[25] M. Dai, Y. Zhang, and D. Loguinov, "A unified traffic model for MPEG-4 and H.264 video traces," *IEEE Transactions on Multimedia*, vol. 11, no. 5, pp. 1010–1023, 2009.

[26] D. Rao, Z. Huang, and D. Yang, "An emperical traffic model of M2M mobile streaming services," in *Proceedings of the Fourth International Conference on Multimedia Information Networking and Security (MINES '12))*, pp. 400–404, November 2012.

[27] FFmpeg Documentation, http://ffmpeg.org/ffmpeg.html.

[28] Open Source Streaming Server, http://developer.apple.com/ opensource/server/streaming/index.html.

[29] S. Xu, Z. Huang, and Y. Yao, "An analytically tractable model for video conference traffic," *IEEE Transactions on Circuits and Systems for Video Technology*, vol. 10, no. 1, pp. 63–67, 2000.

[30] A. Erramilli, O. Narayan, and W. Willinger, "Experimental queueing analysis with long-range dependent packet traffic," *IEEE/ACM Transactions on Networking*, vol. 4, no. 2, pp. 209–223, 1996.

[31] A. Drigas, S. Kouremenos, Y. Bakopoulos, and V. Loumos, "A study of H.263 traffic modeling in multipoint videoconference sessions over IP networks," *Computer Communications*, vol. 29, no. 3, pp. 372–391, 2006.

9

ARQ-Aware Scheduling and Link Adaptation for Video Transmission over Mobile Broadband Networks

Victoria Sgardoni,[1,2] **David R. Bull,**[1] **and Andrew R. Nix**[1]

[1] *Department of Electrical and Electronic Engineering, University of Bristol, Bristol BS8 1UB, UK*
[2] *Department of Aircraft Technology, Technological Educational Institute (ATEI) of Chalkis, Psachna, 34400 Evia, Greece*

Correspondence should be addressed to Victoria Sgardoni, victoria.sgardoni@bristol.ac.uk

Academic Editor: Martin Fleury

This paper studies the effect of ARQ retransmissions on packet error rate, delay, and jitter at the application layer for a real-time video transmission at 1.03 Mbps over a mobile broadband network. The effect of time-correlated channel errors for various Mobile Station (MS) velocities is evaluated. In the context of mobile WiMAX, the role of the ARQ Retry Timeout parameter and the maximum number of ARQ retransmissions is taken into account. ARQ-aware and channel-aware scheduling is assumed in order to allocate adequate resources according to the level of packet error rate and the number of ARQ retransmissions required. A novel metric, namely, *goodput per frame*, is proposed as a measure of transmission efficiency. Results show that to attain quasi error free transmission and low jitter (for real-time video QoS), only QPSK 1/2 can be used at mean channel SNR values between 12 dB and 16 dB, while 16QAM 1/2 can be used below 20 dB at walking speeds. However, these modes are shown to result in low transmission efficiency, attaining, for example, a total goodput of 3 Mbps at an SNR of 14 dB, for a block lifetime of 90 ms. It is shown that ARQ retransmissions are more effective at higher MS speeds.

1. Introduction

Mobile WiMAX (IEEE 802.16e) [1] and 3GPP LTE (Long-Term Evolution) [2] represent mobile broadband standards that offer high user data rates and support for bandwidth hungry video applications. Both standards use very similar PHY and MAC layer techniques, especially for downlink (DL) transmission. In order to provide strong QoS, cross-layer adaptive strategies must be implemented in the wireless network [3, 4]. Video applications demand a low Packet Error Rate (PER), which may be achieved via the use of MAC layer Automatic Repeat ReQuest (ARQ) and the choice of suitable Modulation and Coding Schemes (MCS). However, ARQ consumes additional bandwidth and causes increased end-to-end latency and jitter. ARQ is controlled in the MAC layer by the block lifetime and ARQ Retry Timer parameters, which define how many and how frequently retransmissions may occur. Link adaptation is used in mobile broadband networks to improve the PER by matching the QAM constellation and forward error correction coding rate to the

time varying channel quality. The impact of specific ARQ parameters and mechanisms has been extensively studied in the literature, for example, [5–9].

In [8], the authors analyze delay and throughput using probabilistic PHY layer error modelling. In [9], packet errors were modelled as an uncorrelated process in time. Often packet errors are modelled using statistical channel models, such as Markov chains, for example, [3, 10, 11], based on statistical measurements that have limited scalability and adaptability to a variety of fading, shadowing, or mobility circumstances. However, this type of modelling fails to represent the bursty nature of errors in a fading channel and the impact it has on ARQ retransmission performance.

To deliver video QoS the mobile WiMAX and LTE standards specify a number of scheduling mechanisms, such as Unsolicited Grant Service (UGS), rtPS (real-time Polling Service), and BE (Best Effort). As scheduling of resources is not specified in the standards, but instead left open for vendor implementation, this is an area of considerable research interest. In [12], a survey of several scheduling algorithms showed that, due to the nature of the wireless medium and user mobility, the scheduler should take into account the PER and the Carrier-to-Interference-plus-Noise Ratio (CINR) reported by the channel quality indicator (CQI) per connection. These schedulers are denoted as *"channel aware."* A channel-aware scheduler must take into consideration the MCS mode selected through link adaptation. The scheduling of resources must also take into account ARQ retransmissions, as discussed in [6, 8, 12, 13]. The authors of [8, 13] propose an *ARQ-aware* scheduler, where ARQ retransmissions have priority over new data. For applications that are very sensitive to jitter and delay, such as video, the QoS guarantees a maximum delay and error rate for a given bitrate. If ARQ is enabled on these connections, the BS scheduler must allocate sufficient resources in each frame to accommodate new data and ARQ retransmissions. The resources required per connection vary also according to the MCS mode selected by the Link Adaptation (LA) process.

Many recent publications have studied video streaming over WiMAX, for example, [10, 11, 14], but very few investigate unicast video with ARQ retransmission [4, 9]. In [4], the authors proposed cross-layer parameter optimization to achieve the required QoS, using queuing theory to minimize the required bandwidth while assuming stop-and-wait ARQ retransmission. None of the ARQ mechanisms specied in the 802.16e standard were considered in [4]. In [3, 14], the issue of "bandwidth hungry" video applications was highlighted. Nevertheless, the only video transmissions considered in recent publications are based on low resolution video (CIF, QVGA) with bitrates up to 400 kbps [8, 11, 14].

This work focuses on the transmission of high resolution real-time video, at a bitrate of 1.03 Mbps, over the downlink (DL) of a mobile broadband connection. The simulated transmission of a ow of UDP packets corresponds to the o w of video packets. Simulations are performed for a UDP unicast DL transmission, with Selective ACK (S-ACK) ARQ enabled. Moreover, multicast transmission without ARQ enabled is also included in the analysis. The transmission efficiency of ARQ enabled mobile WiMAX networks is computed by proposing a novel efficiency metric, the *goodput per frame*, which takes into account the amount of radio resources required per DL subframe and the PER attained. Channel-aware and ARQ-aware scheduling at the MAC layer is assumed. Very importantly, block errors are time-correlated, based on the use of the accurate time-correlated 3GPP SCM fading channel model [15]. Results are based on the WiMAX Forum recommendations [16, 17] for the ARQ Retry Timeout parameter and the maximum number of ARQ retransmissions. The study shows for the rst time how PER and delay/jitter are affected by scheduling sufficient (or insufficient) channel resources per frame, to cater for ARQ retransmissions, according to the MCS mode selected. The work identies which MCS modes are suitable to deliver QoS for real-time video, by maintaining quasi-zero PER and low jitter at the application layer. Our previous work [18] focused on received video quality (based on PSNR), for a 7.63 Mbps HD video sequence, when no limitations were applied to the ARQ Retry Timeout parameter and the maximum number of ARQ retransmissions, as assumed in

[8, 9] (since the frequency of ACK is not specied in the IEEE 802.16e standard [1]). The effect of ARQ-aware scheduling was not investigated in our previous work.

In this paper, the effect of MS velocity on ARQ retransmissions is explored. This is made possible by the use of an accurate time-correlated fading channel model. MS velocities of 1 and 10 km/h are considered.

Mobile WiMAX [1], together with 3GPP LTE [2], is key technology for next-generation broadband wireless access (BWA) networks [19]. Both technologies have very similar DL PHY layers and strong similarities in their MAC layers. For both technologies, radio resource management techniques, such as scheduling and resource allocation, are pivotal in research work on QoS support for multimedia services [19].

In the next section, key aspects of the mobile WiMAX PHY and MAC layers are described along with the time-varying channel model. In Section 3, the MAC-PHY simulator is described, detailing the assumptions made. Sections 4, 5, and 6 present an analysis of the simulation results. Conclusions are presented in Section 7.

2. Overview of Mobile WiMAX and the SCM Channel Model

Medium Access Control (MAC) Layer. The 802.16e MAC layer [20] includes a number of adjustable features, such as adaptive MCS, ARQ, packet fragmentation and aggregation, variable size MAC Protocol Data Units (PDU), and application-speci c service o ws and PDU scheduling based on QoS. Packets from the higher layers arrive in the convergence sublayer (CS) of the MAC as MAC Service Data Units (SDUs). Based on their QoS requirements, MAC SDUs are classied into service o ws. There is the option for SDU fragmentation into PDUs, and this feature is assumed here. SDUs are partitioned into ARQ blocks of x ed size when ARQ is enabled. The MAC PDU is the data unit exchanged between the BS and MS MAC layers. Once a PDU has been constructed, it is placed in the appropriate service o w queue and managed by the scheduler, which determines the PHY resource allocation (i.e., bandwidth and OFDMA symbol allocation) on a frame-by-frame basis.

Each transmitted PDU is either received correctly or in error, depending on the channel response at the time of transmission. The time-varying PHY layer PER is accurately calculated based on the channel model for each ARQ block in the transmitted PDU. The standard speci es a number of ARQ feedback mechanisms, such as Cumulative ACK, Cumulative and Selective ACK, and Selective ACK (S-ACK) [1]. Here S-ACK feedback is used. An S-ACK feedback message is generated for each transmission burst and any PDUs containing errors are placed in the retransmission queue [6]. No block rearrangement is enabled. The retransmission of PDUs in error continues until they are received correctly or their ARQ block lifetimes expire. The number of retransmissions is determined by the block lifetime and the ARQ Retry Timeout Timer, as shown in (1). The ARQ Retry Timeout represents the minimum number of OFDMA frames a transmitter will wait to retransmit an

TABLE 1: OFDMA PHY pro le parameters in 802.16e.

Parameters	Values			
Channel bandwidth (MHz)	1.25	5	*10*	20
FFT size	128	512	*1024*	2048
Sampling frequency (MHz)	1.4	5.6	*11.2*	22.4
Subcarrier frequency spacing (kHz)	10.94			
Useful symbol time T_b (μs)	91.4			
Guard time T_g (μs)	11.4			
OFDMA symbol duration ($T_s = T_b + T_g$) (μs)	102.9			
Number of OFDMA symbols (5 ms frame)	47			

TABLE 2: 802.16e link speeds.

No.	Link speed	Bits per slot	Total data rate (Mbps)
0	QPSK 1/2	48	6.14
1	QPSK 3/4	72	9.21
2	16QAM 1/2	96	12.29
3	16QAM 3/4	144	18.43
4	64QAM 1/2	144	18.43
5	64QAM 2/3	192	24.58
6	64QAM 3/4	216	27.64

unacknowledged block [1]. This retry period begins from the frame when the ARQ block was last transmitted. If the block lifetime expires before it is received correctly then the block is discarded.

Physical Layer (PHY). The mobile WiMAX standard has adopted Scalable-OFDMA (S-OFDMA) [1]. Table 1 shows the relevant parameters for the S-OFDMA PHY. Simulations for this paper were performed for the 10 MHz channel bandwidth pro le (highlighted in italics in Table 1). The payload data is modulated using the full range of link speeds (MCS modes) as de ned in the standard [1] and shown in Table 2. Assuming a PUSC DL [1], the modulation symbols allocated to a sequence of slots in each DL OFDMA frame are assigned to a number of logical subchannels. An OFDMA slot is the minimum possible data allocation unit. For PUSC DL, it is de ned as one subchannel by two OFDMA symbols. For the 10 MHz channel, an OFDMA symbol consists of 30 subchannels for PUSC DL, each containing 24 data subcarriers [21]. Hence, a slot contains 48 data subcarriers. Based on this, the slot payload capacity P_{sl} for each MCS mode is computed for PUSC DL. It is shown in Table 3, where m represents the MCS modulation order and r the coding rate. The channel resources (in terms of slots) required for data transmission over a mobile WiMAX network are evaluated based on the slot payload capacity for each MCS mode.

PHY Layer Abstraction. To simplify the interface between the link and system level simulators, whilst still modelling dynamic system behaviour, a technique known as Effective

SINR Mapping (ESM) is used. This method, which can also be used to model the LTE PHY layer, compresses the SINR (per subcarrier) vector into a single effective SINR (ESINR). The technique is described in detail in [22]. The PHY abstraction model is described and validated in [23]. This PHY abstraction model allows the instantaneous Block Error Rate (BLER) to be computed for each channel realization, based on the instantaneous fading channel and the length of the ARQ block. Although many commercial network simulators exist, such as OpNet and QualNet, these tend to provide simpli ed physical layer support. For example, QualNet uses bit error rate look up tables that average the effects of time-varying fast fading. Video analysis requires the use of time-varying instantaneous BLER in a fading channel (not averaged BLER), since the bursty nature of the errors has a detrimental effect on video quality, as shown in [24].

Wideband Channel Model. The channel model follows the ETSI 3GPP spatial channel model (SCM), as described in [15]. A time varying "urban micro" tapped delay line (TDL) was generated for each channel snapshot. The TDL consists of 6 time-correlated fading taps with nonuniform delays. The carrier frequency is 2.3 GHz and the FFT size is 1024. Each radio channel is made up of a number of channel samples (sampled every 2.5 ms) corresponding to a duration of 85 seconds.

3. WiMAX MAC-PHY Simulator

Unicast and multicast transmission of high resolution video is simulated over the mobile WiMAX system. This work is based on a MAC-PHY simulator developed according to the standard [1] and presented in [18]. The mobile WiMAX PHY layer simulator is described in [25]. As discussed in Section 2, the PHY layer PER is generated from the ESM PHY layer abstraction method developed in [23].

3.1. Simulator Assumptions. The following key assumptions were made for the design of the mobile WiMAX MAC-PHY simulator. MAC SDU fragmentation (not packing) is assumed, according to the 802.16e standard [1]. The MAC PDU size is xed for all MCS modes. It is small (less than 200 Bytes) to improve the error rate, according to [5]. The simulated ARQ mechanism is Selective ACK (S-ACK) [1]. It is assumed that no errors occur in the ARQ feedback messages. When errors occur during PDU transmission, no block rearrangement is performed within the PDUs. PDUs that are not acknowledged are placed in a separate queue within the user o w, known as the retransmission queue [6, 26]. The scheduler gives priority to PDUs from the retransmissions queue. SDUs are delivered in order at the receiver, since the ARQ-DELIVER_IN_ORDER MAC parameter is enabled.

Video is assumed to be sent at a constant bit rate (CBR), with x ed size packets; therefore, the use of UGS scheduling is assumed. The scheduler allocates a x ed amount of resources per MAC frame for each DL burst, according to the operation of UGS scheduling. As the standard [1] does not specify how the scheduling of resources is performed,

TABLE 3: Slot payload capacity per MCS for PUSC DL.

MCS	m	r	Slot payload P_{sl} (bits)
QPSK 1/2	4	1/2	48
QPSK 3/4	4	3/4	72
16QAM 1/2	16	1/2	96
16QAM 3/4	16	3/4	144
64QAM 1/2	64	1/2	144
64QAM 2/3	64	2/3	192
64QAM 3/4	64	3/4	216

but instead leaves the issue open for vendor implementation, it is assumed that a "channel-aware scheduler" is used that allocates resources according to the MCS mode selected with an overallocation for ARQ retransmissions [13]. If additional resources (i.e., overallocation) are not provided, when retransmissions occur they will take up resources from the new arriving data, since retransmissions have priority. This would result in a queuing delay that is unacceptable for real-time video applications. It is assumed that adequate additional resources for ARQ are available per frame, as required to cater for the expected number of retransmissions depending on the BLER.

The data payload that each slot can carry for each MCS mode is given in Table 3. The number of PDUs that can fit within the allocated resource is calculated according to the MCS mode and the size of retransmission PDU queue. For each DL burst the retransmission PDUs are included in the allocated resources, taking priority over new PDUs.

3.2. Simulator Functionality. The 802.16e MAC-PHY simulator provides an error modelling tool that predicts the loss patterns for a sequence of RTP/UDP packets and thus the losses in the sequence of video packets at the receiver. The PHY abstraction model allows the instantaneous BLER to be computed for each channel realization, based on the instantaneous fading channel and the length of the ARQ block. Thus, the computed BLER is time-correlated. A flow of fixed size RTP/UDP packets arrive at the MAC layer and are passed into the simulator. It is assumed that UDP packets arrive at a constant rate. Each UDP packet corresponds one-to-one to a MAC SDU. More details on the MAC-PHY simulator are given in [18].

At the receiver, SDUs are reassembled from the appropriate ARQ blocks. Since the MAC parameter ARQ_DELIVER_IN_ORDER is enabled, SDUs are delivered in sequential order to the transport layer, as UDP packets. This means that an SDU cannot be delivered to the higher layers unless all the SDUs preceding it in the flow have been received correctly, or have been discarded. If an ARQ block is finally discarded, despite retransmissions, the IEEE 802.16e standard mandates that the SDU to which it belongs cannot be delivered to the higher layers [1]. A block diagram of the simulator is shown in Figure 1.

The MAC-PHY simulator provides an accurate way to determine the MAC BLER and SDU error rate (SER) for the SDUs that are discarded, taking into account the MAC layer parameters, data encapsulation, and the ARQ process. Importantly, the BLER for contiguous blocks is not independent due to the time-correlated nature of the fading channel, and this is enabled by modelling the instantaneous PHY PER $P_e(t)$. The simulator computes the following as a function of mean channel SNR, MCS mode, ARQ block lifetime, and MS velocity, taking into account MAC layer parameters such as packet size, the ARQ Retry timer, and the ARQ feedback time:

  (i) block error rate (BLER),

  (ii) SDU error rate (SER), equivalent to UDP PER (one-to-one mapping of SDUs to UDP packets),

  (iii) the time pattern of the ARQ block and SDU losses,

  (iv) end-to-end delay and jitter for blocks and SDUs,

  (v) channel capacity consumed during each DL subframe, measured in physical slots,

  (vi) transmission throughput and goodput.

The simulator records the transmission times for each ARQ block and SDU for a flow of N SDUs. The number of ARQ retransmissions k_{re} is estimated from the total ARQ block transmission time T_{ARQ}, computed as

$$T_{ARQ} = k_{re} \cdot (ARQRetry \cdot T_{OFDMA}) + T_{OFDMA}, \quad (1)$$

where T_{OFDMA} is the duration of an OFDMA frame (i.e., 5 ms) and *ARQRetry* is the *ARQRetry* Timeout parameter (number of frames).

The number of ARQ retransmissions k_{re} is estimated when a bound is imposed on T_{ARQ} by the block lifetime l_{bl}, as

$$T_{ARQ} \leq l_{bl}, \quad (2)$$

$$\max(k_{re}) = \left\lfloor \frac{l_{bl} - T_{OFDMA}}{ARQRetry \cdot T_{OFDMA}} \right\rfloor. \quad (3)$$

In general, if insufficient resources are allocated for all retransmissions in the frame where the PDU is to be resent, according to the ARQ Retry Timeout timer, an additional queuing time, Tq, will be added in (1). This represents the block queuing time in the retransmission queue. In this case, the number of retransmissions that will take place will be less than $\max(k_{re})$, as T_{ARQ} is limited by (2). Hence, k_{re} is not deterministic for all blocks.

The simulator calculates the end-to-end SDU latency and jitter for a flow of N SDUs $\in \{1, 2, 3, \ldots, j, j+1, j+2, \ldots, N\}$. The SDU end-to-end latency for SDU j, D_j is calculated as the time difference between the arrival of the MAC SDU j at the MAC layer transmitter, $T_{arr,j}$, and the delivery of the SDU j to the transport layer at the receiver, $T_{rec,j}$, as shown in (4)

$$D_j = T_{rec,j} - T_{arr,j}, \quad (4)$$

$$D_j = D_{tx} + D_{del}. \quad (5)$$

The end-to-end latency of an SDU j, D_j, consists of the transmission time D_{tx} and the delivery time D_{del}.

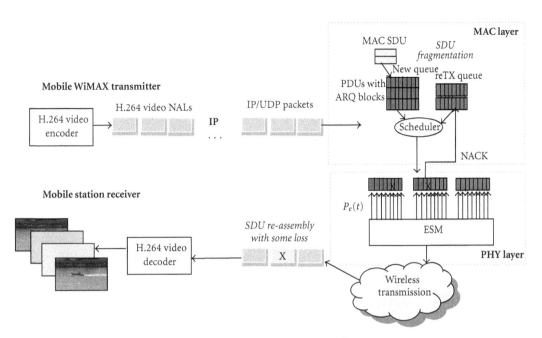

FIGURE 1: WiMAX MAC-PHY simulator.

The transmission time D_{tx} includes the retransmission time for the PDUs containing blocks of SDU j and the waiting time in the retransmission buffer, if any of the ARQ blocks contained in the SDU were retransmitted. An SDU is delivered to the receiver (at the transport layer) when all the ARQ blocks it consists of have been correctly received, after retransmission. Also, SDU packets are delivered in order. This is because the receiver must first receive correctly and reassemble all the ARQ blocks of SDU j and then deliver the SDUs following j. This means that if the ARQ blocks in SDU j have undergone retransmission, the SDUs $j + 1, j + 2, \ldots$ which follow SDU j will be delayed as well, even if no errors and retransmissions occurred for them. Therefore, retransmissions can cause a build up of delay, not only for the SDU which suffered the transmission errors, but also for SDUs following it. If the channel is poor and errors occur frequently, the delay build-up can be significant.

Figure 2 depicts the delay build-up for a number of SDUs, when some of the ARQ blocks of SDU S3 are lost and later retransmitted. Although SDUs S4, S5, and S6, succeeding S3, are received correctly, they are not delivered to the higher layers until all the ARQ blocks from SDU S3 have been received correctly (after ARQ retransmission). So SDUs S4 to S6 are delayed.

The variation in the end-to-end delay (latency) of the SDUs, for a flow of SDUs, is referred to as jitter. Another term commonly used is Packet Delay Variation (PDV), defined in ITU-T Recommendation Y.1540. Jitter is calculated as the variance of the SDU delay as follows

$$\text{jitter} = \text{var}(D_{\text{SDU}}) = \frac{1}{N}\sum_{i=1}^{N}(D_i - \mu_D)^2, \qquad (6)$$

where D_{SDU} is the discrete function of the SDU latency. D_i is the end-to-end delay of SDU i, μ_D is the mean SDU delay, and N is the total number of SDUs transmitted.

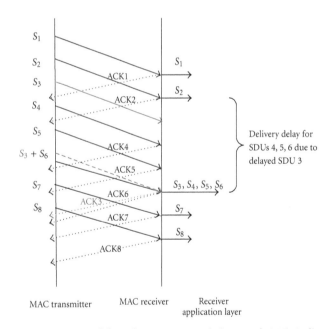

FIGURE 2: SDU delays due to retransmissions and ARQ_Deliver_In_Order.

In accordance with 802.16e recommendations [16, 17], here it is assumed that retransmissions cannot occur in the next frame but are sent at the earliest on the 4th DL subframe after transmission. Furthermore, the maximum number of retransmissions is limited to 4. These values result from processing time at the receiver and transmission delays in the radio network. The MAC parameter ARQ Retry Timeout is set to 4 and performance is simulated for 1–4 retransmissions, corresponding to 30–90 ms block lifetimes, according to (3).

TABLE 4: Mobile WiMAX simulator parameters.

Parameter	Value
OFDMA	
Carrier frequency	2.3 GHz
Channel bandwidth	10 MHz
FFT length	1024
Subcarrier frequency spacing	10.94 kHz
Frame length	5 ms (48 OFDMA symbols)
Guard interval	1/8
DL subcarrier permutation scheme	PUSC DL
Number of active DL subcarriers	840
Number of subchannels	30 DL/35 UL
Data subcarriers per subchannel	24
OFDMA data symbols	22 DL/15 UL
DL capacity	330 slots
DL/UL ratio	60/40
MAC	
MAC SDU size	815 bytes
ARQ block size	32 bytes
MAC PDU size	max 200 bytes
PDU packing	No
SDU fragmentation	Yes
QoS scheduling	UGS
Block rearrangement	No
ARQ feedback type	Selective-ACK
ARQ retry timeout	4 frames
ARQ block lifetime	0–90 ms
Max no. retransmissions	4
ARQ_DELIVER_IN_ORDER	Yes

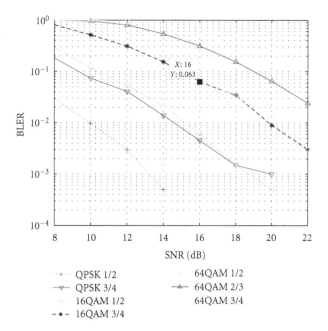

FIGURE 3: BLER versus SNR when block lifetime is 65 ms and MS $v = 1$ km/h.

3.3. Simulation Parameters. Table 4 summarises the PHY and MAC layer parameters used in the MAC-PHY mobile WiMAX simulator. Simulation results are presented in the next sections for a ow of UDP packets corresponding to the "ICE" video sequence [27] (704×576 pixels at 30 fps) encoded using H.264 at 1.03 Mbps, with I, P, and B frames.

The simulator captures the transmission of 2000 UDP packets, 815 Bytes each, transmitted through the 802.16e PHY and MAC layers. UDP packets correspond 1 : 1 to MAC SDUs, also 815 Bytes long. Each MAC SDU was fragmented into ARQ blocks, 32 bytes long. Simulations were carried out for MS velocities $v = 1$ km/h and 10 km/h for mean channel SNR values varying from 8 dB–22 dB.

4. Analysis of BLER and UDP PER

In Figures 3 and 4, the BLER and SDU error rate are compared for an ARQ lifetime of 65 ms (i.e., up to 3 retransmissions may have occurred). The simulated MS speed is 1 km/h. It is observed that the BLER seen at the MAC layer after the retransmissions is projected to a much higher SER and UDP PER at the higher layers. For example, at SNR = 16 dB 16QAM 3/4 results in 0.063 BLER, which corresponds to 0.089 SER. This is because, according to the standard [1],

even if just one ARQ block in an SDU is discarded it will result in the whole SDU being discarded. The SDU error rate is accentuated more for higher BLER, for example, at 14 dB 64QAM 2/3 gives 0.53 BLER and 0.65 SER. This shows that in order to achieve high video quality and quasi-zero PER at the video receiver (i.e., SER), the ARQ retransmissions must achieve quasi-zero BLER. However, with the number of retransmissions limited to 3, only lower modes can deliver error free data in a slowly time-varying channel. From Figure 3, it is obvious that only the QPSK modes and 16QAM 1/2 can deliver SER $\leq 10^{-2}$ for SNR ≤ 18 dB, when the MS speed is 1 km/h and the block lifetime is 65 ms.

In Figure 5, SER versus channel SNR is shown for an MS speed of 1 km/h, when up to 4 retransmissions are allowed, for a block lifetime of 90 ms. It is shown that the SER is lower with a longer block lifetime. QPSK 1/2 delivers error free data for SNR ≥ 12 dB and 16QAM 1/2 attains an SER $<$ 0.02 for SNR ≥ 14 dB.

Our previous work in [18] focused on the BLER attained (rather than SER) when ARQ retransmissions occurred in the next DL subframe, without limitation on the maximum number of retransmissions (since the ARQ retransmission frequency is not speci ed in the 802.16e standard [1]). In [18], it was shown that the BLER achieved was below 10^{-2} at a mean channel SNR of 8 dB, for a block lifetime of 100 ms, with MCS modes 16QAM 1/2 or lower. All MCS modes up to 64QAM 1/2 attained quasi error free transmission when the mean channel SNR was 12 dB and block lifetimes were greater than 70 ms. This was possible because, in that scenario, the maximum number of permitted retransmissions was 7 for a block lifetime of 70 ms; this resulted in more favorable ARQ performance. In this work, it is shown that imposing practical limitations on the ARQ Retry Timeout parameter and the maximum number of retransmissions (as

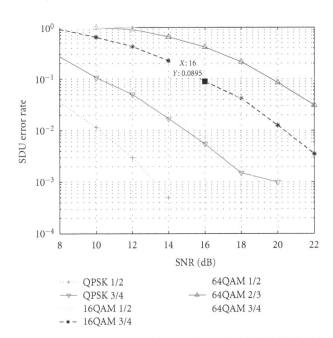

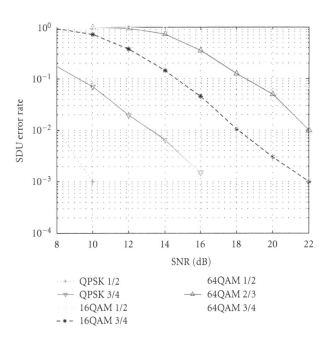

FIGURE 4: SER (or UDP PER) versus SNR when block lifetime is 65 ms and MS $v = 1$ km/h.

FIGURE 6: SER versus SNR when block lifetime is 65 ms and MS $v = 10$ km/h.

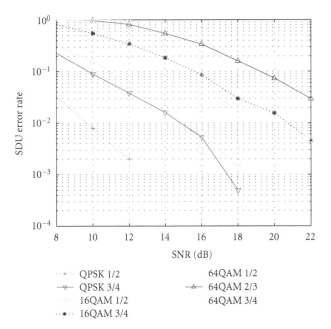

FIGURE 5: SER versus SNR for a block lifetime of 90 ms and MS $v = 1$ km/h.

recommended in [16, 17]) results in a residual BLER. This residual BLER is further accentuated as UDP PER at the higher layers.

In Figure 6, the SER versus SNR across all MCS modes for an MS speed of 10 km/h is compared with the SER versus SNR for an MS speed of 1 km/h, as shown in Figure 4. The maximum number of retransmissions in both cases is determined by a 65 ms block lifetime. It is clear that the SER attained for the 1 km/h channel is higher than the SER for

the 10 km/h channel at all channel SNR values. For example, at 16 dB 16QAM 3/4 attains SER = 0.089 at 1 km/h while this drops to SER = 0.045 at 10 km/h. QPSK 1/2 at 12 dB attains SER = 0.03 for 1 km/h speed, whereas it gives SER = 0 (below the simulation accuracy level) for a 10 km/h MS speed. The low MS speed means that the channel coherence time is longer and the channel decorrelates slower in time. Hence, more ARQ retransmissions are required at the slower speed to achieve a quasi-zero level of SER. The effect of channel coherence time on ARQ retransmissions was also studied in [24] for 802.11 a/g networks, where ARQ retransmission was implemented according to a stop-and-wait mechanism and was governed by the CSMA/CA access protocol.

Next, the BLER and SER attained when multicasting is studied. In Figures 7 and 8 ARQ is not enabled, as is the case for multicasting. The MS speed is 1 km/h. It can be seen that the SER in Figure 8 is much higher than the BLER for the same channel SNR and MCS mode. For example, at 14 dB QPSK 3/4 delivers BLER = 0.039, while the SER is 0.15. The lack of ARQ error correction limits the video broadcast performance over mobile WiMAX, as explained in [11]. Without additional error correction, real-time video multicasting could not be offered for an SNR range below 16 dB (as SER > 10^{-2} [28]), and even then only with the lowest throughput mode QPSK 1/2, which consumes considerable channel capacity.

5. ARQ-Aware Scheduling and Latency/Jitter

Another very important aspect of video transmission with ARQ is the latency and jitter that occurs. As discussed in [29–31], for video applications the playback buffer that masks network jitter can take values in the order of 250 ms, while latency is acceptable up to 100–150 ms, depending on

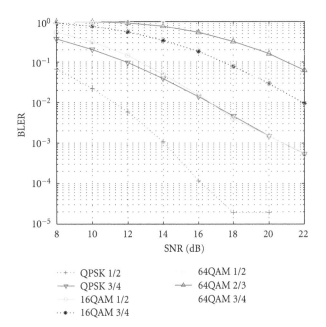

FIGURE 7: BLER versus SNR without ARQ, MS $v = 1$ km/h.

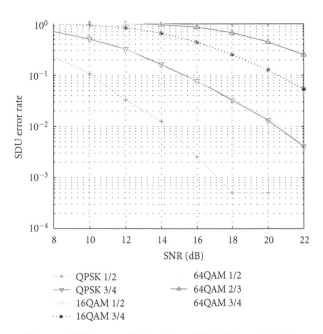

FIGURE 8: SER versus SNR without ARQ, MS $v = 1$ km/h.

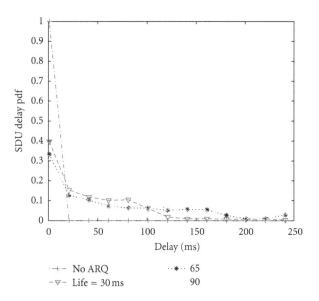

FIGURE 9: PDF of end-to-end SDU delay, SNR = 12 dB, mode = 1, $v = 1$ km/h.

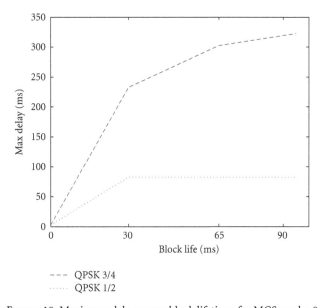

FIGURE 10: Maximum delay versus block lifetime, for MCS modes 0 and 1 when channel SNR = 12 dB and MS $v = 1$ km/h.

the specic video characteristics and applications. Assuming ARQ-aware scheduling, here the latency and jitter associated with ARQ retransmissions is studied over an 802.16e network.

For the 2000 transmitted SDUs, the simulator calculates the total latency for each SDU. Figure 9 shows the PDF of the end-to-end SDU delay computed during the transmission of 2000 SDUs at a channel SNR = 12 dB, MCS mode 1 (QPSK 3/4), and MS speed 1 km/h, for block lifetimes of 30 ms (up to 1 retransmission), 65 ms (up to 3 retransmissions), and 90 ms (up to 4 retransmissions).

The simulator computes the latency during transmission and the jitter as the variance of the SDU latency across the 2000 SDUs, for each SNR, MCS mode, and block lifetime. Figure 10 shows the maximum latency attained versus block lifetime, when the mean channel SNR is 12 dB and the MS speed is 1 km/h. It is observed that at SNR = 12 dB (when the channel is poor) the maximum latency is xed to approximately 82 ms for block lifetimes of 30–90 ms when QPSK 1/2 is used. This MCS mode delivers SER = 0.003 (see Figure 4). If QPSK 3/4 is used, the maximum delay increases for each block lifetime, reaching over 300 ms for a block lifetime of 90 ms. This occurs because a very large number of ARQ blocks are in error and many retransmissions occur.

TABLE 5: Overallocation of resources for lifetime 65 ms.

MCS	SNR = 10 dB	SNR = 22 dB
0	0.06	0
1	0.42	0
2	0.68	0
3	2.48	0.03
4	3.05	0.02
5	3.98	0.15
6	3.99	0.36

This MCS mode attains SER = 0.05 when the block lifetime is 65 ms, despite the retransmissions that take place (see Figure 4). This mode would not be selected for transmission at SNR = 12 dB by the link adaptation algorithm because the BLER is very high for the amount of retransmissions allowed. The amount of resources allocated by the scheduler in this case does not cater for the very large number of retransmissions that occur, resulting in a buildup of queuing delay and also a large increase in jitter. The amount of "overallocation" of resources the ARQ-aware scheduler predicts is related to the level of PER attained by the selected MCS mode and the ARQ block lifetime.

In Table 5, the overallocation γ required for different MCS modes is given for mean channel SNR values of 10 dB and 22 dB, when the block lifetime is 65 ms. If S is the number of slots required per DL frame, for a given bitrate and MCS mode, the scheduler needs to allocate $(1 + \gamma) \cdot S$ slots per DL frame. The overallocation γ is calculated by dividing the number of slots required per DL frame for the desired number of ARQ retransmissions (according to the MCS mode), by S. From this table, it is obvious that, for example, if mode 1 was selected at SNR = 10 dB, the scheduler would need to allocate $\gamma = 0.42$ more resources than that required if ARQ was not enabled. A smaller allocation than this results in queuing delays. It is also obvious that the overallocation required for the higher modes at low SNR values is unacceptable (i.e., three times the amount of resources required for the video bitrate).

Figures 11 and 12 show jitter versus block lifetime for SNR = 22 dB at an MS speed of 1 km/h and for SNR = 12 dB at an MS speed of 10 km/h, correspondingly. Jitter is studied for the MCS modes that attain SER ≤ 0.02 and that can deliver quality video. In Figure 11, where the mean channel SNR = 22 dB, the jitter is below 100 ms when the block lifetime is 65 ms, for MCS modes 0 to 4. All of these modes deliver quasi error free data.

Figure 12 shows the jitter when the MS speed is 10 km/h at SNR = 12 dB. The jitter is approximately 100 ms for mode 1 when the block lifetime is 65 ms. Both QPSK 3/4 and 16QAM 1/2 attain an SER of approximately 0.02, but for 16QAM 1/2 more retransmissions occur and therefore higher jitter ensues.

The study of the simulation results on SER, latency and jitter, when the recommendations from [17, 32] regarding ARQ parameters are applied, leads to the conclusion that when the channel SNR is poor (SNR ≤ 14 dB) only the lower

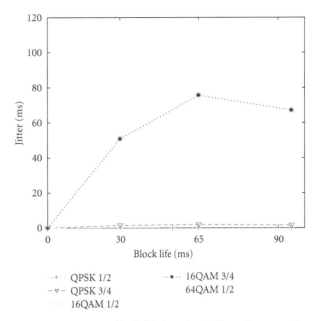

FIGURE 11: Jitter versus block lifetime, for MCS modes 0 to 4 when channel SNR = 22 dB and MS v = 1 km/h.

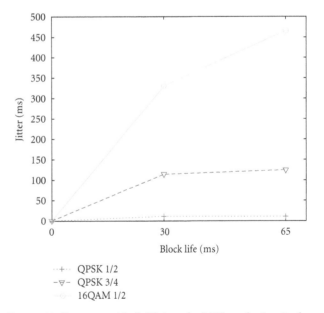

FIGURE 12: Jitter versus block lifetime, for MCS modes 0 to 3 when channel SNR = 12 dB and MS v = 10 km/h.

QPSK modes can deliver quality video with acceptable jitter. For a UDP unicast video transmission, in order to attain quasi error free SER, and at the same time limit jitter to below 100 ms, QPSK modes should be used with up to 3 retransmissions. When the channel has a long coherence time more retransmissions are required in order to deliver the ARQ blocks error free, and only QPSK 1/2 can be used. However, even then the SER attained (0.03) is not quasi error free.

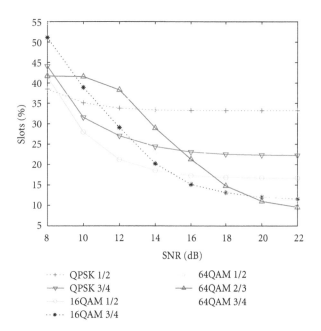

FIGURE 13: Percentage of physical DL slots required versus SNR, block lifetime = 65 ms, v = 1 km/h.

6. Transmission Efficiency

Having discussed the mobile WiMAX performance in terms of SER and jitter when ARQ is enabled, the channel resources required during unicast video transmission are now studied. The simulator estimates the total number of physical slots required for the transmission of 2000 SDUs, at each mean channel SNR and MCS mode, including all ARQ retransmissions. Then the channel capacity required is calculated as a percentage of the total number of DL slots available, for the duration of the transmission. This work focuses on the goodput attained. A novel transmission efficiency metric is proposed, namely the goodput per frame, which takes into account the goodput achieved for the amount of channel resources required per DL subframe.

Figure 13 shows the channel capacity required, as a percentage of the total physical DL slots available per DL subframe, versus the mean channel SNR, for all MCS modes when up to 3 retransmissions are allowed. It is shown that for QPSK 1/2 there is a very small differentiation in the channel resources required for SNR $\geq$ 14 dB, as resource requirements drop from 38.5% of slots at SNR = 8 dB to 33%. This is because very few retransmissions occur for higher channel SNR values with QPSK 1/2, therefore the resources required are constant, corresponding to the new data arrivals. In other cases, the differentiation of resources required across SNR values is much greater. For example, for 64QAM 1/2 at SNR = 8 dB approximately 55% of the total slots are required, whereas for SNR = 22 dB only 11.5% of the total slots are required. This is because more ARQ retransmissions are required at low SNR values. It is also obvious that the higher throughput modes require less resources than the lower modes, even at low SNR values when retransmissions occur. For example, 16QAM

3/4 requires 29% of the total resources at SNR = 12 dB, while QPSK 1/2 requires 34% of the resources. This is because the lower modes pack less data bits per slot, as shown in Table 3.

It is clear that greater bandwidth efficiency can be achieved when higher MCS modes are used. However, as shown by the SDU loss rate, in order to support QoS for real time video transmission, only lower MCS modes can be successfully used at lower SNR values.

The goodput delivered per OFDMA frame for one ow of data, $G_{\text{o w}}(s, l, m)$, is computed as the correct number of bits received, $CorrectBits$, divided by transmission duration, F_T, in number of OFDMA frames, required for the transmission of N UDP packets. The goodput delivered per OFDMA frame is calculated for each mean channel SNR s, MCS mode m, and block lifetime l, as

$$G_{\text{o w}}(s, l, m) = \frac{CorrectBits(s, l, m)}{F_T(s, l, m) \cdot T_{\text{OFDMA}}}, \qquad (7)$$

where T_{OFDMA} is the duration of an OFDMA frame (i.e., 5 ms).

The average channel capacity, in slots, required for the data ow per OFDMA frame, $\theta_{\text{o w,fr}}$, is calculated as the total number of required physical slots C_T divided by the transmission duration, F_T, for each mean channel SNR s, MCS mode m, and block lifetime l

$$\theta_{\text{o w,fr}}(s, l, m) = \frac{C_T(s, l, m)}{F_T(s, l, m)}. \qquad (8)$$

Therefore, a $\theta_{\text{o w,fr}}$ capacity per DL frame delivers $G_{\text{o w}}$ goodput per frame, for each channel SNR, MCS mode, and block lifetime. The goodput-per-frame efficiency metric measures the goodput $G_{\text{o w}}$ delivered per frame taking into account the average capacity required per frame (in slots), $\theta_{\text{o w,fr}}$. Hence goodput per frame, g_{fr}, is de ned as

$$g_{\text{fr}}(s, l, m) = \frac{G_{\text{o w}}(s, l, m)}{\theta_{\text{o w,fr}}(s, l, m)}. \qquad (9)$$

If the total capacity of the DL frame, S_{fr}, is used, the system can support a total goodput per frame Gdp_{fr}, calculated using (10). The total capacity of a DL frame, S_{fr}, in slots, is a system dependent parameter and for the mobile WiMAX system simulated, assuming a PUSC enabled DL, S_{fr} = 330 slots (Table 1). The system therefore can support a total goodput per frame Gdp_{fr} given by

$$Gdp_{\text{fr}}(s, l, m) = \frac{G_{\text{o w}}(s, l, m) \cdot S_{\text{fr}}}{\theta_{\text{o w,fr}}(s, l, m)}. \qquad (10)$$

Figure 14 shows the total goodput per frame versus channel SNR, estimated for all MCS modes when the block lifetime is 90 ms and the MS speed is 1 km/h. It can be seen that QPSK 1/2 offers the highest transmission efficiency for SNR $\leq$ 10 dB and 16QAM 1/2 for SNR values in the range 10 dB to 16 dB. For higher SNR values 16QAM 3/4 is more efficient. 16QAM 3/4 can support 7-8 Mbps when the mean channel SNR is 18–20 dB. The goodput per frame metric helps identify the most efficient mode per channel SNR for

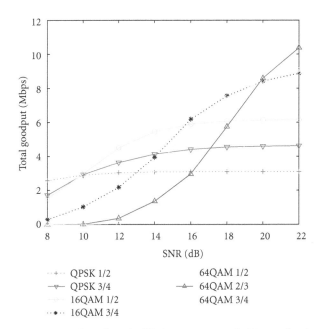

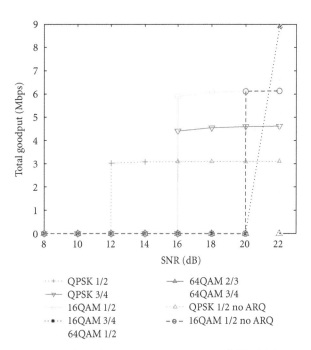

FIGURE 14: Total goodput for lifetime = 90 ms and MS v = 1 km/h.

FIGURE 15: Total goodput versus SNR, PER $\leq 10^{-2}$, block lifetime = 90 ms, and no ARQ, MS v = 1 km/h.

a particular block lifetime. It can also be seen that only lower throughput modes (up to mode 3) are selected for SNR values below 20 dB.

In order to select the most efficient MCS mode that also delivers zero PER, or the PER below a minimum acceptable value (such that video QoS can be guaranteed), a constraint should be applied based on the PER attained at the application layer per channel SNR. Loss of packets can seriously degrade the quality of received video [28, 33]. In the following, UDP PER is constrained to less than 1%. Figure 15 shows the total goodput per frame versus channel SNR, for all MCS modes with UDP PER $\leq 10^{-2}$, when the block lifetime is 90 ms and the MS speed is 1 km/h. If the PER attained for a particular MCS mode and SNR value is higher than 10^{-2}, then the total goodput is set to zero. It is observed that below an SNR value of 12 dB no MCS mode can achieve quasi error free transmission. Therefore, quality unicast video cannot be offered for channel SNR below 12 dB. For SNR values in the range 12 dB to 16 dB only QPSK 1/2 can achieve the desired PER. For SNR values in the range 16 dB to 20 dB the most efficient MCS mode that offers quasi error free transmission is 16QAM 1/2, whereas for SNR = 22 dB mode 64QAM 1/2 offers the highest transmission efficiency, for a PER below 10^{-2}. In Figure 15, the total goodput attained for multicast transmission (no ARQ enabled) is also shown. The multicast transmission also observes the PER $\leq 10^{-2}$ constraint. It can be seen that the multicast video service cannot be offered quasi error free for SNR values below about 16 dB. For SNR values in the range 16 dB to 18 dB only QPSK 1/2 can achieve the desired PER. For SNR values in the range 20 dB to 22 dB mode 16QAM 1/2 offers the highest transmission efficiency while keeping the PER below 10^{-2}. This comparison shows that using ARQ with a block lifetime of 90 ms offers a signi cant gain of approximately 3 Mbps (i.e., double the goodput) for

16 dB $\leq$ SNR $\leq$ 18 dB and a gain of 2.8 Mbps at a channel SNR of 22 dB. Also the range of the service is extended by approximately 4 dB when ARQ is enabled with a block lifetime of 90 ms.

7. Conclusions

From the simulation results presented in this work, it has been possible to study the performance of different MCS modes and block lifetimes for various channel SNR values in a mobile broadband network. The performance of ARQ retransmissions was shown to depend on the MS velocity. It was shown that at walking speeds (e.g., 1 km/h) ARQ retransmissions are less efficient. Only mode 0 succeeds in delivering data with PER $\leq 10^{-2}$ for 12 $\leq$ SNR < 16 dB, and only modes 1 and 2 for SNR $\leq$ 20 dB, with up to 4 retransmissions. The SER attained is lower for the same MCS mode, block lifetime and channel SNR, when the channel coherence time is short.

It was demonstrated that a channel-aware and ARQ-aware scheduler should be used in order to predict and provide sufficient resources per frame for delay sensitive services, such as real-time video. The novel efficiency metric, goodput per frame, has enabled a performance comparison in terms of PER achieved and radio resources required when S-ACK ARQ is enabled, for various MCS modes. This efficiency metric showed the total goodput that each MCS mode could support for each channel SNR for a given block lifetime. The goodput per frame metric was found to be a valuable tool for radio resource management in broadband wireless networks.

Insight has been gained on the importance of the ARQ Retry Timeout MAC parameter and how it affects system performance, not only in terms of SDU delay, but PER as well. When practical considerations are taken into account regarding the frequency and number of possible retransmissions based on the WiMAX Forum recommendations, only modes 0, 1, and 2 can deliver quasi error free data. Jitter in these cases is maintained within acceptable limits for video QoS. However, the lower modes, 0 and 2, that attain quasi error free transmission, require 35% and 18% of the total channel resources, correspondingly, to successfully deliver video at 1.03 Mbps quasi error free. The total goodput attained is 3Mbps for SNR ≤ 16 dB (with MCS mode 0) and 6 Mbps for channel SNR values in the range 16 dB to 20 dB (with MCS mode 2). A quality unicast video service cannot be offered for channel SNR values below 12 dB.

Multicasting real-time video, while observing a QoS without ARQ retransmissions, is ineffective below about 16 dB SNR. Additional error correction mechanisms are necessary in order to support high quality multicast video, such as the Application Layer Forward Error Correction (FEC) mechanism based on Raptor codes, endorsed by the 3GPP MBMS [34].

References

[1] *IEEE Standard for Local and metropolitan area networks part 16: 802.16*, IEEE Std., 2006.

[2] LTE, *Evolved Universal Terrestrial Radio Access (E-UTRA) and Evolved Universal Terrestrial Radio Access Network (E-UTRAN); Overall description; Stage 2 (3GPP TS 36.300 version 10.5.0 Release 10)*, 3GPP Std., http://www.3gpp.org/ftp/Specs/html-info/36300.htm.

[3] O. Oyman, J. Foerster, Y. J. Tcha, and S. C. Lee, "Toward enhanced mobile video services over WiMAX and LTE," *IEEE Communications Magazine*, vol. 48, no. 8, pp. 68–76, 2010.

[4] I. Cerutti, F. Meucci, P. Castoldi, and L. Pierucci, "An adaptive cross-layer strategy for QoS-guaranteed links in 4G networks," in *Proceedings of the IEEE Global Telecommunications Conference (GLOBECOM '08)*, pp. 1–5, New Orleans, La, USA, December 2008.

[5] H. Martikainen, A. Sayenko, O. Alanen, and V. Tykhomyrov, "Optimal MAC PDU size in IEEE 802.16," in *Proceedings of the 4th International Telecommunication Networking Workshop on QoS in Multiservice IP Networks (IT-NEWS '08)*, pp. 66–71, Venice, Italy, February 2008.

[6] A. Sayenko, V. Tykhomyrov, H. Martikainen, and O. Alanen, "Performance analysis of the IEEE 802.16 ARQ mechanism," in *Proceedings of the 10th ACM Symposium on Modeling, Analysis, and Simulation of Wireless and Mobile Systems (MSWiM '07)*, pp. 314–322, ACM, October 2007.

[7] F. Hou, J. She, P. H. Ho, and X. Shen, "Performance analysis of ARQ with opportunistic scheduling in IEEE 802.16 networks," in *Proceedings of the 50th Annual IEEE Global Telecommunications Conference (GLOBECOM '07)*, pp. 4759–4763, Washington, DC, USA, November 2007.

[8] W. Wang, Z. Guo, X. Shen, and C. Chen, "Performance analysis of ARQ scheme in IEEE 802.16," in *Proceedings of the IEEE Global Telecommunications Conference (GLOBECOM '06)*, pp. 1–5, San Francisco, Calif, USA, December 2006.

[9] W. Wang, Z. Guo, X. Shen, C. Chen, and J. Cai, "Dynamic bandwidth allocation for QoS provisioning in IEEE 802.16 networks with ARQ-SA," *IEEE Transactions on Wireless Communications*, vol. 7, no. 9, pp. 3477–3487, 2008.

[10] M. Chatterjee, S. Sengupta, and S. Ganguly, "Feedback-based real-time streaming over WiMax," *IEEE Wireless Communications*, vol. 14, no. 1, pp. 64–71, 2007.

[11] W. Jianfeng, M. Venkatachalam, and F. Yuguang, "System architecture and cross-layer optimization of video broadcast over WiMAX," *IEEE Journal on Selected Areas in Communications*, vol. 25, no. 4, pp. 712–721, 2007.

[12] C. So-In, R. Jain, and A. K. Tamimi, "Scheduling in IEEE 802.16e mobile WiMAX networks: key issues and a survey," *IEEE Journal on Selected Areas in Communications*, vol. 27, no. 2, pp. 156–171, 2009.

[13] A. Sayenko, O. Alanen, and T. Hämäläinen, "ARQ aware scheduling for the IEEE 802.16 base station," in *Proceedings of the IEEE International Conference on Communications (ICC '08)*, pp. 2667–2673, Beijing, China, May 2008.

[14] S. Deb, S. Jaiswal, and K. Nagaraj, "Real-time video multicast in WiMAX networks," in *Proceedings of the 27th IEEE Communications Society Conference on Computer Communications (INFOCOM '08)*, pp. 1579–1587, Phoenix, Ariz, USA, April 2008.

[15] *3GPP TR 25.996 V6.1.0 Spatial channel model for Multiple Input Multiple Output (MIMO) simulations (Release 6)*, 3GPP Std., 2009.

[16] Mobile System Pro le, *WMF-T23-001-R010v09*, WiMAX Forum Std., 2010.

[17] *IEEE 802.16m Evaluation Methodology Document (EMD) IEEE 802.16m-08/004r5*, IEEE 802.16 Broadband Wireless Access Working Group Std., 2009, http://ieee802.org/16.

[18] V. Sgardoni, D. Halls, S. M. M. Bokhari, D. Bull, and A. Nix, "Mobile WiMAX video quality and transmission efficiency," in *Proceedings of the IEEE 22nd International Symposium on Personal Indoor and Mobile Radio Communications (PIMRC '11)*, pp. 1077–1082, September 2011.

[19] A. Esmailpour and N. Nasser, "Dynamic QoS-based bandwidth allocation framework for broadband wireless networks," *IEEE Transactions on Vehicular Technology*, vol. 60, no. 6, pp. 2690–2700, 2011.

[20] *IEEE Standard for Local and metropolitan area networks part 16: Air Interface for Broadband WirelessAccess Systems 802.16-2009*, IEEE Std., 2009.

[21] *Mobile WiMAX—part I: A Technical Overview and Performance Evaluation*, WiMAX Forum Std., 2006.

[22] L. Wan, S. Tsai, and M. Almgren, "A fading-insensitive performance metric for a uni ed link quality model," in *Proceedings of the IEEE Wireless Communications and Networking Conference (WCNC '06)*, pp. 2110–2114, April 2006.

[23] D. Halls, A. Nix, and M. Beach, "System level evaluation of UL and DL interference in OFDMA mobile broadband networks," in *Proceedings of the IEEE Wireless Communications and Networking Conference (WCNC '11)*, pp. 1271–1276, Quintana Roo, Mexico, March 2011.

[24] V. Sgardoni, P. Ferré, A. Doufexi, A. Nix, and D. Bull, "Frame delay and loss analysis for video transmission over time-correlated 802.11A/G channels," in *Proceedings of the 18th Annual IEEE International Symposium on Personal, Indoor and Mobile Radio Communications (PIMRC '07)*, pp. 1–5, Athens, Greece, September 2007.

[25] M. Tran, D. Halls, A. Nix, A. Doufexi, and M. Beach, "Mobile WiMAX: MIMO performance analysis from a quality of service (QoS) viewpoint," in *Proceedings of the IEEE Wireless Communications and Networking Conference (WCNC '09)*, pp. 1–6, Budapest, Hungary, April 2009.

[26] C. Cicconetti, A. Erta, L. Lenzini, and E. Mingozzi, "Performance evaluation of the IEEE 802.16 MAC for QoS support," *IEEE Transactions on Mobile Computing*, vol. 6, no. 1, pp. 26–38, 2007.

[27] "video test sequences," http://media.xiph.org/video/derf/.

[28] H. Jenkac, T. Stockhammer, and G. Liebl, "H.264/AVC video transmission over MBMS in GERAN," in *Proceedings of the IEEE 6th Workshop on Multimedia Signal Processing*, pp. 191–194, October 2004.

[29] T. Stockhammer and M. M. Hannuksela, "H.264/AVC video for wireless transmission," *IEEE Wireless Communications*, vol. 12, no. 4, pp. 6–13, 2005.

[30] M. Baldi and Y. Ofek, "End-to-end delay analysis of videoconferencing over packet-switched networks," *IEEE/ACM Transactions on Networking*, vol. 8, no. 4, pp. 479–492, 2000.

[31] S. Liang and D. Cheriton, "TCP-RTM: using TCP for real time multimedia applications," in *International Conference on Network Protocols*, 2002.

[32] WiMAX Forum Air Interface Speci cations, *WiMAX Forum Mobile System Profile, Release 1.0, WMF-T23- 001-R010v09*, WiMAX Forum Std., 2007.

[33] D. Wu, Y. T. Hou, and Y. Q. Zhang, "Transporting real-time video over the Internet: challenges and approaches," *Proceedings of the IEEE*, vol. 88, no. 12, pp. 1855–1877, 2000.

[34] *3GPP TS 26.346 V8.0.0 (2008-10) Universal Mobile Telecommunications System (UMTS); Multimedia Broadcast/Multicast Service (MBMS); Protocols and codecs*, ETSI Std., 2008.

10

Available Bandwidth Estimation in Network-Aware Applications for Wireless Campus e-Learning System

Mohd Faisal Ibrahim,[1] Masita Jamal,[1] Saadiah Yahya,[1] and Mohd Nasir Taib[2]

[1] *Faculty of Computer and Mathematical Sciences, Universiti Teknologi MARA, 40450 Shah Alam, Malaysia*
[2] *Faculty of Electrical Engineering, Universiti Teknologi MARA, 40450 Shah Alam, Malaysia*

Correspondence should be addressed to Mohd Faisal Ibrahim, faisal@tmsk.uitm.edu.my

Academic Editor: Youyun Xu

The constraint of a wireless network has motivated many researchers to develop network-aware applications that can dynamically adjust the users' demand based on network resources. For this to happen, applications need to have some mechanism that can estimate the network bandwidth by simply adjusting their behavior based on the collected network characteristics information. In the past, there have been several proposals that provide passive and active bandwidth estimation approaches for wired and wireless network. However, little effort has been spent to address the crucial issues of reliability and congestion control especially in a wireless network environment, which stay as a sticking point for the success of network-aware application. This paper focuses on providing accurate, low-intrusiveness, and fast-convergence time bandwidth estimation for network-aware application architecture. The experimental results validate the efficiency of the proposed solution in terms of accuracy, intrusiveness, and timelines.

1. Introduction

Wireless local area networks (WLANs) are becoming more widely used in homes, offices, public facilities, and university campuses. Recently, the focus is to establish Wi-Fi hotspots in convention centers, airports, shopping malls, hotels, public libraries, and cafes in which people can access email, download attachments, browse web sites or establish VPN connections to corporate networks while on the move. WLANs can be implemented as an extension or alternative for a wired LAN within a building or campus. As the number of hotspot locations is increasing, academic and industrial research have started to think of applications that can effectively utilize the network, which in return could satisfy their users' demands for reliable wireless Internet or web access. This trend has initiated the needs of network-aware applications that can dynamically adapt the users' demands to match the varying supply of network resources.

In order to make it possible for the user to use suitable application or download appropriate file based on the current bandwidth condition, the application must be aware of network resource availability which is also known as network-aware application. With the exception of [1, 2], most of the approaches are directed mostly towards conceptual framework or have been pursued to address network-aware application issues for wired network. Furthermore, network-aware applications in wireless networks are difficult to develop [3] and implement due to the fact that bandwidth estimation techniques can be affected by reception signal strength [4], path loss [4], fading [4], interference [5], resource sharing [5, 6], and fluctuating nature [6–8]. This results in imprecise estimates with high convergence times and intrusiveness.

In this paper, we incorporate active available bandwidth estimation technique to our proposed network-aware application architecture for e-learning system. To address accuracy, convergence, and intrusiveness issues, we employ WBest algorithm to deal with the significant quality fluctuations, performance degradation, and weak connectivity of wireless network.

The rest of the paper is structured as follows. Section 2 describes bandwidth estimation, packet dispersion techniques, WBest algorithm, and related works. Section 3 explains the architecture of NApEL, and Section 4 clarifies the goals and usage scenario of NApEL. Section 5 examines the experimental results. Finally, we briefly discuss future work and conclude in Section 6.

2. Preliminaries

2.1. Bandwidth Estimation. End-to-end measurement of bandwidth-related metrics is referred to as bandwidth estimation. Its features consist of capacity, available bandwidth, and bulk TCP transfer capacity. Within this paper, the term available bandwidth (AB) refers to the maximum unused bandwidth at a link or end-to-end path in a network. AB depends on the link capacity and the traffic load during a certain time period. In a given hop i the available bandwidth A_i of end-to-end link during time interval $(t; t + \tau)$ is given by the unutilized part of the capacity:

$$A_i(t, t + \tau) = \frac{1}{\tau} C_i \int_t^{t+\tau} [1 - \lambda i(t)] dt, \qquad (1)$$

where λ_i is the average utilization of hop i in the given time interval, and C_i is the capacity of hop i. By considering the available bandwidth definition to an n number of hops in a path the available bandwidth of the end-to-end path A will be the minimum available bandwidth of all n hops:

$$A(t, t + \tau) = \min_{i=1...n} \{A_i(t, t + \tau)\}. \qquad (2)$$

The term tight link of a network path is employed to illustrate the minimum available bandwidth along the path and the term narrow link is used to portray the minimum capacity of the end-to-end path.

2.2. Packet Dispersion Techniques. There has been several bandwidth estimation techniques such as packet dispersion, probe gap model, and self-loading periodic streams aimed at measuring the end-to-end available bandwidth of a network path. Since in our solution we employ WBest algorithm [4], packet dispersion techniques will be discussed in detail in this section.

Figure 1 illustrates the basic concept of packet dispersion. Packet train probing sends packet train of length N with the same back-to-back packets of size L to travel into the network. After the packet traverses the narrow link C_i, the receiver measures the time spacing between the arrival of the first packet and the arrival of the last packet as follows:

$$b(N) = (N - 1) \times \frac{L}{\Delta(N)}, \qquad (3)$$

where $b(N)$ is the bandwidth estimate, N is the length of the packet train, L is the size of each packet, and $\Delta(N)$ is the difference in time between (dispersion) the first packet and the final packet of the train.

The probe packet size can significantly affect the performance of the bandwidth estimation [9]. Sending larger packets will lead to a wider dispersion and can cause additional traffic. However, if packets are small, the estimation tends to be overrating because of shorter dispersion times [10].

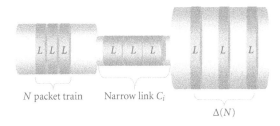

FIGURE 1: Illustration of bandwidth estimation using packet train probing.

---

(1) Send n packet pairs to client
(2) $C_e \leftarrow \text{median}(C_i), \quad i = 1, \dots, n$
(3) Send m packet train at rate C_e to Client
(4) $R \leftarrow L/\text{mean}(T_i), \quad (i = 1, \dots, m - 1)$
(5) **If** $R \geq C_e/2$ then AB $\Leftarrow C_e [2 - C_e/R]$
(6) **Else** AB $\Leftarrow 0$
(7) $p \Leftarrow$ packet loss rate in train
(8) **if** $p > 0$ then AB $\Leftarrow$ AB $\times (1 - p)$

ALGORITHM 1: WBest algorithm.

2.3. WBest Algorithm. This section briefly describes the WBest algorithm that estimates the available bandwidth of an end-to-end path. A more detail information regarding WBest can be found in [4]. The WBest algorithm, summarized in Algorithm 1, has two phases: effective capacity measurement phase and available bandwidth estimation phase. In the first phase, a packet pair technique estimates the effective capacity of the wireless network. In the second phase a packet train scheme determines achievable throughput and infers available bandwidth.

2.3.1. Effective Capacity Measurement Phase. During the effective capacity measurement phase, the algorithm sends n packet pairs to estimate the effective capacity C_e. In order to minimize the impact of crossing and contending traffic, the median of the n packet pair capacity estimates is used to approximate C_e in the estimation time period:

$$C_e = \text{median}(C_i), \quad i = 1, \dots, n. \qquad (4)$$

This will allow the algorithm to capture the impact of rate adaptation measurements of effective capacity.

2.3.2. Available Bandwidth Estimation Phase. For the second phase of the algorithm (lines (3–8)), the available bandwidth is estimated by sending m packet train at rate C_e. The available bandwidth AB can be derived by using the following equation:

$$AB \Leftarrow C_e \left[2 - \frac{C_e}{R} \right], \qquad (5)$$

where R is the average dispersion rate at the receiver.

For a wireless network, achievable throughput is the average dispersion rate at the receiver for a probing rate of C_e [11]. If the achievable throughput is greater or equal to half of C_e then the AB can be calculated by using (5), otherwise the AB is zero. A suitable pair of packet pairs and trains will be removed from the computation once WBest algorithm identifies a packet loss in order to reduce estimation errors and convergence time. Loss rate p will be recorded in each packet train to reduce the available bandwidth estimation (lines (7–8) of Algorithm 1).

2.4. Related Work. This section describes previous work in bandwidth estimation and network-aware application. Research in these two areas has become increasingly widespread in recent years. As our work stresses the need for a web application to be sensitive to the dynamic network conditions, some of the previous works have concentrated mainly on bandwidth estimation algorithms. The efforts have been strongly oriented towards either proposing improvements to bandwidth estimation algorithm specific to wired or wireless networks.

For example, pathload [12], TOPP [13, 14], pathChirp [15], and PTR [16] present the end-to-end AB estimations for wired networks. They are based on self-loading techniques, including the Self-loading Periodic Streams (SLoPS) [12] and Train of Packet Pairs (TOPP) [13, 14], which applies multiple rate traffic, linearly increased probing rate, or exponentially increased probing rate. In SLoPS, if a flow is inserted that induces a temporal congestion in the bottleneck link of the path, the input and the output probing packet rate can be compared in order to find the ABW.

Other methods such as IGI [16], Spruce [17], and Delphi [18], use Probe Gap Model (PGM) to estimate the AB. This technique calculates the cross-traffic rate by measuring the time gap between the arrivals of two successive probes at the receiver and then estimates the AB indirectly.

However, these probe-based techniques provide unreliable bandwidth estimation for wireless network [19, 20], due to the characteristics of wireless networks such as contention, link layer retransmissions, fading, and interference. Furthermore, these estimation methods presume that they are dealing with an unvarying characteristic of wired networks, which does not apply to wireless networks due to the shared physical medium, unreliable nature of the transmission medium, and the multiaccess coordination function.

Nevertheless, all these existing bandwidth estimation techniques have been the basis for many wireless bandwidth estimators such as SenProbe [21], AdhocProbe [22, 23], WBest [4], DietTOPP [9], and SLOT [24]. AdhocProbe and SenProbe are an end-to-end path capacity estimation tools for ad hoc and wireless sensor networks.

SLOT, combines two packet probing techniques which are SLoPS and TOPP. The estimated AB is obtained by implementing two different probing strategies which are linear (incremental) and binary (dichotomy).

Another method, DietTOPP, determines the AB by modifying and reducing TOPP search algorithm. Although this technique improves accuracy, it does not consider convergence time and intrusiveness.

WBest measures the effective capacity and available bandwidth of wireless networks by utilizing packet dispersion techniques. It uses a two-step estimation algorithm: (1) the effective capacity estimation based on a packet pair technique and (2) the achievable throughput and available bandwidth estimation based on a packet train technique.

A lot of effort has been spent in the field of network-aware application to address the issues of heterogeneity and bandwidth variations of pervasive web environment. Some of the works such as Bolliger and T. Gross [25], Bates et al. [26], and Tierney et al. [27] were aimed towards architecture or conceptual framework of network-aware application. Transend [28] is a proxy-based architecture, employing so-called distillation services, that automatically converts image formats (e.g., from TIFF format to JPEG) or adjusts the image by reducing the resolution or color depth based on a given client's network bandwidth. Odyssey [1] provides adaptation for mobile information access application that adapts to changing network environments. It was designed to cope with network heterogeneity and dynamic changes of wireless environments [29]. However, the adaptation strategy in Odyssey is not suitable for Internet-based hosts and the approach is towards passive measurements rather than active Mobiware [2], which is based on CORBA and Java distributed object technology, and is a middleware toolkit that supports the adaptation of applications to varying mobile network conditions.

Although Odyssey and Mobiware have shown promise in providing a network-aware application solution that can adapt to mobile devices' network constraints, they have not taken into consideration the tradeoffs of bandwidth estimation approach with respect to timeliness, accuracy, and overhead in real systems. The usefulness of bandwidth estimator for the needs of network-aware applications rests on the accuracy of the information. This is important because accurate AB estimation will be very useful especially for applications that have critical response time requirements.

If an application wants to adjust to network changes by adapting the content, it is important to make sure that the AB estimation is accurate. The intrusiveness and convergence time required for bandwidth estimation process are also important because the time taken to estimate the AB and the probing packet sent to the network traffic should be low [30].

3. Architecture—NApEL

In this section we elaborate on the architectural design of the network-aware applications for E-Learning System (NApEL). The term "network-aware applications" refers to the capability to monitor network conditions such as available bandwidth, network capacity, packet loss rate, and delay that can be used by the application to adjust their behavior to best utilize the network resources availability [25, 31]. It can be divided into two parts which are network awareness and network adaptation. Network awareness implies the capability of the web application to monitor network conditions and

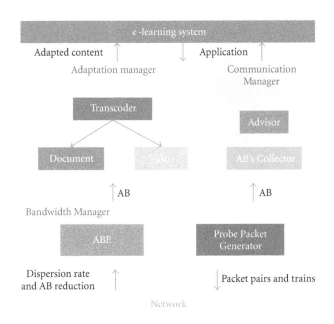

FIGURE 2: Architectural overview of Network-Aware Application for e-Learning System (NApEL).

network adaptation refers to the ability of utilizing network resources and optimizing content delivery.

The architecture of NApEL is illustrated in Figure 2, contains three important components which are Adaptation Manager, Communication Manager, and Bandwidth Manager. These components are explained in what follows in more detail.

3.1. Bandwidth Manager.

This section presents an overview of the Bandwidth Manager and its two components, the Probe Packet Generator (PPGen) and Available Bandwidth Estimator (ABE). We will explain how PPGen sends network probes to capture raw estimation data and then how ABE collects these data to estimate available bandwidth. We have customized WBest in order to deploy ABE in NApEL. To automate the bandwidth estimation loops, we added the loop command *for (Loop=0; loop < MaxLoop; loop++)* in *wbest_snd.c*. This instruction will get the maximum number of loops *MaxLoop* as well as the IP address (*hostname*) of the sender node *SND* from a text file. Then *SND* starts to establish connection with the receiver node *RCV* by executing this command: "*./wbest_rcv -s %s*", *hostname*. To change the packet probe size, we altered the *i_PktNumbPP* and *i_PktNumbPT* variables in wbest_snd.c file. The main idea of ABE is to supply information regarding the AB to users or applications in a database server which can be accessed by the web server. Therefore, we have modified some parts of the original code to allow AB estimation results to be stored in the database.

3.1.1. Available Bandwidth Estimator (ABE).

The main function of ABE is to provide the information regarding the end-to-end available bandwidth estimation. ABE will use the average dispersion rate R and the available bandwidth reduction S values obtained from PPGen to estimate available bandwidth.

3.1.2. Probe Packet Generator (PPGen).

PPGen is responsible for sending at an effective capacity (C_e) rate, a packet train of length m to estimate available bandwidth. C_e is defined as follows:

$$C_e = \frac{\int_{t_0}^{t_1} (L/T(t))dt}{t_1 - t_0},$$ (6)

where $T(t)$ is the dispersion time t between packets and L is the packet size.

3.2. Communication Manager

3.2.1. Advisor.

The purpose of Advisor in Communication Manager is to give some suggestions on suitable communication tool to be used by users based on network condition. A dialog box will come up on user's screen whenever Advisor's recommendation is invoked. If the available bandwidth is low, a user can decide whether to still choose the same communication tool or not.

3.2.2. AB's Collector.

The function of AB's Collector is to collect all information concerning each AP's network condition by performing a system call to periodically obtain up-to-date bandwidth information

3.3. Adaptation Manager.

When Adaptation Manager receives available bandwidth information from Bandwidth Manager, it simply calls the transcoder to transcode the content and generates the adapted content. An open-source FFMPEG tool version 0.8.2 is used for transcoding and it is running under aWindows XP machine. Currently, the transcoding process is being implemented by utilizing the knowledge of the network characteristics only.

4. Goals and Usage Scenario of NApEL in Campus Learning Environment

The NApEL project has been developed at the faculty of Computer and Mathematical Sciences, Universiti Teknologi MARA, in order to provide a prototype which could demonstrate how the architecture can be implemented. With the intention of introducing the goals of NApEL, in this section we present the scenario to describe the requirements of network-aware applications and demonstrate an application of the scenario.

Melissa is working on a class project together with her other friends Sam and Natasha. All of them agree to meet at the cafeteria for aquick project discussion at 10 am. Upon arrival, she discovered that her friends have not yet arrived. So, she grabs her notebook and connects to NApEL through access point 1. She needs to check the status of "who is online now" (Figure 3) to see whether Sam and Natasha are connecting to NApEL because she suspects that both of

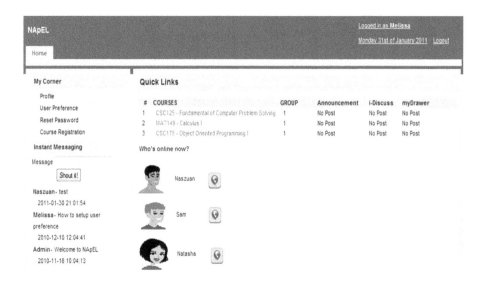

FIGURE 3: NApEL user interface. We have integrated Skype into NApEL. Each Skype user on a PC, notebook, or PDA can send messages to other Skype users and check online or offline presence of these users in real time.

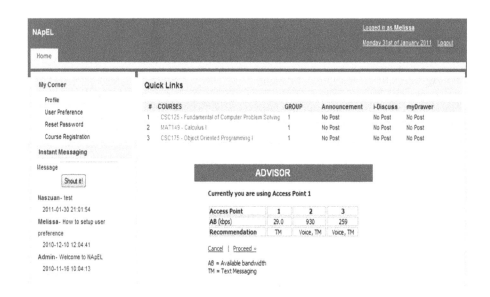

FIGURE 4: NApEL provides a mechanism for detecting insufficient bandwidth and providing recommendation on suitable communication tools to be used based on available bandwidth.

them forget about this meeting. When she opens NApEL, she sees that both of her friends are online now. She decided to contact Natasha using VOIP. Unfortunately, bandwidth is miserable because many students at the cafeteria are surfing the web using AP1. NApEL observes that at the current bandwidth Melissa will not be able to communicate with Natasha smoothly. By checking other APs nearby, NApEL discovers that wireless bandwidth is excellent at AP2, and if Melissa still wants to communicate through AP1 she can still use text messaging. A dialog box (Figure 4) pops up on Melissa's screen suggesting that she can still use AP1 if she wants to communicate through text messaging or go to AP2 if she still prefers VOIP. Melissa accepts NApEL's advice and

connects her notebook to AP2. She realizes that the avail-able bandwidth at AP2 is more than 900 Kbps. She manages to contact Natasha and ask her to quickly come to the cafeteria.

5. Experimental Design and Results

The goal of our experiments is to quantify how effectively NApEL platforms are able to track the dynamic rate adaptation of highly varying characteristics of wireless network in a timely and accurate manner. In addition, we quantify the effectiveness of the platforms under reproducible and controllable conditions for different traffic loads in order to ensure a fair comparison. We describe the network test-beds, the evaluation metrics, the experimental setup, and validation methodology used for our experiments. We have performed several experiments to validate our proposed method. The first aims at comparing the ABE result with passive monitoring tools. The second experiment is to determine whether the fleet of packet trains sent will stress the network. The third experiment is to evaluate how long does it take for ABE to have the estimation.

5.1. Performance Metrics. The usefulness of bandwidth estimation algorithm for network-aware adaptation relies on the accuracy of the estimation, the convergence time, and intrusiveness. In order to measure the accurateness of the bandwidth estimation, ABE error is computed as the difference between the actual bandwidth AB measured using passive monitoring technique and the estimated AB. We also used relative error given below to evaluate the accurateness of the AB:

$$\text{Rel}_{\text{Error}} = \frac{\text{AB}_{\text{estimated}} - \text{AB}_{\text{actual}}}{\text{AB}_{\text{actual}}}, \tag{7}$$

where $\text{AB}_{\text{estimated}}$ is the available bandwidth estimates generated by ABE, and $\text{AB}_{\text{actual}}$ is the actual available bandwidth detected by WRM.

In the evaluation of ABE, one of the main interests is intrusiveness. The intrusiveness of bandwidth estimation expresses to what extent its heavy packets probing affects the existing network traffic. In other words, low intrusiveness is vital for decreasing the impact initiated by the probing traffic. We defined intrusiveness as follows:

$$\text{Intrusive}_{\text{BEM}(\%)} = \frac{T_{\text{ABE}}}{\text{AB}} \times 100, \tag{8}$$

where AB is the actual bandwidth available identified by WRM and T_{ABE} is the amount of traffics (in bits) sent by ABE during probing time.

Convergence time is the total estimation time used by ABE to complete an estimation.

5.2. Experimental Setup. We verify the measured available bandwidth by comparing it with WRM [32] and by measuring how ABE responds to induce changes in available bandwidth. Both ABE and WRM use the same machines.

It is essential to use test traffic that closely simulates traffic on real networks and reproduces its most critical characteristics. In our study we conducted two series of laboratory experiments using Nuttcp to generate and send different volume of contending traffic to the network. The dynamic traffic conditions that typify actual wireless links are being replicated under varying levels of traffic load from 0%, 25%, 50%, and 75%.

5.3. Testbed Topology. A laboratory testbed was set up in order to evaluate the ability and efficiency of the proposed ABE to compute the available bandwidth. The testbed topology is shown in Figure 5. It contains two PCs (PC1 and PC2)

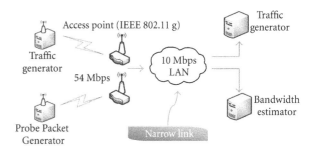

FIGURE 5: 10 Mbps single hop tight link.

running Nuttcp traffic generator to produce controllable synthetic cross-traffic and two Dell Dimension PCs (PC3 and PC4) running under Ubuntu 7.08 which are used as the sender and the receiver to generate probe traffic. The stream which originated in PC5 is sent to PC6 and PC5 is wirelessly connected to the AP by means of a 54 Mbps WiFi segment and PC6 is directly connected using a 10BaseT network connection to the same AP.

5.4. Experimental Results

5.4.1. Accuracy. From Figure 6, we observe that as we decrease the packet pairs and trains to 15, the relative error are higher for 25%, 50%, and 75% cross traffic. Packet pairs and trains of 30 and 45 provide more accurate estimation. We realize that the estimation algorithm depends on the size of packet pairs and trains as what have been discovered by [33]. As the number of packets decreases, accuracy will also decrease.

5.4.2. Intrusiveness. The intrusiveness of ABE is assessed on its capacity of generating a result while transferring the minimum amount of additional traffic. The main aim of this experiment is to determine whether the total amount of probing bytes generated by ABE causes a considerable decline in the AB. Figure 7 shows the results of a 60-minute experiment, performed similarly with the experiment 1. As expected, sending 15 packet pairs and trains will make the ABE intrusiveness decreases. When we used 30 and 45 packet pairs and trains, the intrusiveness was between 5 to 17% for all traffic loads. This indicates that even if we use 30 or 45 packet pairs and trains, ABE can still be considered as nonintrusive because the average probing traffic rate does not encompass a substantial load on the network during the measurement process. This result is in agreement with Prasad et al.'s [34] finding which suggests that ABE is noninvasive.

5.4.3. Convergence Time. Figure 8 depicts, respectively, the result of convergence time for each traffic load with packet pairs and trains of 15, 30, and 45. The results show that on average if we use 30 packet pairs and trains, we can effectively achieve the convergence time between 0.3 to 0.4 seconds. ABE requires a short convergence time due to the fact that WBest algorithm estimates the available bandwidth without using searching algorithms [4]. Furthermore, according to

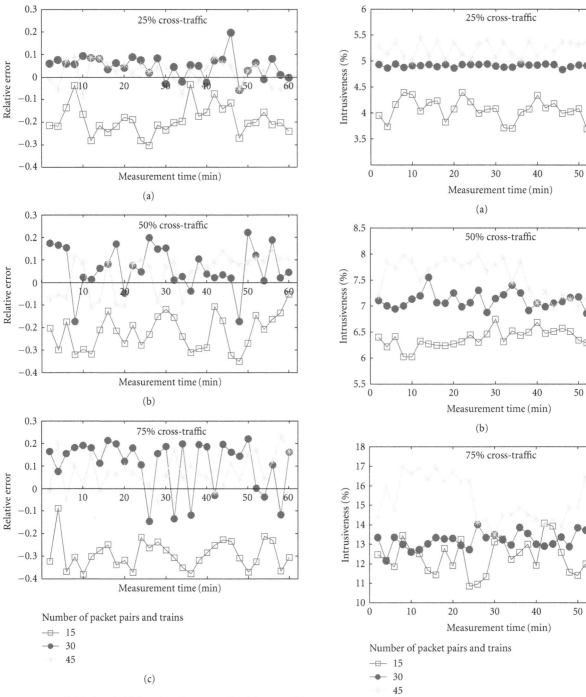

FIGURE 6: Available bandwidth estimation error for (a) 25%, (b) 50%, and (c) 75% cross-traffic.

FIGURE 7: Intrusiveness for (a) 25%, (b) 50%, and (c) 75% cross-traffic.

[4] this algorithm does not rely on delay measurements to measure the AB which in return will make it more robust and yield accurate results with lower convergence times and intrusiveness.

6. Conclusion

This paper proposes the NApEL architecture for wireless campus e-learning system that includes an end-to-end available bandwidth estimation module called ABE. It allows bandwidth estimator algorithm to be executed separately from applications, tracks the network bandwidth, and then sends this information to web applications. We have conducted several experiments to estimate the effectiveness of available bandwidth based on accuracy, intrusiveness, and convergence time by investigating how it reacts when the cross traffic is present on the single hop narrow links. Based

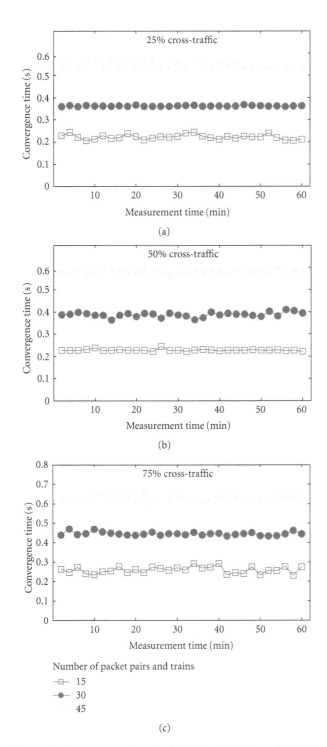

Number of packet pairs and trains
- □ 15
- ● 30
  45

(c)

FIGURE 8: Convergence time for (a) 25%, (b) 50%, and (c) 75% cross-traffic.

on the experiments, the estimations are very close to the passive measurement with low probe packets generation and probing time.

Future research activity will aim at providing adapted content not only according to the network resources constraints but also device capabilities limitations. The limitation of mobile devices such as processing power, screen size, small memory, and storage should be considered when

developing and implementing network-aware applications so that appropriate content can be delivered and presented in any heterogeneous devices.

Finally, it is interesting to notice that the network-aware adaptation approach described in this paper could further strengthen the advantages and benefits of network-aware application over wireless campus environment in terms of the utilization of mobile application, multimedia content, and network resources. One of the main reasons of deploying this approach is to improve users' productivity by optimizing the utilization of resources. Our work here is towards providing the wireless campus communities to access multimedia content anywhere, anytime, and on any device.

References

[1] B. D. Noble, M. Satyanarayanan, D. Narayanan, J. E. Tilton, J. Flinn, and K. R. Walker, "Agile application-aware adaptation for mobility," in *Proceedings of the 16th ACM Symposium on Operating Systems and Principles*, pp. 276–287, 1997.

[2] O. Angin, A. T. Campbell, M. E. Kounavis, and R. R. F. Liao, "The mobiware toolkit: programmable support for adaptive mobile networking," *IEEE Personal Communications*, vol. 5, no. 4, pp. 32–43, 1998.

[3] M. Kim and B. Noble, "Mobile network estimation," in *Proceedings of the 7th Annual International Conference on Mobile Computing and Networking*, pp. 298–309, July 2001.

[4] M. Li, M. Claypool, and R. Kinicki, "WBest: a bandwidth estimation tool for IEEE 802.11 wireless networks," in *Proceedings of the 33rd IEEE Conference on Local Computer Networks (LCN '08)*, pp. 374–381, October 2008.

[5] H. Zhao, E. Garcia-Palacios, J. Wei, and Y. Xi, "Accurate available bandwidth estimation in IEEE 802.11-based ad hoc networks," *Computer Communications*, vol. 32, no. 6, pp. 1050–1057, 2009.

[6] S. Tursunova, K. Inoyatov, and Y. T. Kim, "Cognitive passive estimation of available bandwidth (cPEAB) in overlapped ieee 802.11 WiFi WLANs," in *Proceedings of the 12th IEEE/IFIP Network Operations and Management Symposium (NOMS '10)*, pp. 448–454, April 2010.

[7] T. Nadeem, "Network-aware applications in wireless networks," in *Proceedings of the 2nd Workshop on Research Directions in Situational-aware Self-managed Proactive Computing in Wireless Adhoc Networks*, 2009.

[8] K. Lee, "Adaptive network support for mobile multimedia," in *Proceedings of the 1st Annual International Conference on Mobile Computing and Networking*, pp. 62–74, November 1995.

[9] A. Johnsson, B. Melander, and M. Björkman, "Bandwidth measurement in wireless networks," in *Proceedings of the 4th Annual Mediterranean Ad Hoc Networking Workshop*, 2005.

[10] C. Dovrolis, P. Ramanathan, and D. Moore, "Packet-dispersion techniques and a capacity-estimation methodology," *IEEE/ACM Transactions on Networking*, vol. 12, no. 6, pp. 963–977, 2004.

[11] M. Li, M. Claypool, and R. Kinicki, "Modeling and simulating packet dispersion in wireless 802.11 networks," Tech. Rep. WPI-CS-TR-06-03, Computer Science Department at Worcester Polytechnic Institute, 2006.

[12] M. Jain and C. Dovrolis, "End-to-end available bandwidth: measurement methodology, dynamics, and relation with TCP

throughput," *IEEE/ACM Transactions on Networking*, vol. 11, no. 4, pp. 537–549, 2003.

[13] B. Melander, M. Bjorkman, and P. Gunningberg, "A new end-to-end probing and analysis method for estimating bandwidth bottlenecks," in *Proceedings of IEEE GLOBECOM–Global Internet Symposium*, pp. 415–420, 2000.

[14] B. Melander, M. Bjorkman, and P. Gunningberg, "Regression-based available bandwidth measurements," in *Proceedings of the International Symposium on Performance Evaluation of Computer and Telecommunications Systems*, 2002.

[15] V. Ribeiro, R. Riedi, R. Baraniuk, J. Navratil, and L. Cottrell, "PathChirp: efficient available bandwidth estimation for network paths," in *Proceedings of the Passive and Active Measurements Workshop*, 2003.

[16] N. Hu and P. Steenkiste, "Evaluation and characterization of available bandwidth probing techniques," *IEEE Journal on Selected Areas in Communications*, vol. 21, no. 6, pp. 879–894, 2003.

[17] J. Strauss, D. Katabi, and F. Kaashoek, "A measurement study of available bandwidth estimation tools," in *Proceedings of the ACM SIGCOMM Internet Measurement Conference (IMC '03)*, pp. 39–44, October 2003.

[18] V. Ribeiro, M. Coates, R. Riedi, S. Sarvotham, B. Hendricks, and R. Baraniuk, "Multifractal cross-traffic estimation," in *Proceedings of the ITC Conference on IP Traffic, Modeling and Management*, 2000.

[19] K. Lakshminarayanan, V. N. Padmanabhan, and J. Padhye, "Bandwidth estimation in broadband access networks," in *Proceedings of the ACM SIGCOMM Internet Measurement Conference (IMC '04)*, pp. 314–321, October 2004.

[20] D. Gupta, D. Wu, P. Mohapatra, and C. N. Chuah, "Experimental comparison of bandwidth estimation tools for wireless mesh networks," in *Proceedings of the 28th IEEE Conference on Computer Communications (INFOCOM '09)*, pp. 2891–2895, April 2009.

[21] T. Sun, L. J. Chen, G. Yang, M. Y. Sanadidi, and M. Gerla, "SenProbe: path capacity estimation in wireless sensor networks," in *Proceedings of the 3rd International Workshop on Measurement, Modelling, and Performance Analysis of Wireless Sensor Networks*, 2005.

[22] L. J. Chen, T. Sun, G. Yang, M. Y. Sanadidi, and M. Gerla, "AdHoc probe: path capacity probing in wireless ad hoc networks," in *Proceedings of the 1st International Conference on Wireless Internet (WICON '05)*, pp. 156–163, July 2005.

[23] L. J. Chen, T. Sun, G. Yang, M. Y. Sanadidi, and M. Gerla, "AdHoc Probe: end-to-end capacity probing in wireless ad hoc networks," *Wireless Networks*, vol. 15, no. 1, pp. 111–126, 2009.

[24] A. Amamra and K. M. Hou, "Bandwidth estimation in broadband access networks," in *Proceedings of the 10th International Conference on Computer Modeling and Simulation*, pp. 46–51, 2008.

[25] J. Bolliger and T. Gross, "A framework-based approach to the development of network-aware applications," *IEEE Transactions on Software Engineering*, vol. 24, no. 5, pp. 376–390, 1998.

[26] J. Bates, D. Halls, and J. Bacon, "A framework to support mobile users of multimedia applications," *Mobile Networks and Applications*, vol. 1, no. 4, pp. 409–419, 1996.

[27] B. L. Tierney, D. Gunter, J. Lee, M. Stoufer, and J. B. Evans, "Enabling network-aware applications," in *Proceedings of the 10th IEEE Interantionsl Symposium on High Performance Distributed Computing*, pp. 281–288, August 2001.

[28] A. Fox, S. D. Gribble, E. A. Brewer, and E. Amir, "Adapting to network and client variability via on-demand dynamic distillation," in *Proceedings of the 7th International Conference of Architectural Support for Programming Languages and Operating Systems*, pp. 160–173, 1996.

[29] B. Badrinath, A. Fox, L. Kleinrock, G. Popek, P. Reiher, and M. Satyanarayanan, "Conceptual framework for network and client adaptation," *Mobile Networks and Applications*, vol. 5, no. 4, pp. 221–231, 2000.

[30] D. M. Batista, N. L. S. da Fonseca, F. K. Miyazawa, and F. Granelli, "Self-adjustment of resource allocation for grid applications," *Computer Networks*, vol. 52, no. 9, pp. 1762–1781, 2008.

[31] J. Cao, K. M. McNeill, D. Zhang, and J. F. Nunamaker, "An overview of network-aware applications for mobile multimedia delivery," in *Proceedings of the Hawaii International Conference on System Sciences*, vol. 9, pp. 4663–4672, January 2004.

[32] M. Davis, "A wireless traffic probe∗ for radio resource management and QoS provisioning in IEEE 802.11 WLANs," in *Proceedings of the 7th ACM Symposium on Modeling, Analysis and Simulation of Wireless and Mobile Systems*, pp. 234–243, October 2004.

[33] M. Bredel and M. Fidler, "A measurement study of bandwidth estimation in IEEE 802.11g wireless LANs using the DCF," in *Proceedings of the Networking Ad Hoc and Sensor Networks, Wireless Networks, Next Generation Internet*, vol. 4982 of *Lecture Notes in Computer Science*, pp. 314–325, 2008.

[34] R. Prasad, C. Dovrolis, M. Murray, and K. Claffy, "Bandwidth estimation: metrics, measurement techniques, and tools," *IEEE Network*, vol. 17, no. 6, pp. 27–35, 2003.

11

PAPR Reduction of FBMC by Clipping and Its Iterative Compensation

Zsolt Kollár and Péter Horváth

Department of Broadband Infocommunications and Electromagnetic Theory, Budapest University of Technology and Economics, Budapest 1111, Hungary

Correspondence should be addressed to Zsolt Kollár, kollar@mht.bme.hu

Academic Editor: Dov Wulich

Physical layers of communication systems using Filter Bank Multicarrier (FBMC) as a modulation scheme provide low out-of-band leakage but suffer from the large Peak-to-Average Power Ratio (PAPR) of the transmitted signal. Two special FBMC schemes are investigated in this paper: the Orthogonal Frequency Division Multiplexing (OFDM) and the Staggered Multitone (SMT). To reduce the PAPR of the signal, time domain clipping is applied in both schemes. If the clipping is not compensated, the system performance is severely affected. To avoid this degradation, an iterative noise cancelation technique, Bussgang Noise Cancelation (BNC), is applied in the receiver. It is shown that clipping can be a good means for reducing the PAPR, especially for the SMT scheme. A novel modified BNC receiver is presented for SMT. It is shown how this technique can be implemented in real-life applications where special requirements must be met regarding the spectral characteristics of the transmitted signal.

1. Introduction

In wireless communications the frequency spectrum is an essential resource. As the unlicensed spectrum is used by an increasing number of devices, the possibility of communication collision is increasing. To avoid this collision, two solutions are possible: extending the frequency limits higher to unused frequency bands at the upper end of the spectrum or reaggregating the densely used licensed frequency bands. Both ideas have disadvantages: the use of higher frequencies requires expensive specially designed analog devices; the reuse of the spectrum calls for complex, intelligent, and adaptive systems. In this paper the focus is on the reuse of the spectrum with multicarrier modulations tailored for spectrally efficient applications.

Future applications operating in the licensed bands, for example, cognitive radios, favor spectrally efficient FBMC schemes with low out-of-band leakage, minimizing harmful interference between devices using adjacent channels. In this paper two subclasses of FBMC are investigated, both allowing the use of a complex modulation alphabet: OFDM and SMT. Both of these schemes provide relatively low out-of-band leakage.

Today OFDM [1] is the de-facto standard technique for high-speed wireless data transmission. Using OFDM, low-complexity modulation and demodulation can be performed by the "Inverse Fast Fourier Transform (IFFT)" and the Fast Fourier Transform (FFT), respectively. With Cyclic Prefix (CP), channel equalization can be efficiently implemented in the frequency domain. This scheme also has some drawbacks. As the PAPR of the transmitted signal is large, OFDM is highly sensitive to the nonlinear characteristics of the Power Amplifier (PA) and the D/A-A/D converters [2]. Signal preprocessing has to be applied to reduce the high PAPR of the OFDM signal, otherwise power amplification would not be efficient. Nevertheless, if the linear range of the PA is smaller than required, nonlinear effects also degrade the performance of the OFDM system. The nonlinearity introduces in-band and out-of-band distortion as well.

Numerous signal processing methods have been proposed to reduce the PAPR of OFDM [3, 4] such as, amplitude clipping [5], coding [6], interleaving [7], partial transmit sequence [8], selected mapping [9], tone reservation [10], tone injection [11], and active constellation extension [12]. Each has its own advantage and drawback. Clipping introduces distortion, some methods may require higher power, others cause data rate loss, and in some cases additional information must be transmitted to the receiver. Furthermore, the computation complexity varies for each technique.

Besides OFDM, another FBMC-based multicarrier family is being strongly investigated: the SMT [13, 14] scheme, which is also known as OFDM/Offset-QAM [15]. The SMT scheme has significantly reduced out-of-band leakage compared to OFDM. However, due to the absence of CP, it is more sensitive to effects of multipath propagation. The SMT signal suffers from large PAPR similarly to OFDM, which makes it especially vulnerable against nonlinearities present in the transceiver chain. For PAPR reduction of SMT signals, only the clipping technique can be applied as the consecutive symbols are overlapping, therefore it is not possible to treat them separately as in OFDM.

In this paper the baseband amplitude clipping method [5] is applied for reducing the PAPR of OFDM and SMT signals. Clipping is applied to the transmitted signal in order to align it to the linear range of the PA. Although the PAPR of the signal can be easily limited by clipping, nonlinear effects are introduced, degrading the system performance. Therefore clipping must be compensated in the receiver. The receiver-oriented turbo principle is a good candidate for the compensation of the negative side effect of clipping. Two different iterative techniques are described for OFDM receivers:

(i) Decision Aided Reconstruction (DAR) [16], where the receiver aims to reconstruct the peaks of the time domain signal.

(ii) Bussgang Noise Cancellation (BNC) [17], where the objective is to remove the clipping noise in the frequency domain.

Both methods were originally proposed using hard-decision-based decoding procedures. Modified receivers using soft decisions are introduced in [18]. Using the soft information the receiver takes full advantage of the turbo principle, yielding better Bit Error Rates (BER). In this paper the focus is on the BNC algorithm using soft decision because it outperforms the DAR method [18].

This paper is organized as follows. First the system model applying clipping on coded FBMC signals is introduced. A short description is given of OFDM and SMT. The PAPRs and the spectral characteristics of the transmitted signals are compared. The mathematical description of the clipping effects is also presented. In the next section, a detailed description is given of the soft BNC receiver algorithm, introducing modifications to the method presented in [18, 19] in order to be applicable to SMT. The technique is explained both for OFDM and SMT schemes. The convergence analysis is given based on Extrinsic Information Transfer (EXIT) chart. The possibility to apply clipping on a real-life system is considered and modified transmitter architectures are also presented. In the closing section BER simulations are shown over ideal and frequency selective channels with Additive

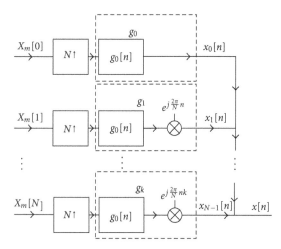

FIGURE 1: Block diagram of an FBMC modulation scheme.

White Gaussian Noise (AWGN). The paper concludes with a summary of the most important results.

2. System Model

2.1. FBMC Modulation Scheme. The FBMC transmit signal is constructed from N parallel streams as shown in Figure 1. The input for the mth symbol in the kth branch $X_k[m]$ is selected from the complex modulation alphabet $\mathcal{A}$. The modulation symbols are upsampled by a factor of N to achieve maximum data rate with critical sampling. For each upsampled signal a specially designed complex modulated prototype filter is applied having the impulse response $g_k[n]$ and Z-transform $G_k(z)$ as

$$g_k[n] = g_0[n]e^{jk(2\pi/N)}, \quad 0 < n < KN, \tag{1}$$

$$G_k(z) = G_0\left(W_N^k z\right), \tag{2}$$

where $j = \sqrt{-1}$ is the imaginary unit, $W_N = e^{j(2\pi/N)}$, and K is the overlapping factor giving the number of overlapping impulses. The $x_k[n]$ output streams are summed to form the transmit signal $x[n]$ which can be expressed using (1) as

$$x[n] = \sum_{m=-\infty}^{\infty} \sum_{k=0}^{N-1} X_m[k]g_0[n-mN]e^{jk(n-mN)(2\pi/N)}. \tag{3}$$

In the receiver a similar filter bank is used to separate the N data streams. The separated streams are downsampled to retrieve the transmitted complex modulation values. The FBMC scheme can be implemented in a computationally efficient way using IFFT and a polyphase decomposition of the filters $G_k(z)$ [20].

2.1.1. OFDM Transmitter. The OFDM scheme is a special class of FBMC where a prototype filter with a rectangular impulse response is applied. This leads to a simplified structure where the consecutive symbols do not overlap,

FIGURE 2: Block diagram of an OFDM transmitter.

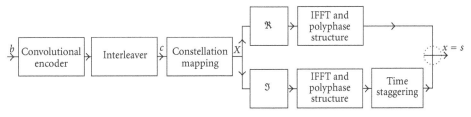

FIGURE 3: Block diagram of an SMT transmitter.

that is, $K = 1$. As a result, the samples of an OFDM symbol can be expressed by simplifying (3) as described in [1]:

$$x[n] = \sum_{k=0}^{N-1} X[k] e^{jkn(2\pi/N)}, \quad 0 \leq n < N. \qquad (4)$$

The block diagram of an OFDM transmitter is shown in Figure 2. The binary information data b are encoded by a rate-R convolutional encoder and the encoded bits are interleaved. The interleaved bits are mapped to X complex constellation symbols from the set $\mathcal{A}$. Each $a_k \in \mathcal{A}$ symbol maps M encoded and interleaved bits. Finally IFFT is used to modulate the subcarriers. Then, prior to transmission, a CP with P samples is added to each symbol to form the transmitted signal s.

2.1.2. SMT Transmitter. In the SMT scheme prototype filters with overlapping impulse responses fulfilling the Nyquist criterion are applied. Due to the advantageous properties of the prototype filter bank, the SMT signal will have a better Adjacent Channel Leakage Ratio (ACLR) than OFDM. With the use of offset-QAM modulation, where the real and imaginary data are transmitted with a time offset of a half symbol duration, no data rate loss will occur compared to OFDM. Prior to transmission, the symbols are overlapped such that they can be separated at the receiver. In order to maintain orthogonality of the filter bank structure, CP can not be used in SMT systems. As a result, techniques with higher complexity must be applied in comparison to OFDM in order to combat the channel-induced intersymbol interference [21, 22]. The modulated signal for the SMT scheme can be expressed as:

$$x[n] = \sum_{m=-\infty}^{\infty} \sum_{k=0}^{N-1} \left(\theta_k \mathcal{R}\{X_m[k]\} g_0[n - mN] \right.$$

$$\left. + \theta_{k+1} \mathfrak{I}\{X_m[k]\} g_0\left[n - mN - \frac{N}{2} \right] \right) \qquad (5)$$

$$\times e^{jk(n-mN)(2\pi/N)},$$

where

$$\theta_k = \begin{cases} 1, & \text{if } k \text{ is even}; \\ j, & \text{if } k \text{ is odd}. \end{cases} \qquad (6)$$

An efficient implementation of (5) is to use two separate polyphase filter banks where two output signals are time staggered and added. This polyphase structure of the SMT scheme can be seen in Figure 3. A major difference compared to OFDM is the no CP is applied. The SMT transmit signal is identical to the modulated signal $s[n] = x[n]$.

2.2. Properties of The Transmitted Signal

2.2.1. PAPR. The PAPR is one of the quantities that describes the dynamic properties of the transmitted signal $s[n]$. The PAPR is defined as:

$$\text{PAPR}(s[n])_{\text{dB}} = 10 \log_{10} \left(\frac{\max\left\{|s[n]|^2\right\}}{P_s} \right), \qquad (7)$$

where $|s[n]|$ is the amplitude and P_s is the average power of the transmitted signal. The PAPR curves of the transmitted symbols are analyzed in Figure 4, where the Complementary Cumulative Distribution Functions (CCDFs) of the PAPR are depicted as a function of the number of subchannels N with an oversampling ratio of 4. It can be seen that as the number of subchannels increases, the probability that the amplitude exceeds a certain PAPR threshold (PAPR$_0$) increases for both systems.

2.2.2. Power Spectrum Density. Spectral behavior especially regarding the ACLR is also an important property of the transmitted signal. The power spectrum density function of the transmitted signal with an oversampling factor of 4 is depicted in Figure 5 as a function of the number of subchannels. In case of OFDM the length of the CP is set to 1/4 symbol duration. The adjacent channel leakage is considerably lower in SMT than in OFDM. The low out-of-band radiation makes SMT a more suitable solution for cognitive

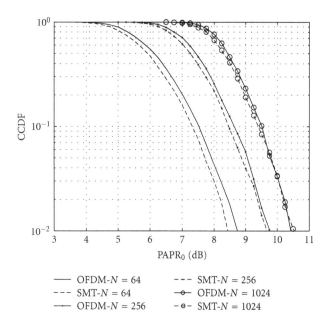

—— OFDM-$N = 64$ - - - SMT-$N = 256$
- - - SMT-$N = 64$ -○- OFDM-$N = 1024$
—— OFDM-$N = 256$ -●- SMT-$N = 1024$

FIGURE 4: CCDF of the PAPR of the transmitted signal of OFDM and SMT for various number of subchannels. The probability that an amplitude value exceeds a certain threshold PAPR$_0$ is visible.

radio applications where strict ACLR limits are enforced. If the number of subchannels increases, the PAPR also increases, but the spectral characteristics become more efficient, out-of-band radiation is reduced. It has been shown in [23] that in the presence of a nonlinear PA the performance of both systems degrades severely. The spectral mask is distorted, leading to a considerable amount of out-of-band leakage. A detailed analysis of the out-of-band radiation for OFDM and SMT schemes is given in [24].

2.3. Clipping. Clipping is applied to the baseband transmit signal $s[n]$ in order to reduce the PAPR. The amplitude values are limited to a threshold of A_{max}. The clipped signal $s^c[n]$ is given as

$$s^c[n] = \begin{cases} s[n] & |s[n]| \leq A_{max} \\ A_{max}e^{j\varphi(s[n])} & |s[n]| > A_{max}, \end{cases} \quad (8)$$

where $\varphi(s[n])$ is the phase of the complex signal $s[n]$. The limiter is characterized by the clipping ratio (CR),

$$CR_{dB} = 20\log_{10}(\gamma), \quad (9)$$

with $\gamma = A_{max}/\sqrt{P_s}$. According to Bussgang's theorem [25], the signal at the output of the limiter can be expressed as

$$s^c[n] = \alpha s[n] + d[n]. \quad (10)$$

The clipping noise $d[n]$ is assumed to be complex Gaussian distributed and uncorrelated with the useful signal $s[n]$ and the attenuation factor α is calculated as [25]

$$\alpha = 1 - e^{-\gamma^2} + \frac{\sqrt{\pi}}{2}\gamma\,\mathrm{erfc}(\gamma). \quad (11)$$

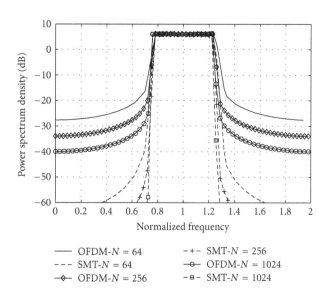

—— OFDM-$N = 64$ -+- SMT-$N = 256$
- - - SMT-$N = 64$ -○- OFDM-$N = 1024$
-◇- OFDM-$N = 256$ -□- SMT-$N = 1024$

FIGURE 5: Power spectrum density comparison of the transmitted signals of OFDM and SMT with various number of subchannels.

FIGURE 6: Block diagram of the baseband transceiver chain.

The output power of the limiter is given by

$$P_{out} = \left(1 - e^{-\gamma^2}\right)P_s. \quad (12)$$

Using (10) and (12), the clipping noise power can be calculated as

$$P_d = \left(1 - e^{-\gamma^2} - \alpha^2\right)P_s. \quad (13)$$

As clipping is performed on the baseband digital signal nonlinear distortions will only occur in the baseband, that is, all distortions terms will fall in-band.

2.4. Transceiver Chain. For modeling the transceiver chain the digital baseband equivalent is used. The model of the transceiver is presented in Figure 6. The radio channel is modeled as a FIR filter having a discrete impulse response $h[n]$ and a sampled AWGN term $w[n]$ with variance $\sigma_0^2 = N_0/2$ per complex dimension. The sampled received signal can be expressed as:

$$y[n] = s[n] * h[n] + w[n]. \quad (14)$$

The receiver is assumed to have the knowledge of the channel coefficients $h[n]$.

3. Bussgang Noise Cancellation

3.1. BNC Turbo Detection for OFDM Systems. In OFDM systems, the CP of P samples is assumed to be longer than the channel's maximum excess delay. As a result, the received symbols on the kth subcarrier after OFDM demodulation can be expressed using (10) as

$$
\begin{aligned}
Y[k] &= X^c[k]H[k] + W[k] \\
&= \alpha X[k]H[k] + D[k]H[k] + W[k], \quad 0 \le k < N,
\end{aligned}
\tag{15}
$$

where $X[k]$, $X^c[k]$, $D[k]$, $H[k]$, and $W[k]$ are the discrete Fourier transforms of the sampled signals $x[n]$, $x^c[n]$, $d[n]$, $h[n]$, and $w[n]$, respectively. The BNC receiver performs iterative equalization and detection [26]. The basic block diagram of a BNC receiver for OFDM according to [18] is shown in Figure 7. Two main subblocks are present in the figure: the BNC detector and the channel decoder. The BNC detector consists of a forward and feedback signal processing path.

3.1.1. Forward Path.

The extrinsic Log-Likelihood Ratio (LLR) for each channel observation $\hat{Y}[k]$ is calculated according to [27] as

$$
L\left(b_{u,v} \mid \hat{Y}[k]\right) = \ln \frac{\sum\limits_{a_l \in \mathscr{A}^1_{u,v}} p\left(\hat{Y}[k] \mid a_u = a_l\right)}{\sum\limits_{a_l \in \mathscr{A}^0_{u,v}} p\left(\hat{Y}[k] \mid a_u = a_l\right)},
\tag{16}
$$

where $\mathscr{A}^1_{u,v}$ and $\mathscr{A}^0_{u,v}$ are subsets of $\mathscr{A}_u$. The vth bit in a_u can be either 1 or 0. The conditional probability density function $p(\hat{Y} = a_l)$ is given by [16]

$$
p\left(\hat{Y}[k] \mid a\right) = \exp\left(\frac{\left(\hat{Y}[k] - \alpha H[k]a\right)^2}{N_0 + |H[k]|^2 P_D^i}\right),
\tag{17}
$$

where P_D^i is the power of the remaining clipping noise after the ith iteration. Taking into account the large number of samples and applying the central limit theorem, the clipping noise $d[n]$ can be modeled as a Gaussian distributed random variable, which is independent of the channel noise $w[n]$. Based on this assumption, passing through the linear channel filter, the power of the Bussgang noise P_D is multiplied by $|H[k]|^2$. For the 0th iteration, with no feedback, P_D^0 is calculated according to (13). For the next iterations, P_D^i can be approximated as

$$
P_D^i = E\left\{\left|D[k] - \hat{D}[k]\right|^2\right\}.
\tag{18}
$$

As the receiver does not know $D[k]$, the power of the remaining clipping noise is to be estimated as

$$
P_D^i = P_D^0 - E\left\{\left|\hat{D}[k]\right|^2\right\}.
\tag{19}
$$

3.1.2. Feedback Path.

After interleaving the extrinsic LLRs provided by the channel decoder, the soft symbols are calculated as [16]

$$
\tilde{X}_n = \sum_{l=0}^{2^M-1} a_l \prod_{u=0}^{M-1} P(b_{l,u}), \quad a_l \in \mathscr{A}.
\tag{20}
$$

Each symbol is first weighted by the probability of the mapped bits and then summed up. Using these soft symbols a time domain estimation of the OFDM signal is performed. Clipping is applied with a level of $A_{\max}$, and the signal is converted back to the frequency domain. The attenuation factor α^i must be set in accordance with the output power of the soft mapper. If the estimated extrinsic information for the coded bits is rather low due to low channel SNR values, no clipping compensation will be performed. The clipping ratio for the ith iteration can be calculated as

$$
\gamma^i = \frac{A_{\max}}{\sqrt{P_{\tilde{x}}}}.
\tag{21}
$$

The attenuation factor for the ith iteration is calculated according to (11) using (21) as

$$
\alpha^i = 1 - e^{-(\gamma^i)^2} + \frac{\sqrt{\pi}}{2}\gamma^i \operatorname{erfc}\left(\gamma^i\right).
\tag{22}
$$

Following each iteration the attenuation factor in the feedback loop decreases from 1 to α as the estimation becomes more and more precise.

Subtracting the attenuated symbols from the clipped symbols, the estimated clipping noise can be expressed as

$$
\hat{D}[k] = \tilde{X}^c[k] - \alpha^i \tilde{X}[k], \quad 0 \le k < N.
\tag{23}
$$

The estimated noise term $\hat{D}$, multiplied by the channel coefficient, is then subtracted from the received symbols (15) to suppress the clipping noise

$$
\begin{aligned}
\hat{Y}[k] &= \alpha H[k]X[k] + H[k]\left(D[k] - \hat{D}[k]\right) \\
&\quad + W[k], \quad 0 \le k < N.
\end{aligned}
\tag{24}
$$

The 0th iteration is the case when no feedback loop is used, that is, $\hat{Y}[k] = Y[k]$. The attenuation factor α^i is monotonously decreasing, so the iteration can stop when consecutive iterations give less difference in α than a given limit.

The BCJR channel decoder [28] computes the extrinsic information of the deinterleaved LLRs, which are provided by the BNC detector. These extrinsic LLRs are used to suppress the clipping noise in the feedback path of the BNC detector.

3.2. Convergence Analysis.

The convergence behavior of a turbo loop can be examined using the Extrinsic Information Transfer (EXIT) chart, developed by ten Brink [26]. It is used to investigate the iteration behavior of a turbo loop based on the exchange of mutual information. This powerful tool enables the tracing of mutual information exchange between the BNC detector and the channel decoder over the iterations.

The LLRs defined by (16) are modeled with an equivalent Gaussian channel [26]. The mutual information between these LLRs and the transmitted symbols U which

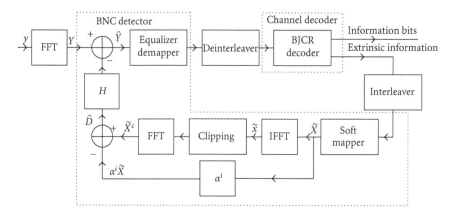

FIGURE 7: Block diagram of the Bussgang noise cancelation for OFDM.

are the realizations of $u \in \{-1, +1\}$ can be expressed with the conditional probability density function [26] as

$$I_A(U; \mathrm{LLR}) = \frac{1}{2} \sum_{u=-1,1} \int_{-\infty}^{\infty} p_A(\xi \mid U = u)$$

$$\cdot \log_2 \frac{2 p_A(\xi \mid U = u)}{p_A(\xi \mid U = -1) + p_A(\xi \mid U = 1)} \mathrm{d}\xi, \tag{25}$$

where $0 \leq I_A \leq 1$. The binary variable $u_k = -1$ and $u_k = 1$ represents the digital bits $b_k = 0$ and $b_k = 1$, respectively. To measure the mutual information content of the output extrinsic LLR values, the following expression is applied:

$$I_E(U; \mathrm{LLR}) = 1 - E\left\{\log_2\left(1 + e^{-\mathrm{LLR}}\right)\right\}$$

$$\approx 1 - E\left\{\log_2\left(1 + e^{-u_k \mathrm{LLR}_k}\right)\right\}. \tag{26}$$

The EXIT function of the BNC detector is not only a function of the a priori mutual information I_A provided by the channel decoder, but it also depends on E_b/N_0 as $I_{E1} = f(I_{A1}, E_b/N_0)$. The EXIT function of the channel decoder only depends on the a priori LLRs provided by the BNC detector as $I_{E2} = f(I_{A2})$. The iteration steps of the turbo loop can be visualized using the EXIT functions of the BNC detector and the channel decoder. The output of the channel decoder becomes the input of the BNC detector, and the output of the detector will be the new input of the decoder in the next iteration:

$$I_{E1} = f\left(I_{A1} = I_{E2}, \frac{E_b}{N_0}\right),$$

$$I_{E2} = f(I_{A2} = I_{E1}). \tag{27}$$

To observe the mutual information transfer of the turbo loop, the EXIT chart is constructed from the two EXIT functions. The EXIT function of the channel decoder is plotted with swapped x-y axes on top of the BNC detectors to visualize the iteration trajectory. An iteration trajectory can be seen for $E_b/N_0 = 4\,\mathrm{dB}$ and $E_b/N_0 = 12\,\mathrm{dB}$ with a channel

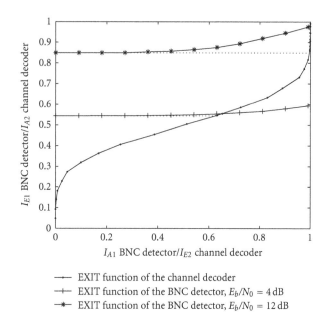

—•— EXIT function of the channel decoder
—+— EXIT function of the BNC detector, $E_b/N_0 = 4\,\mathrm{dB}$
—*— EXIT function of the BNC detector, $E_b/N_0 = 12\,\mathrm{dB}$
······ Decoding trajectory

FIGURE 8: EXIT chart, with iteration trajectories of the BNC turbo receiver with an $R = 1/2$ rate channel decoder for $E_b/N_0 = 4\,\mathrm{dB}$ and $E_b/N_0 = 12\,\mathrm{dB}$ values with CR = 1 dB

decoder rate of 12 in Figure 8. In iterative receivers the EXIT functions of both decoders have to be monotonically increasing in order to achieve convergence. It can be observed in Figure 8 that the monotony of the BNC detector is satisfactory. As the input mutual information I_{A1} increases, a growing output mutual information I_{E1} can be observed. If the extrinsic information in the feedback loop has reached the value of 1, that is, a perfect reconstruction is achieved, meaning that the clipping noise can be fully removed and unclipped system performance can be achieved.

3.3. Modified BNC Turbo Detector for SMT Systems. For SMT scheme the blocks of the BNC receiver presented for OFDM in Figure 7 must be modified and extended. Both, the feedforward and the feedback path should be altered, due to

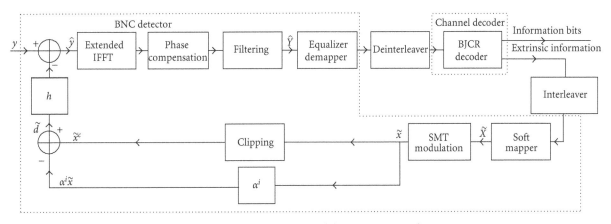

FIGURE 9: Block diagram of the modified BNC receiver for SMT.

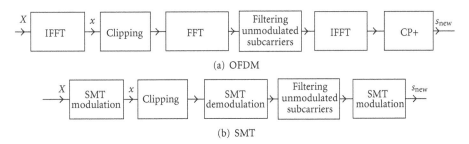

(a) OFDM

(b) SMT

FIGURE 10: Block diagram of the modified transmitter of OFDM (a) and SMT (b) systems.

the overlapping nature of the symbols and the absence of the CP, as it can be seen in Figure 9:

(i) The compensation of the clipping noise is performed in time domain before demodulation.

(ii) In the presence of ISI only a quasi Maximum Likelihood (ML) detection of the received modulation symbols $\hat{Y}$ can be performed.

(iii) The demapping blocks have to be extended with additional signal processing blocks.

First, an enlarged FFT operation is applied [29] with a length equal to the time domain impulse duration of the prototype filter. The phase compensation of the transmission channels effect for each subcarrier in each subchannel is performed in the frequency domain. After the phase compensation, filtering is performed in the frequency domain [29]. Finally, a quasi-ML detection of the transmitted, channel distorted complex modulation values is calculated similar to the case of OFDM. Equation (17) has to be modified taking ISI into account. The probability function is approximated as

$$p\left(\hat{Y}[k] \mid a\right) \approx \exp\left(\frac{\left(\hat{Y}[k] - \alpha H[k]a\right)^2}{I + N_0 + |H[k]|^2 P_D^i}\right), \quad (28)$$

where I is the ISI term which can be calculated according to [21].

4. Practical Application

In real-life systems not all subcarriers are used for data transmission. Usually the DC subcarrier and some carriers at the edge of the transmission band are not used due to technical difficulties and guard band purposes in the spectrum. Clipping introduces nonlinear distortions in the entire baseband, so the originally unused subcarriers will contain components introduced by clipping. This also negatively affects the spectral behavior of the transmission signal, that is, leakage will appear. These components have to be suppressed. Digital filtering is not sufficient to suppress the clipping components on the unused subcarriers and analog filtering introduces modulation errors. Instead of filtering, the clipped transmit signal is demodulated again. The modulation values for each symbols of the used subcarriers are selected and the unused subcarriers are set to zero, and repeated modulation is performed similar as described in [30]. The described modification of the transmitter for OFDM and SMT systems can be seen in Figure 10. In the receiver the BNC detector for the OFDM system remains the same, as the compensation of the clipping noise is performed in the frequency domain. On the other hand, the BNC receiver for the SMT scheme has to be modified. The same scheme as presented in Figure 10 must be implemented in the feedback loop to reconstruct the clipping noise in the time domain.

The results of clipping and resetting the unmodulated subcarriers to zero for OFDM and SMT can be seen in Figures 11 and 12. In Figure 11 a spectrum regrowth can be

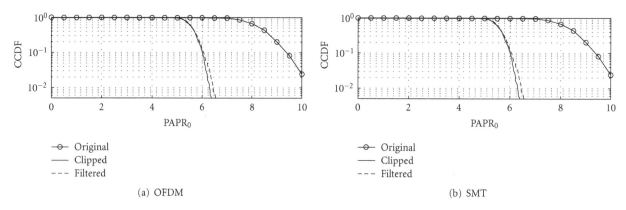

FIGURE 11: CCDF of the PAPR values of the transmitted signal with clipping and additional signal processing for OFDM (a) and SMT (b).

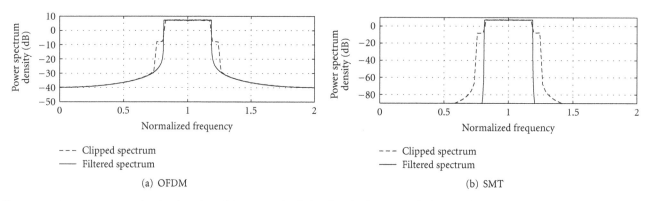

FIGURE 12: Power spectrum density function of the transmitted signal with clipping and additional signal processing for OFDM (a) and SMT (b).

observed for the PAPR of both systems as a result of the filtering. The regrowth of PAPR is strongly dependent on number of unused subcarriers. If more unmodulated subcarriers are applied, more nonlinear distortion will be removed from the signal leading to the regrowth of the peaks. In Figure 12 on the spectral characteristics the effects of clipping can be well observed as the nonlinear products appear in the baseband causing a large side lobe. This leakage disappears with the filtering of the unused subcarriers. As a positive side-effect of the filtering the power of the clipping noise will also be reduced, so the receiver will operate with a reduced P_d.

5. Simulation Results

Table 1 shows the summary of the simulation parameters for the two modulation schemes.

The binary data are encoded with a code rate of 1/2, using a 4-state recursive systematic convolutional encoder with polynomials $(1, 5/7)_8$ in octal notation. The interleaved bits are mapped according to a 16-QAM constellation with Gray mapping. The clipping level (CR) is set to 1 dB. For the prototype filter of the SMT system the coefficients presented in [31] are applied.

TABLE 1: Simulation parameters for SMT and OFDM system.

Parameter	SMT	OFDM
Bandwidth	8 MHz	
Cyclic prefix (P) length	0	128
Available subcarriers/subbands (N)	1024	
Modulated subcarriers/subbands (N_c)	768	
Overlapping factor (K)	4	1
Mapping (M)	4 (16-QAM)	
Clipping ratio	1 dB	

To obtain comparable bit error rates, the SNR normalized to one bit energy is defined. The noise power of the AWGN channel is calculated according to the following definition:

$$\text{SNR}_{dB} = 10 \log_{10} \left(\frac{P_b}{N_0} \right)$$
$$= 10 \log_{10} \left(\frac{P_{\text{out}}(N + P)}{N_0 MRN_c} \right), \tag{29}$$

where P_b is the bit power, N is the number of the subcarriers/subbands available, and N_c is the number of subcarriers/subbands used. P is the length of the CP, M is the number

TABLE 2: Excess delay and relative amplitude for IEEE 802.22 B and C channel profiles.

Profile B	Path 1	Path 2	Path 3	Path 4	Path 5	Path 6
Excess d.	$-3\,\mu s$	$0\,\mu s$	$2\,\mu s$	$4\,\mu s$	$7\,\mu s$	$11\,\mu s$
Rel. amp.	$-6\,dB$	$0\,dB$	$-7\,dB$	$-22\,dB$	$-16\,dB$	$-20\,dB$
Profile C	Path 1	Path 2	Path 3	Path 4	Path 5	Path 6
Excess d.	$-2\,\mu s$	$0\,\mu s$	$5\,\mu s$	$16\,\mu s$	$24\,\mu s$	$33\,\mu s$
Rel. amp.	$-9\,dB$	$0\,dB$	$-19\,dB$	$-14\,dB$	$-24\,dB$	$-16\,dB$

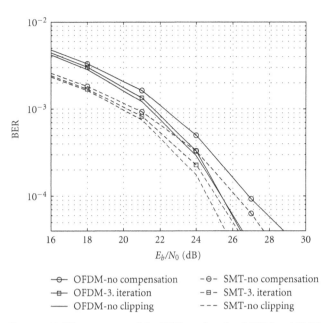

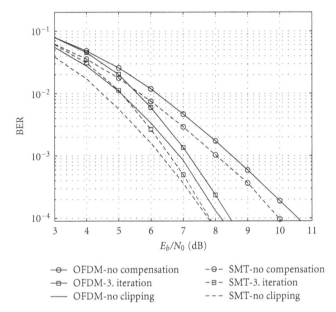

- ○ OFDM-no compensation   - ⊖ - SMT-no compensation
- ☐ OFDM-3. iteration   - ⊟ - SMT-3. iteration
- —— OFDM-no clipping   - - - SMT-no clipping

FIGURE 13: Bit error rates of the BNC receiver for OFDM and SMT signaling over AWGN channel.

- ○ OFDM-no compensation   - ⊖ - SMT-no compensation
- ☐ OFDM-3. iteration   - ⊟ - SMT-3. iteration
- —— OFDM-no clipping   - - - SMT-no clipping

FIGURE 14: Bit error rates of the BNC receiver for OFDM and SMT signaling over channel B.

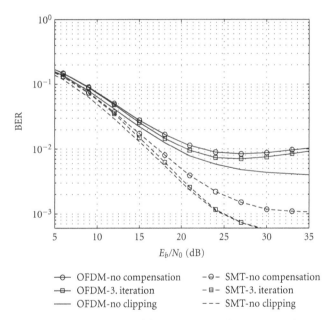

- ○ OFDM-no compensation   - ⊖ - SMT-no compensation
- ☐ OFDM-3. iteration   - ⊟ - SMT-3. iteration
- —— OFDM-no clipping   - - - SMT-no clipping

FIGURE 15: Bit error rates of the BNC receiver for OFDM and SMT signaling over channel C.

of bits transmitted by one subcarrier/subband, and R is the coding rate. Assuming a normalized symbol duration T, the energy of a single bit can be expressed as $E_b = P_b T = P_b$. The parameters of the applied IEEE 802.22 channel profiles B and C can be found in Table 2 [32]. For decoding of the received bits BJCR decoder was suggested, but due to arithmetic overflow issues the log-map decoder [33] is used.

The simulated BERs over AWGN channel can be seen in Figure 13. Due to the absence of CP, SMT outperforms OFDM. It can be observed for both techniques that clipping severely degrades the overall system performance if it is not compensated, that is, no feedback loop is active. With iterative compensation the system performance can be improved, if the SNR acceded a limit the BER results approach the performance of the case without clipping.

The BER simulations for Channel B can be seen in Figure 14. For OFDM the CP is longer than the maximal channel delay, therefore ISI is not affecting the OFDM system, and the effects of clipping can be compensated. For SMT the effect of the ISI does not severely degrade the system performance, it still outperforms OFDM. For both techniques the effect of clipping can be compensated and the BER after the third iteration approaches the results where no clipping was applied.

The BER simulations for Channel C are shown in Figure 15. In this scenario the CP of OFDM is shorter than the channel impulse response so an error floor caused by the residual ISI can be observed. The presence of ISI results in an error floor also for FBMC systems but at a much lower SMT.

6. Conclusion

In this paper a modified BNC structure suitable for clipped SMT signal processing was presented. Based on the EXIT chart, it was shown that the proposed iterative scheme is convergent. It was also described how the clipping technique can be applied in real-life systems for both OFDM and SMT modulation. Finally, the performance of the BNC SMT receiver was verified and compared to OFDM based on BER simulations over AWGN and Rayleigh channels. For both systems the clipping compensation can be performed and the performance without clipping can be approached.

Acknowledgment

The research leading to these results was derived from the European Community's Seventh Framework Programme (FP7) under Grant Agreement no. 248454 (QoSMOS).

References

[1] A. R. S. Bahai, B. R. Saltzberg, and M. Ergen, *Multi Carrier Digital Communications: Theory and Applications of OFDM*, Springer, 2004.

[2] J. Gazda, P. Drotár, D. Kocur, P. Galajda, and R. Blicha, "Joint evaluation of nonlinear distortion effects and signal metrics in OFDM based transmission systems," *Acta Electrotechnica et Informatica*, vol. 9, no. 4, pp. 55–60, 2009.

[3] S. H. Han and J. H. Lee, "An overview of peak-to-average power ratio reduction techniques for multicarrier transmission," *IEEE Wireless Communications*, vol. 12, no. 2, pp. 56–65, 2005.

[4] P. Foomooljareon and W. Fernando, "PAPR reduction in OFDM systems," *Thammasat International Journal of Science and Technology*, vol. 7, no. 3, 2002.

[5] X. Li and L. J. Cimini, "Effects of clipping and filtering on the performance of OFDM," *IEEE Communications Letters*, vol. 2, no. 5, pp. 131–133, 1998.

[6] A. E. Jones, T. A. Wilkinson, and S. K. Barton, "Block coding scheme for reduction of peak to mean envelope power ratio of multicarrier transmission schemes," *Electronics Letters*, vol. 30, no. 25, pp. 2098–2099, 1994.

[7] A. D. S. Jayalath and C. Tellambura, "The use of interleaving to reduce the peak to average power ratio of an OFDM signal," in *Proceedings of the IEEE Global Telecommunication Conference (GLOBECOM '00)*, vol. 1, pp. 82–86, 2000.

[8] S. H. Müller and J. B. Huber, "OFDM with reduced peak-to-average power ratio by optimum combination of partial transmit sequences," *Electronics Letters*, vol. 33, no. 5, pp. 368–369, 1997.

[9] A. Mobasher and A. K. Khandani, "Integer-based constellation-shaping method for PAPR reduction in OFDM systems," *IEEE Transactions on Communications*, vol. 54, no. 1, pp. 119–127, 2006.

[10] S.-E. Park, Y. Sung-Ryul, J. Y. Kim, D. S. Park, and P. Y. Joo, "Tone reservation method for PAPR reduction scheme," Tech. Rep. IEEE 802.16e Task Group, IEEE 802.16e-03n60, 2003.

[11] S. H. Han, J. M. Cioffi, and J. H. Lee, "Tone injection with hexagonal constellation for peak-to-average power ratio reduction in OFDM," *IEEE Communications Letters*, vol. 10, no. 9, pp. 646–648, 2006.

[12] B. S. Krongold and D. L. Jones, "PAR reduction in OFDM via active constellation extension," *IEEE Transactions on Broadcasting*, vol. 49, no. 3, pp. 258–268, 2003.

[13] B. Farhang-Boroujeny and C. H. Yuen, "Cosine modulated and offset QAM filter bank multicarrier techniques: a continuous-time prospect," *Eurasip Journal on Advances in Signal Processing*, vol. 2010, Article ID 165654, 2010.

[14] F. Schaich, "Filterbank based multi carrier transmission (FBMC)—evolving OFDM: FBMC in the context of WiMAX," in *Proceedings of the European Wireless Conference (EW '10)*, pp. 1051–1058, April 2010.

[15] P. Siohan, C. Siclet, and N. Lacaille, "Analysis and design of OFDM/OQAM systems based on filterbank theory," *IEEE Transactions on Signal Processing*, vol. 50, no. 5, pp. 1170–1183, 2002.

[16] M. Colas, G. Gelle, and D. Declercq, "Analysis of iterative receivers for clipped COFDM signaling based on soft Turbo-DAR," in *Proceedings of the 1st International Symposium on Wireless Communication Systems (ISWCS '04)*, pp. 110–114, September 2004.

[17] H. Chen and A. Haimovich, "An iterative method to restore the performance of clipped and filtered OFDM signals," in *Proceedings of the International Conference on Communications (ICC '03)*, pp. 3438–3442, May 2003.

[18] R. Djardin, M. Colas, and G. Gelle, "Comparison of iterative receivers mitigating the clipping noise of OFDM based system," in *Proceedings of the European Wireless Conference*, 2007.

[19] Z. Kollár, M. Grossmann, and R. Thomä, "Convergence analysis of BNC turbo detection for clipped OFDM signalling," in *Proceedings of the 13th International OFDM-Workshop (InOWo'08)*, pp. 241–245, Hamburg, Germany, 2008.

[20] D. S. Waldhauser and J. A. Nossek, "Multicarrier systems and filter banks," *Advances in Radio Science*, vol. 4, pp. 165–169, 2006.

[21] Z. Kollár, G. Péceli, and P. Horváth, "Iterative decision feedback equalization for FBMC systems," in *Proceedings of the 1st International Conference on Advances in Cognitive Radio (COCORA '11)*, Budapest, Hungary, 2011.

[22] T. Ihalainen, T. H. Stitz, and M. Renfors, "Efficient per-carrier channel equalizer for filter bank based multicarrier systems," in *Proceedings of the IEEE International Symposium on Circuits and Systems (ISCAS '05)*, pp. 3175–3178, jpn, May 2005.

[23] Z. Kollár and P. Horváth, "Modulation schemes for cognitive radio in white spaces," *Radioengineering*, vol. 19, no. 4, pp. 511–517, 2010.

[24] L. Baltar, D. S. Waldhauser, and J. A. Nossek, "Out-of-band radiation in multicarrier systems: a comparison," *Multi-Carrier Spread Spectrum*, vol. 1, pp. 107–116, 2007.

[25] H. E. Rowe, "Memoryless non-linearities with gaussian inputs: elementary results," *The Bell System Technical Journal*, vol. 61, no. 7, pp. 1519–1525, 1982.

[26] S. Ten Brink, "Designing iterative decoding schemes with the extrinsic information transfer chart," *AEU-Archiv fur Elektronik und Ubertragungstechnik*, vol. 54, no. 6, pp. 389–398, 2000.

[27] S. ten Brink, J. Speidel, and R. H. Yan, "Iterative demapping and decoding for multilevel modulation," in *Proceedings of the Global Telecommunications Conference, (GLOBECOM '98)*, pp. 579–584, November 1998.

[28] L. R. Bahl, J. Cocke, F. Jelinek, and J. Raviv, "Optimal decoding of linear codes for minimizing symbol error rate," *IEEE Transactions on Information Theory*, vol. IT-20, no. 2, pp. 284–287, 1974.

[29] "Phydas project: documents D2.1 and D3.1," 2008, http://www.ict-phydyas.org/.

[30] P. Sharma, S. Verma, and A. Basu, "Modified clipping and filtering technique for peak-to-average power ratio reduction

of OFDM signals used in WLAN," *International Journal of Engineering Science and Technology*, vol. 2, no. 10, pp. 5337–5343, 2010.

[31] M. Bellanger, "Physical layer for future broadband radio systems," in *Proceedings of the IEEE Radio and Wireless Symposium (RWW '10)*, pp. 436–439, January 2010.

[32] E. Sofer and G. Chouinard, "WRAN channel modeling," IEEE 802.22-05/0055r7, 2005.

[33] G. Bauch, *Turbo-Entzerrung, und Sendeantennen Diversity mit Space-Time-Codes im Mobilfunk*, VDI Verlag GmbH, Düsseldorf, Germany, 2001.

12

Wireless Sensing Based on RFID and Capacitive Technologies for Safety in Marble Industry Process Control

Fabrizio Iacopetti, Sergio Saponara, Luca Fanucci, and Bruno Neri

Department of Information Engineering, University of Pisa, Via Caruso 16, 56122 Pisa, Italy

Correspondence should be addressed to Fabrizio Iacopetti; fabrizio.iacopetti@iet.unipi.it

Academic Editor: Agusti Solanas

This paper presents wireless sensing systems to increase safety and robustness in industrial process control, particularly in industrial machines for marble slab working. The process is performed by abrasive or cutting heads activated independently by the machine controller when the slab, transported on a conveyer belt, is under them. Current slab detection systems are based on electromechanical or optical devices at the machine entrance stage, suffering from deterioration and from the harsh environment. Slab displacement or break inside the machine due to the working stress may result in safety issues and damages to the conveyer belt due to incorrect driving of the working tools. The experimented contactless sensing techniques are based on four RFID and two capacitive sensing technologies and on customized hardware/software. The proposed solutions aim at overcoming some limitations of current state-of-the-art detection systems, allowing for reliable slab detection, outside and/or inside the machine, while maintaining low complexity and at the same time robustness to industrial harsh conditions. The proposed sensing devices may implement a wireless or wired sensor network feeding detection data to the machine controller. Data integrity check and process control algorithms have to be implemented for the safety and reliability of the overall industrial process.

1. Introduction

The transformation of stone blocks coming from quarries into finished products, for example, tiles, sculptures, building materials, stone powder, and so forth, is performed through several different industrial processes. In the case of slab-shaped products (e.g., tiles), marble blocks coming from quarries are firstly sawn by a gangsaw [1] into marble slabs with a resulting irregular contour and with rough surfaces. Slabs are afterwards polished in a polishing machine [2], cut into smaller and regular slabs by means of cutting machines, and finally become end products. The process control of marble slab working is nowadays mainly based on a feed-forward control scheme: the marble slab is transported inside the machine by a conveyer belt; at the entrance of the machine, contact or optical sensing technologies are used to derive information on the presence and shape of the slab which are then used by the machine controlling system to drive the working heads on the slab when it is passing under them. Due to unforeseen events that may occur to the slab

inside the machine, mainly slab displacement and cracks, the controlling system may drive the working heads on the base of not up-to-date or wrong information on the shape and position of the slab. This leads to damages for the machine, in particular for the conveyer belt, with resulting costs due to the need of replacing damaged parts and above all to the machine stop. The detection of slab cracks and of other working problems is nowadays still demanded to operators supervising the machine during the course of the working, who stop the machine in case of suspected or occurred problems. This approach may result in late intervention and in consequent machine damages but also may increase the safety risks for the workers. Moreover, the currently industrially used slab sensing technologies suffer from some issues like deterioration and performance problem in the dirty and wet working environment (mud, water, and stone residuals).

For the above-mentioned reasons, a feedback control scheme on the slab position inside the machine would turn into an improvement for the reliability and safety of the industrial process control.

This paper deals in particular with the use of contactless sensing technologies, specifically based on RFID (radio frequency identification) and capacitive techniques, and to a multipoint wireless sensing data generation approach to improve the reliability and safety in industrial machines for marble slabs polishing. The proposed approach can be generally applied to other machines for stone slab working (cutting, waxing, etc.). The use of wireless technologies in industrial applications is an interesting and emerging trend, aiming at reducing cabling and installation complexity and costs and at avoiding the danger of cables and connectors failure especially on moving parts of industrial machines. Several works have been proposed in the literature [3] mainly addressing wireless systems for industrial communication or, in the case of RFID techniques, for positioning and logistics. On the contrary this work exploits RFID wireless technologies both for contactless multipoint sensing and wireless data communication; the work proposes and examines also the use of multipoint capacitive sensing techniques. For both RFID- and capacitive-based sensing applications, hardware and software components have been developed or COTS (commercial off the shelf) devices have been characterized and proposed for an integration within the machine process control architecture. This approach is supported by experimental campaigns on sensor performance using both sensing wireless technologies (RFID and capacitive) and considering working environments representative of those found in real industrial applications.

After this introduction this work briefly reviews in Section 2 the working principle of industrial marble machines and the state-of-the-art solutions based on optical and mechanical sensors and their limits. Section 3 introduces 4 RFID systems analyzed and tested in the present work, each one based on a different RFID technology, to try overcoming through contactless and wireless sensing the limits of the state-of-the-art process control applications. Then, in Section 4 to 7, the work presents the applications and results concerning the test of the 4 mentioned RFID technologies applied to the case of slab detection in conditions representative of a real industrial working scenario. Section 8 presents the basic principle for capacitive sensing (capacitive sensor and the relevant front-end acquisition circuitry), while Section 9 presents two different types of capacitive sensors that have been designed, implemented, and tested in a test setup representative of real industrial working conditions. A comparison among the different analyzed contactless and wireless sensing solutions, based on RFID and capacitive technologies, is reported in Section 10. Conclusions are drawn in Section 11.

2. Process Control and Sensors in Industrial Marble Machines

Figure 1 shows the schematic diagram of a typical industrial marble machine for slab working. Marble machines are typically made up of consecutive working heads (up to a few tens) under which the marble slab, initially brought to the machine by means of a roller system, is transported by a plastic conveyer belt [2]. A marble slab is typically sized 2 m × 3 m and

has a thickness of some cm. The typical conveyer belt speed amounts to a few cm/s. As an example, the polishing machine in [2] has a total length of 13.5 m and up to 18 abrasive heads.

In Figure 2 the schematic illustration of a section constituted by the different materials/parts inside the machine is reported.

The working environment inside a marble machine is dirty, due to mud, marble, and abrasive residuals, and wet, due to a water level of few cm needed for heads cooling, elimination of residuals, and easing of the conveyer belt sliding on the machine metallic plane. These mentioned issues add up to the other classic problems of wireless systems in industrial scenarios, such as electromagnetic signal attenuation, multipath, and interference from other electromagnetic sources like electrical motors.

As mentioned in Section 1, the process control for marble slab working is currently based on the following scheme: mechanical or optical sensors, arranged in a linear array at the entrance of the machine, are sampled at regular intervals (i.e., each second) to detect the presence of the marble slab on the conveyer belt at the entrance of the industrial machine (profile reader in Figure 1). Such approach results in a spatial sampling of the slab area, with sample step of a few cm, which is used by the PLC (programmable logic controller) controlling the entire machine, including the conveyer belt speed, as the reference time to drive down each cutting/abrasive head when the marble slab is available and to drive up the head in the initial position when the slab is overpassing the working tool. The above-mentioned feed-forward control rule is based on the assumptions that the position and speed of the conveyer belt, the position of the marble slab on the belt, and therefore the relative positions of the heads are constantly known. If one of such assumptions is not verified, in particular the position of the slab on the belt, then the marble slab may not be present when the head is driven down, so that the latter reaches and damages the conveyer belt which must be repaired or replaced causing a long stop of the machine and of the industrial production. During the long travel inside the machine, the slab might indeed move on the conveyer belt due to the working forces or due to breaks under the working mechanical stress. Hence a feedback detection signal should be provided to the heads control system about the real presence of the marble slab under the head inside the machine.

In addition to the missing feedback to the heads control system inside the machine, the state-of-the-art sensors for slab detection outside the machine have problems still to overcome: mechanical sensors suffer from deterioration due to the continuous contact with the slab, while optical sensors [4] need frequent cleaning and recalibration due to the dirty working environment; see Figure 3.

Due to the wet and dirty working conditions and to the nonhomogeneous and nonconstant environmental physical properties, also other contactless sensors proposed or potentially suitable for marble machines, based on LASER or vision systems or ultrasonic waves [5–8], turned out not to be suitable for successful industrial applications.

Capacitive sensors for marble [9] and more complex ultrasound- or georadar-based systems [6, 8, 10] have been studied in the literature. However, their target is the

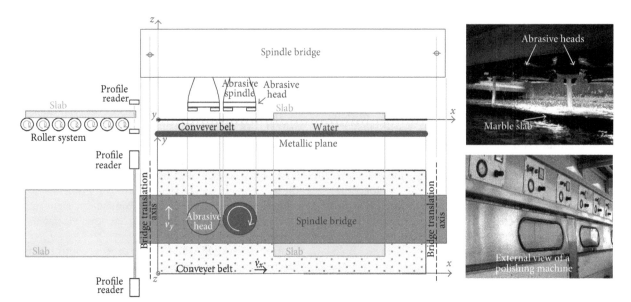

FIGURE 1: Schematic diagram of a marble machine and a snapshot of the abrasive heads over a marble slab.

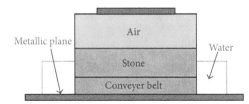

FIGURE 2: Schematic representation of a section of the different materials/parts inside the machine.

fine-grain analysis of the porosity and defects of stone materials (e.g., measuring the dielectric permittivity variations) in a controlled working environment (dry, clean, and with still stone samples) rather than the real-time detection of the presence of a marble slab during the working process inside an industrial machine.

In [11] we have presented preliminary results from experimental tests exploiting capacitive sensing for the detection of the marble slab at the entrance and inside the marble machine, which are further illustrated in Sections 9.1 and 9.2.

Proximity capacitive sensors have also been proposed by semiconductor industry in [12] but targeting small distances mainly for touch sensing applications.

Marble detection through RFID systems, exploiting the interaction between stones and RF radiations, has been preliminary discussed by us in [13] and will be further detailed in the following Section 3 to Section 8.

Also the techniques proposed in [5–8, 14, 15] aim at classification and fine-grain analysis of the texture and surface of stone slabs in a static and controlled environment, with conditions different from those found inside a marble machine. Moreover, for marble machines a simpler on/off detection is required, but with the possibility to be performed in real time, with higher robustness, to be easily integrated with the machine controlling system, having low

maintenance costs. Finally, the computational power needed to implement computing techniques based on wavelets, Gabor filters, or neural networks as in [6, 7, 14] is not compatible with the utilization of the PLC devices commonly used in marble machines controlling systems, above all if such techniques must be applied in several points inside the machine.

To address some of the issues of the state-of-the-art slab detection, in this paper we present the experimental characterization of 4 different RFID systems and of 2 capacitive sensing systems in the detection of the presence of the marble slab outside and/or inside the marble machine. Our work aims at a multipoint sensing scheme being contactless, nearly maintenance-free, operating in real-time, robust to harsh environment conditions. The detection aims at providing the machine controlling system with an on/off information concerning the presence of the marble slab under the working tools and is not intended to provide low-scale information on the properties of the material-like composition, thickness, unhomogeneousness due to small cracks, and so forth.

The target of the work, concerning the RFID and capacitive wireless sensing technologies, is highlighting the advantages and the limits of them when applied to detection tasks, mainly in the marble industry process control, and suggesting which technologies are most suitable and how they can be used.

3. RFID for Process Control in Marble Machines

RFID is a mean of identifying, but also tracking and detecting, an item using radio frequency communication, which takes place between a transmitter, usually called "reader," and a transponder (silicon chip connected to an antenna), usually called "tag." The physical coupling is based on magnetic or electromagnetic fields. Tags can either be passive, that is, powered by the reader field, semipassive or active, that is,

(a)

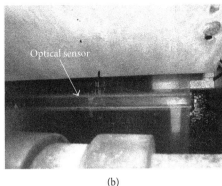

(b)

FIGURE 3: Mechanical sensors and optical sensors at the machine entrance stage.

powered by a battery; in this last case the transmitter is usually the tag itself [16].

At the state-of-the-art the application of RFID technologies has been analyzed and implemented for logistics (for which commercial solutions are available, as an example in the marble industry [17, 18] using 13.56 MHz passive tags and handheld RFID reader), for the management of production [19, 20], and even for localization [21], but less for industrial machine process control and sensing.

In marble machines, the effects on reader-tag communication depend on various parameters: the composition and shape of the stone slab, the operating frequency and power levels of the RFID system, the radiation pattern of the antennas, the distance between tag and reader and their relative orientation, and the working environment (presence of water or dust or a mixture of both, presence of metallic planes in the machine, and composition of the conveyer belt). Hence an experimental test campaign on real case studies using different RFID systems is required. Such experimental campaign, missing in the literature, is the main objective of the present part of the work on RFID technologies.

Since marble machines are not produced in large numbers, therefore not justifying the development of ASICs, in our experiments we implemented 4 RFID systems starting from commercially available tags and readers and customizing the hardware components and/or the relevant software for proper configuration of the experimental setup and for acquisition and processing of test results. Due to the poor availability of experimental data in the literature, we have investigated the application of RFID systems ranging from the low frequencies (LF) to the ultrahigh frequencies (UHF) bands. The four considered RFID systems are shown in Figure 4. The low-frequency RFID system of Figure 4(a) [22] uses passive tags and a communication frequency of 125 kHz; the high-frequency (HF) system of Figure 4(c) at 13.56 MHz uses passive tags [23]; two ultrahigh-frequency systems, at 868 MHz [24], see Figure 4(b), and at 2.45 GHz [25], see Figure 4(d), use, respectively, passive tags and active tags.

The following experiments and related hardware and/or software customizations of the systems in Figure 4 have been realized: (i) measurement and comparison with a given threshold of the amplitude of the signal modulated by the tag

and decoded by the reader; (ii) proper setting, through the control software, of the power radiated by the reader antenna; (iii) detection and comparison with a given threshold of the packet reception error rate in the tag-reader communication.

The above solutions are alternatives of each other, and the most suited depends on the possibility of configuration offered by RFID components. As an example in the considered systems [24, 25] the reader power level may be configured. The software of [25] allows processing of communication data to determine the packet error rate. For the test campaign sixteen stone samples, different in size and shape (typically rectangular with the larger sizes in the order of some tens of cm and height of up to a few cm) and representative of the possible materials processed in marble industry (e.g., onyx, marble, granite, etc.), have been considered. In Figure 5 six of the sixteen stone samples are shown.

4. Experimental Analysis of the LF RFID System

The 125 kHz LF RFID system has been firstly characterized in a test setup reproducing the environment inside the marble machine; as sketched in Figure 6 the passive tags have been embedded in fixed positions in the conveyer belt which is made of plastic/rubber and is transparent to LF (the scheme in Figure 6 realizes a smart conveyer belt) or placed under it. The aim of the first test has been the determination of the maximum distances in the 3D space where the tags are detected by the reader without the interposition of the stone samples. In this test the observed output is the data output of the RFID LF reader, see Figure 7, sent to a PC connected to the reader and shown by means of an application providing on/off detection information (plus the code of the tag in case of detection). The LF reader, using a coil antenna with a diameter of about 20 cm (see Figure 4(a)), communicates with passive tags of size 8 cm × 5 cm through inductive coupling. The output power of the reader is 100 mW. Figure 7 also shows the schematic waveform of the signal on the reader coil, highlighting the carrier and its modulation (communication data).

The experimental results, reported in Figure 8, show that the tags can be detected up to a distance of roughly 20 cm in the 3D space. The experiment has been repeated with all

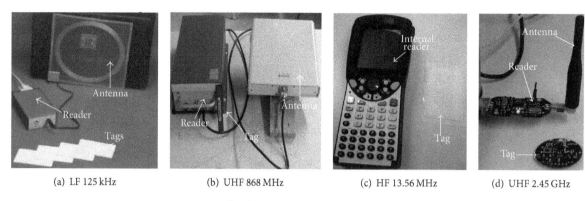

(a) LF 125 kHz   (b) UHF 868 MHz   (c) HF 13.56 MHz   (d) UHF 2.45 GHz

FIGURE 4: Considered RFID systems (reader, antenna, and tag).

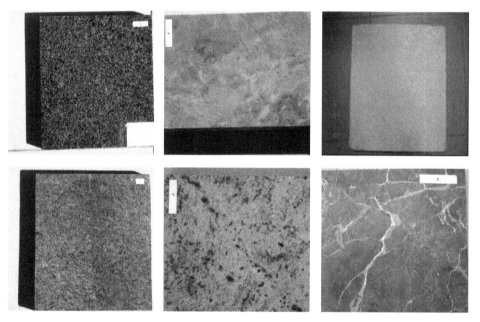

FIGURE 5: Six of the 16 marble slabs used for the test campaign.

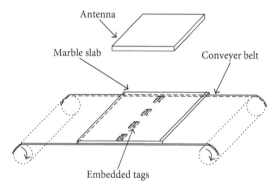

FIGURE 6: Test configuration with tags embedded in the conveyer belt.

the different stone samples interposed between the tags and the reader coil antenna, with and without the presence of a water layer of some cm and with and without the presence of

marble dust and mud. The obtained results are substantially the same of those reported in Figure 8, in which only results on the ZY plane are reported, due to the circular symmetry of the antenna lying on the XY plane.

Experimental results prove that, as expected at the test frequency, stones, water, and mud are almost transparent to LF radiations. Finally we repeated all the above tests analyzing the analog decoded signal in the LF reader, see Figure 7, considering a fixed distance of 10 cm (compliant with the use of the system inside the machine) between the nearest tag and the reader coil antenna. The analyzed signal is obtained through a custom circuit that we added to the reader circuitry in order to filter and measure the amplitude of the decoded signal (envelope of the received signal). Results of these tests are showed in Figure 9. Each reported measurement is generated by averaging ten measurements of the peak-to-peak signal amplitude, with and without interposition of the stone slab between the tag and the reader. The peak-to-peak voltage level measured in absence of stone samples resulted to be 120 mV. Repeating the tests with the stones interposed (more

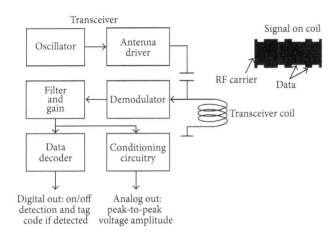

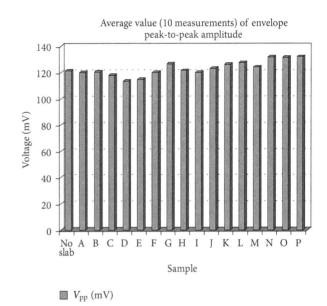

FIGURE 7: Architecture of the reader, LF RFID system, and schematic illustration of data modulation.

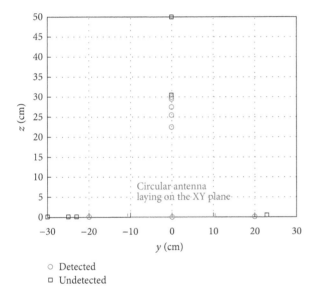

○ Detected
□ Undetected

FIGURE 8: Experimental points of detection, LF RFID system.

FIGURE 9: Peak-to-peak amplitude of the decoded signal picked up on the reader by a custom circuitry.

and of the corresponding marble slab when the tag is passing in the area covered by the reader antenna. For the considered LF system the antenna-tag distance should be within 15 cm. Such distance allows the application both outside and inside the machine.

5. Experimental Analysis of the HF RFID System

For the RFID HF system in Figure 4(c), communicating through magnetic coupling with passive tags at 13.56 MHz, by means of a Windows CE application on the handheld device we implemented similar tests and obtained similar results as in the case of the RFID LF system. Figure 10 shows the experimental results concerning the detection limit points in the 3D space without any stone sample interposition. The only difference with the LF system is that the HF system is based on a handheld battery-powered device [23] with an internal tag reader and an internal antenna. Due to the limited radiated power, in the range of tens of mW (typical of HF RFID readers for handheld applications [26, 27]), the maximum reachable distance is below 8 cm. Using an HF RFID reader, not battery powered, a higher power level could be irradiated and hence we expect the achievement of performances similar to those of the LF system concerning the maximum distance of tag reading. As an example, the RFID HF reader [28] technical specifications report a maximum output power of about 4 W and a tag reading distance above 80 cm.

6. Experimental Analysis of the UHF RFID System

For the RFID UHF system, shown in Figure 4(b) and working at 868 MHz, we have firstly repeated the characterization with the test setup in Figure 6 reproducing the marble machine

than 16 different stone samples labeled with letters from A to P in Figure 9, with/without water or mud or marble dust), the revealed signal ranged between 115 mV and 125 mV with small differences (within ±4%) versus the 120 mV reference (see Figure 9). Since the measured value slightly depends on the specific type of stone the above detecting technique could possibly be used for industrial applications involving a specific stone type but not in a machinery where the type of stone samples varies from slab to slab.

To solve this issue for the LF RFID system a different detecting strategy has been adopted: instead of embedding the tags in the conveyer belt as in Figure 6, the tag has been applied on the side surface of each marble slab through a fast dry resin as in [17]. The tag is not placed on the top surface of the marble slab in order to avoid any damage by the polishing abrasive heads. The tag has in this case the function of confirming the presence of the slab on the conveyer belt in the position expected by the PLC. This configuration allows the detection, even in presence of water and dirt, of the tag

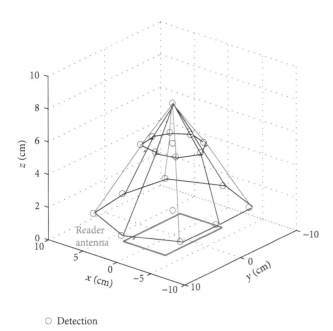

○ Detection

FIGURE 10: Experimental surface of maximum detection distance, HF RFID system.

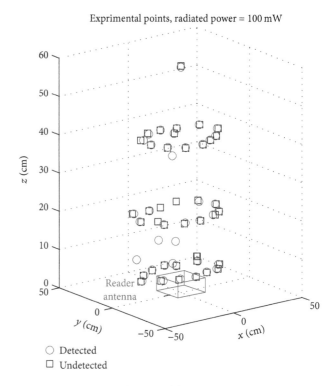

○ Detected
□ Undetected

FIGURE 11: Experimental points of detection, UHF RFID system, for a radiated power of 100 mW.

working environment, embedding the passive tags in fixed positions in or below the conveyer belt. The aim of the first test was the determination of the maximum distances in the 3D space at which the tags are detected by the UHF reader for a defined tag-antenna relative orientation, without interposition of stone samples, at different radiated power levels. Experimental results are reported in Figure 11 for the case example of the reader radiating a 100 mW power. At UHF frequencies the coupling between RFID reader and tags is electromagnetic.

The power level irradiated by the UHF reader antenna is programmable in the range [100 mW, 4 W]. To be noted is that power regulations in Europe are characterized by a limit of 500 mW while the maximum level of 4 W is permitted by US regulations.

Besides the irradiated power level also the working frequency of the selected UHF reader [24] is programmable in order to support both European and US regulations. The used tags are passive devices compliant with the ISO18000-6B standard and compliant with both US and European regulations concerning frequency and power levels. The antenna is a planar one with a wide frequency working range from roughly 800 MHz to 960 MHz. To carry out the test campaign, the Microsoft Visual C++ PC application controlling the UHF reader has been modified and customized in order to provide an interface suitable for testing purposes. In Figure 12 the customized graphical user interface (GUI) is shown. Figure 13 reports the maximum distance at which the tag is still detected as a function of the reader antenna power level.

The experiment has been repeated with all the different stone samples interposed between the tags and the reader antenna, with and without the presence of a water level of few cm and with and without the presence of marble dust

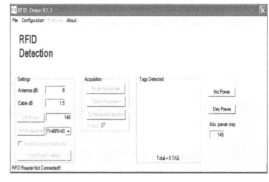

FIGURE 12: The customized GUI of the application for the UHF reader control.

and mud. Differently from what measured in the case of LF and HF systems, at UHF frequencies the communication is completely shielded by water, that is, in presence of a thin layer of water, or in some cases just with a few water drops wetting the tag, the tags are not detected. These experimental results are aligned with studies [29] on water properties, see Figure 14, proving that in the UHF range the intensity of a plane incident wave decreases to $1/e$ (i.e., 63% absorbed) in a penetration distance of about 1 cm or lower depending on the test conditions (note that in our application the water layer can be of some cm). Therefore UHF systems cannot be used inside the marble machine.

The results of the test campaign applied using the configuration of Figure 6 with different types of stones interposed (in a dry environment) prove that at UHF frequencies a stone

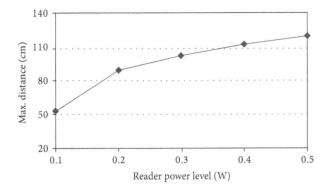

FIGURE 13: Max. distance of tag detection versus radiated power.

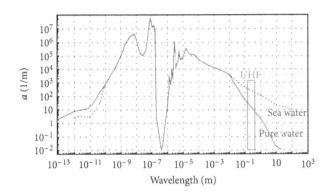

FIGURE 14: Water absorption spectrum.

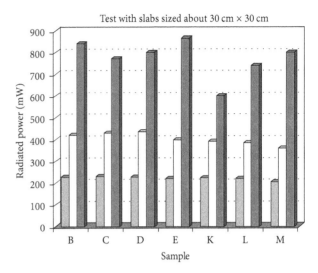

☐ Minimum detection power (mW), no slab, no conveyer belt
☐ Maximum non-detection power (mW), no slab, with conveyer belt
■ Minimum detection power (mW), with slab and conveyer belt

FIGURE 15: Experimental results showing the radiated power in the on/off detection strategy test.

sample attenuates the RF signal. Therefore the tags embedded in the conveyer belt can be detected or not depending on the distance and power level radiated by the reader.

According to this result the detection of the marble slab with UHF systems is possible following the strategy described hereafter. First, as sketched in Figure 6, the tags should be embedded in the conveyer belt while the reader antenna should be attached on the upper part of the machinery in a fixed position (e.g., 40 cm above the conveyer belt in our case study). Secondly, the emitted power level should be properly configured so that (a) when the stone sample is interposed between the tag and the reader antenna the RF signal is attenuated under a certain bound and the tag cannot be detected by the reader; (b) when the stone sample is not present the tag communicates correctly with the reader. After the test campaign in a dry environment we determined that configuring the UHF reader with a radiated power ranging from about 400 mW to 600 mW the detection of stone samples is allowed according to the above on/off strategy. The experimental results of this test are reported in Figure 15 for a case study of slabs sized about 30 cm × 30 cm. Hence configuring the reader with a proper power level in this range (e.g., 500 mW) and embedding the tags in the belt, a RFID UHF system can be used for automatic detection in the process control of marble industry. It must be pointed out that this type of detection is possible only in a dry environment; therefore it cannot be used inside the machine where a water layer of several millimeters is always present.

On the contrary, outside the machine, in a dry environment, the UHF RFID system represents an interesting alternative to traditional mechanical and optical systems to detect the presence of the marble slab at the entrance of the machine. With respect to mechanical sensors, the UHF RFID systems benefit of being contactless. With respect to optical systems the UHF RFID solution is more robust to the presence of a dirty environment.

7. Experimental Analysis of the Microwave Active RFID System

For the RFID UHF system at 2.45 GHz we implemented tests similar to those carried out for the RFID system at 868 MHz. One of the main differences is represented by the fact that the 2.45 GHz solution, shown in Figure 4(d), uses active tags and its maximum detection distance, without the marble slab, is up to 20 m at 1 mW of effective radiated power. Since the distance to be covered in marble machine applications is below 50 cm, during the tests we configured the 2.45 GHz RFID tags for 1/16 mW effective radiated power in order to limit the operating range at a few tens of cm when the marble slab is not present. For the 2.45 GHz active system, the slab detection strategy is not based on the reception/no reception of data packets transmitted by the active tag but on the measure of the reception error ratio and its change in the two cases of slab interposed and not interposed between the tag and the receiver antenna. Reception errors are due to RF absorption and/or scattering by the stone. In the following, the reception ratio refers to the number of correctly received packets divided by the number of expected (i.e., transmitted) packets. For the considered 2.45 GHz RFID system, a data packet is transmitted every about 250 ms (4 packets per second); transmission power is cyclically changed every data

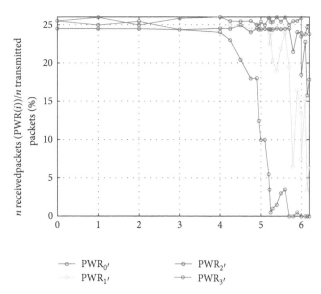

FIGURE 16: Reception ratio versus tag-reader distance for the ith emitted power level (1/64 mW, 1/16 mW, 1/4 mW, and 1 mW, resp., PWR_0, PWR_1, PWR_2, and PWR_3).

TABLE 1: Relative dielectric permittivity of different materials.

Material	Dielectric permittivity, ε_r
Bianco Carrara	5.7
Rosa Portogallo	6.8
Pietra di Trani	13.8
Granito Grigio	29.9
Pietra del Cardoso	9.2
Ceramics	4.3–6.7
Plastic (PVC, Plexiglass)	2–3

packet in the set of 4 different radiated power levels: 1/64 mW, 1/16 mW, 1/4 mW, and 1 mW. Obviously the reception error rate can be calculated as 1 minus the reception rate of correct data packets.

In order to collect experimental data, we developed an ad hoc Matlab (from the Mathworks) application on a PC processing data received by a USB 2.45 GHz receiver. Packets received with errors are discarded and therefore counted as nonreceived. The original firmware (C) on the tag and on the receiver was customized in order to format data packets according to data processing needs.

Preliminary tests were carried out in order to confirm that with transmitter and receiver placed at a short distance the reception rate was 100% for each power level, therefore excluding buffer overflow problems on the receiving PC (e.g., due to application overhead problems). To be noticed is that the packet distribution is not exactly 25.0% for each power level, but about 25.5%, 24.25%, 24.5%, and 25.75% for packets at 1/64 mW, 1/16 mW, 1/4 mW, and 1 mW power, respectively, as measured in several experiments and in conditions of no packet loss. Figure 16 shows the reception ratio in percentage for each power level as a function of the tag-reader distance, measured in a first experiment carried out in a mixed indoor/outdoor environment.

For the power of 1/64 mW, Figure 16 shows a monotonic decrease and a knee in the curve of reception ratio versus distance. Curves at different power levels have not exactly the same trend of the curve for the power of 1/64 mW, probably due to reflections and/or other scattering effects in the working environment, that should of course be characterized and/or avoided in on-field applications.

To achieve the best sensitivity in the reception ratio, the experimental setup for slab detection was arranged by properly displacing tag and receiver antenna so that the reception ratio without the slab was below 100%, ideally on

a working point in the decreasing part of the curve after the knee, in order to have a good sensitivity of the reception ratio versus slab interposition.

During tests with the sixteen slabs we carried out about five measurements of the error ratio just a few seconds before any slab interposition in order to avoid drifts due to possible environmental effects and then during slab interposition. The two sets of measured values are reported in Figure 17, linked by a line identifying the progression of the experiment. With this configuration, when the marble slab is not passing, the reception ratio is from 40% to 80% while with slab interposition, in most cases, the reception ratio drops below 10%–20% (i.e., the reception error rate is up to 80%–90%); this decrease is interpreted as detection of the stone sample, but in some cases (slab B, E, J, L) the presence of the slab causes an increase of the detection ratio instead of a decrease. Since the behavior of the system depends on the specific type of stone, the described detecting technique could possibly be used only for applications involving a specific stone type but not in a machine where the type of stone sample is not known a priori.

To be noted is that the considered 2.45 GHz RFID system has two main disadvantages:

(i) its use is possible only at the entrance of the marble machine in a dry environment since, as in case of the 868 MHz RFID system of Section 6, also microwave signals are absorbed by water;

(ii) the use of active tags causes a higher cost for the tags. Therefore the solution with passive tags should be preferred for process control applications in the marble industry.

8. Capacitive Sensing Principle and Front-End Circuitry for Marble Detection

To address some issues of the currently used and of other proposed slab detection techniques, this section of the work proposes novel capacitive sensors for the detection of stone samples during the industrial process, inside and outside the machine, and by means of contactless and low-complexity devices. Indeed, as reported in Table 1, the stone samples used in the marble industry have relative dielectric permittivity ε_r in the range 5 to 30 [5, 9, 10] that can be used to reveal the presence of a stone sample being different from those of air ($\varepsilon_r = 1$), water ($\varepsilon_r = 81$), or plastic (ε_r between 2 and 3).

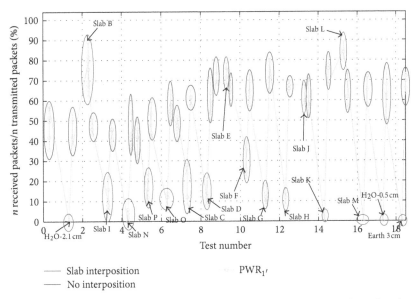

FIGURE 17: Reception ratio normalized to 100% measured with/without slab interposition for radiated power of 1/16 mW.

As mentioned in Section 2, capacitive sensors have been studied in the literature [9] but the solutions proposed are optimized for a fine-grain analysis of the porosity and surface defects of the stone material in a controlled working environment (dry and clean) rather than the real-time detection of a marble slab in an industrial machine. Furthermore in [9] the realized sensor should be taken in contact with the stone sample with a controlled force of 1 N and the stone sample should be held in a fixed position. Instead the aim of our work is the contactless detection of the presence of stone samples moving on the conveyer belt and considering a real industrial environment characterized by the presence of mud, water, and stone residuals and is not intended to measure or give information about material properties (e.g., thickness, composition, unhomogeneousness, etc.).

The basic scheme exploited in this work is the capacitor with parallel metallic plates filled with multiple layers of different dielectric materials; see Figure 18 for the schematic representation in case of a number of dielectric layers $n = 3$.

The value of the capacitance can be determined considering the series of n capacitors each of value $C_i = \varepsilon_o \cdot \varepsilon_{ri} \cdot S/d_i$ with $i = 1, \ldots n$, being S the area of the metallic plates, and d_i and ε_{ri} the thickness and the relative dielectric permittivity of each layer.

Firstly we realized a capacitive sensor with plates sized 6.5 cm × 12.5 cm (S roughly 80 cm^2) in a test-bed reproducing a marble machine working environment found at the machine entrance stage, without the presence of water (note that the characterization of the sensing system with a test-bed considering the presence of water will be discussed in Sections 9.1 and 9.2). The total distance D between the plates has been fixed at 4.5 cm to allow the contactless interposition of different stone samples which have a typical thickness between 1 and 3 cm. The reported analysis is still valid for case studies with maximum thickness higher than 3 cm by increasing, accordingly, the distance D between the

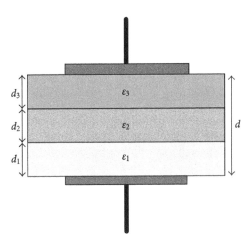

FIGURE 18: Multidielectric layer capacitive sensor.

plates. Mounted at the entrance of the marble machine, the capacitance value, when the marble sample is not present, is expressed by (1) and amounts to about 1.6 pF:

$$C_0 = \varepsilon_o \cdot \frac{S}{D}. \tag{1}$$

In this case the filling dielectric is just air. When a stone sample of relative dielectric permittivity ε_r and thickness x is passing through the metallic plates, see Figure 19, the capacitor value C_{sens} is expressed by (2), and the ratio C_{sens}/C_0 is expressed by (3):

$$C_{\text{sens}} = \varepsilon_o \cdot \varepsilon_r \cdot \frac{S}{[x + \varepsilon_r (D - x)]}, \tag{2}$$

$$\frac{C_{\text{sens}}}{C_0} = \varepsilon_r \cdot \frac{D}{[x + \varepsilon_r \cdot (D - x)]}$$

$$= \frac{\varepsilon_r}{[x/D + \varepsilon_r \cdot (1 - x/D)]}. \tag{3}$$

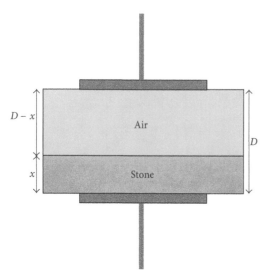

FIGURE 19: Multidielectric layer (air/stone) capacitive sensor.

For typical stone samples ε_r ranges from 5 to 30, see Table 1, and x/D ranges from 0.25 to 0.75 for the selected value $D = 4.5$ cm. Therefore, when a stone sample is passing, the capacitor value is increased with a ratio C_{sens}/C_0 expressed by (3). As a consequence, the detection of the stone sample can be simply realized by revealing a change in the capacitor value higher than a given threshold. The easiest way [30, 31] to reveal this change is inserting the capacitive sensor in an astable circuit and measuring the shift of the oscillating frequency with a microcontroller-based circuit, as shown in Figure 20. The astable circuit is realized with a simple 555 IC and has a theoretical oscillating frequency expressed by

$$F = \frac{1}{\left[\ln(2) \cdot (R_A + 2R_B) \cdot \left(C_{sens} + C_p + C_{ext}\right)\right]}. \quad (4)$$

In (4) C_{sens} refers to the capacitive sensor, C_p to the open-circuit parasitic capacitor due to wire connections and astable component input capacity, and C_{ext} to an external capacitor inserted to set at a desired value F_0 the oscillation frequency when $C_{sens} = C_0$. This way the capacitance change is transformed in a frequency change, easily revealed through a low-cost low-power [32] 8-bit microcontroller.

With marble interposition the value of C_{sens} in (2) increases and hence the oscillation frequency in (4) decreases. To be noticed is that the size of the surface plates S does not influence the change of the capacitance ratio $C_{sens} = C_0$; the value of S is important to determine absolute values of C_{sens} and C_0 giving measurable variation in (4).

After realizing the circuit we implemented a test campaign using 16 stone samples, different in size and shapes (typically rectangular with horizontal size in the order of several tens of cm and height of up to a few cm), representative of the possible materials processed in marble industry (e.g., onyx, marble, and granite). Snapshots of 6 of the 16 different stone samples used during the testing campaign are reported in Figure 5.

The obtained results are summarized in Figure 21 which reports the frequency change with respect to F_0 for each stone sample (labeled with a letter in the range [A,...,P]). The frequency changes in Figure 21 range from a minimum of 2.6 kHz (sample K in Figure 21) to a maximum of 26 kHz (sample I in Figure 21) allowing a reliable detection of the stone presence. The astable circuit reference frequency is set at $F_0 = 219$ kHz, see in Figure 22 the snapshot of the signal generated by the circuit in Figure 20 when $C_{sens} = C_0$. The tests have been carried out also in the presence of mud, marble dust, and powder, obtaining results similar to those in Figure 21.

In the test campaign, we used a threshold for frequency change detection of 1 kHz which ensures a margin of 1 kHz against false detections and higher than 1.6 kHz (the minimum 2.6 kHz decrease when a stone is present minus 1 kHz threshold) against missed detections. Since our goal is an on/off detection, the above margins are sufficient to avoid errors caused by changes in the reference frequency during the time occurring for a typical slab to pass under the sensor (up to tens of seconds); such reference frequency changes can be caused by parasitic capacitance change, deposition of marble dust or mud, and change of temperature conditions. To face slow variations of the reference frequency, the microcontroller via software can monitor F_0 and manage adaptive thresholds.

It is worth noting that in our proposed front-end circuitry the capacitance change (due to the stone slab presence) is detected through a frequency change with respect to the fixed frequency value F_0. To further increase the robustness of our system to electromagnetic interference (EMI), typical of industrial environments, a variable resistor R_B can be used in the scheme of Figure 20 to tune the value of F_0 according to (4). This way when applying the proposed sensing system in a specific industrial environment during the system calibration phase the frequency F_0 can be set in a range where the EMI is null or minimal by changing the value of R_B. To this aim Figure 23 shows that to change F_0 in the range [100 kHz–500 kHz] it is enough to change R_B in the range [5 kΩ–100 kΩ]. These values have been sized under the hypothesis, which is always verified in our experimental tests and in industrial systems we considered, that in the selected range [100 kHz–500 kHz] there is at least a pass-band channel of several kHz where the level of EMI does not interfere with the signals in the circuitry of Figure 20.

The change of R_B can be implemented directly by the microcontroller in Figure 20 by using a digital-controlled potentiometer. The control of R_B has been preferred to the control of R_A since in (4) R_B has a weight double of the one of R_A.

9. Capacitive Detection

9.1. Multidielectric Capacitive Sensing for Marble Industry. Once demonstrated in Section 8 the effectiveness of the sensing and reading principle some modifications have been applied to the schemes in Figures 18, 19, and 20 for a successful integration in a real marble machine. Indeed, as discussed in Section 2 and illustrated in Figure 24, in a marble machine the stone samples are placed on a plastic belt with a thickness B less than 1 cm (0.5 cm typical) sliding

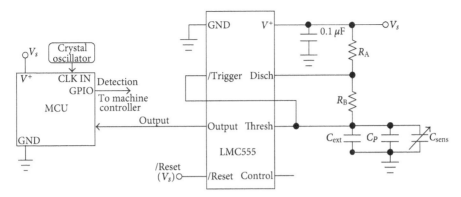

FIGURE 20: Front-end circuitry for capacitance change detection.

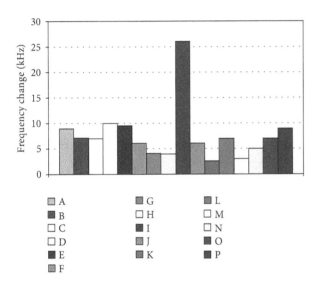

FIGURE 21: Frequency change for different stone samples, 2-plate capacitor.

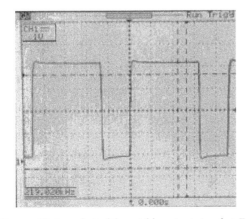

FIGURE 22: Snapshot of the astable output signal at F_0.

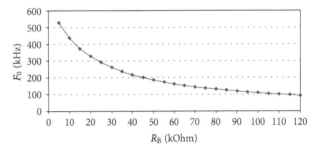

FIGURE 23: Change in F_0 versus change in R_B for the circuit in Figure 20.

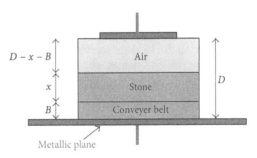

FIGURE 24: Multidielectric layer (air/stone/plastic belt) capacitive sensor inside the marble machine.

the metallic plate one, the method of image charges [33] can be applied: the new capacitor is equivalent to that of Section 8, (1) to (3), but with an effective distance $2D$. With respect to the analysis in Section 8 we have also to consider that in absence of the stone sample the filling dielectric is made up of a layer of $B = 0.5$ cm of plastic material (with ε_{rb} between 2 and 3) and a layer of air of thickness $D - B$. The reference capacitance C_0 is now determined by

$$C_0^{-1} = \left[\varepsilon_o \cdot \frac{S}{2(D-B)} \right]^{-1} + \left[\varepsilon_{rb} \varepsilon_o \frac{S}{2B} \right]^{-1}. \qquad (5)$$

Considering $D = 4.5$ cm and $S = 80$ cm^2, C_0 in (5) amounts to roughly 1 pF. When a stone sample of constant ε_{rx} and thickness x is passing through the metallic plates, a change in the capacitance value occurs since the capacitor is

on a metallic plane. Hence the capacitive sensor can be simply realized suspending a conductive plate (top plate of the capacitor) over the already existing metallic plane of the industrial machine (bottom plate of the capacitor) at a distance D. Since the metallic plane surface is larger than

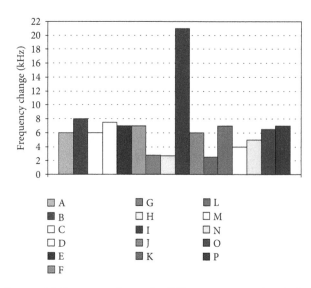

FIGURE 25: Frequency change for different stone samples, 1 plate capacitor.

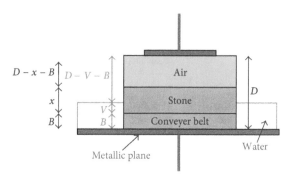

FIGURE 26: Multidielectric layer (air/stone/plastic belt) capacitive sensor inside the marble machine with water.

filled by three dielectric layers: a layer of $B = 0.5$ cm due to the plastic belt, a layer of x cm due to the stone, and a layer of air of size $D-x-B$. As a result of the stone interposition there will be a change of the capacitance C_{sens} (the value increases) that can be read as a frequency change in the circuit of Figure 20 (the oscillation frequency decreases with respect to the reference value F_0 obtained when $C_{\text{sens}} = C_0$).

Implementing a test campaign with the new designed sensing circuit using the 16 stone samples mentioned in Section 3, different in size and shapes, and representative of the possible materials processed in marble industry (e.g., onyx, marble, granite,...etc.) the results of Figure 25 are obtained: the frequency change ranges from a minimum of 2.5 kHz (K sample in Figure 25) to a maximum of 21 kHz (I sample in Figure 25) allowing a reliable detection of the stone samples.

The tests have been implemented also in presence of mud, marble dust, and powder obtaining similar results. As discussed in Section 8, since our goal is an on/off detection, a frequency change threshold of about 1 kHz allows for sufficient margins against false or missing detections due to parasitic capacitance change, deposition of marble dust or mud, and changing of temperature conditions during the typical measure time (1 second and up to tens of seconds). Reference frequency variations in a larger time scale can be managed through the microcontrollers via software by monitoring F_0 and adapting the thresholds accordingly.

The correct behavior of the capacitive detection system with capacitive to frequency conversion has been confirmed also considering the presence of water inside the machinery.

In this case, see Figure 26, when the stone sample is not passing the reference capacitor value C_0 can be calculated considering a layer of size B of roughly 0.5 cm due to the plastic belt in series with a layer of size V (few cm) filled by water and a layer of size $D - (V + B)$ filled by air. When the marble stone is interposed between the metallic plates it removes the water and the new capacitor value C_{sens} can be

calculated considering a layer of size B for the conveyer belt in series with a layer of size x and dielectric constant ε_{rx} and a layer of size $D-(x+B)$ filled by air. By detecting the capacitor change through a frequency change reusing the astable circuit (see Figure 20) the presence of a stone sample can be revealed in a reliable way. Repeating the test campaign using the 16 stone samples, different in size and shape, and in presence of water the frequency change is at minimum 1.5 kHz.

Summarizing, the proposed scheme can be easily implemented in a real marble machine, it is a low-complexity scheme with low maintenance cost, it is contactless, and it allows the reliable detection of stone samples also in presence of water, mud, and marble dust with enough margins against miss detections or false hits. The detection signal generated by the microcontroller may be sent to the main PLC controlling the working heads (see Figure 20). Though presenting a lower value of C_0 for a given surface S of the plate, the single-plate capacitor solution has the great advantage versus the 2-plate capacitor discussed in Section 8 of not requiring the positioning of the second metallic plate under the conveyer belt, since the already existing metallic plane of the industrial machine is used. This way cabling and system maintenance are simplified.

9.2. Surface Capacitive Sensing for Marble Industry. In this section we propose a new capacitive sensor configuration, derived as an adaptation of the theory developed by Bozzi and Bramanti in [9]. Then we compare the obtained solution with the one proposed in Section 9.1.

In [9] Bozzi and Bramanti realized a capacitive sensor, see Figure 27, through the use of three copper conductive lines printed over a piece of FR4 dielectric material ($\varepsilon_r \sim = 4.5$) with a thickness T of 10 mm: the central copper line, acting as signal line, is separated by a narrow gap W from the two other lines, joined together at one end and acting as ground lines. The lines are separated by a distance $W = 1$ mm, and therefore $W \ll T$.

As proved in [9] this device is sensitive to the average value of the dielectric permittivity (ε_{r2} in Figure 27), of the material which is present at a distance H from its surface, with $H \leq W$. As an example if the device in Figure 27 is put in contact with a material with dielectric value ε_{r2}, the device has a capacitance expressed by (6) where k is a constant whose

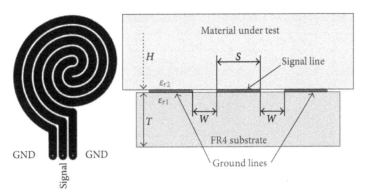

FIGURE 27: Surface capacitive sensor from [9].

FIGURE 28: Modified surface capacitive sensor.

size depends on the ratio between the width of the lines, S, and their distance, W.

As suggested in [9] and realized in Figure 27, S should be comparable to W while the total track length L should be much higher than S and W:

$$C = 2 \left(\varepsilon_{rFR4} + \varepsilon_{r2} \right) \cdot \varepsilon_o \cdot k. \tag{6}$$

The above sensor has been used in [9] to reveal, on static samples, the surface value of the dielectric constant of materials by reading through a capacimeter the value of the capacitance between the signal and the ground lines. The sensor devised by Bozzi and Bramanti is a contact sensor for surface analysis: it is sensitive to the material property within a distance H of about 1 mm from its surface.

Starting from the Bozzi and Bramanti theory we modified the sensor in order to

(a) use an FR4 plane with a thickness of 1.6 mm, compliant with standard printed circuit board (PCB) technology and much lower than the 10 mm used in [9]; indeed the size used in [8] is not compliant with standard PCB technologies and hence implies a high device cost in case of industrial production;

(b) change the shape and size, see our new device in Figure 28, of the printed capacitor to be sensitive within a range H of at least 2 cm from the surface.

The condition in the above point (b) is essential to allow a contactless detection of the presence of a stone sample. However, for the device in Figure 28, as in [9], the thickness of the sensitive area H is determined by the distance W between the conductive lines printed over the FR4 substrate.

To achieve a thickness H of roughly 2 cm the device in Figure 28 has to be sized with a distance between the lines W of about 2 cm. The width S of the printed conductive lines in Figure 28 is 2.5 cm, while the larger side of the sensor has a size $L = 22$ cm (according to the approach of Bozzi and Bramanti in [9] L should be much higher than W). As a result, to achieve a thickness H of roughly 2 cm a total area of 220 cm^2 is required for the surface capacitive sensor, 2.75 times larger than the area of the capacitive sensors in Sections 8 and 9.1 which is 80 cm^2. This is a bottleneck of the surface capacitive sensor presented in this section when compared to the capacitive sensor in Section 9.1. Indeed scaling all dimensions of Figure 28 to achieve a sensing thickness of 4 cm, as in Section 9.1, the required area will increase up to 1300 cm^2. For this reason the device in Figure 28 has been sized for a value of $H = 2$ cm, a good tradeoff between sensitive thickness and sensor area.

Figure 29 reports the impedance Z_{in}, real and imaginary (absolute value) parts, offered by the sensor in Figure 28 as a function of the frequency, derived from an analysis with the electromagnetic simulator ADS (advanced design system) by Agilent Technologies. For sake of clarity two figures are reported referring to a frequency range from 10 Hz to 1 kHz and a frequency range from 1 kHz to 1 MHz.

The proposed sensor in Figure 28 can be suspended over the conveyer belt at a height of 3 cm (to leave enough space for the stone samples in the considered application case study of a thickness ranging from 1 to 3 cm). When there is not any stone to detect ε_{r2} in (6) is 1 (air) and the sensed capacitive value represents the reference value C_0. When a stone is passing, the device can reveal its presence as a change in the capacitance value that can be converted through the astable circuit of Figure 20 in a frequency change. As already discussed when the stone is detected the capacitance value from (6) is increased and the oscillation frequency from (4) is decreased.

Implementing a test campaign with the sensing circuit designed in Figure 28 using the 16 stone samples, different in size and shape, already adopted in Sections 8 and 9.1, the results of Figure 30 are obtained.

The frequency changes in Figure 30 range from a minimum of 2 kHz to a maximum of 7 kHz allowing a reliable detection of the stone samples.

TABLE 2: Main performance of the RFID systems (passive tags) for marble slab detection.

RFID System	LF 125 kHz	HF 13.56 MHz	UHF 868 MHz
Radiated power	100 mW	<50 mW	<500 mW
Max. stone detection distance	15 cm	<8 cm	<40 cm
Best tag placement	Side surface of the marble slab		Embedded in the conveyer belt or under it
With water	Works		Does not work
With dust/dirt/stone residuals		Works	

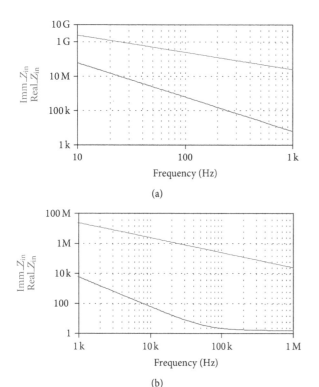

FIGURE 29: Real and imaginary (absolute value) parts of the surface capacitive sensor in Figure 28 (10 Hz–1 kHz and 1 kHz–1 MHz ranges) versus frequency.

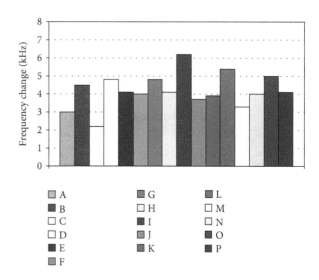

FIGURE 30: Frequency change versus stone sample, surface capacitor.

Repeating the test in presence of water, marble dust, or mud we obtained similar results.

10. Discussion on the Application of the Analyzed Sensing Technologies

10.1. Comparison among the Different Analyzed Contactless Sensing Solutions. As illustrated in Section 4 to Section 7, the experimental analysis of the 4 RFID technologies has been carried out using a test setup reproducing environmental conditions representative of those found inside the marble machine, with water, mud, marble dust, and considering more than 16 different types of stones. The experimental results are schematically reported in Table 2.

Test results proved the following.

(i) Passive tags have to be preferred to active tags since the marble slab detection can be implemented with lower costs and easier system maintenance (e.g., no battery to be replaced). Table 2 summarizes the main performances of the analyzed RF detection systems using passive tags.

(ii) All types of stones are transparent to the tested 125 kHz LF and 13.56 MHz HF radiations; hence for these RFID systems the most suitable strategy for a reliable detection is applying the tag on the side surface of each marble slab by means of a fast dry resin. This allows the detection, even in presence of water and dirt, of the tag and of the corresponding marble slab when the tag is passing in the area covered by the reader antenna. This strategy is useful anyway to confirm to the heads controlling system the presence of the marble slab in the expected point of the machine. The tag, placed in this position, can be used also to store information for logistic applications and for the traceability of the different industrial processes applied to each slab [17].

(iii) UHF communication at 868 MHz and 2.45 GHz is shielded by water and hence UHF systems can be used just outside the machine (dry environment): with respect to mechanical sensors, the RFID systems benefit of being contactless. With respect to optical systems the RFID ones are more robust to the presence of marble dust and dirt. The detection of the marble slab is possible according to the on/off strategy described in Section 6 by properly configuring the UHF system and possibly to the detection strategy presented in Section 7 concerning active RFIDs at 2.45 GHz. In the latter case, anyway, the behavior of the RFID system depends on the specific type of stone, and therefore the described detecting technique could be suitable just for applications involving a stone type a priori known.

It is worth noting that the above-described detecting techniques using passive tags require low-cost tags (one for each marble slab or a set embedded in the conveyer belt) and an antenna for each head of the machine or serving a few consecutive heads. Multiple antennas (e.g., up to 4 for the RFID system in [24]) can be controlled by the same reader positioned outside the machinery since the reader and its antenna are typically connected through cables whose length amounts to some meters.

The application of contactless sensing of the presence and/or the position of the marble slab by means of RFID technologies also have a direct benefit on the possibility to avoid or reduce cabling inside or outside the machine for sensor data transmission to the machine controlling system. For passive RFID tags, no cabling among them is needed, while in the case of active RFID tags (usable only outside the machine) supply should be provided to tags (batteries need maintenance, and energy harvesting appears not to be practical or possible at the required transmission rate).

Passive RFID tags implement a wireless sensor network coordinated by the RFID reader.

The possibility offered by RFID technologies of multitag detection and collision management system allows for the implementation of linear sensor (tag) arrays placed under the conveyer belt at the machine entrance stage. For a typical case study, a tag spacing of 10 cm would allow a usable spatial resolution in slab sampling. At this aim, about 30 tags can constitute a tag array covering the conveyer belt width (in the order of 3 m), and, depending on the particular RFID technology used, multitag reading is possible at a rate sufficient to read a tag array every one-two seconds by means of one or more RFID antennas and/or readers. In such a way, slab presence detection and slab shape detection may be realized for process control. The tag IDs are provided as data output by the RFID readers on a serial or Ethernet port. RFID readers may be connected through a point-to-point (or multipoint-to-point) connection to

(i) the PLC, if its processing power is sufficient to command/configure the RFID readers, receive detected tag IDs, and transform them into slab sampling information;

(ii) an intermediate intelligent data collecting and processing device, for example, a microcontroller-based one, able to command/configure the reader and to apply detection algorithms, sending to the PLC only the final detection data.

Concerning the LF and HF RFID systems, tags are only one or a few for each slab, the reader and its antenna are mounted on the moving spindle bridge, and tag ID data may be transmitted to the PLC wirelessly or by means of a wired bus. In the latter case there are some additional issues due to the movement of the spindle bridge.

Concerning the two capacitive sensing solutions we proposed in Sections 9.1 and 9.2, the experimental campaign carried out with real working conditions highlighted the main advantages and disadvantages of each approach.

As already discussed in Section 9.2, if the two sensors are realized with a comparable area occupation then the PCB-printed surface capacitor offers a reduced detection distance. Obviously, to achieve a similar detection distance the surface capacitor requires a larger area. Indeed for the marble machine application case study a total area of $220\,cm^2$ is required for the surface capacitive sensor in Section 9.2, 2.75 times larger than the area of the sensor in Section 9.1 which is $80\,cm^2$.

As far as the detection robustness is concerned it is clear that, in average, the frequency changes in Figure 30 for the surface capacitor are lower than those in Figure 25 for the single-plate capacitor suspended over the machine metallic plane. However the minimum detected frequency change value in both solutions is comparable: 2.5 kHz in Figures 25 and 2 kHz in Figure 30. Since our goal is an on/off detection of the stone samples, as previously discussed a threshold of about 1 kHz is adequate for both capacitive sensor systems in Sections 9.1 and 9.2. This allows, for both systems, sufficient margins against false or missing detections due to parasitic capacitance change, deposition of marble dust or mud, and change of temperature conditions.

The main advantages of the capacitor described in Section 9.2 versus the solution in Section 9.1 are

(i) the possibility to avoid cabling between the suspended plate and the metallic base of the marble machine;

(ii) the possibility to implement on the same PCB the capacitive sensor, the front-end measurement circuitry, and the interface for data communication (wired or wireless).

With the surface sensing approach, cabling and connection problems are reduced and system maintenance is simplified.

10.2. Case Study Application of Networked Sensing Data Collection in Marble Machines. In this section we discuss the application of the detection sensors outside and inside the machine and the concerning data generation. As application case study, we consider the surface capacitive sensors, as the collection of their output data is performed by means of an architecture resulting in an extension of the one used for the UHF RFID detection and data collection technologies applied at the machine entrance stage.

The arrangement of several sensors into a linear array implements a multipoint sensing scheme for the spatial sampling of the slab, as currently done by mechanical or optical sensors just at the entrance stage of the machine.

The linear array is mounted perpendicularly to the movement direction of the conveyer belt and spans for its entire width, see Figure 31. We indicate with w_{cb} the width of the

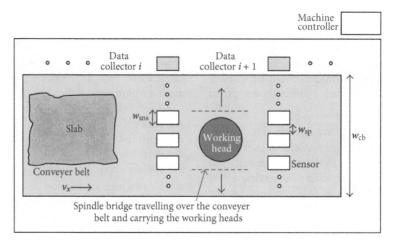

FIGURE 31: Schematic representation of the machine sensing and data collection architecture.

conveyer belt, with w_{sn} the width of each sensor, and with w_{sp} the spacing among two sensors in the array.

We have therefore a number of sensors n_{sns} given by

$$n_{sns} = \text{floor}\left(\frac{w_{cb}}{(w_{sn} + w_{sp})}\right). \tag{7}$$

Sensor output data have to be collected, processed, and transmitted to the machine controller, which, in case of the sensors mounted inside the machine, compares sensor data with data previously drawn from the sensors at the entrance stage, being therefore able to be aware of unexpected slab displacements.

As already mentioned in the beginning of the present Section 10.2, as a case study we consider an array of capacitive sensors usable also inside the machine.

Each capacitive sensor and the relevant front-end circuitry for oscillation generation and frequency detection implement a node of the sensing array, connected to the other sensing nodes through a wired bus (e.g., RS-485, I^2C, CAN, etc.).

For the implemented surface capacitive sensors of Figure 28, whose lower side is 10 cm long, we consider the following data:

$w_{sn} = 10$ cm, width of the surface capacitor PCB;

$w_{sp} = 10$ cm, spacing among capacitive sensors;

$w_{cb} = 3.0$ m, width of the conveyer belt.

We have therefore a number of sensors given by (7) which leads to $n_{sns} = 15$.

As illustrated in the schematic representation in Figure 20, we propose a surface capacitive sensor connected to a small supplementary PCB (that can be further integrated with the sensor on the same PCB) integrating an oscillator (555 timer), a low-cost 8-bit microcontroller (Atmel ATmega 16, which has been chosen for demonstration purposes and is largely sufficient in terms of the features needed), and a communication interface for multidrop bus communication that in the application case study was chosen as the I^2C

bus directly driven by the microcontroller in slave mode. Of course, such a communication bus may be substituted by other industrial data buses in an on-field application. The data collector (see Figure 31) is a microcontroller-based (Atmel ATmega 16) device acting as I^2C master, reading frequency data from the different sensors and implementing proper slab detection and slab shape sampling algorithms whose results are transmitted to the machine controller.

More specifically, the microcontroller on each capacitor enables/disables the oscillating circuit, measures the capacitor oscillation frequency, and sends it every regular interval to the master microcontroller.

The slab detection and slab shape sampling strategies are devolved to the master microcontroller and not to the onboard intelligence of each sensor, as the master microcontroller is aware of the oscillation frequencies of all the sensors in the array, and can therefore

(i) detect quiescent oscillation frequency during a learning/calibration phase performed periodically (without any slab passing) or at machine start and set different detection threshold levels for frequencies of the different sensors; moreover, quiescent frequency may be quite different from sensor to sensor due to the spread in physical and electrical characteristics of its components and to the surrounding environment, for example, proximity to metallic parts of the machine, and so forth;

(ii) detect, during operations, frequency derating due to variations in the water level, in the environment temperature, and so forth, and change detection threshold accordingly.

The master microcontroller (data collector) communicates with the main machine controller wirelessly or through a wired data bus, sharing the communication channel with the other master microcontrollers managing other sensor arrays, and transmits to the machine controller detection data. Each data collector also receives commands from the machine controller, for example, to activate/deactivate sensor arrays, and so forth. The above architecture, in which single sensor arrays and the respective data collector devices are connected to the same cables (supply and, for wired communication, to the data bus), allows for reduced cabling: in the mechanical sensors at the machine entrance stage, see Figure 3, tens of cables, one for each sensor tip, are connected to the PLC. The communication between each sensor and the array data collector occurs with a relatively low rate. In the application case study, the oscillation frequency is coded using 2 bytes (8 Hz resolution for a full scale frequency of 524288 Hz); the number of sensors for each array is $n_{sns} = 15$, and each sensor is assigned a 1-byte I^2C address; sensor data is transmitted every $T = 1$ s; the slab is transported on the conveyer belt at a $v_x = 5$ cm/s. In such a case, the obtained spatial sampling is $s_x = v_x \cdot T = 5$ cm and $s_y = w_{sn} + w_{sp} = 20$ cm.

If no transmission data integrity check or redundancy is used, the needed transmission rate is about $f_{TX} = n_{sns} \cdot 3/T = 45$ B/s, that is, well under 1 kbit/s, a communication speed reachable on commonly used data buses, even in an industrial scenario.

Of course, in an industrial, electrically noisy environment, and due to the impact on the process safety itself, it is necessary to implement data integrity check and filtering schemes, at the sensor raw data output level (a checksum byte for frequency data) and at processing level by the data collector (e.g., removing isolated detection/nondetection points near frequency threshold).

Concerning the implementation costs, a capacitive-based sensing solution could in general be less expensive than a RFID-based sensing one. As an example, a cost estimation for a RFID-based linear array sensor (UHF system, 4 antennas) leads to a cost higher than the corresponding capacitive linear array sensor. It should be anyway noticed that the price of machines for marble slab working is in the order of one to several hundreds of thousands of euros, and therefore the cost of electronics (estimation in the order of thousands of euros) would have a limited impact on the whole machine cost. Anyway, for a correct comparison of the implementation cost, also the impact on the mechanics of the machine sections involved (e.g., the metallic basement) should be evaluated by means of a detailed mechanical design review, that is beyond the scope of the present paper, but the impact appears reasonably limited in comparison to the overall machine cost. As marble machines can operate for several years, the overall cost saving due to the possibility to prevent or reduce damages to the conveyer belt and the consequent machine stops also contributes to justify the extra cost needed for the sensing application. Moreover, the RFID technology might be used not only for slab detection and process control but also to manage the marble logistics during the entire travel and stocking in the working facility, as an example in [34].

11. Conclusion

The paper has presented an experimental analysis towards the application of RFID and capacitive wireless sensing technologies to process control in the marble industry. The final aim was the detection of the presence of a marble slab under the abrasive/cutting head inside an industrial machine or outside at the machine entrance stage. The proposed techniques try to overcome issues related to currently used detection sensors: mechanical or optical devices which suffer from deterioration and dirt-related problems and do not provide the main machine controlling system with feedback signals about the correct alignment between each marble slab and the corresponding cutting/abrasive head inside the machine. This may result in safety issues, costly damages for the machine itself, and a long production stop.

The experimental results for the analyzed RFID technologies using a test setup reproducing the marble machine environment (with water, mud, marble dust) and considering more than 16 different types of stones have led to depict advantages and limits for each tested technology and to define their possibility of use at the entrance stage and/or inside the machine.

The proposed capacitive sensing solutions are optimized for the contactless detection of stone samples inside the industrial machine. Compared to the state-of-the-art detection systems, the proposed solutions allow for a reliable detection while being of low complexity and with low maintenance cost, can be easily integrated with the machine controlling system and are robust to harsh environment conditions. We have then proposed an application case study for surface capacitive sensors representative of a sensing and data collecting network architecture for slab detection outside and inside the machine, providing the machine controlling system with information about the slab position during working. Such architecture is suitable to a more general application, not limited to cutting/polishing processes in marble industry, exploiting the proposed contactless sensing techniques applied in the automation of industrial machinery.

Acknowledgments

This work has been supported by the Tuscany Region DOCUP program in collaboration with Celver Elettronica srl. Discussions with R. Massini, A. Carrafiello, and E. Valentini are gratefully acknowledged.

References

[1] Barsanti Spa, "Gangsaw TLD 60A/80A machine," 2009, http://www.barsantimacchine.it.

[2] Barsanti Spa, "LCA200 marble polishing machine," 2008, http://www.barsantimacchine.it.

[3] D. Miorandi, E. Uhlemann, S. Vitturi et al., "Guest editorial: special section on wireless technologies in factory and industrial automation," *IEEE Transactions on Industrial Informatics*, vol. 3, no. 2, pp. 95–98, 2007.

[4] Celver srl, "Archimedes optical system," http://www.celver.it/new-site/prodotti/prodotti-archimedes.asp.

[5] M. Bramanti et al., "A procedure to detect flaws inside large sized marble blocks by ultrasound," *Subsurface Sensing Technologies and Applications*, vol. 2, no. 1, pp. 1–13, 2001.

[6] M. A. Selver, O. Akay, E. Ardali, B. A. Yavuz, O. Önal, and G. Özden, "Cascaded and hierarchical neural networks for classifying surface images of marble slabs," *IEEE Transactions on*

Systems, Man and Cybernetics Part C, vol. 39, no. 4, pp. 426–439, 2009.

[7] J. D. Luis-Delgado, J. Martínez-Alajarín, and L. M. Tomás-Balibrea, "Classification of marble surfaces using wavelets," *Electronics Letters*, vol. 39, no. 9, pp. 714–715, 2003.

[8] S. A. Coker and Y. C. Shin, "In-process control of surface roughness due to tool wear using a new ultrasonic system," *International Journal of Machine Tools and Manufacture*, vol. 36, no. 3, pp. 411–422, 1996.

[9] E. Bozzi and M. Bramanti, "A planar applicator for measuring surface dielectric constant of materials," *IEEE Transactions on Instrumentation and Measurement*, vol. 49, no. 4, pp. 773–775, 2000.

[10] D. Vaccaneo, L. Sambuelli, P. Marini, R. Tascone, and R. Orta, "Measurement system of complex permittivity of ornamental rocks in L frequency band," *IEEE Transactions on Geoscience and Remote Sensing*, vol. 42, no. 11, pp. 2490–2498, 2004.

[11] S. Saponara, F. Iacopetti, A. Carrafiello, E. Valentini, L. Fanucci, and B. Neri, "Capacitive sensors for process control in industrial marble machines," in *Proceedings of the 5th IEEE International Workshop on Intelligent Data Acquisition and Advanced Computing Systems: Technology and Applications (IDAACS '09)*, pp. 142–147, Rende, Italy, September 2009.

[12] B. Osoincah, "Proximity capacitive sensor technology for touch sensing applications," Freescale White Paper, 2007.

[13] S. Saponara, F. Iacopetti, A. Carrafiello, L. Fanucci, B. Neri, and R. Massini, "Experimental analysis towards the application of RFID technologies in industrial marble machines," in *Proceedings of the 5th IEEE International Workshop on Intelligent Data Acquisition and Advanced Computing Systems: Technology and Applications (IDAACS '09)*, pp. 67–71, Rende, Italy, September 2009.

[14] I. Ar and Y. S. Akgul, "A generic system for the classification of marble tiles using Gabor filters," in *Proceedings of the 23rd International Symposium on Computer and Information Sciences (ISCIS '08)*, pp. 1–6, October 2008.

[15] J. Martínez-Alajarín, J. D. Luis-Delgado, and L. M. Tomás-Balibrea, "Automatic system for quality-based classification of marble textures," *IEEE Transactions on Systems, Man and Cybernetics Part C*, vol. 35, no. 4, pp. 488–497, 2005.

[16] K. Finkenzeller, *RFID Handbook: Fundamentals and Applications in Contactless Smart Cards, Radio Frequency Identification and Near-Field Communication*, John Wiley & Sons, 3rd edition, 2010.

[17] RFIDline, "RFid project: special technology on marble and granite," 2007, http://www.rfidstone.com.

[18] R. Wessel, "Italian stone supplier uses RFID to track marble, granite," RFIDJournal, 2007.

[19] K. Kwon, J. Ryu, J. Sohn, and I. Chung, "Intelligent process control system with RFID cuboid," in *Proceedings of the 11th International Conference on Electronic Commerce (ICEC '09)*, pp. 1–8, Taipei, Taiwan, 2009.

[20] G. Fenu and P. Garau, "RFID- based supply chain traceability system," in *Proceedings of the 35th Annual Conference of the IEEE Industrial Electronics Society (IECON '09)*, pp. 2672–2677, November 2009.

[21] B. S. Choi, J. W. Lee, and J. J. Lee, "An improved localization system with RFID technology for a mobile robot," in *Proceedings of the 34th Annual Conference of the IEEE Industrial Electronics Society (IECON '08)*, pp. 3409–3413, November 2008.

[22] EM Microelectronic, "EM4102 Read only contact less identification device," 2005.

[23] PSION Teklogic, "Workabout Pro guide," 2004.

[24] CAEN SpA, "A928 long range UHF reader data sheet," 2007, http://www.caen.it/rfid.

[25] Open 2.4 GHz RFID Sputnik, http://www.openbeacon.org.

[26] Y.-C. Choi, M.-W. Seo, Y.-H. Kim, and H.-J. Yoo, "A multi standard 13.56 MHz RFID reader system," in *Proceedings of the International Technical Conference on Circuit/System, Computers and Communications (ITC-CSCC '08)*, pp. 1073–1076, 2008.

[27] N. Choi et al., "Design of a 13.56 MHz RFID system," in *Proceedings of the 14th International Conference on Advanced Communication Technology (ICACT '12)*, pp. 840–843, 2006.

[28] Beijing Hongchangtag Tech-Sci Development Inc, "HCT-HFR-80507," 2012, http://www.hongchangtag.com/product.asp?id=15&f1id=1&f2id=19&f1=3.

[29] M. Chaplin, "Water structure and science; water and microwaves," http://www.lsbu.ac.uk/water.

[30] M. Kollar, "Measurement of capacitances based on a flip-flop sensor," *Sensors & Transducers Magazine*, vol. 35, no. 8-9, pp. 1–7, 2003.

[31] G. Brasseur, "Design rules for robust capacitive sensors," *IEEE Transactions on Instrumentation and Measurement*, vol. 52, no. 4, pp. 1261–1265, 2003.

[32] L. Fanucci, S. Saponara, and A. Morello, "Power optimization of an 8051-compliant IP microcontroller," *IEICE Transactions on Electronics*, vol. 88, no. 4, pp. 597–600, 2005.

[33] D. Dugdale, *Essentials of Electromagnetism*, The Macmillan Press, London, UK, 1993.

[34] F. Marco, System and method for a plant for working natural stones. European Patent Application 10425405.7, 2010.

13

Obtaining More Realistic Cross-Layer QoS Measurements: A VoIP over LTE Use Case

F. Javier Rivas, Almudena Díaz, and Pedro Merino

Department of Languages and Computer Science, University of Malaga, UMA, Campus Teatinos, 29071 Malaga, Spain

Correspondence should be addressed to Almudena Díaz; almudiaz@lcc.uma.es

Academic Editor: Maria G. Martini

We introduce a real-time experimentation testbed in this paper which enables more realistic analysis of quality of service (QoS) in LTE networks. This testbed is envisioned for the improvement of QoS and quality of experience (QoE) through the experimentation with real devices, services, and radio configurations. Radio configurations suggested in the literature typically arise from simulations; the testbed provides a real and controlled testing environment where such configurations can be validated. The added value of this testbed goes a long way not only in the provision of more realistic results but also in the provision of QoS and QoE cross-layer measurements through the correlation of information collected at different layers: from service and IP levels to radio and protocol parameters. Analyzing the interlayer dependencies will allow us to identify optimal settings for the radio access network and service parameters. This information can be used to suggest new cross-layer optimizations to further improve quality of experience of mobile subscribers. As a use case, we examine VoIP service over LTE, which is currently an open issue.

1. Introduction

The enhancement of QoS in a sustainable manner is a critical goal for network operators as management tasks are becoming increasingly complex. Although some initial efforts have been carried out by the standardization bodies, there is still a significant gap to be covered in QoS and also in QoE optimization. Actually, current efforts towards improving QoS and QoE are typically based on estimations derived from costly drive test campaigns. Furthermore, involvement of human expertise is required to manually tune network configurations. On the other hand, most of the service and network configurations available in the literature are derived from simulations [1–6]. As is widely known, in the process of modeling communication systems to simulate them, some details may be missed, and thus, misleading results may be derived. For example, it is very common to find that the consumption of control resources is ignored when evaluating different scheduling methods. In this context, providing optimized network configurations based on measurements obtained directly from the subscribers' terminals and correlated with the information collected at the network will pave the way for a reduction of costs and more accurate tuning

of network operation from the point of view of the QoS perceived by final users. Moreover, as stated by standards organizations (SDOs) or alliances with the participation of network operators such as NGMN [7], *the optimization of QoS still requires "real" developments to further study the direction in which to move forward.*

In this paper, we propose the use of an experimental testbed [8] implemented by our research group to carry out specific long term evolution (LTE) experiences in a real context and to extract the correlation between LTE radio configurations and QoS parameters perceived at the application level. The execution of exhaustive measurements campaigns using this testbed will enable the identification of specific performance counters, correlations between them, and use cases for QoS and QoE optimization in LTE networks.

The focus of the paper is on VoIP calls over LTE, which pose new challenges over previous technologies. In LTE, voice calls are now delivered through an all-IP network (VoIP) instead of a circuit switched one, which means that voice has to compete for bandwidth with other services provided in the network. It is vital to at least guarantee the same QoE for VoIP calls that was available in pre-LTE technologies such as global system mobile communications (GSM) and

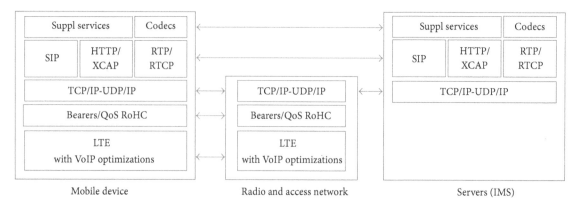

FIGURE 1: Scope of VoIP deployment over LTE by GSMA PRD IR.92 v6.0.

universal mobile telecommunications (UMTS). This will be required to avoid significant impact on customers, who will demand a good service in all-IP mobile networks. Due to situations like this, the testbed has been conceived to validate the performance of the network configurations and problems presented in the research literature. Specifically for VoIP service we have correlated layer 1 and layer 2 LTE radio parameters with IP performance parameters and mean opinion score (MOS) measurements base on perceptual evaluation of speech quality (PESQ) algorithm.

The organization of the paper is as follows. Section 2 introduces the necessity of obtaining performance measurements which capture the QoS and QoE as perceived by final users and the new challenges presented in the provision of voice call services in LTE. This section provides also a brief state of the art on VoIP over LTE and some noteworthy LTE configurations proposed in the literature to optimize its performance. Section 3 presents the testbed and the configuration under which the measurements were collected. Section 4 provides the results obtained during the analysis of IP performance parameters and Section 5 provides their correlation with LTE parameters. Finally, in Section 6, we present conclusions and future work.

2. Voice Calls over LTE: A Regular Data Service, the Same Quality as before

Third generation partnership project (3GPP) has standard-ized two solutions for the deployment of voice call service over LTE. The first is circuit-switched fallback (CSFB) [9], which implies a shift of the user equipment (UE) access from LTE to 2G/3G during a voice call. The second is VoLTE [10] which on the contrary is based on IP multimedia subsystem (IMS) and does not require the use of legacy technologies. Another alternative available in the market is voice over LTE via generic access (VoLGA) [11]. That specification has been developed by the VoLGA forum, based on the existing 3GPP Generic Access Network (GAN) standard [12]. CSFB and VoLGA provide interim solutions for early LTE deployments, while VoLTE offers a long term opportunity for mobile operators. VoLTE allows integrating voice and Internet services and delivering new multimedia services in a

permanent environment. This will enable the exploitation of the potential offered by mature LTE networks. In this context, VoLTE has emerged as the preferred solution by carriers and the GSM association (GSMA) is developing a specification for delivering integrated telephony services over LTE.

Specifically, the GSMA defines in [10], the minimum mandatory set of features that a wireless device and a network should implement to support a high quality IMS-based telephony service over LTE radio access. The scope provided by GSMA is shown in Figure 1.

Standardization bodies are confident about the necessity of introducing specific LTE configurations for the deploy-ment of VoIP service. In [10] GSMA proposes a list of LTE configurations which we aim to extend with new ones obtained and validated in the testbed proposed.

As stated in the 3GPP initiative, the multiservice forum has already demonstrated successful VoLTE calls, and also multi media telephony (MMTel) services [13]. During these tests, equipment from 19 manufacturers was used. The tests performed focused on validating the interoperability between the interfaces defined in the 3GPP technical specifications.

Network operators have also performed testings experi-ments for quality of service (QoS) measuring. For example, different performance metrics such as latency or throughput are evaluated for the TeliaSonera network in [14]. How-ever, our work aims to go a step beyond and not only measure the performance of interfaces and terminals using individual metrics but also correlate all these measurements with specific LTE parameters in order to identify optimum configurations.

2.1. Some Considerations about the Transport of VoIP over LTE. As proposed by GSMA in [10] session initiation protocol (SIP) is the protocol used to register UE in the IMS server. real-time transport protocol (RTP) and user datagram proto-col (UDP) are the protocols recommended to voice transport, and RTP control protocol (RTCP) to provide link aliveness information, while the media are on hold.

The most restrictive performance indicators for inter-active real-time services such as VoIP are the end-to-end delay and jitter. The maximum allowed one-way delay for voice service is 300 ms as stated in [15], with a recommended value lower than 150 ms. The low latency of LTE access

(20–30 ms) reduces the end-to-end delay obtained in previous cellular technologies. However, LTE radio bearers do not employ fixed delay. Instead, fast retransmissions are used to repair erroneous transmissions, and uplink and downlink transmissions are controlled by schedulers. Consequently, LTE transmissions introduce jitter, which implies that UE must implement efficient dejitter buffers. The minimum performance requirements for jitter buffer management of voice media are described in [16]. In Section 4, IP parameters will be analyzed in more detail, while in this section, we will continue with the introduction of some concepts which will identify exactly what is standardized in VoIP over LTE, what is not, and how to generate specific configurations to improve the performance of VoIP over LTE.

The objective of radio resource management (RRM) procedures in LTE is to ensure an efficient use of the resources [17]. RRM algorithms at the eNodeB involve functionalities from layer 1 to layer 3. Admission control mechanisms, QoS management, and semipersistent scheduling are deployed at layer 3, while hybrid adaptive repeat and reQuest (HARQ) management, dynamic scheduling, and link adaptation are in layer 2 and channel quality indicator (CQI) manager and power control in layer 1.

3GPP specifies RRM signaling, but the actual RRM algorithms are not provided [17]. The combination of radio bearers that a UE must support for voice over IMS profile is defined in [18] Annex B. Concretely, the voice traffic requires a guaranteed bit rate (GBR) bearer, as described in [19]. The network resources associated with the evolved packet system (EPS) bearer supporting GBR must be permanently allocated by admission control function in the eNodeB at bearer establishment. Reports from UE, including buffer status and measurements of UE's radio environment, must be required to enable the scheduling of the GBR as described in [20]. In uplink, it is the UE's responsibility to comply with GBR requirements.

In the following subsections, we will analyze separately those parameters and configurations which have been identified in the current state of the art as optimized LTE solutions for VoIP.

2.1.1. Quality Class Indicator. The characteristics of the bearers are signalled with a QoS class identifier (QCI). The QCI is a pointer to a more detailed set of QoS attributes, including layer 2 packet delay budget, packet loss rate, and scheduling priority. As defined in [21], QCI 1 is intended for conversational voice.

2.1.2. RLC Mode Configuration. As specified in [10], the unacknowledged mode (UM) should be configured at radio link control (RLC) layer for EPS bearers with QCI 1 to reduce traffic and latency.

2.1.3. DRX Mode. Support of LTE discontinuous reception (DRX) methods for both UE and network is mandatory to reduce power consumption on mobile devices. The idea behind DRX methods is that the terminal pauses the monitorization of control channels during some periods of time, allowing it to turn the radio off. DRX parameters can be tuned

depending on radio resource control (RRC) status or service. Decisions about when the radio should be activated again can be based on QoS indicators. The simulations conducted in [1] give, for VoIP applications, a potential saving of about 60 percent.

2.1.4. Compression. In order to optimize, radio resources the UE and the network must support robust header compression (RoHC) to minimize the size of IP packets during VoIP calls [10]. As we have already said, the use of UM at RLC and reduced sequence number sizes also decrease overhead. The reduction of packet size will enable the improvement of coding efficiency which is especially important for uplink scenarios and to improve the quality of data connection in areas with poor coverage.

2.1.5. Semipersistent Scheduling. The mechanisms involved in packet scheduling at the eNode-B are three: dynamic packet scheduling, link adaptation, and hybrid adaptive repeat and request management (H-ARQ). Semipersistent scheduling significantly reduces control channel overhead for applications that require persistent radio resource allocations such as VoIP. There are many different ways in which semipersistent scheduling can configure persistent allocations.

Simulated results obtained in [2] show that in uplink direction, semi-persistent scheduling can support higher capacity than dynamic scheduling while at the same time guaranteeing VoIP QoS requirement, but with the cost of sacrificing some statistical multiplexing gains from HARQ. As dynamic scheduling is already needed for other services, they suggest using dynamic scheduling by default for VoIP. As an exception, semi-persistent scheduling should be applied for some VoIP users only in situations where the signaling load becomes too high.

2.1.6. Admission Control. Admission control mechanisms determine whether a new evolve packet system (EPS) bearer request should be admitted by checking that QoS requirements of at least all the bearers with high priority are fulfilled. Specific rules and algorithms for admission control are not specified by 3GPP. An interesting technique is proposed by AT&T Labs Research in [3] based on an intelligent blocking algorithm (IBA) for the admission process of VoIP calls subject to individual customers' blocking objectives and which is only invoked when the total bandwidth in use is close to its engineering limit. The algorithm has also been validated with simulations.

2.1.7. Packet Bundling in Downlink. Traffic generated by voice codecs can be very bursty due to the nature of the service, that is, silences in the conversations, and the nature of the codecs, for example, traffic from the adaptive multi-rate (AMR) codec. The combination between VoIP traffic patterns with dynamic packet scheduling can lead to inefficient resource utilization that might be improved by the use of packet bundling in the downlink. Several simulation studies have been done for both universal terrestrial radio access network (UTRAN) [4] and evolved universal terrestrial radio

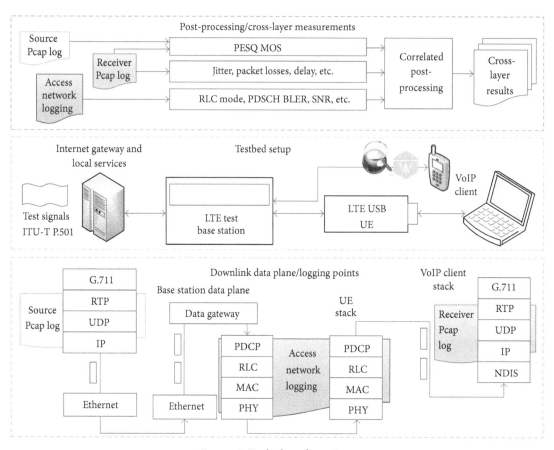

FIGURE 2: Testbed configuration.

access (E-UTRAN) [5] probing that dynamic packet bundling approaches improve VoIP services.

2.1.8. RLC Segmentation and TTI Bundling in Uplink. UE has limited transmission power, and at the edge of LTE cells, there is a high probability of obtaining an error in the transmission of VoIP packets because the device is not able to gather enough energy during one transmission time interval (TTI) (1 ms) to send the packet. In the case of unsuccessful transmission, HARQ retransmissions are required, which will imply the introduction of 8 ms delay per retransmissions. A large number of retransmissions will involve an intolerable increase in the delay for a conversational voice service and reduction of the transmission efficiency.

The conventional approach used to reduce delays and improve the coverage at the cell edge is RLC segmentation. It consists of the segmentation of service data unit (RLC SDU) and their transmission in consecutive TTIs. However, this is not an optimum solution from the point of view of the overhead introduced in the control signaling and the increase of the vulnerability of packet loss due to HARQ feedback errors. The idea behind TTI bundling is that for a given transport block a fixed number of transmissions is done in consecutive TTIs without waiting for the HARQ feedback. The eNodeB sends the corresponding HARQ feedback only when it has received the whole bundle of transmissions. This approach

reduces the amount of HARQ feedback significantly [6]. The L2 header overhead is also reduced because there is a lower need for segmentation, as well as the signaling overhead required for uplink grants (i.e., resource allocations) because a single grant is required for each TTI bundle.

3. Testbed Configuration for VoIP Testing

We have composed an experimental testbed [8] with the aim of providing a realistic test scenario where previous and new radio configurations could be deployed. Additionally, it is possible to analyze their interactions and to verify cross-layer performance of Internet applications and services over LTE. Moreover, the testbed can be used to reproduce, in a controlled environment, behaviors captured in field test campaigns [8].

The testbed includes an LTE test base station from AT4 wireless which provides high performance protocol and radio capabilities behaving as an actual LTE radio access network (RAN), as shown in Figure 2. It also includes features such as emulation of channel propagation that allows modeling fading and additive white gaussian noise impairments, in addition to a high degree of configurability of the LTE stack and logging functions. The LTE test base station supports the connection of real LTE terminals and the transport of IP traffic generated by commercial applications installed on them. The non access stratum (NAS) signalling exchange is provided by a core network emulation. Although the effect of core network transportation is also important for QoS, it has not been analyzed in the present work because of the focus on RAN and will be addressed in the future. The mobile terminals also incorporate advanced monitoring software [22, 23]. Finally, the testbed includes postprocessing tools which enable the testing and identification of IP connectivity issues and LTE mismatches through the correlation of logs collected at different points as shown in Figure 2.

During the experiment, VoIP calls are initiated by a commercial VoIP client running in a laptop. The laptop uses the Samsung GT-B3730 USB LTE modem connected, via a radio frequency (RF) wire, to the E2010 eNodeB emulator from AT4 wireless. The emulator is connected to the Internet and to a local Asterisk server via a proprietary data gateway. The core network is not presented in the current version of the testbed. In this work, we focus on the study of radio access interface performance from the point of view of QoS and QoE perceived at the user equipment (UE). In order to automate the establishment of the calls, the Asterisk server is configured to provide a callback service, so that this service reproduces a 30-second recording each time a call is received in a preconfigured VoIP extension. Records have been extracted from audio samples provided in the (international telegraph union telecommunication standardization sector (ITU-T) recommendation P.501 to speech quality evaluation on telephone networks. The codec used during the transmission is the G.711 because it is well known and its constant bit rate eases the initial analysis of the impact in throughput and similar metrics. Other codecs such as AMR (codec recommended for VoLTE profile in [10]) or SILK (Skype) will be addressed in future experiments.

Wireshark is used to capture the IP traffic on both sides. The emulator also provides low level EUTRAN traces that are valuable for detailed examination of behaviors of interest. The postprocessing of the results collected is carried out using a tool developed in our research group which, among other things, obtains delay, packet losses, jitter, and MOS values of the VoIP calls. perceptual evaluation of speech quality (PESQ) algorithm defined in [24] is used to calculate MOS. PESQ analyzes relative degradation between the original and the received voice signals. In order to apply the algorithm, both waveforms have to be provided as input. The source signal is directly fed to the server, but for comparison purposes, we obtain it from the generated IP traffic to isolate it from server encoding effects, whereas the received voice is reconstructed from the IP traffic recorded by Wireshark at the destination end.

Table 1 contains an example configuration deployed in the LTE test base station.

Different fading and noise propagation conditions have been applied. Multipath fading conditions are typically experienced in mobile environments as a result of the user mobility. A typical environment with low delay spread is represented with the EPA5 profile as defined in [25]. EPA stands for Extended Pedestrian A channel model, which contains 7 channel taps with an average delay spread of 45 ns and a maximum tap delay of 410 ns. The EPA5 profile has

TABLE 1: Resource scheduling and radio frequency configuration in the LTE test base station.

Parameter	Configuration
MIMO configuration	2×2
Channel bandwidth	10 MHz
Reference signal power	−60 dBm/15 kHz
Noise power	−67 to −73 dBm/15 KHz
Max HARQ retransmissions	3
RLC transmission mode	UM
RLC sequence number size	5
PDCP discard policy	No discard
PDCP sequence number size	7
Peak PDSCH bandwidth	120 Kbps
Resource allocation	Periodic, 5 ms
Modulation	16QAM
MCS (mod.& coding index)	13
PHICH duration	Normal
PHICH resources	1/6
Number of PDCCH symbols	1
Specific aggregation level	2
Fading profile	EPA5

TABLE 2: Extended Pedestrian A channel model.

Excess tap delay (ns)	Relative power (dB)
0	0.0
30	−1.0
70	−2.0
90	−3.0
110	−8.0
190	−17.2
410	−20.8

an associated maximum Doppler frequency of 5 Hz, and the associated tap delay and relative power is shown in Table 2.

As demonstrated in the table, the signal to noise ratio (SNR) has been swept in a range of 7 to 13 dB to analyze the results under moderate packet loss conditions. As the VoIP service has real-time requirements, the RLC layer is configured to operate in unacknowledged mode (UM), that does not retransmit. However, although the RLC UM does not retransmit unconfirmed data, the hybrid automatic repeat request (HARQ) at medium access control (MAC) level provides convenient fast retransmission with incremental redundancy. Thus, even in the presence of a moderate Physical downlink shared channel (PDSCH) bLock error rate (BLER), a higher layer protocol data unit (PDU), will only be lost if the maximum number of HARQ retransmissions is reached at MAC level.

4. Analysis of IP Performance

The aim of this paper is not only to introduce a reference framework for measurements of IP services deployed over LTE but also the importance of cross-layer results in the context of the VoIP service. Using the testbed described in the previous section, a campaign of experiments have been carried out to obtain the results referred to. Also cross-layer correlations between LTE mechanism and IP performance are explained.

4.1. IP Parameters. As we have stated in previous sections, some variable bit rate codecs are expected to be used in VoIP over LTE however, in this approach we have chosen the G.711 codec to compare because it is a standard and widely studied codec with constant bit rate (CBR). G.711 codec has a 64 kbps voice bandwidth. The constant sampled rate of 20 ms and the fixed 160 bytes of the payload plus 40 bytes of IP/UDP/RTP header produce a flow with a bandwidth of 80 kbps at the IP level. At the radio access a peak PDSCH bit rate of 120 kbps has been scheduled to provide enough throughput headroom. We have analyzed the IP bandwidth of the flow received by the mobile device during 10 consecutive VoIP calls in the worst-case scenario, that is, the scenario with 7 dB of SNR. The call length is 30 seconds. Results are depicted in Figure 3(a). The instantaneous evolution of the IP bandwidth for the 10 calls is compared with the nominal 80 kbps constant bit rate generated by the source. The IP bandwidth fluctuations obtained at the destination are caused by lost and delayed packets, which cause instantaneous decrements of the received bit rate. Successful retransmissions generate bandwidth peaks one second after the decrement, because the calculation is made averaging the received packets during the last second. Although we have used the LTE same fading profile and nominal signal to noise ratio in all the calls, different instantaneous results have been obtained because of the random nature of the fading and noise generators.

A packet loss rate close to 0% and a jitter lower than 2 ms can provide good quality VoIP calls, even comparable with a public switched telephone network (PSTN) call. However most codecs used in the VoIP service are not tolerant of higher packet losses. For the "standard" G.711 codec or the G.729 codec, a 1% packet loss rate significantly degrades a call [26]. In Figure 3(b), we depict packet losses obtained during sessions where different SNR were configured. We can see that packet losses are higher than 1% only for VoIP call with the lower configured SNR, 7 dB.

The interarrival jitter is calculated as defined in [27] using the IP traces captured at the mobile subscriber terminal. Each RTP packet contains a timestamp which reflects the sampling instant of the first octet in the RTP data packet. The instantaneous variation of the delay is obtained by comparing the elapsed time between two received packets with the difference between their timestamp. The jitter is then derived applying a filter to the instantaneous delay variation. In Figure 3(c), we observe the temporal evolution of instant jitter during VoIP calls conducted in the scenario configured with 7 dB of SNR, while Figure 3(d) shows the mean jitter obtained in all the scenarios. This is a traditional analysis based on only IP parameters, which is very useful to characterize the performance of the service under study. However, it is not enough for the adaptation and optimization of the service to the underlying transport technology. This can be better appreciated by observing Figure 3(d). Concretely,

it can be seen that despite the delay variations introduced by HARQ retransmissions, the average jitter is kept in only a few ms, although eventually the instantaneous delay may vary in the order of tens of ms. However, to obtain a better comprehension of VoIP performance over LTE, it is necessary to monitor low level parameters and correlate them with IP parameters. In the following section, we will analyze the correlations between parameters monitored at different LTE layers.

5. Cross-Layer Measurement Analysis

In this section, a further analysis of the results obtained in previous experiments is provided. Specifically, we will present a correlation of the SNR configured in the experiments with different IP and RF measured parameters. In addition, we will also depict the mapping of voice quality measurements. Known functions (linear, polynomial, exponential, and logarithmic functions) have been applied to obtain the correlation between the parameters. To retrieve the degree of correlation, the coefficient of determination R^2 has been calculated. R^2 ranges from 0 (indicating the absence of a systematic correlation) to 1 (indicating a perfect correlation).

5.1. HARQ and Packet Losses. Figure 4(a) shows the effect of the SNR on the packet loss rate. We have represented the mean value, as well as the minimum and the maximum packet loss rate to illustrate the maximum variability for a given SNR value. It must be noted that although in some points the slope seems to change, these effects may appear because of the randomness of the propagation conditions, these magnitudes require large statistical analysis and in a limited set of experiments small deviations may appear in the results.

We have also compared the PDSCH BLER with the IP packet loss rate. The PDSCH BLER represents the ratio of correctly acknowledged transport blocks to the total number of transmitted transport blocks. As the SNR decreases, the effect of the noise makes the PDSCH BLER increase. In Figure 4(b), we correlate the PDSCH BLER with the packet loss rate. In absence of HARQ, the PDSCH BLER should match the packet loss rate, but HARQ reduces the rate of packet losses at the cost of additional use of PDSCH resources to allocate retransmissions. As we are operating in relatively ideal conditions, the relation between the BLER and the effective bandwidth reduction is approximately linear as a single retransmission will succeed typically. In worse SNR conditions, the ratio of lost packets rate to PDSCH BLER would be even further reduced at the expense of a more noticeable impact on the bandwidth.

Other useful magnitudes are also related with SNR and parameters. The CQI is a magnitude reported by a mobile device, with a configurable periodicity, that provides an estimation of the instantaneous quality of the channel. The larger the reported CQI, the higher the coding rate (lower redundancy) that can be used for transmission. We have verified that the reported average CQI decreases consistently as the noise increases, and in future work, we will provide

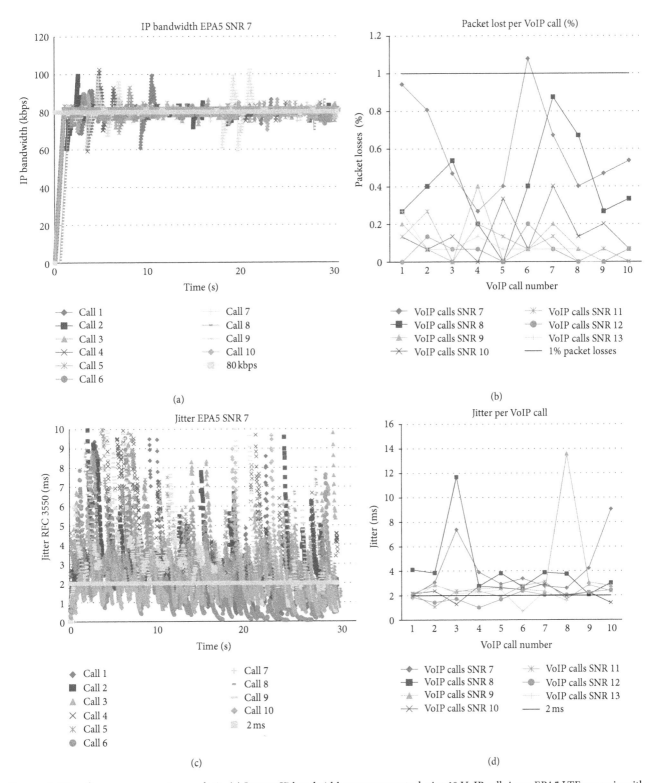

FIGURE 3: IP performance parameters analysis. (a) Instant IP bandwidth measurements during 10 VoIP calls in an EPA5 LTE scenario with a 7 dB of SNR. (b) Packet losses per VoIP call for different levels of SNR in an EPA5 scenario. (c) Instant jitter measurements during 10 VoIP calls in a EPA5 LTE scenario with a 7 dB of SNR. (d) Mean Jitter per VoIP call for different levels of SNR.

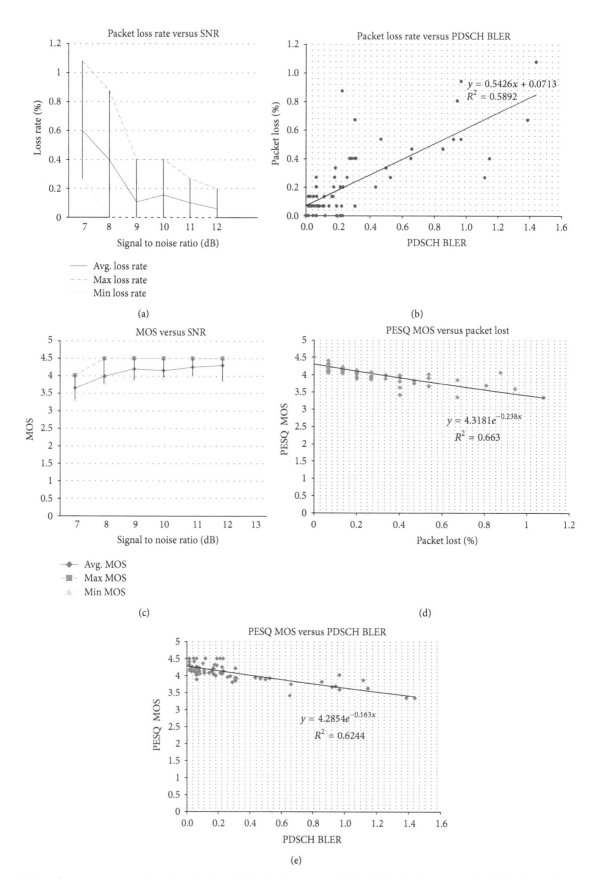

FIGURE 4: Cross-layer measurements and correlations. (a) Packet Loss versus SNR. (b) Packet Loss versus PDSCH BLER. (c) MOS versus SNR. (d) PESQ MOS versus packet lost. (e) PESQ MOS versus PDSCH BLER.

detailed results of the mapping of PDSCH BLER to reported CQI for different cell configurations and propagation conditions. Furthermore, we will also analyze different CQI adaptive schedulers, that will react to the instantaneous received CQI to provide appropriate resource allocations.

In general, low R^2 values have been obtained (0.7 or less) with the equations used, which exposes the complexity of the relationships between the cross-layer parameters analyzed. In future work, we will apply objective-driven simulations [28] to obtain more accurate patterns between cross-layer parameters under study.

5.2. Voice Quality Measurements. In this section, we provide the voice quality results associated to the former experiments. VoIP voice quality has been calculated using the objective PESQ algorithm standardized by ITU-T. The PESQ algorithm outcome provides a quality metric mapped to the MOS. The algorithm requires injecting a known speech signal into the system under test, and the degraded output signal is compared with the original (reference) input. Values between 4 and 4.5 represent toll quality, which is the typical quality offered by the PSTN, while values below 3.5 are often considered by some users. In Figure 4(c), we can see that an SNR of 8 dB or higher produces a an average MOS higher than 4, whereas an SNR of 7 dB results in an MOS of below 3.5 for some calls.

Although the mapping of MOS to packet losses has been analyzed in the literature, it is also represented in Figure 4(d) to verify that a linear estimation can be derived. Particularly, it can be verified that for packet losses close to 0%, the maximum quality is reported by PESQ, whose maximum output is 4.5. It must be noted that the PESQ algorithm does not consider factors such as the end to end delay that affect the subjective quality and are considered in other methods such as the E-model.

In Figure 4(e), the mapping of MOS to the PDSCH BLER is represented. Although it will depend on the cell configuration, in future work, we will consider using delay aware quality algorithms such as E-model to review the relation between MOS and PDSCH BLER, as the delay introduced by HARQ retransmissions could have also an impact on quality depending on the configuration and the end to end delay budget.

6. Conclusions

In this paper, we have provided a detailed state of the art of LTE improvements for enhanced VoIP support. It has also been identified that standardization organizations, alliances, and network operators demand more realistic measurements to improve the QoS and QoE of LTE deployments in general and VoIP over LTE in particular. To that end, we have proposed an experimental testing setup based on a real-time implementation of the LTE radio access where it is possible to test LTE protocol settings, commercial devices, and real applications.

We have also shown the results obtained by the provision of relevant reference performance measurements carried out for a specific configuration at different levels of the communication, covering LTE physical level, IP performance and voice quality evaluation. Moreover, the measurements are correlated to check the consistency of the results and extract the relationships between them. For example, the number of configured HARQ retransmissions has impact on the tradeoff between maximum delay and packet losses. These results will also complement the limited nonsimulated results currently available in the scientific literature.

During the experiments, it has been identified a noticeable variability of the results because of the use of realistic impairments such as fading and noise. Real-time test environment where the experiments can be largely repeated, as the proposed one, will definitely contribute to improve the statistical relevance of the results with shorter test times.

For future work we plan to extend the number of fading profiles, increase the parameters logged at the emulated environment, and automate the execution of the tests to increase the number of VoIP calls under study, which will improve statistical validity of the results. With these automation features, we will apply the presented methodology to validate the proposals identified in the summarized state of the art. The testbed will be also extended with a core network which will enable to evaluate the impact of the transport in the evolved packet core (EPC) and study the performance of mobility procedures such as S1- and X2-based handovers.

Acknowledgments

This work has been funded by the Government of Andalusia under Grant ITC-20111046, the Spanish Ministry of Innovation and Science under Grant IPT-2011-1034-370000 and FEDER from the European Commission.

References

[1] C. S. Bontu and E. Illidge, "DRX mechanism for power saving in LTE," *IEEE Communications Magazine*, vol. 47, no. 6, pp. 48–55, 2009.

[2] D. Jiang, H. Wang, E. Malkamaki, and E. Tuomaala, "Principle and performance of semi-persistent scheduling for VoIP in LTE system," in *Proceedings of the International Conference on Wireless Communications, Networking and Mobile Computing (WiCOM '07)*, pp. 2861–2864, September 2007.

[3] X. Mang, Y. Levy, C. Johnson, and D. Hoeflin, "Admission control for VoIP calls with heterogeneous codecs," in *Proceedings of the 18th Annual Wireless and Optical Communications Conference (WOCC '09)*, pp. 1–4, May 2009.

[4] O. Fresan, T. Chen, K. Ranta-aho, and T. Ristaniemi, "Dynamic packet bundling for VoIP transmission over Rel'7 HSUPA with 10ms TTI length," in *Proceedings of the 4th IEEE International Symposium on Wireless Communication Systems (ISWCS '07)*, pp. 508–512, October 2007.

[5] J. Puttonen, T. Henttonen, N. Kolehmainen, K. Aschan, M. Moisio, and P. Kela, "Voice-over-IP performance in UTRA long term evolution Downlink," in *Proceedings of the IEEE 67th Vehicular Technology Conference (VTC Spring '08)*, pp. 2502–2506, May 2008.

[6] R. Susitaival and M. Meyer, "LTE coverage improvement by TTI bundling," in *Proceedings of the IEEE 69th Vehicular Technology Conference (VTC Spring '09)*, esp, April 2009.

[7] NGMN, "NGMN top OPE recommendations version 1.0.21," Tech. Rep., NGMN Alliance, 2010.

[8] A. Diaz, P. Merino, and F. J. Rivas, "Test environment for QoS testing of VoIP over LTE," in *Proceedings of the IEEE Network Operations and Management Symposium (NOMS '12)*, pp. 780–794, 2012.

[9] 3GPP, "Digital cellular telecommunications system (Phase 2+), Universal Mobile Telecommunications System (UMTS), Circuit Switched (CS) fallback in Evolved Packet System (EPS), stage 2," TS 23.272.

[10] GSMA, "Permanent Reference Document (PRD) IP Multimedia Subsystem (IMS) profile for voice and SMS," GSMA IR92, 2012.

[11] V. Forum, "Voice over LTE via generic access, requirements specification, phasel," TS 1.4.0, 2010.

[12] ETSI, "Digital cellular telecommunications system (Phase 2+), Generic Access Network (GAN), stage 2," TS 43.318, 2012.

[13] M. Forum, "MSF VoLTE interoperability event 2011. Multivendor testing in global LTE and IMS Networks," WhitePaper, 2011.

[14] Epitiro, "LTE "Real World" Performance Study. Broadband and voice over LTE, (VoLTE) quality analysis: TeliaSonera," Tech. Rep., Epitiro, 2011.

[15] 3GPP, "Digital cellular telecommunications system (Phase 2+), Universal Mobile Telecommunications System (UMTS), LTE, Services and service capabilities," TS 22.105.

[16] 3GPP, "Universal Mobile Telecommunications System (UMTS); LTE; IP Multimedia Subsystem (IMS); Multimedia telephony; Media handling and interaction," TS 26.114.

[17] A. T. Harri Holma, *LTE for UMTS: Evolution to LTEAdvanced*, chapter 8, Wiley, 2011.

[18] 3GPP, "LTE; Evolved Universal Terrestrial Radio Access (E-UTRA); Radio Resource Control (RRC); Protocol specification," TS 36.331.

[19] 3GPP, "LTE; General Packet Radio Service (GPRS) enhancements for Evolved Universal Terrestrial Radio Access Network (E-UTRAN) access," TS 23.401.

[20] 3GPP, "LTE; Evolved Universal Terrestrial Radio Access (E-UTRA) and Evolved Universal Terrestrial Radio Access Network (E-UTRAN); Overall description; stage 2," TS 36.300.

[21] 3GPP, "Digital cellular telecommunications system (Phase 2+); Universal Mobile Telecommunications System (UMTS); LTE; Policy and charging control architecture," TS 23.203.

[22] A. Díaz, P. Merino Gomez, and F. Rivas Tocado, "Mobile application profiling for connected mobile devices," *IEEE Pervasive Computing*, vol. 9, no. 1, pp. 54–61, 2010.

[23] A. Alvarez, A. Diaz, P. Merino, and F. J. Rivas, "Field measurements of mobile services with android smartphones," in *Proceedings of the IEEE Consumer Communications and Networking Conference (CCNC '12)*, pp. 105–109, 2012.

[24] I. T. U. -T, "Perceptual evaluation of speech quality (PESQ): an objective method for end-to-end speech quality assessment of narrow-band telephone networks and speech codecs," Recommendation P.862.

[25] 3GPP, "Evolved Universal Terrestrial Radio Access (EUTRA); User Equipment (UE) conformance specification; radio transmission and reception; part 1: conformance testing," Tech. Rep. 36.521-1, TS.

[26] O. Heckmann, *The Competitive Internet Service Provider: Network Architecture, Interconnection, Traffic Engineering and Network Design*, Wiley, 2007, Edited by, D. Hutchison.

[27] H. Schulzrinne, S. Casner, R. Frederick, and V. Jacobson, *RTP: A Transport Protocol For Real-Time Applications*, Internet Engineering Task Force, RFC.

[28] A. Díaz, P. Merino, and A. Salmerón, "Obtaining models for realistic mobile network simulations using real traces," *IEEE Communications Letters*, vol. 15, no. 7, pp. 782–784, 2011.

14

Infrastructure Sharing as an Opportunity to Promote Competition in Local Access Networks

João Paulo Pereira[1] and Pedro Ferreira[2]

[1] School of Technology and Management, Polytechnic Institute of Bragança (IPB), 5301-857 Bragança, Portugal
[2] Institute for Systems and Robotics, Technical University of Lisbon (IST), 1049-001 Lisbon, Portugal

Correspondence should be addressed to João Paulo Pereira, jprp@ipb.pt

Academic Editor: John Doucette

Telecom infrastructures are facing unprecedented challenges, with increasing demands on network capacity. Today, network operators must determine how to expand the existing access network infrastructure into networks capable of satisfying the user's requirements. Thus, in this context, providers need to identify the technological solutions that enable them to profitably serve customers and support future needs. However, the identification of the "best" solution is a difficult task. Although the cost of bandwidth in the active layer has reduced significantly (and continually) in recent years, the cost of the civil works—such as digging and trenching—represents a major barrier for operators to deploy NGA infrastructure. Duct is a critical part of the next-generation access networks, and its sharing would reduce or eliminate this capital cost and this barrier to entry. The aim of this paper is to provide a better understanding of the economics of broadband access networks technologies (wireline and wireless), their role in the deployment of several services in different regions, and the development of competition in the access networks.

1. Introduction

The need for telecommunication networks with higher capacity is becoming a reality all over the world. However, there is a recognized disparity between broadband availability in urban and rural areas. Preexisting rural telecommunications infrastructure is generally poor and unevenly distributed in favor of urban centers [1]. In most rural areas, low population density and high deployment costs discourage private investment, creating a negative feedback of limited capacity, high prices, and low service demand. It is costly to build telecommunications networks in rural areas. Further, in many cases, there is not a good commercial business case for rural deployments; established, competitive service providers already offer solutions for urban and suburban areas, yet there is little or no commitment to connect areas that include smaller towns and rural villages [2]. The deployment of access network broadband services in low competition areas is characterized by low subscriber densities, longer loop lengths, lower duct availability, and, consequently, higher infrastructure costs compared to high competition areas.

The rapid development of new-generation applications requires upgrading the access infrastructure a necessity for higher throughput requirements and communication demands. These applications include high-definition television (HDTV), peer-to-peer (P2P) applications, video on demand, interactive games, e-learning, and use of multiple personal computers (PCs) at home. Other ubiquitous broadband access requires a minimum bit rate sufficient to allow all citizens to benefit from these services. As a result, to run voice, data, video, and advanced Internet applications, residential users might soon need connections of more than 30 Mbps [3].

Service and network providers are challenged to provide this higher-capacity access to the end user and offer wider services. Consequently, new Internet infrastructure and technologies that are capable of providing high-speed and high-quality services are needed to accommodate multimedia applications with diverse QoS requirements. Until a few years ago, Internet access for residential users was almost exclusively provided via public switched telephone networks (PSTN) over the twisted copper pair [4]. The new quadruple play services (i.e., voice, video, data, and mobility) require high-speed broadband access, which created new challenges for the modern broadband wireless/wired access networks [5]. The new services led both to the development of several different last-mile solutions to make the access network capable of supporting the requirements and to a stronger integration of optical and wireless access networks.

2. Next-Generation Networks (NGNs)

The move toward NGNs has significant implications for the technical architecture and design of access network infrastructure, as well as the value chains and business models of electronic communications service provision [6]. This migration has begun to transform the telecommunication sector from distinct single-service markets into converging markets [7]. NGNs allow consumers to choose from among different access network technologies to access their service environment. In our work, the NGN architecture will be limited to the current and future developments of network architectures in the access network (local loop), referred to as the "next-generation access network" (NGAN).

2.1. Next-Generation Access Networks. NGANs are being deployed across the world with technologies, such as fiber, copper utilizing xDSL technologies, coaxial cable, power line communications (PLC), wireless solutions, or hybrid deployments of these technologies. Wireless networks typically use a range of different technologies, including high speed packet access (HSPA), HSPA+, worldwide interoperability for microwave access (WiMAX), and long-term evolution (LTE). Further, wireline networks increasingly employ some form of fiber, such as fiber-to-the-home (FTTH) and fiber-to-the-curb/cabinet (FTTC). NGN access in a fixed network is initially broadband access-based on the copper loops; however, many countries are in the process of enhancing these networks over time to provide higher speed using fiber-based technology, such as very high-speed digital subscriber line (VDSL) or FTTB/H. For cable networks, often the only voice service is IP based, whereas for mobile networks, the migration to IP voice is more complex [6].

2.2. Competition in Next-Generation Access. The choice of a specific technology for NGAN can be different among countries, geographic areas, and operators. In recent years, there has been an increase in the number, coverage, and market share of "alternative" networks or operators, such as resellers, unbundling operators, cable network operators, operators using frequencies for WLL/WiMAX, and operators deploying optical fiber in the local loop [8]. This has resulted in differences in competitive conditions among geographic areas, leading to increasing arguments (especially from incumbent operators) that geographical aspects should be recognized in market/competition analyses and regulatory decisions. There are several factors that might be responsible for this discrepancy [9]: state and age of the existing network infrastructure; length of the local loop; population density and structure of the housing market; distribution of the number of users and street cabinets for local exchange;

level of intermodal competition in the market; willingness to pay for broadband services; existence of ad hoc national government plans for broadband development.

3. Model Overview

3.1. Description. The proposed model compares seven NGA broadband technologies—FTTH-PON, xDSL, HFC, PLC, Fixed WiMAX, UMTS, and LTE—in different scenarios, focusing on the access segment of the network (between CO and customer premises). Some assets within the access network include (1) feeder, distribution segment, and the final drop connection to the customer's premises (we assume that the cost associated with final drop connection is included in the activation fee of the service); (2) trenches/ducts from CO and customer premises; (3) cable (optical fiber, copper, and coax) in feeder and distribution part of the network; (4) radio systems (wireless solutions); (5) equipment, such as repeaters, line cards, DSLAMs, ONU, and OLTs.

The programming language used to implement the model was Microsoft Excel with Visual Basic for Applications (VBA), which includes all relevant capital and operating expenditures for the several technologies. The proposed tool calculates the required total expenditure in terms of CAPEX, OPEX, and other several economic indicators.

3.2. Model Structure. The proposed model is divided into four main parts (Figure 1): input parameters, engineering model (applies engineering criteria to determine the volumes of components), economic model (provides information for several kinds of information), and a sensitivity analysis model that shows the effects of uncertainties.

4. Business Case (Case Study) Definition

The definition of a "business case" implies a great number of assumptions, such as the penetration rate, components prices, and the market share rate. However, it is difficult to get an exact forecast of its performance. The utility of a business case is offering a more approximated estimation that allows for the construction of future scenarios. It is fundamental that the business case be as realistic as possible to be useful and reflect all the variables of interest of the market as well as its own evolution and expected behavior [11].

In each business case, several scenarios can be defined by network alternatives, service portfolio, market segments, and external factors such as regulatory issues, competition, and demand evolution [12]. A "scenario" is the description of the network situation to provide a given set of services to a number of users within a certain area and study period, including one or several operators [13, 14]. In summary, the scenario description is defined in terms of regulation, services, competition, and technology. Scenario-based technoeconomics uses scenarios to estimate several economic results of a technology in different circumstances.

4.1. Main Assumptions and Input Parameters. The first step is to collect all input relevant to the business case. Each network

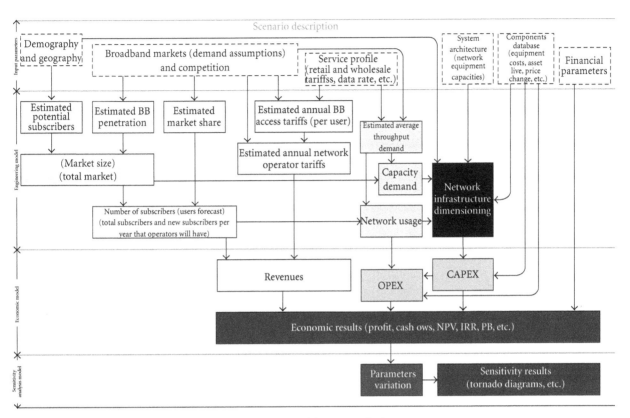

FIGURE 1: Model structure [10].

deployment has a unique set of financial, technical, and business parameters that need to be modeled and analyzed [15]. The base case was developed to study the costs and other economic results of two technologies (FTTH: PON and LTE) in two different regions (urban and rural) and different competitive markets. The analysis horizon is 10 years.

The network is built for the total number of homes passed in advance of subscriber turn on (fixed costs). All construction work (trench, ducts, cable, cabinets, base stations, etc.) required to provide service to all homes passed takes place in the first year. Therefore, all infrastructure costs (e.g., housing construction, electronics, and cable deployment) are incurred for all homes passed. Equipment is deployed based on take rate assumptions. This implies that in areas with low penetration rates, the cost per subscriber would be higher than at high take rates, where it would be low [16]. However, the deployment costs of the CPE, the drop cable/installation, and the ports in the aggregate node are incurred only when a home subscribes (marginal costs). We also assume there is maximum sharing of trenching, which means that all wires run over a common trench for as far as possible. The method used to calculate the reduction factor for trench sharing is based on previous Europe economic projects [17]. Table 1 presents the main general assumptions considered for the business case.

4.2. Territory and Demography. For the rural area, the rollout strategy does not cover the whole area; the target area is limited to 34.04 km^2 with 23,000 inhabitants (see Table 2).

Several studies and models [19, 20] assume that in urban areas, the duct availability rate is about 60% for feeder segments and 40% for the distribution segment. In rural areas, the duct availability rate is 25% for feeder and 0% for the distribution segment. The report from Analysys-Mason [21] assumes that a substantial proportion (80% near to the CO and 30% nearer to the premises) of existing ducts can be reused for fiber deployment (see Table 3).

For mobile solutions, [22] assumes a site sharing of 90% in urban areas (lower in less-populated areas) as regulation declares that masts for UMTS must be shared between operators.

4.3. Service Profiles Assumptions. Service profile is key driver of the business model, and some assumptions have to be made. The service profile drives the revenue and traffic forecasts, and the traffic forecast drives capital and operating expenses. The traffic generated by users is required to calculate economic results. For all services, we need to define the type (e.g., triple play and phone), bandwidths, mobility, and so on.

So, as the network services are used and the number of users connected in the network is increasing, the throughput demand tends to grow quite rapidly over time. Several studies propose some 20% to 50% growth every year in the long run [14, 23–26]. Since the average traffic demand per user is increasing exponentially, the network is initially dimensioned for the whole demand growth in the study period.

TABLE 1: General assumptions summary.

Input assumption	Description
Analysis horizon	10 years
Operator type	Incumbent, CLEC (Competitive Local Exchange Carrier) and new entrants
Geographical profiles	Urban coverage and rural coverage. An urban area was chosen due to the high-density population and to the high data demand. A rural area was chosen due to its low-density population and its relatively low service demand compared with urban areas.
Technology scenarios	The cost model considers two different technological options for the provision of next-generation broadband services: FTTH(PON) and LTE. We assume that each region has only one CO.
CPE costs	Subscriber's proportion on CPE costs: 100% for Fiber and 50% for LTE. This means that the network operator is assumed to subsidize the LTE CPEs in order to make the service offering competitive with Fiber offerings.
Target market	Consumer (Households)
Broadband service profile	S1—2 Mbps (10% annual variation) S2— 20 Mbps (20% annual variation)
Rollout scenario	Fast rollout—1st year (100%) for both regions
Financial inputs	We apply a unique WACC to represent the risk associated with the wireline operators (9.96%) and other WACC to wireless operators (11.9%).

TABLE 2: Territorial and demographic scenarios.

Parameters	Region 1	Region 2
Geographic area type	Urban	Rural
Size of Area: Surface (km²)	45.90	1.173
Population	172,063	34.000
Trend (% per year)	0.62%	−0.04%
Density (pop/km²)	3.748	29
Target area		
Target area (km²)	45.90	34.04
Target Population	172.063	23.000
Trend (% per year)	0.62%	0.01%
Density (pop/km²)	3,748	676
Inhabitants per household	1.99	1.54
Total no. of potential subscribers (HH)	86.565	14.921
Number of buildings in serving area	18.249	6.596

Let us assume the growth ratio of throughput demand to be 1.12 (12%) per year for Service 2 and 1.1 (10%) per year for Service 1 (see Table 4).

As the average traffic demand per user increases, the network is initially dimensioned for the whole demand growth in the study period.

TABLE 3: Infrastructure reuse assumptions [18].

Component	Proportion of existing infrastructure reused
Feeder segment duct	50%
Distribution segment duct	80%
Final drop	50%
Street cabinet	100%

TABLE 4: Service profile technical features.

Service profiles	Data rate per subscriber (Mbps)	Annual variation
Service 1	2 (DS)/0.200 (US)	10%
Service 2	20 (DS)/2 (US)	12%

The expected tariff evolution (factor by which the tariff is expected to increase or decrease annually) is defined for both tariffs (see Table 5). We assume that one provider charges the same retail price in all regions. We observe that several studies and deployments [27–29] use the yearly price erosion of between 5% and 15%.

4.4. Broadband Market Penetration (Penetration Rates). It is challenging to forecast the number of subscribers an operator can expect to sign over the life of the network. Specially, it is hard to predict consumers' behavior when faced with new technologies, new services, or if is required to opt for a new provider of that service [30].

For fixed broadband, the European research project CELTIC/MARCH estimates a penetration rate of 67.2% in 2018 (60% in 2010). As we can see in Figure 2, the fixed broadband penetration is reaching a saturation level. For mobile broadband, the long-term broadband saturation level in the consumer market (Western EU) is estimated to be between 32% [31] and 34% [28, 32, 33] in 2020. In 2010, the average penetration in Western EU was 6% and is estimated that penetration will be 20% in 2015 [34]. During the study period, there will be churn effect caused by mobile broadband substitution. Reference [28] argues that specific reasons are the cheaper prices of mobile broadband compared with fixed broadband. The market forecast is based on Gompertz model. Figures 2 and 3 show the penetration forecast for fixed and mobile technologies. In 2020, the expected penetration rates for the fixed technologies are 1.5% for WiMAX, 14.25% for HFC, 22.71% for fiber, and 30.97% for DSL.

To better plan the network capacity, we also segment the estimated broadband penetration into services classes; it is important to characterize how many subscribers are assigned to each service in each region/segment. We estimate that in Year 1, 40% of all subscribers in the urban area (for the residential market segment) are assigned to Service 1 (2 Mbps) and 60% are Service 2 (20 Mbps). We also assume that market share of Service 1 has a decrease about 5% in the urban area and 3% in the rural area.

TABLE 5: Service profile characteristics (retail prices).

Service profiles	Activation fees	Annual variation	Monthly fees	Annual variation
Service 1	100 €	−5%	20 € /month	−5%
Service 2	100 €	−5%	50 € /month	−7%

TABLE 6: FTTH (PON) architecture components by category.

Cost categories	Costs
Equipment costs	(1) OLT (ports and chassis); (2) splitter (primary split); (3) splitter (secondary split); (4) ONU; (5) fiber modem; (6) optical repeater.
Installation costs (Equip.)	(1) OLT (ports and chassis); (2) splitter (primary split and secondary split); (3) ONU and CPE; (4) optical repeater.
Housing costs	Cost of building remote nodes—splitter cabinet/closures (secondary split). The cost for building the CO is not included.
Civil works (Labor)	Cost of the labor required and include (1) trenching costs (digging and ducting costs) of feeder and distribution plant; (2) cable installation—pulling (cable not included) the cable on the feeder and distribution plant.
Cable costs	Cost of the necessary fiber optics (installation not included). Include the fiber cable required for the feeder and distribution plant.

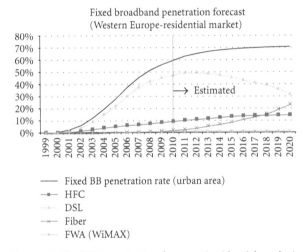

FIGURE 2: Fixed BB penetration forecasts (residential market).

4.5. Competition and Market Share (Deployment Strategies). In this section, we define the number of competitors (players) in the service operator market, the number of competitors (players) in the network operator market, and the market shares of the competitors.

In the urban area, the new entrant is faced with three players (competitors) in broadband fixed access technologies and three competitors in the broadband mobile access technologies: (1) DSL: one incumbent operator and one competitive operator (also known as alternative operators). It is assumed that the three operators (incumbent, competitive, and new entrant) control the entire market (100%); (2) HFC: one incumbent operator; (3) UMTS: three incumbent operators. In the rural market, the new entrant has one competitor in broadband fixed access technologies and three competitors in the broadband mobile access technologies: (1) DSL: one incumbent operator; (2) UMTS: three incumbent operators.

5. Network Architecture Assumptions

With this business case, we want to compare two solutions (FTTH: PON and LTE) from the point of view of the existent competitors and a new entrant (i.e., an operator that does not have its own network infrastructure in the service area). Figure 4 shows the architecture defined in our case.

5.1. Network Components. For FTTH architecture, we assume that in the central office, the OLT card (with one or several ports) ensures the interface between the switching equipment and the ODN (Optical Distribution Network). The OLT line cards are aggregated on shelves that are placed in racks. The OM (Optical Monitoring) module surveys the ODN quality and an MDF (Main Distribution Frame), which provides a connection point between equipment and outside cables. For outside plant construction, it is necessary to consider the hardware parts (fiber cables, splices, splitters, connectors, and enclosures) together with civil work (e.g.,

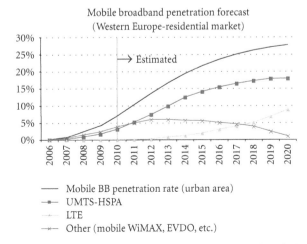

FIGURE 3: Mobile BB penetration forecasts (residential market).

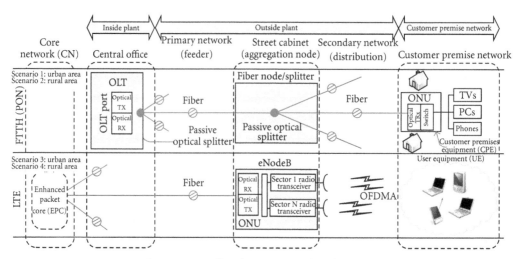

FIGURE 4: Broadband access network architecture.

TABLE 7: LTE architecture components.

Segment		Components
Evolved Packet Core (EPC)		OLT ports; chassis; splitter (primary split); installation (ports, chassis, and split).
Outside Plant	Feeder (EPC-eNodeB)	Optical repeater; repeater installation; aerial/buried trenches/ducts (trenching costs); fiber cable (cable cost); cable installation.
	eNodeB	Site acquisition or site lease; civil works BS/cabinets; housing cabinet/closures for each BS; TRXs; BS installation cost (including sectors); ONU (per BS) and installation.
	Distribution	Wireless PMP access
End User		LTE terminal (include antenna, transceiver, radio modem) and installation.

TABLE 8: CAPEX costs.

Component name	Cost value	Installation cost	Source
Equipment costs per unit			
Fiber modem	80 €	100 €	CSMG
Fiber splitter	100 €	50 €	CSMG
Fiber OLT card (Ports32)	60000 €	20 €	CSMG
OLT Chassis cards 32	5000 €	150 €	CSMG
Fiber Optical repeater	10000 €	60 €	Optilab
Fiber_ONU	106 €	50 €	CSMG
LTE_CPE	75 €	100 €	LUCENT
LTE ENodeB	34000 €		WiROI LTE
LTE TRX	5000 €	1000 €	WiROI LTE
Housing (structure)			
FNode Cab. 512user	2450 €		CSMG
FNode Cab. 2048user	3200 €		CSMG
LTE Site BuildOut	17000 €		WiMAX Forum
Civil works costs			
Digging/ducting costs: urban (per km)	60000 € (urban) 40000 € (rural)	CSMG	
LTE_BS_CivilWorks	1000 €		WiMAX Forum
Cable costs (per km)			
OpticalCable24Fiber	1220 €	900 €	Analysys Mason
OpticalCable96Fiber	2934 €	900 €	Analysys Mason

TABLE 9: Operation and administration costs (OPEX).

Operation and administration costs	OAM cost	Assumptions	Source
Equipment maintenance	7.00%	of CAPEX for equipment	
Installation equipment	5.00%	of CAPEX for Installation	
Housing: cabinets/closures	5.00%	of CAPEX for closures	Analysys Consulting 2009
Cables (copper, coax, fiber)	4.00%	of CAPEX for cables	
Civil works	3.00%	of CAPEX for Civil Works	
Network operations	10.00%	of gross revenue	
Site rental, per MSC/GMSC		Urban areas: 3000 €/Year Rural areas: 1000 €/Year	EC 2009

TABLE 10: Technical assumptions.

Technical parameters	Value
Downstream rate (Mbps) per OLT port	622
Upstream rate (Mbps) per OLT port	155
Number of OLT ports per Card	08
Number of OLT card slots per OLT Chassis	16
Primary split	04
Secondary split	08
Feeder cable type (Optical Cable)	24 Fiber
Distribution cable type	8 Fiber
Capacity per optical cable (Mbps)	1000
Distance between optical repeater (km)	5
Max. ONUs per OLT port	64
Max. nodeB per RNC	100
Max. capacity per RNC (Mbps)	250
LTE (evolved node B)	
Maximum DS capacity per ONU (Mbps)	2000
Number of sectors per NodeB	3
Maximum number of TRX per sector	6
Max. Base Station range—radius (km)	1.0
Downstream TRX capacity (Mbps)	20.00
Upstream TRX capacity (Mbps)	0.512

trenching) and installation techniques. Each fiber cable is composed of several fibers.

Digging and ducting are the major cost items in access networks, outweighing by far the costs of the transmission medium and the line terminating equipment. Civil works typically take some 85% of fiber to the home (FTTH) first installed network costs, while the fiber cable and the optical components take only 3%; the remainder is taken by other hardware, installation activities, and other services [35]. Hence, in Greenfield situations, the costs of introducing FTTH may not differ much from twisted copper pair or coaxial cable access solutions (see Table 6).

Based on LTE system architecture presented previously, the LTE system consists of two main blocks: the E-UTRAN and the EPC. The E-UTRAN segment is characterized by a network of eNBs that support OFDMA and advanced antenna techniques. Each eNB is composed of an antenna system (radio tower), building, and base station equipment (transceivers and antenna interface equipment). In the UE

segment, users who connect using LTE mobile broadband will require an LTE modem to access the network, which will be available using PCMCIA cards; internally embedded modems inside laptops; ExpressCard; or a USB modem. Any users with mobile phones or PDA devices will also eventually have the ability to access the Internet using LTE mobile broadband services. For home Network Termination Units (NTUs), a receiver assembly that can produce one or more outputs can be connected to devices such as home telephones, computers, or television sets (see Table 7).

5.2. Capital Expense (CAPEX) Items. For each technology, a number of cost components are assigned to different parts of the networks. The major CAPEX components for each technology are described in Table 8. For each component cost, we also use a set of parameters required to calculate final costs, depreciation, economies of scale, and so on.

5.3. Operating Expense (OPEX) Items. Like network components costs, operation, and administration costs (OAM) have to be included in the calculations analyses. Table 9 presents the OPEX costs (per annum) as a percentage of initial CAPEX.

5.4. Technical Specifications. Several key network design assumptions used in our model are combined with the service profile as an additional input to the business model. These assumptions are presented in Table 10. These values are used to calculated network traffic, capital expenses, and operations expenses.

5.5. Scenarios. Several business case scenarios are studied and the economical results are presented (see Table 11).

6. Business Case Evaluation (Results)

In Scenario 9 (upgrade DSL/HFC to FTTH(PON), urban area), the NPV is positive (23 M€), IRR is 42%, and payback period is five years. However, in the rural area (Scenario 10), the NPV and IRR are negative, and the payback period is greater than this study period (see Table 12).

Results show that the strategy of new entrant to deploy fiber deeper into the access network is not economically viable (Scenarios 11 and 12). In the urban area (Scenario 11),

TABLE 11: Scenarios description.

Scenario	Description
9 and 10 Upgrade	Upgrade of DSL to FTTH(PON) in both regions. This scenario analyses the incumbent player that has an existing DSL network and aims evolve to FTTH(PON).
11 and 12 New entrant	New entrant deploy FTTH(PON) in both regions. BB access fiber deployment strategy used is the infrastructure deployment (Fiber deployment deeper in the AN).
17 and 18 Upgrade	This scenario analyzes the incumbent player that has an existing UMTS network and wants to deploy its own LTE network. Many operators already have 2G/3G networks with BS, which means that an important part of the investments have been carried out.
19 and 20 New entrant	New entrant with LTE license in both regions.

TABLE 12: General economic results: FTTH(PON).

Indicator	Region 1			Region 2		
	Scenario 9	Scenario 11		Scenario 10	Scenario 12	
	Operator 1	Operator 2	Operator 3	Operator 1	Operator 2	Operator 3
Type of operator	**Incumbent**	**New entrant**	—	**Incumbent**	**New entrant**	—
Payback period	5	> Study Period	—	> Study Period	> Study Period	—
Payback period (DCF)	5	> Study Period	—	> Study Period	> Study Period	—
NPV—year 10	23.525.114 €	77.930.761 €	—	2.891.438 €	74.554.064 €	—
IRR	42.60%	−15.42%	—	−2.69%	−35.24%	—
Cost per subsc. Y1 (CAPEX+OPEX)	3.037 €	92.052 €	—	14.331 €	3.494.104 €	—
Cost per subsc Yn (CAPEX+OPEX)	102 €	225 €	—	68 €	234 €	—
Total 10-year cumulative CAPEX	17.024.848 €	108.287.583 €	—	6.617.710 €	81.922.300 €	—
Total 10-year cumulative OPEX	8.630.924 €	7.914.193 €	—	892.505 €	2.920.012 €	—

TABLE 13: General economic results of FTTH(PON) with infrastructure sharing.

Indicator	Region 1			Region 2		
	Scenario 9	Scenario 11		Scenario 10	Scenario 12	
	Operator 1	Operator 2	Operator 3	Operator 1	Operator 2	Operator 3
Type of operator	**Incumbent**	**New entrant**	—	**Incumbent**	**New entrant**	—
Payback period	4	10	—	7	> Study Period	—
Payback period (DCF)	5	> Study Period	—	10	> Study Period	—
NPV—year 10	28.631.692 €	6.494.183 €	—	359.689 €	5.515.438 €	—
IRR	32.91%	−4.30%	—	1.82%	−20.12%	—
Cost per subsc. Y1 (CAPEX+OPEX)	3.127 €	25.595 €	—	9.608 €	287.934 €	—
Cost per subsc Yn (CAPEX+OPEX)	103 €	193 €	—	84 €	261 €	—
Total 10-year cumulative CAPEX	15.922.467 €	31.696.364 €	—	4.470.139 €	7.122.407 €	—
Total 10-year cumulative OPEX	9.632.985 €	7.012.172 €	—	1.067.618 €	2.367.722 €	—

TABLE 14: General economic results of LTE.

Indicator	Region 1			Region 2		
	Scenario 17	Scenario 19		Scenario 18	Scenario 20	
	Operator 1	Operator 2	Operator 3	Operator 1	Operator 2	Operator 3
Type of operator	**Incumbent**	**New entrant**	—	**Incumbent**	**New entrant**	—
Payback period	8	> Study Period	—	9	> Study Period	—
Payback period (DCF)	10	> Study Period	—	> Study Period	> Study Period	—
NPV—10 year	741.070 €	305.266.868 €	—	37.747 €	38.237.147 €	—
IRR	14.56%	−30.02%	—	10.99%	−30.10%	—
Cost per subsc. Y1 (CAPEX+OPEX)	138.160 €	7.776.688 €	—	151.019 €	6.971.479 €	—
Cost per subsc Yn (CAPEX+OPEX)	93 €	110 €	—	87 €	104 €	—
Total 10-year cumulative CAPEX	5.254.196 €	330.436.601 €	—	793.222 €	41.469.144 €	—
Total 10-year cumulative OPEX	1.902.605 €	25.798.773 €	—	244.684 €	3.145.164 €	—

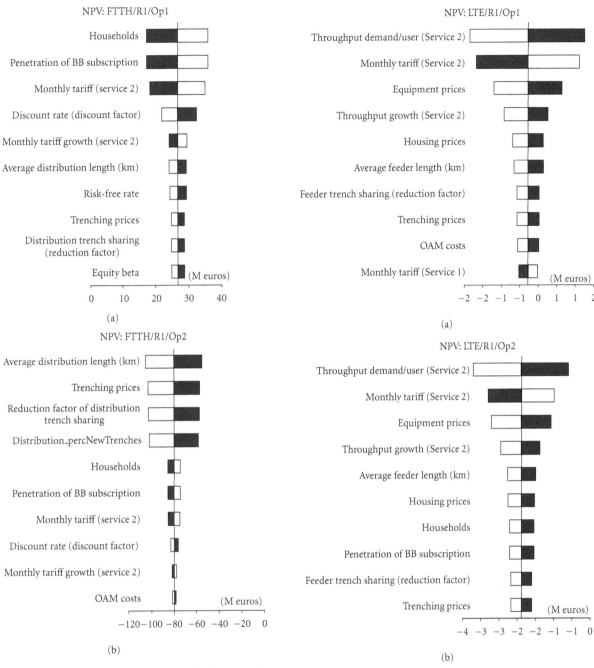

FIGURE 5: Sensitivity analysis results, FTTH(PON)/urban area/Op. 1 and 2.

FIGURE 6: Sensitivity analysis results, LTE/rural area/Op. 1 and 2.

the NPV is −77.9 M€ and IRR is −15.42%. In Scenario 12 (rural area), the estimated NPV in the end of Year 10 is −74.5 M€ and IRR is −35.2%. The cumulated CAPEX in Year 10 for the urban area is six times superior to the incumbent costs. In the rural area, the CAPEX is 13 times superior (see Table 12).

For Scenarios 11 and 12, we also compute the economic results when the new entrant uses the passive infrastructure (ducts) from the incumbent operator (see Table 13). Table 14 presents the economic results if the new entrant (Operator 2) decides to lease (instead of build) the ducts from incumbent

(Operator 1). We assume, in the urban area, duct availability (number of ducts available for leasing) of 100% in the feeder segment and 100% in the distribution segment. For the rural area, we assume 75% and 75% for both feeder and distribution segments. The results clearly indicate that the economic results improve significantly. The NPV of Operator 1 increases from 23 M€ to 28.6 M€, and the payback period is reduced to 4 years; this occurs because of the value paid by Operator 2 to use Operator 1's infrastructure. Operator 2 also gets positive effects with the increase of NPV, about 70 M€,

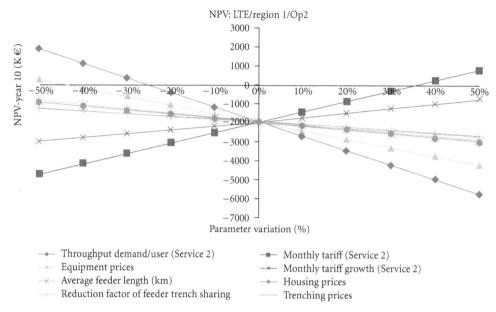

FIGURE 7: Sensitivity analysis results, LTE/urban area/new entrant.

a decrease in the payback period, and a significant reduction of CAPEX.

For LTE technology, we define two main scenarios (upgrade of UMTS network to LTE and the deployment of a new network by a new entrant) that are applied in both regions. In Scenario 17 (upgrade in the urban area), the NPV is positive but low, and the IRR is 14.5%; the discounted payback period is estimated to be nine years. In the rural area (Scenario 18), the discounted payback period is greater than 10 years. The upgrade scenario in the rural area has a negative NPV, but the IRR is positive, although the Greenfield deployment (Scenarios 19 and 20) has higher costs in both regions. The IRR is negative and similar in both regions (−30.02% and −30.1%), and NPV (besides negative) is higher in the rural area. Like other technologies, LTE will benefit from an adequate infrastructure sharing (see Table 14).

7. Sensitivity Analysis

These results are based on assumptions, forecasting, and estimation of several parameters; therefore, it is essential to investigate which are the most significant parameters to influence the results (sensitivity) and, if possible, verify such factors as increased profits or other negative results. With the sensitivity analysis, we can understand the influence of several input parameters (e.g., HH, penetration rates, segments length, bandwidth, retail price, discount rate, trench/duct infrastructure sharing) on the economic indicators results (NPV, IRR, CAPEX, OPEX, and PB).

Comparing the relative importance of variables (Figure 5), we can verify that the number of HH, penetration of BB subscription, and monthly tariff of Service 2 has a big impact on the NPV of Operator 1 (Region 1). For new entrants (Operator 2), the most significant parameters are

distribution segment length, trenching prices, and trench/duct share. Less sensitive parameters are omitted.

In the LTE operator cases (Figure 6), the demand required per user (Service 2), BB subscription, equipment price, risk free rate, and start market share are the most sensitive variables.

Figure 7 shows the result of the linearly variation (−50% to 50%) of the input parameters for LTE technology, urban area (Region 1), and Operator 2 (New entrant). For example, if the throughput demand/user (Service 2) decreases 30%, the NPV will be positive.

8. Conclusion

The case study results illustrate the importance of infrastructure sharing for new entrants both in FTTH and LTE. The presented results give important information about the two different solutions in urban and rural areas, indicating that both technologies can provide for sustainable business in Scenario 1. We also identified the critical input parameters for each technology; with this analysis, we examine how technology decisions can change as a function of the input parameters. However, LTE is the better solution for rural areas besides the capacity constraints. The offered capacity per user is the most critical parameter.

References

[1] H. Galperin, "Wireless networks and rural development: opportunities for latin America," *Information Technologies and International Development*, vol. 2, no. 3, pp. 47–56, 2005.

[2] J. P. Pereira and P. Ferreira, "A cost model for broadband access networks: FTTx versus WiMAX," in *Proceedings of the 2nd International Conference on Access Networks (AccessNets '07)*, Ottawa, Canada, 2007.

[3] P. Chanclou, Z. Belfqih, B. Charbonnier et al., "Access network evolution: optical fibre to the subscribers and impact on the metropolitan and home networks," *Comptes Rendus Physique*, vol. 9, no. 9-10, pp. 935–946, 2008.

[4] O. C. Ibe, *Fixed Broadband Wireless Access Networks and Services*, John Wiley & Sons, 2002.

[5] J. P. Pereira and P. Ferreira, "Access networks for mobility: a techno-economic model for broadband access technologies," in *Proceedings of the 5th International Conference on Testbeds and Research Infrastructures for the Development of Networks and Communities and Workshops (TridentCom '09)*, Washington, DC, USA, April 2009.

[6] J. S. Marcus and D. Elixmann, "Regulatory approaches to NGNs: an international comparison," *Communications & Strategies*, vol. 69, p. 21, 2008.

[7] F. Kirsch and C. V. Hirschhausen, "Regulation of next generation networks: structural separation, access regulation, or no regulation at all?" in *Proceedings of the 1st International Conference on Infrastructure Systems and Services: Building Networks for a Brighter Future (INFRA '08)*, Rotterdam, The Netherlands, 2008.

[8] P. Xavier, "Geographically segmented regulation for telecommunications," in *Proceedings of the Working Party on Communication Infrastructures and Services Policy (OECD '10)*, p. 77, 2010.

[9] G. B. Amendola and L. M. Pupillo, "The economics of next generation access networks and regulatory governance in Europe: one size does not fit all," in *Proceedings of the 18th ITS Regional Conference*, Istanbul, Turkey, 2007.

[10] J. P. Pereira and P. Ferreira, "Next generation access networks (NGANs) and the geographical segmentation of markets," in *Proceedings of the 10th International Conference on Networks (ICN '11)*, St. Maarten, The Netherlands, 2011.

[11] J. Rendón, F. Kuhlmann, and J. P. Alanis, "A business case for the deployment of a 4G wireless heterogeneous network in Spain," in *Proceedings of the 18th European Regional International Telecommunications Society*, Istanbul, Turkey, 2007.

[12] J. Harno, "Impact of 3G and beyond technology development and pricing on mobile data service provisioning, usage and diffusion," *Telematics and Informatics*, vol. 27, no. 3, pp. 269–282, 2010.

[13] EURESCOM, "Techno-economic analysis of integrated wireless-optical networks," in *Proceedings of the EURESCOM*, pp. 1–71, 2000.

[14] T. Smura, *Competitive Potential of WiMAX in the Broadband Access Market: A Techno-Economic Analysis*, Helsinki University of Technology, 2006.

[15] H. Sarkissian and R. Schwartz, "A comprehensive WiMAX Operator Business Case Process," 2007.

[16] J. P. Pereira, "The role of WiMAX technology on broadband access networks," in *WIMAX, New Developments*, U. D. Dalal and Y. P. Kosta, Eds., pp. 17–45, N-TECH, Vienna, Austria, 2010.

[17] Analysys-Consulting, *Analysys Cost Model for Australian Fixed Network Services*, ACCC, Australia, 2009.

[18] CSMG, *Economics of Shared Infrastructure*, London, UK, 2010.

[19] B. T. Olsen, D. Katsianis, D. Varoutas et al., "Technoeconomic evaluation of the major telecommunication investment options for european players," *IEEE Network*, vol. 20, no. 4, pp. 6–15, 2006.

[20] T. Monath, N. K. Elnegaard, P. Cadro, D. Katsianis, and D. Varoutas, "Economics of fixed broadband access network strategies," *IEEE Communications Magazine*, vol. 41, no. 9, pp. 132–139, 2003.

[21] Analysys-Mason, *The Costs of Deploying Fibre-Based Next-Generation Broadband Infrastructure*, Broadband Stakeholder Group, Cambridge, UK, 2008, Edited by Analysys-Maso.

[22] M. Kantor, K. Wajda, B. Lannoo et al., "General framework for techno-economic analysis of next generation access networks," in *Proceedings of the 12th International Conference on Transparent Optical Networks (ICTON '10)*, July 2010.

[23] L. E. Braten, "Requirements to and architecture of hybrid broadband access networks," *Telektronikk*, vol. 2, pp. 22–38, 2006.

[24] H. R. Anderson, *Fixed Broadband Wireless System Design*, John Wiley & Sons, Chichester, UK, 2003.

[25] T. Smura et al., *Final Techno-Economic Results on Mobile Services and Technologies Beyond 3G*, ECOSYS, 2006, Edited by J. Harno.

[26] V. Riihimäki, "Managing Uncertainties in Broadband Investments-Case Studies of Real Options for Rural Area Access Networks," in Department of Communications and Networking, Aalto, Fla, USA, Aalto University, p. 166, 2010.

[27] K. Stordahl, "Broadband demand and the role of new technologies," in *Proceedings of the 13th International Telecommunications Network Strategy and Planning Symposium*, 2008.

[28] K. Stordahl, "Market development up to 2015," MARCH—Multilink architecture for multiplay services, p. 72, 2010.

[29] European-Union, "Europe's digital competitiveness report 2010," Tech. Rep., European Union, Luxembourg, UK, 2010.

[30] R. Prasad and F. J. Velez, *WiMAX Networks: Techno-Economic Vision and Challenges*, Springer, New York, NY, USA, 1st edition, 2010.

[31] N. K. Elnegaard, K. Stordahl, J. Lydersen et al., "Mobile broadband evolution and the possibilities," *Telektronikk*, vol. 3, no. 4, p. 11, 2008.

[32] G. Rosston, S. Savage, and D. Waldman, "Household demand for broadband internet service," *Communications of the Acm*, vol. 54, no. 2, pp. 29–31, 2011.

[33] European-Commission, "Electronic Communications Market Indicators," European Commission, 2011.

[34] Analysys-Mason, "Mobile and fixed broadband: co-habitation or competition?" in *Webinar*, Analysys Mason, London, UK, 2008.

[35] T. Koonen, "Fiber to the home/fiber to the premises: what, where, and when?" *Proceedings of the IEEE*, vol. 94, no. 5, pp. 911–934, 2006.

15

Dealing with Energy-QoE Trade-Offs in Mobile Video

Fidel Liberal, Ianire Taboada, and Jose-Oscar Fajardo

University of the Basque Country UPV/EHU, Faculty of Engineering of Bilbao, Alameda Urquijo s/n, 48013 Bilbao, Spain

Correspondence should be addressed to Fidel Liberal; fidel.liberal@ehu.es

Academic Editor: Maria G. Martini

Scalable video coding allows an efficient provision of video services at different quality levels with different energy demands. According to the specific type of service and network scenario, end users and/or operators may decide to choose among different energy versus quality combinations. In order to deal with the resulting trade-off, in this paper we analyze the number of video layers that are worth to be received taking into account the energy constraints. A single-objective optimization is proposed based on dynamically selecting the number of layers, which is able to minimize the energy consumption with the constraint of a minimal quality threshold to be reached. However, this approach cannot reflect the fact that the same increment of energy consumption may result in different increments of visual quality. Thus, a multiobjective optimization is proposed and a utility function is defined in order to weight the energy consumption and the visual quality criteria. Finally, since the optimization solving mechanism is computationally expensive to be implemented in mobile devices, a heuristic algorithm is proposed. This way, significant energy consumption reduction will be achieved while keeping reasonable quality levels.

1. Introduction

The evolution of multimedia encoding techniques allows efficiently provisioning video services at different quality levels. However, resulting streams lead also to different energy consumptions making it difficult to simultaneously satisfy both energy consumption and quality requirements. Therefore, an energy versus quality compromise solution is commonly required. In commercial cellular networks, users are used to dealing with these trade-offs either manually or automatically (i.e., using small widgets to reduce display brightness, disable radio interfaces, etc.) and normally maintaining the same play-out quality. However, reduced energy consumption becomes a truly severe constraint in specific communication scenarios such as mobile emergency networks or distributed sensors. Additionally, any solution will also depend on the characteristics of the video players although higher resolution video could improve visual quality for high-end mobile devices, for others no visible quality improvement is achieved due to available screen resolution, codecs, or CPU power. So, additional energy consumption, higher data bandwidth, and spectrum use would have no real impact on users satisfaction. Energy- and visual quality-aware video dynamic

transmission schemes would allow network operators and users to avoid such waste of resources.

In order to cope with the heterogeneity of mobile devices and user requirements for efficient mobile video delivery, a multilayer scheme is broadly considered as the best solution. In this paradigm, each video is encoded into a single stream with multiple layers, where each layer is only transmitted once. Scalable Video Coding (SVC) standard, an extension for H.264/AVC standard, makes this multilayering possible, becoming the most promising encoding technology for solving the problem of multiuser video streaming in most mobile environments (see [1, 2]). This mechanism for content delivery provides quality differentiation, so that the same content is sent simultaneously in different qualities without replicating the original information. This way, users that demand lower energy consumption can maintain the reproduction but accepting lower quality level.

For example, [3–5] have proposed broadcasting schemes that would allow mobile devices to receive and decode the most suitable number of layers, maintaining the perceived video quality proportional to the consumed energy in a DVB-H scenario. Under typical system parameters of mobile TV networks, the proposed schemes allow mobile devices to achieve energy savings between 60% and 95% depending on how many layers they receive. In [5], not only does the proposed scheme enable each device to achieve energy saving proportional to perceived quality but also low channel switching delays are guaranteed, which is also important to user experience.

However, in these works the expected visual quality level as perceived by the user is not quantified, which is fundamental to find a relation between energy consumption and user Quality of Experience (QoE).

In [6], authors follow a similar approach but in a 802.11e environment by using sleep cycles of wireless adapter for energy saving. In this case, a simple QoE estimation algorithm is used to trigger specific power save protocol operations. However, they only modify the behaviour of the receiver with a single version of the content. Furthermore, no analysis of the optimality of their approach is included.

Such kind of optimization in 802.11 is carried out in [7], including both linear programming techniques and heuristics. Unfortunately, only energy is considered as optimization criteria and no effect into quality is analyzed.

Finally, [8] proposes a method for statically selecting the best number of layers for the whole duration of a video with energy constraints. However, no compromise solution is provided and DVB-H scenarios only are considered.

In order to cover these lacks, in this paper we analyze the optimal strategy to be applied if we can modify dynamically the number of layers during the video reproduction considering energy and quality constraints. Therefore, the main contributions of the paper are as follows. (1) We analyze the energy versus QoE trade-offs considering either energy or quality as constraints. (2) We formulate the aforementioned scenarios in terms of single-objective linear programming (SOLP) problems and analyze the optimal sets in both the input and the objective space. (3) We study the multiobjective problem therefore allowing deployers to fine tune the relative weights of green consciousness and quality criteria. (4) We propose lightweight heuristics for energy- and QoE-aware optimization that ensure a feasible implementation on the end user while providing near-optimal solutions.

Therefore, the rest of this paper is structured as follows. In Section 2, we analyze the dual energy minimizing and QoE maximizing problem while alternating the number of reproduced layers during a video session. Section 3 considers users that have both energy and QoE related criteria, and Section 4 summarizes achieved results.

2. Energy/QoE Single Optimization

In this section, we will express the Energy versus QoE trade-off in terms of a typical optimization problem with different objectives and constraints, analyze the optimal strategy, and compare it with the traditional ones.

Traditional QoE-aware energy-constrained video reproduction strategies select the maximum number of layers that the available battery [8] and/or CPU load [9] would allow for the full video playout in an static way, so that the decision is taken just once. We will generalize and refer to this kind of strategies as basic strategy.

Considering (1) that each additional layer provides different QoE level (see, e.g., [10, 11]) and energy consumption and (2) that SVC players [12] support switching from a layer to another, we will instead propose a dynamic method for triggering layer switching considering energy constraints.

We will therefore focus on selecting the best set of different time periods t_i so that during $t_i(s)i$ layers will be reproduced.

For simplicity purposes, we will consider 4 layers to illustrate the method. For a video of duration $T(s)$ it is clear then that $t_1 + t_2 + t_3 + t_4 = T$. In our optimization problem $\mathbf{t} = [t_1 \quad t_2 \quad t_3 \quad t_4]$ will be the input variables.

In order to define our optimization problem completely, we will consider that the average of the satisfaction over the whole video reproduction $\widehat{\text{QoE}}$ is a good estimator of video quality. Then, we have an optimization problem consisting of the following.

(A2.1) Minimizing energy consumption for a given video and certain minimum acceptable visual quality.

(A2.2) Maximizing user QoE for a given video and certain maximum energy constraint.

Any single-objective optimization problem (SOP) [13] like (A2.1) and (A2.2) aims at choosing the "best" possible combination of input parameters in order to optimize the one considered criterion.

Let $\mathbf{x} \in \mathbb{R}^M$ be a vector of M input variables of the optimization problem.

The SOP can be stated as follows:

$$\begin{aligned} \max \quad & \{f(\mathbf{x}) = z\} \\ \text{s.t.} \quad & \mathbf{x} \in S, \quad z \in \mathbb{R}, \end{aligned} \tag{1}$$

where S is the set of feasible points in the input space delimited by i inequalities and j equalities such as

$$\mathbf{x} \in S \Longleftrightarrow \begin{cases} g(\mathbf{x}) \leq \mathbf{b}, & (b_1, b_2, \ldots, b_i) \\ h(\mathbf{x}) = \mathbf{c}, & (c_1, c_2, \ldots, c_j). \end{cases} \tag{2}$$

Thus, the SOP could be summarized as "finding the set of input variables $\mathbf{x_{opt}}$ belonging to S region so that $f(\mathbf{x_{opt}}) = z_{opt}$ is max," where S is constrained by inequalities $g(\mathbf{x}) \leq \mathbf{b}$ and equalities $h(\mathbf{x}) = \mathbf{c}$.

If both $f(\mathbf{x})$ is linear and S is defined by linear conditions (therefore both $g(\mathbf{x})$ and $h(\mathbf{x})$ are linear functions as well), then the SOP is called single objective linear programming problem (SOLP) [14].

The basic metric that we will use for estimating the whole user satisfaction regarding video quality will be the average value of the Mean Opinion Score (MOS) according to the number of layers reproduced along each time period. Therefore,

$$\widehat{\text{QoE}} = \frac{1}{T} \sum_{i=1}^{4} \int_{t_i} \text{MOS}_i(t) \cdot dt, \tag{3}$$

where $\text{MOS}_i(t)$ is the evolution of the QoE measured in the MOS scale along the ith period.

If the visual quality is considered roughly constant for a certain bitrate or number of layers and we denote $1 \leq \mathrm{MOS}_i \leq 5$ as the MOS estimated for a certain number of layers according to subjective tests, then $\mathrm{MOS}_i(t) \approx \mathrm{MOS}_i$ for the whole period. Therefore,

$$\mathbf{Q} = [Q_1 \quad Q_2 \quad Q_3 \quad Q_4], \qquad Q_i = \frac{\mathrm{MOS}_i}{T} \qquad (4)$$

are the normalized quality coefficients, and (3) can be expressed as follows:

$$\widehat{\mathrm{QoE}} = \mathbf{Q} \cdot \mathbf{t}^\mathsf{T}. \qquad (5)$$

Similarly, according to [8, 15], the battery consumption in mobile video players shows some kind of dependence on the number of layers received. Therefore, the total energy consumption will depend on the number of layers that will be received so that total consumption P along the whole reproduction time can be expressed as follows:

$$P = \mathbf{B} \cdot \mathbf{t}^\mathsf{T}, \qquad (6)$$

where $\mathbf{B} = [B_1 \quad B_2 \quad B_3 \quad B_4]$ is the vector of normalized coefficients of battery consumption.

This way, problem (1) can be expressed as a SOLP problem for both (A2.1) and (A2.2).

2.1. Minimizing Energy Consumption Assuring a QoE Threshold (A2.1).

In this case, the objective function to be minimized is the energy consumption so that $f(\mathbf{x}) = P$. Minimum energy consumption will be constrained by the QoE threshold, the user will stand (E) in terms of $\widehat{\mathrm{QoE}} \geq E$. This constraint will lead to the associated inequality in (7). Similarly, the sum of the time period for all the layer numbers must be the total duration of the video T leading to an equality constraint expressed with the identity vector $\mathbf{i} = [1 \quad 1 \quad 1 \quad 1]$. Consider the following:

$$\max \quad \{-\mathbf{B} \cdot \mathbf{t}^\mathsf{T}\}$$

$$\mathrm{s.t.} \quad \begin{bmatrix} [\mathbf{I}] \\ \mathbf{Q} \end{bmatrix} \cdot \mathbf{t}^\mathsf{T} \geq \begin{bmatrix} [\mathbf{0}] \\ E \end{bmatrix} \qquad (7)$$

$$\mathbf{i} \cdot \mathbf{t}^\mathsf{T} = T,$$

where the natural condition $t_i \geq 0$ for all i is included in the matrix notation in (7) using the identity 4×4 matrix $[\mathbf{I}]$.

Then, the SOLP problem in (7) can be solved by typical well-known optimization problem resolution mechanisms such as the simplex method [16]. Therefore, we can easily calculate the solution of the SOLP for a wide range of constraints and $\mathbf{Q}$ parameters. In fact, considering the proposed transmission scheme in [8], we have carried out the optimization for the parameters collected in Table 1 and obtained Figures 1 and 2. Note that the normalized available battery is measured in seconds to avoid specific details about battery characteristics (like voltage and capacity in mAh).

For mobile videos with different motion levels or Content Types (CTs) (referred to as Low Motion (LM), Medium

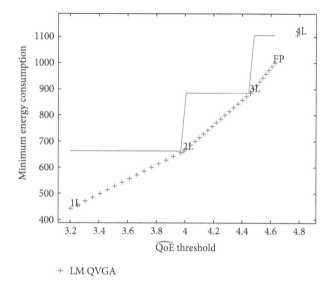

+ LM QVGA

FIGURE 1: Comparison between basic strategy and energy optimization.

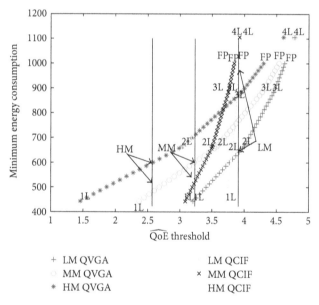

+ LM QVGA	LM QCIF
○ MM QVGA	× MM QCIF
* HM QVGA	HM QCIF

FIGURE 2: Static versus dynamic energy optimization for different CTs and SRs.

Motion (MM), and High Motion (HM)) and Spatial Resolutions (SRs) we have calculated the QoE-optimal layer selection strategy with the energy constraint. Note that, although we have considered a specific scenario in our study, the method can be applied to any multilayer broadcasting technology just by considering related $\mathbf{Q}$ and MOS_i coefficients.

In order to calculate realistic QoE constraints, we must consider $E_{\min}$ and $E_{\max}$: the minimum and maximum achievable $\widehat{\mathrm{QoE}}$ considering $t_1 = T$ and $t_4 = T$, respectively (i.e., receiving only 1 layer—worst quality—or 4 layers—best quality—during the whole video length). According to the metric used $E_{\min} = \mathrm{MOS}_1$ and $E_{\max} = \mathrm{MOS}_4$. Finally, since

TABLE 1: Values for coefficients for battery minimizing SOLP obtained from [8].

Concept			Value		
Video length T (s)			7200		
QoE threshold E			$E_{min} \leq E \leq E_{max}$		
Available battery (s)			1000		
	Content Type	SR	Values per layer		
MOS$_i$	LM	QVGA	$\begin{bmatrix} 3.20 & 3.99 & 4.45 & 4.78 \end{bmatrix}$		
	MM	QVGA	$\begin{bmatrix} 2.36 & 3.57 & 4.27 & 4.77 \end{bmatrix}$		
	HM	QVGA	$\begin{bmatrix} 1.45 & 3.03 & 3.95 & 4.60 \end{bmatrix}$		
	LM	QCIF	$\begin{bmatrix} 3.71 & 3.82 & 3.89 & 3.93 \end{bmatrix}$		
	MM	QCIF	$\begin{bmatrix} 3.08 & 3.50 & 3.74 & 3.92 \end{bmatrix}$		
	HM	QCIF	$\begin{bmatrix} 2.29 & 3.07 & 3.52 & 3.85 \end{bmatrix}$		
B			$K \cdot \begin{bmatrix} 2 & 3 & 4 & 5 \end{bmatrix}$ where the constant K depends on the transmission scheme only regardless of the CT and resulting spatial resolution		

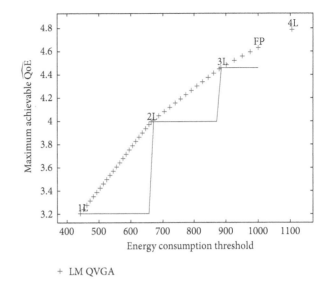

+ LM QVGA

FIGURE 3: Comparison between basic strategy and QoE optimization.

the additional constraint of the total energy consumption must be less than the available battery (if a handheld device) or the energy budget, not all points will be feasible.

In Figure 1, the objective space (namely, minimum battery consumption versus QoE threshold) and the finite decision points associated to the traditional selection of a fixed number of layers for the whole video are shown for a certain CT/SR combination. Considered remaining battery constraint results in a Feasible Point (FP) that represents the maximum achievable QoE level. Both this FP and discrete no. L points are shown (the points related to reproducing a certain number of layers during the whole play-out time, T).

We can see how, by changing the number of layers reproduced along the video duration, we can optimize the energy consumption with finer grain QoE constraints. This way, for $MOS_1 \leq \widehat{QoE} < MOS_2$ traditional static strategies would result in selecting 2 layers (2L) for the whole duration of the video and consuming associated energy. Our dynamic approach would instead allow the selection of different (energy, QoE) points. On the other hand, if we compare in detail both approaches for this concrete CT and SR (LM and QVGA), obtained optimum strategy does not match the simplest one in 2L point. This clearly reflects the energy saving achieved as for the same MOS less energy is consumed.

Additional results are depicted in Figure 2 for every combination of video types and encoding resolutions considered. Examining in detail the figure we can see how optimization strategy does not match the traditional static approaches (fixed no. L points). Furthermore, vertical lines show the result of ensuring certain QoE levels for different CTs. For example, for selected $\widehat{QoE}$ thresholds, the QCIF versions are better in terms of energy consumption for HM and MM

videos, while QVGA is better for the threshold considered in the LM case.

2.2. Maximizing User QoE Constrained by Maximum Energy Consumption (A2.2). For (A2.2), in an analogous way to Section 2.1, the objective function to be maximized is the MOS so that $f = \widehat{QoE}$. Maximum achievable QoE will be constrained by the maximum battery consumption C. This constraint will lead to the associated inequality in the following:

$$\max \quad \{\mathbf{Q} \cdot \mathbf{t}^\mathsf{T}\}$$
$$\text{s.t.} \quad \begin{bmatrix} [\mathbf{I}] \\ -\mathbf{B} \end{bmatrix} \cdot \mathbf{t}^\mathsf{T} \geq \begin{bmatrix} [\mathbf{0}] \\ -C \end{bmatrix} \quad (8)$$
$$\mathbf{I} \cdot \mathbf{t}^\mathsf{T} = T.$$

Figure 3 depicts the evolution in the objective space of the proposed optimal strategy in comparison with the basic one considering #L points only. Once more, we can see how the proposed scheme allows us to set a continuous range of energy constraints resulting in different values of $\widehat{QoE}$. In this case, an available energy budget in the $[E_1, E_2)$ range would collapse into the same 1L point, therefore allowing only minimum $\widehat{QoE}$.

When we compare the obtained results for different CT/SR combinations (in Figure 4), we can see, again, how the QoE maximizing quality selection mechanism would choose QCIF (for the particular energy saving constraints marked with a vertical line in the figure) for LM and MM videos, while QVGA for the HM one.

2.3. Comparison between SOLP Approaches. In Sections 2.1 and 2.2, we have used the simplex optimization method for SOLPs in order to optimize either energy for a given QoE

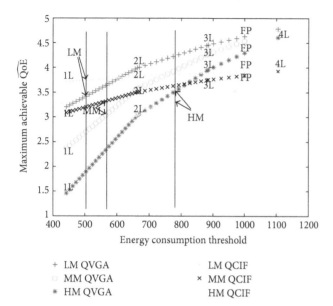

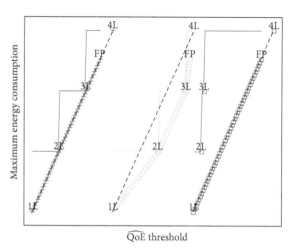

FIGURE 5: Pareto fronts for 3 different MOS_i and **B**.

FIGURE 4: Static versus dynamic QoE optimization for different CTs and SRs.

threshold or QoE for a given maximum battery consumption. Due to the nature of the linear optimization problem, if we compare both optimization approaches, we can see in Figure 6 that both lead to the same shape in the objective space. This conclusion is consistent with the nature of the dual problem itself, since energy and QoE are opposite objectives, and the constraint in one problem becomes the objective function in the other.

Since carrying out the simplex method for the optimization of every video reproduction would be inviable for handheld devices due to the high CPU power needed, we focus on developing heuristics capable of providing near-optimal solutions. This way, both video operators and end users themselves would be able to reduce their energy consumption while maintaining QoE levels. In order to do so, we have analyzed more deeply the shape of the optimal set (namely, Pareto front in the objective space) for three different situations and compared it with the #L points. We can see (Figure 5) how the optimal strategy for energy versus QoE, depending on MOS_i and **B** evolution:

(1) follows exactly the line between 1L and 4L (including 2L and 3L), constrained by the FP;

(2) follows the polygon (the 2D polytope in the objective space) 1L-2L-3L-4L constrained by the FP;

(3) follows the 1L and 4L but without going through 2L and 3L points.

We conclude that, regardless of the specific parameters of the SOLP problem to be solved, the optimal strategy always includes 1L and 4L points (or associated FP point if 4L is not feasible due to the battery constraint). This result is quite evident since reproducing just 1 or all the 4 layers gives the minimum and maximum QoE and battery. However, both 2L ([0 *T* 0 0]) and 3L ([0 0 *T* 0]) points are not always

optimal points (i.e., they do not belong to the Pareto front). As a result, the simple strategy of following the 1L-2L-3L-4L path must be carefully reviewed.

Therefore, in order to propose an optimization strategy, we must evaluate the evolution of the Pareto front in both the objective and the input space for every possible situation (1, 2, and 3).

In Figures 6 and 7, we can see such evolution for the objective and input space in the aforementioned Situations 1 and 2. Figure 6 confirms the superposition of both (A2.1) and (A2.2) Pareto fronts in the objective space for both situations. In Figure 7, we depict the 4D input space with the points that belong to the Pareto front in both situations. In order to do so, (x, y, z) space coordinates correspond to t_1, t_2, and t_3, respectively. The fourth dimension (t_4) is represented by the area of the sphere in the (t_1, t_2, t_3) point. Finally, the result of the objective function is represented by the color of the sphere according to the colormap shown. $(T, 0, 0, 0)$, $(0, T, 0, 0)$, $(0, 0, T, 0)$, and $(0, 0, 0, T)$ points are also depicted with spheres.

When comparing Situations 1 and 2 in the input space, we can see how, for the former, the optimal path does not follow any simple strategy. However, the latter follows a linear path in a set of consecutive planes, which leads to easy-to-implement heuristics.

After comparing the figures for MOS_i for every considered video CTs and SRs and the evolution of the energy consumption versus the number of layers, we conclude that all of them follow the Situation 2. In fact, if we analyze the sufficient conditions leading to Situation 2 it is clear that, if the function max MOS = f(min Energy) in the objective space is convex, the resulting shape would belong to this group. Most QoE studies aiming at mapping satisfaction versus network performance parameters use logarithmic expressions (see [17]), so that they are convex. In our case, due to this convexity of the MOS expression and the proportional $K \cdot (i + 1)$ dependency of the energy with $\mathbf{t}(i)$ for all i, an increment achieved by the simplex algorithm in terms of

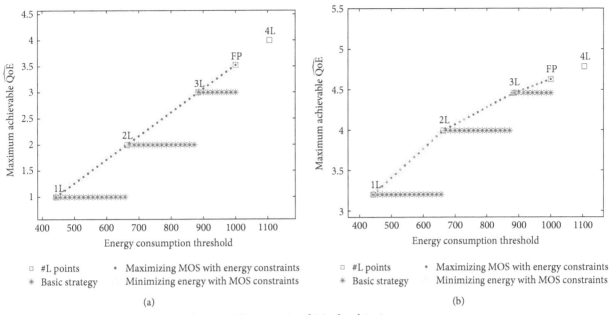

(a)

(b)

FIGURE 6: Situations 1 and 2 in the objective space.

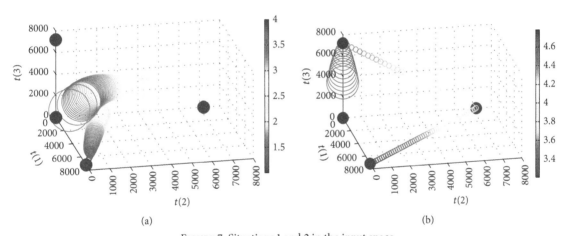

(a)

(b)

FIGURE 7: Situations 1 and 2 in the input space.

MOS$'$ = MOS + ΔMOS would be caused by a displacement vector $\mathbf{t}' = \mathbf{t} + \Delta\mathbf{t}$ leading to a (P', MOS') point above the 1L–4L line in the objective space. An equivalent conclusion will be obtained if we calculate the gradient of both MOS and energy, or if we consider that many optimization methods indeed provide the convex part of the Pareto front.

Therefore, in this case the associated optimization heuristic is straightforward, regardless either optimization approach 1 (minimize energy for a certain QoE) or 2 (maximize QoE for a certain energy budget) is applied. Algorithm 1 shows the complete optimization heuristic procedure. The algorithm is based on the fact that the optimal polytope will follow the 1L-2L-3L-4L path (constrained by the FP). Additionally, we take into account that, due to the linear constraints, the polytope will be formed by the intersection of planes leading to lines in the different 2D planes formed by the successive input parameters. So, since $\mathbf{t} = [t_1 \ t_2 \ t_3 \ t_4]$ is the 4D input space, the optimization heuristic will consider

the polytope delimited by 1L, 2L, 3L, and 4L/FP points and planes $[t_1 \ t_2 \ 0 \ 0]$, $[0 \ t_2 \ t_3 \ 0]$, and $[0 \ 0 \ t_3 \ t_4]$. Note here that along the different figures in this paper, we have set a maximum energy constraint leading to an FP between 3L and 4L for illustration purposes. In a real scenario, the FP could be anywhere in the 1L–4L Pareto Front.

Regardless our aim is minimizing energy for a certain QoE or maximizing QoE with a certain energy budget, we will calculate the 2D plane where the target point in the input space will be located at. Since both energy and QoE are monotonically growing with $\mathbf{t}(i)$ for all i either the QoE or the battery constraint will allow us to select the plane by evaluating the $\text{BAT}_i-\text{BAT}_{i+1}$ or $\text{QoE}_i-\text{QoE}_{i+1}$ intervals where $i = 1 \cdots \text{FP}$. Later, the linear dependence will allow us to express $\mathbf{t}_{\text{opt}}(i)$ as a function of provided constraints (see lines 18–21 and 28–30).

In Figure 8, the results obtained with the heuristics for both Situations 1 and 2 in the objective space are depicted.

(1) $T \leftarrow$ Video Length {Initialize total time to play the whole video}
(2) $\mathbf{B} \leftarrow$ obtain B from Transmission Scheme() {Obtain battery related coefficients}
(3) $\mathbf{Q} \leftarrow$ obtain Q from Subjective Tests (CT, SR) {Obtain QoE related coefficients}
(4) $E_{\max} \leftarrow$ maximum Battery Consumption
(5) **for** $i = 1 \rightarrow 4$ **do**
(6) $\quad \mathbf{t}_i \leftarrow [0 \ 0 \ 0 \ 0]$
(7) $\quad \mathbf{t}_i(i) = L$
(8) $\quad \text{QoE}_i \leftarrow \mathbf{Q} \cdot \mathbf{t}_i^\mathsf{T}$ {Obtain QoE for #L point}
(9) $\quad \text{BAT}_i \leftarrow \mathbf{B} \cdot \mathbf{t}_i^\mathsf{T}$ {Obtain Battery consumption for #L point}
(10) **end for**
(11) $\text{BAT}_{\text{FP}} \leftarrow E_{\max}$ {Maximum battery sets the FP}
(12) $\text{QoE}_{\text{FP}} \leftarrow$ calculate FP($\mathbf{t}_1, \mathbf{t}_2, \mathbf{t}_3, \mathbf{t}_4, \text{BAT}_{\text{FP}}$) {Obtain QoE for FP}
(13) **If** minimize Energy **then** {minimize energy for a given QoE constraint}
(14) $\quad E \leftarrow$ minimum Acceptable QoE
(15) $\quad i \leftarrow$ find Plane($E, \text{QoE}_i, \text{BAT}_i, \text{BAT}_{\text{FP}}, \text{QoE}_{\text{FP}}$)

(16) $\quad a \leftarrow \dfrac{\text{BAT}_{i+1} - \text{BAT}_i}{\text{QoE}_{i+1} - \text{QoE}_i}$

(17) $\quad b \leftarrow \dfrac{\text{BAT}_{i+1} - \text{BAT}_i \cdot \text{QoE}_{i+1}/\text{QoE}_i}{1 - \text{QoE}_{i+1}/\text{QoE}_i}$

(18) $\quad \text{BAT}_{\text{opt}} \leftarrow a \cdot E + b$

(19) $\quad \mathbf{t}_{\text{opt}} \leftarrow [0 \ 0 \ 0 \ 0]$

(20) $\quad \mathbf{t}_{\text{opt}}(i) \leftarrow \dfrac{E - T \cdot \mathbf{Q}(i+1)}{\mathbf{Q}(i) - \mathbf{Q}(i+1)}$

(21) $\quad \mathbf{t}_{\text{opt}}(i+1) \leftarrow T - \mathbf{t}_{\text{opt}}(i)$
(22) **else** {maximize QoE for a given energy constraint}
(23) $\quad C \leftarrow$ maximum Energy Consumption
(24) $\quad i \leftarrow$ find Plane($C, \text{QoE}_i, \text{BAT}_i, \text{BAT}_{\text{FP}}, \text{QoE}_{\text{FP}}$)

(25) $\quad a \leftarrow \dfrac{\text{BAT}_{i+1} - \text{BAT}_i}{\text{QoE}_{i+1} - \text{QoE}_i}$

(26) $\quad b \leftarrow \dfrac{\text{BAT}_{i+1} - \text{BAT}_i \cdot \text{QoE}_{i+1}/\text{QoE}_i}{1 - \text{QoE}_{i+1}/\text{QoE}_i}$

(27) $\quad \text{QoE}_{\text{opt}} \leftarrow \dfrac{C - b}{a}$

(28) $\quad \mathbf{t}_{\text{opt}} \leftarrow [0 \ 0 \ 0 \ 0]$

(29) $\quad \mathbf{t}_{\text{opt}}(i) \leftarrow \dfrac{C - T \cdot \mathbf{B}(i+1)}{\mathbf{B}(i) - \mathbf{B}(i+1)}$

(30) $\quad \mathbf{t}_{\text{opt}}(i+1) \leftarrow T - \mathbf{t}_{\text{opt}}(i)$
(31) **end if**

ALGORITHM 1: Heuristic for both SOLP optimization problems.

Note that, even for Situation 1 the heuristic provides values very close to the Pareto set. The reason is that 2L, 3L and the points in the 1L–4L path belong to the Pareto front. At the same time, when approaching these points from $[t_1 \ t_2^- \ t_3 \ t_4]$ and $[t_1 \ t_2^+ \ t_3 \ t_4]$, there exist different combinations of $\mathbf{t}(i)$ that result in the equivalent point in the objective space. Therefore, depending on the path followed by the simplex algorithm and the stopping thresholds, the simulation would provide different points in the input space, but the heuristic is still capable of providing equivalent optimal points in the objective space.

Figure 9 shows the effect of applying developed algorithm for Situation 3. As already mentioned, although each case should be evaluated in terms of MOS_i and $\mathbf{B}$ in order to estimate associated situation, the convex shape of the MOS function makes this situation highly improbable. Anyway, the equivalent heuristic is again quite simple, since the Pareto front follows the 1L–4L path.

3. Hybrid Approach: Optimizing Energy Consumption and QoE

In the previous section, we have focused on analysing the problem of optimizing one single objective (i.e., either energy or QoE) in our mobile video scenario. Therefore, we have

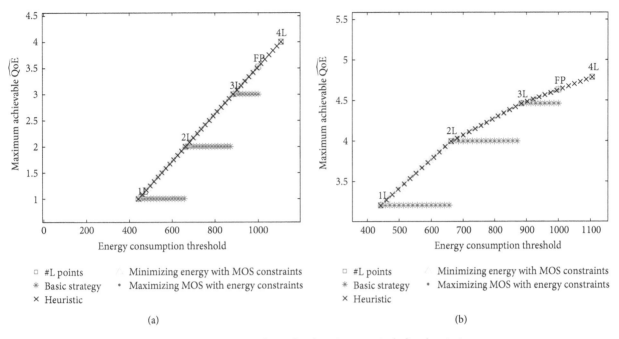

(a)   (b)

FIGURE 8: Situations 1 and 2 in the objective space including heuristics.

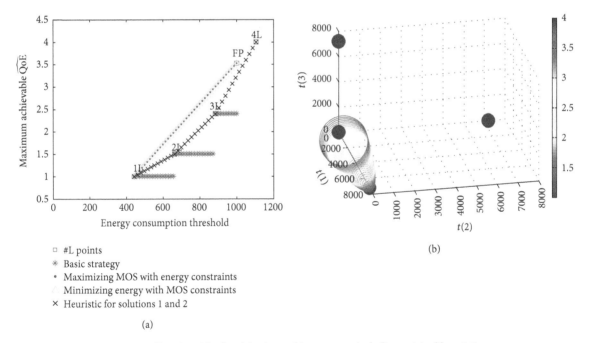

FIGURE 9: Situation 3 in the objective and input space including original heuristics.

expressed both optimization problems in terms of SOP. The considered $\widehat{QoE}$ metric allowed us to reduce such problems to SOLP ones and describe them with the matrix notation in (7) and (8).

However, real users do not usually consider a single criterion while evaluating a product or a service [18]. Generally speaking, most users will not care about energy consumption or quality in an isolated way but will take into account both

criteria. On one hand, commercial users would probably prefer assuring higher quality for playing movies. In other scenarios, such as aforementioned emergency networks, they would instead put the emphasis on preserving battery. However, minimum image quality levels should be also provided to keep quality of information so that, for example, first responders would be still capable of evaluating the risks of an emergency. Therefore, the two original SOPs merge into

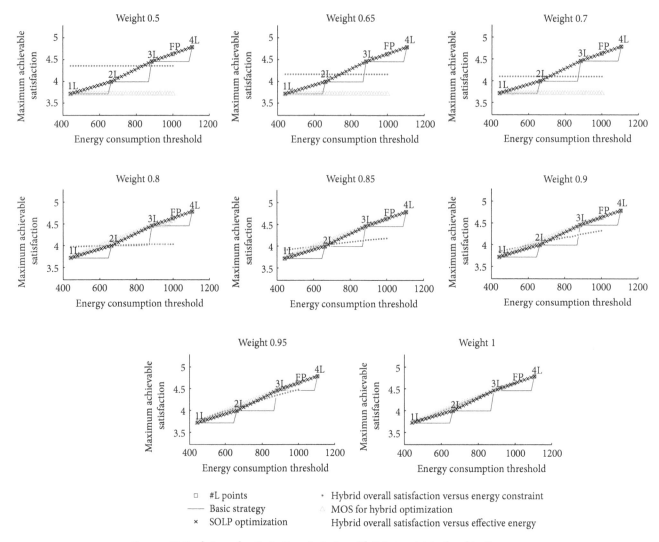

FIGURE 10: Evolution of optimization strategies with $0.5 \leq w \leq 1$ in the objective space.

a more complex Multiple Objective Optimization Problem (MOOP) including two objectives: minimizing energy consumption (i.e., $f_1(\mathbf{t})$) and maximizing QoE (i.e., $f_2(\mathbf{t})$).

Then, the MOOP is an extension of the SOP, which can be defined as follows:

$$
\begin{aligned}
\max \quad & \{f_1(\mathbf{x}) = z_1\} \\
\max \quad & \{f_2(\mathbf{x}) = z_2\} \\
& \vdots \\
\max \quad & \{f_k(\mathbf{x}) = z_k\} \\
\text{s.t.} \quad & \mathbf{x} \in S,
\end{aligned}
\tag{9}
$$

where f_i is the ith criterion function.

The simplest solution for the MOOP problem consists of finding the input vector $\mathbf{x}_{\mathbf{opt}}$ so that

$$
\exists \mathbf{x}_{\mathbf{opt}} \in S \mid \max \left\{ f_i\left(\mathbf{x}_{\mathbf{opt}}\right) = z_{i_{\text{opt}}}\right\} \quad \forall i = 1, 2, \ldots, k. \tag{10}
$$

In most of the cases, there will not exist such $\mathbf{x}_{\mathbf{opt}}$ which maximizes all the criteria simultaneously. So, we will have to redefine the nature of the problem by introducing the concept of utility function, U. Then, the real formulation of the MOOP can be expressed mathematically as follows:

$$
\max \{U(z_1, z_2, \ldots, z_k)\}. \tag{11}
$$

Then, any MOOP requires the definition of a utility function that collects users' preferences regarding different considered criteria as in (11). Many authors have considered the linear composition of preferences with different weights to express the articulation of preferences in communications systems with methods such as the Analytic Hierarchy Process (AHP; see, e.g., [19]) to infer the weight of each criterion out of user surveys. If we consider that our utility function follows this linear approach:

$$
U(\mathbf{x}) = w_1 \cdot f_1(\mathbf{x}) + w_2 \cdot f_2(\mathbf{x}), \tag{12}
$$

where, if we normalize f_1 and f_2 between the same value ranges (i.e., $1 \leq f_i \leq 5$ as in the MOS scale), associated

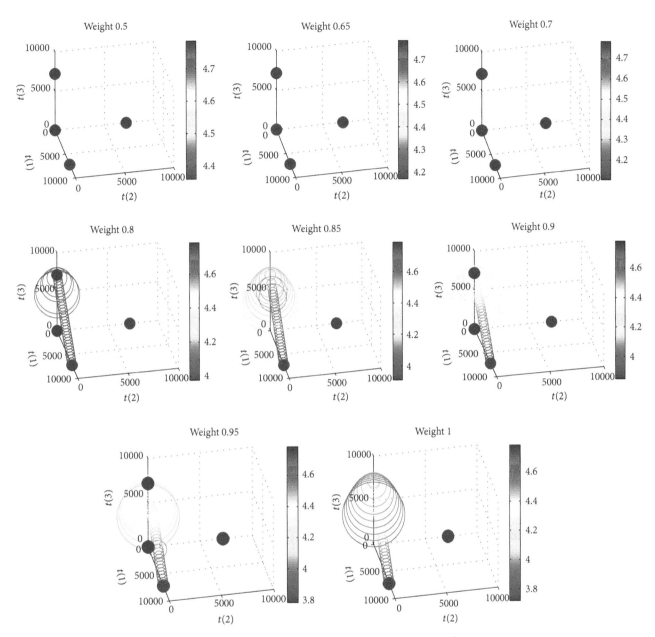

FIGURE 11: Evolution of optimization strategies with $0.5 \leq w \leq 1$ in the input space.

weights will follow $w_1 + w_2 = 1$ so that we could express the utility function in a linear way as in the following:

$$U(\mathbf{x}) = w \cdot f_1(\mathbf{x}) + (1 - w) \cdot f_2'(\mathbf{x}). \qquad (13)$$

Since both f_1 and f_2' (normalized f_2) are related to QoE and battery criteria, respectively, if we consider similar expressions as those in (7) and (8) for the objective functions, we could expand expression (13) as follows:

$$U(\mathbf{t}) = w \cdot \sum_{i=1}^{4} \mathbf{Q}(i) \cdot \mathbf{t}(i) + (1 - w) \cdot \sum_{i=1}^{4} \mathbf{B}'(i) \cdot \mathbf{t}(i), \qquad (14)$$

where $\mathbf{B}'$ is the vector of normalized battery parameters so that $1 \leq f_2' \leq 5$. Note that, contrary to $\mathbf{Q}$, $\mathbf{B}'$ coefficients

will decrease with $i\,\mathbf{B}'(i) > \mathbf{B}'(i + 1)$ for all i since users satisfaction regarding battery will decrease when the number of layers and therefore the battery consumption grows. If we manipulate this expression for the utility function, we can express the complex MOOP into a simplified SOLP similar to (7) and (8) as follows:

$$\max \quad \{\mathbf{M} \cdot \mathbf{t}^{\mathsf{T}}\}$$

$$\text{s.t.} \quad \begin{bmatrix} [\mathbf{I}] \\ -\mathbf{B} \\ \mathbf{Q} \end{bmatrix} \cdot \mathbf{t}^{\mathsf{T}} \geq \begin{bmatrix} [\mathbf{0}] \\ -C \\ E \end{bmatrix} \qquad (15)$$

$$\mathbf{I} \cdot \mathbf{t}^{\mathsf{T}} = T,$$

where $\mathbf{M}(i) = w \cdot \mathbf{Q} + (1 - w) \cdot \mathbf{B}'$. In order to calculate $\mathbf{B}'$, we carry out a mapping between the actual battery consumption and associated satisfaction, where $\mathbf{B}'(1)$ will be associated with the maximum satisfaction and $\mathbf{B}'(4)$ with the lowest one (maximum consumption).

Once $\mathbf{M}$ is calculated and maximum battery and minimum QoE are set, we can use simplex again in order to optimize users' satisfaction considering both battery and QoE. Figure 10 depicts the evolution of the optimal strategy in the objective space for different values of w, the relative weight of both criteria. Both hybrid optimization (with proposed utility function) together with maximizing QoE only policy, static assignment and proposed heuristics are shown. The different values for w represent how important is the "Green characteristic" of the device for the user and/or video provider when compared with video quality (with $w = 1$ completely important and $w = 0$ not important at all).

We have computed only the range $0.5 \leq w \leq 1$, since the same figures were obtained for lower values of w. We can see how, for all $w < 0.7$, the optimal shape is restricted to a single point (corresponding to 1L). The reason is that, considering the low importance of QoE, the optimization algorithm considers that it is always more convenient to restrict the energy consumption rather than receive more layers and obtain better video quality. The higher the w value, the closer the Pareto fronts gets to our original single-objective optimization.

In Figure 11, we carry out the equivalent analysis in the input space. Once again, the Pareto front for considered $\mathbf{Q}$ and $\mathbf{B}'$ leads to a simplified optimization strategy for $\mathbf{t}$. In this case, however, the evolution is from plane $[t_1 \ 0 \ t_3 \ 0]$ to plane $[0 \ 0 \ t_3 \ t_4]$.

In order to get the exact $\mathbf{t}_{opt}$ point for every E and C constraint pair, we carry out the same equations as in lines 18–21 and 28–30 of Algorithm 1.

Therefore, in order to solve the MOLP problem, we could use any LP optimization technique (i.e., simplex or Interior Points Method) or analyze the problem in a case per case basis in order to infer whether a simple per-plane heuristic could be applied. In any case, the complexity of the solution is low. For example, although simplex's complexity analysis is rather a problem dependent leading even to worst-case exponential, due to the small size of the input matrix, results are obtained in less than 20 iterations, and empirical tests have led to less than 30 ms of CPU consumption.

4. Conclusions

In this paper, we analyze the trade-off between energy consumption and visual quality for mobile video systems.

Different optimization approaches have been evaluated. The simplest static strategy comprises receiving the highest number of video layers while coping with the video duration requirements. Thus, taking as inputs the video length and the amount of remaining battery, we always select the best possible visual quality. The main drawback of this approach is that all the battery is available to be used in the video playout.

In Section 2, we introduce a single-objective optimization problem as a way to provide an automated decision making

process to the mobile device. Two approaches have been defined and solved by linear programming: energy consumption minimization constrained to a minimal QoE threshold, and QoE maximization constrained to a maximum level of battery consumption. Contrary to the previous case, the decision maker may provide a noninteger number of layers, providing a finer grain resolution for quality optimization. Yet although we are able to introduce additional energy constraints to the automated decision making, the desired remaining battery level must be a priori computed without further information of the achievable QoE level.

Additionally, once the energy or quality constraints are assured, the single-objective optimization will lead to the feasible point of maximum quality or minimum energy consumption. Therefore, this approach does not explore the intermediate points as possible optimum solutions, where we can make use of the different relations between increased energy consumption and enhanced visual quality.

In order to overcome this drawback, we analyze in Section 3 the problem from a multiobjective optimization standpoint. Both energy and quality are considered as objective functions by means of a weighted utility function, which allows us to solve the problem as a single-objective linear programming problem. Different weights have been evaluated, which entail different priority to energy saving or required quality. These weights could be used to define different user profiles, different device energy saving modes, or dynamically adapted based on the status of the device battery.

Since the implementation of the optimization algorithm in a mobile handset may result on a resource-consuming process, we propose the use of a heuristic algorithm. From the analysis of the evolution of both the objective function and input variable spaces, different alternatives are found for the shape of the Pareto front. However, considering the logarithmic shape of the evolution of most MOS-related utility functions, a simple heuristic has been proposed. As a result, the proposed algorithm can be run on a mobile device as a decision making process to trigger the switching between layers.

Acknowledgments

The research leading to these results has received funding from the European Union Seventh Framework Programme (FP7/2007–2013) under Grant agreement 284863 (FP7 SEC GERYON) and from the Basque Country under BASAJAUN Project.

References

[1] X. Ji, J. Huang, M. Chiang, G. Lafruit, and F. Catthoor, "Scheduling and resource allocation for SVC streaming over OFDM downlink systems," *IEEE Transactions on Circuits and Systems for Video Technology*, vol. 19, no. 10, pp. 1549–1555, 2009.

[2] M. Brandas, M. Martini, M. Uitto, and J. Vehkapera, "Quality assessment and error concealment for svc transmission over unreliable channels," in *Proceedings of the IEEE International Conference on Multimedia and Expo (ICME '11)*, pp. 1–6, 2011.

[3] C. Hsu, M. Hefeeda, and Video broadcasting to heterogeneous mobile devices, in *Proceedings of the 8th International IFIP-TC 6 Networking Conference (NETWORKING '09)*, pp. 600–613, 2009.

[4] C.-H. Hsu and M. Hefeeda, "Flexible broadcasting of scalable video streams to heterogeneous mobile devices," *IEEE Transactions on Mobile Computing*, vol. 10, no. 3, pp. 406–418, 2011.

[5] C. Hsu and M. Hefeeda, "Multi-layer video broadcasting with low channel switching delays," in *Proceedings of the 17th International Packet Video Workshop (PV '09)*, May 2009.

[6] M. Csernai and A. Gulyas, "Wireless adapter sleep scheduling based on video qoe: how to improve battery life when watching streaming video?" in *Proceedings of 20th International Conference on Computer Communications and Networks (ICCCN '11)*, pp. 1–16.

[7] J. Lorincz, M. Bogarelli, A. Capone, and D. Begušić, "Heuristic approach for optimized energy savings in wireless access networks," in *Proceedings of the 18th International Conference on Software, Telecommunications and Computer Networks (SoftCOM '10)*, pp. 60–65, September 2010.

[8] I. Taboada, J. Fajardo, and F. Liberal, "Qoe and energy-awareness for multilayer video broadcasting," in *Proceedings of the IEEE International Conference on Multimedia and Expo (ICME '11)*, pp. 1–6.

[9] A. M. Alt and D. Simon, "Control strategies for H.264 video decoding under resources constraints," in *Proceedings of the 5th International Workshop on Feedback Control Implementation and Design in Computing Systems and Networks (FeBiD '10)*, pp. 13–18, ACM, April 2010.

[10] D. WeiSong and S. Azad, "User-centered video quality assessment for scalable video coding of H. 264/AVC standard," in *Proceedings of the 16th International Multimedia Modeling Conference (MMM '10)*, Advances in Multimedia Modeling, p. 55, Springer, Chongqing, China, January 2010.

[11] D. Migliorini, E. Mingozzi, and C. Vallati, "QoE-oriented performance evaluation of video streaming over WiMAX," in *Proceedings of the 8th International Conference on Wired/Wireless Internet Communications (WWIC '10)*, pp. 240–251, 2010.

[12] M. Blestel and M. Raulet, "Open SVC decoder: a flexible SVC library," in *Proceedings of the 18th ACM International Conference on Multimedia ACM Multimedia (MM '10)*, pp. 1463–1466, October 2010.

[13] J. Nocedal and S. Wright, *Numerical Optimization*, Springer, 1999.

[14] G. Dantzig, *Linear Programming and Extensions*, Princeton University Press, 1998.

[15] F. Pescador, E. Juarez, D. Samper, C. Sanz, and M. Raulet, "A test bench for distortion-energy optimization of a DSP-based H.264/SVC decoder," in *Proceedings of the 13th Euromicro Conference on Digital System Design: Architectures, Methods and Tools (DSD '10)*, pp. 123–129, September 2010.

[16] R. Bartels and G. Golub, "The simplex method of linear programming using LU decomposition," *Communications of the ACM*, vol. 12, pp. 266–268, 1969.

[17] R. M. Salles and J. A. Barria, "Fair and efficient dynamic bandwidth allocation for multi-application networks," *Computer Networks*, vol. 49, no. 6, pp. 856–877, 2005.

[18] B. Erman and E. P. Matthews, "Analysis and realization of IPTV service quality," *Bell Labs Technical Journal*, vol. 12, no. 4, pp. 195–212, 2008.

[19] A. M. S. Alkahtani, M. E. Woodward, and K. Al-Begain, "Prioritised best effort routing with four quality of service metrics applying the concept of the analytic hierarchy process," *Computers and Operations Research*, vol. 33, no. 3, pp. 559–580, 2006.

16

Exploiting Spatial and Frequency Diversity in Spatially Correlated MU-MIMO Downlink Channels

Rosdiadee Nordin

Department of Electrical, Electronics and System Engineering, Faculty of Engineering and Built Environment, Universiti Kebangsaan Malaysia, 43600 Bangi, Selangor, Malaysia

Correspondence should be addressed to Rosdiadee Nordin, adee@eng.ukm.my

Academic Editor: Rui Zhang

The effect of self-interference due to the increase of spatial correlation in a MIMO channel has become one of the limiting factors towards the implementation of future network downlink transmissions. This paper aims to reduce the effect of self-interference in a downlink multiuser- (MU-) MIMO transmission by exploiting the available spatial and frequency diversity. The subcarrier allocation scheme can exploit the frequency diversity to determine the self-interference from the ESINR metric, while the spatial diversity can be exploited by introducing the partial feedback scheme, which offers knowledge of the channel condition to the base station and further reduces the effect before the allocation process takes place. The results have shown that the proposed downlink transmission scheme offers robust bit error rate (BER) performance, even when simulated in a fully correlated channel, without imposing higher feedback requirements on the base controller.

1. Introduction

Dynamic resource assignment from the Orthogonal Frequency Division Multiple Access (OFDMA) in combination with multiplicative increase in throughput from Multiple-Input Multiple-Output (MIMO) technology offers improved spectral diversity in a wireless downlink transmission. The result of this combination is able to provide a highly efficient and low latency with enhanced spectrum flexibility radio interface, as can be seen from the downlink implementation of a Long Term Evolution (LTE) network [1]. In addition, the LTE network benefits from MU-MIMO, a multiuser diversity technique that exploits the spatial diversity from the channel knowledge at the transmitter, that is, channel state information (CSI), to improve the performance gain. However, accurate CSI is obtained at the expense of massive feedback overhead. A partial feedback scheme, which is based on a quantized discrete Fourier transform (DFT), is considered in this paper. Instead of feeding back the full CSI, mobile users update the E-UTRAN Node B (eNodeB) with the preferred precoding matrix based on the channel quality indicator (CQI).

The implementation of the full feedback scheme comes at the expense of CSI; therefore, it requires an enormous amount of feedback to the eNodeB. This scenario is not practical for the downlink implementation because eNodeB requires a higher level of computational overhead to compute the channel matrix. This situation worsens when the channel is severely impaired by channel imperfection, such as spatial correlation, which is also described by Gesbert et al. [2] as an effect of *self-interference*. This is because MIMO system capacity mostly depends on the spatial correlation properties of the radio channel. An obvious way to achieve decorrelation between a set of antenna elements is to place them far away from each other. However, in most cases, the nature of the equipment will limit the antenna spacing.

The core novelty of this paper lies in the fact that it considers the effective exploitation of both the frequency and spatial diversity. The spatial diversity is exploited from the MU-MIMO feedback scheme, while the frequency diversity is implemented by means of dynamic subcarrier allocation. Both of the diversity schemes, spatial diversity (from MU-MIMO feedback scheme) and frequency diversity (dynamic subcarrier allocation), are combined in order to reduce the effect of self-interference at the user equipment (UE) and/or eNodeB (base station). In addition, two feedback schemes are considered: (i) full feedback, which has full information of the channel's CQI and (ii) partial feedback, which represents the channel's CQI in a quantized form. The partial feedback scheme aims to reduce the uplink overhead requirement. The proposed combination of diversity schemes is analyzed against different MIMO-correlated channel environments and codebook sizes to achieve varying degrees of multiuser diversity.

The rest of this paper is organized as follows. Section 2 describes the fundamentals of MU-MIMO, Section 3 presents different types of feedback schemes, Section 4 presents the subcarrier allocation scheme, Section 5 describes the system setup and simulation parameters for the representation of the LTE downlink transmission, Section 6 discusses and analyses the significance of the results from the simulation, and Section 7 concludes the paper with a brief discussion.

2. Spatial Diversity: Multiuser- (MU-) MIMO Scheme

MIMO operation can be classified into two modes: Single-user- (SU-) MIMO and Multiuser- (MU-) MIMO. SU-MIMO only considers access to multiple antennas that are connected to a single UE. However, this configuration does not achieve ideal channel capacity when the channel is highly correlated and thus requires decorrelation between the spatial signatures of the antennas. In an Line-of-Sight LOS situation, a strong correlation between spatial signatures is expected. This correlation limits the use of spatial multiplexing and degrades the overall system throughput.

By scheduling different UEs on different spatial streams over the same time-frequency resource, additional diversity can be exploited in the spatial domain. This spatial diversity scheme is called MU-MIMO. MU-MIMO allows the simultaneous allocation of different spatial subchannels to different UEs in the same time-frequency resource. The earlier work in MU-MIMO can be traced back in 2006, published by Weingarten et al. [3].

In MU-MIMO, the burden of spatially separating the UEs lies at the eNodeB, thus offering reduced complexity at the UE compared to SU-MIMO. MU-MIMO benefits from the knowledge of channel state information (CSI) to properly serve the spatially multiplexed users. CSI, while not essential to SU-MIMO, is of critical importance to downlink MU-MIMO precoding techniques.

3. Feedback Schemes in MU-MIMO

Precoding uses a linear transformation of the symbols at the transmitter to improve the resilience of spatial multiplexing. In a precoded system, CSI allows a transmitter to send data along the strongest eigenmodes of a channel and effectively cope with fading by appropriate weighting from the beamforming.

However, the use of precoding comes at the expense of channel knowledge. Precoding requires an enormous amount of feedback on the uplink to benefit most from the full channel information. Therefore, full and accurate CSI feedback may not be available in a severely impaired channel, reducing the overall spectral efficiency as a result of the quantization error. These challenges have motivated research into the partial feedback scheme.

3.1. Partial Feedback versus Full Feedback. In the full feedback scheme, a UE feeds back a channel quality indicator (CQI) value for every matrix in the codebook, as is illustrated in Figure 1. When a precoding matrix for the RB is chosen, the corresponding SINR can be fed into the scheduler, which provides accurate CQI information. The user with the highest SINR for each spatial subchannel is selected, and the selected users are then precoded to share the same time-frequency resource grid.

While in a partial feedback scheme, the transmitter is provided with quantized information, and most of the gains of a precoded spatial multiplexing system can be achieved at the cost of a few bits of feedback. For example, Sanayei and Nosratinia [4] have shown that a single bit quantized feedback can preserve the multiuser diversity gain. A user selects one or more preferred beamforming matrices out of the codebook by evaluating the SINRs of different beamforming combinations. Thus, each user must signal one or several indices of the preferred vectors. The UE only feeds back a single CQI value for the preferred precoding matrix for each RB, by selecting the highest average SINR perceived by the user. Based on the feedback, the scheduler at the eNodeB chooses the precoding matrix with the highest sum of the average SINR values of all spatial subchannels and applies it to the RB.

In the full feedback scheme, the corresponding SINR is known to the scheduler because the eNodeB has the information from all users. While in the partial feedback scheme, only the users who declare the same preferred matrix are eligible for selection. For MU-MIMO, feedback schemes must be jointly designed with appropriate scheduling and multiple access methods to minimize the CSI inaccuracy and retain the feedback efficiency.

3.2. Unitary Precoding. In unitary precoding (UP), UEs provide accurate and efficient CSI feedback regarding the preferred precoding matrix to the eNodeB on the uplink control channel. Ideally, this information is made available per resource block, thus allowing channel resources to be allocated to different users in an effective manner and allowing the amount of feedback to be greatly reduced. There are several precoding methods (references [5, 6] provide detailed overview of precoding scheme with limited feedback) that have been developed, and one of them, known as the codebook-based precoding method, has recently received considerable attention in the literature.

A codebook consists of a finite number of possible beamforming matrices at both the transmitter and the receiver. Instead of using the physical antenna, the network

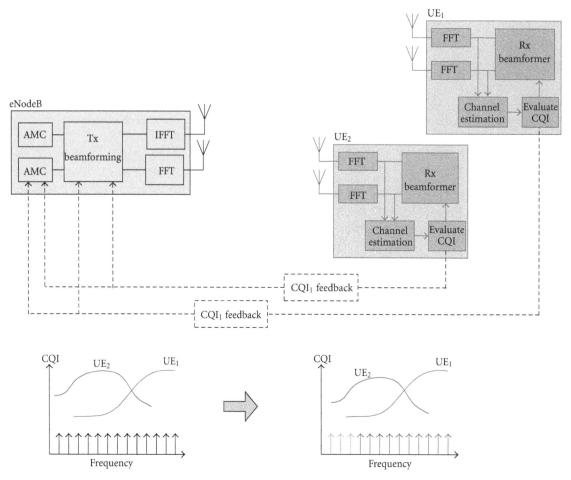

FIGURE 1: MU-MIMO with CQI feedback.

transmits through a codebook-based spatial beam, thus ensuring uniform sector coverage across the cell, as shown by Rohling and Grünheid [7].

This paper considers the use of DFT-based codebooks because it is shown in [8–10] that the DFT-based codebook is effective against a wide range of propagation scenarios, from the uncorrelated [8, 10] to the fully correlated channel [9]. Other than its excellent protection against the effects of self-interference, the DFT-based codebook also has low complexity codebook design, as described in [5].

The DFT-based unitary precoder codebook, $\mathbf{E}$, consists of the unitary matrix set, that is, $\mathbf{E} = \{\mathbf{E}^{(0)} \cdots \mathbf{E}^{(l-1)}\}$, where $\mathbf{E}^{(l)} = [e_0^{(l)} \cdots e_{N_t-1}^{(l)}]$ is the lth precoding matrix and $e_{n_t}^{(l)}$ is the N_tth precoding vector in the set. It is defined in the Fourier basis, as given in [11]:

$$
e_{n_t}^{(l)} = \frac{1}{\sqrt{N_t}} \left[w_{0n_t}^{(l)} \cdots w_{(N_t-1)n_t}^{(l)} \right]^T,
$$

$$
w_{n_r n_t}^{(l)} = \exp\left\{ j \frac{2\pi n_r}{N_t} \left(n_t + \frac{l}{L} \right) \right\},
$$

(1)

where N_t and N_r are the number of receiving and transmitting antennas, respectively; $w_{mn}^{(l)}$ is the codebook index and L is the codebook size. From (1), the precoder matrices sets

TABLE 1: Codebook size for unitary precoding, $L = 2$.

$$
\mathbf{E}_0 = \frac{1}{\sqrt{2}} \begin{bmatrix} 1 & 1 \\ 1 & -1 \end{bmatrix}
$$

$$
\mathbf{E}_1 = \frac{1}{\sqrt{2}} \begin{bmatrix} 1 & 1 \\ j & -j \end{bmatrix}
$$

(also known as the codebooks) of size 2 and 4 are generated; they are shown in Tables 1 and 2.

In codebook unitary precoding, the codebook size contains a set of $L = N_q/N_t$ predefined and fixed unitary beamforming matrices of size $N_t \times N_t$, where N_q is the allocated subcarriers at spatial subchannel q. The codebook indices are then used by the eNodeB to construct the precoding matrix. For each beamforming matrix in the codebook, each UE computes the SINR for each of the N_t beamforming vectors in the matrix assuming that the other spatial subchannels defined by the remaining $N_t - 1$ vectors are used for interfering transmission to the other UEs.

Overall, the UE computes N_q SINRs and signals the codebook index corresponding to the best SINR value

Table 2: Codebook size for unitary precoding, $L = 4$.

$$\mathbf{E}_0 = \frac{1}{\sqrt{2}}\begin{bmatrix} 1 & 1 \\ 1 & -1 \end{bmatrix}$$

$$\mathbf{E}_1 = \frac{1}{\sqrt{2}}\begin{bmatrix} 1 & 1 \\ \frac{1}{\sqrt{2}}(1+j) & \frac{1}{\sqrt{2}}(-1-j) \end{bmatrix}$$

$$\mathbf{E}_2 = \frac{1}{\sqrt{2}}\begin{bmatrix} 1 & 1 \\ j & -j \end{bmatrix}$$

$$\mathbf{E}_3 = \frac{1}{\sqrt{2}}\begin{bmatrix} 1 & 1 \\ \frac{1}{\sqrt{2}}(-1+j) & \frac{1}{\sqrt{2}}(1-j) \end{bmatrix}$$

Table 3: Feedback overhead for the considered MIMO schemes for $L = 2, Q = 2$.

Feedback Scheme	MU-MIMO full feedback	MU-MIMO partial feedback	SU-MIMO
Preferred layer 1 CQI	4 bits	4 bits	4 bits
Preferred layer 2 CQI	4 bits	4 bits	
Alternative layer 1 CQI	4 bits	—	—
Alternative layer 2 CQI	4 bits	—	—
Preferred matrix index	1 bit	1 bit	1 bit
Total bits per RB	17 bits	9 bits	5 bits

back to the eNodeB. The eNodeB then makes use of this information to select the beamforming matrix and schedule the UEs for transmission. In a partial feedback scheme, the eNodeB has a very limited set of unitary precoding matrices from which to choose, and the multiplexing gain is at its maximum when enough UEs in the cell have orthogonal channel signatures that match the vectors in one of the codebook matrices.

For both the MU-MIMO and SU-MIMO cases, the amount of feedback increases with the number of spatial subchannels, Q. In the full feedback MU-MIMO scheme, the amount of feedback is further increased by the codebook size (an L fold increase), resulting in a further increase in the uplink overhead. Otherwise, the same precoding matrix is shared among all of the subcarriers in an RB. The feedback overhead for each RB for the considered MIMO scheme is summarized in Table 3. The reporting scheme for MU-MIMO scheme is based on CQI per layer. A bitmap (e.g., 4 bits) is used to signal the MCS levels. The preferred antennas are implied by filling in the appropriate CQI layer field. The number of "1s" in the bitmap indicates the rank for antenna selection, while a NULL CQI field indicates the corresponding transmit antenna is not preferred. The matrix index represents the preferred DFT matrix by indicating "1" in the corresponding bit position.

4. Frequency Diversity: Interference-Aware Subcarrier Allocation

4.1. SINR Metric. The mathematical model of a received signal in the considered MIMO-OFDMA system, after FFT and guard removal, is described as follows:

$$\mathbf{Y}_k^s = \mathbf{H}_k^s \mathbf{E}_k^s \mathbf{X}_k^s + \mathbf{N}_k^s, \tag{2}$$

where the subscript k denotes the UE index, s denotes the subcarrier index, $\mathbf{H}_k^s$ is a channel matrix containing the frequency responses of the spatial subchannels between N_t and N_r antennas at subcarrier s and applied to the subcarriers of the OFDMA signal on a cluster basis for the kth UE, $\mathbf{E}_k^s$ is the precoding matrix, $\mathbf{N}_k^s$ denotes a complex circular symmetric colored noise with an invertible

covariance matrix, and $\mathbf{X}_k^s$ denotes the $N_t \times 1$ matrix containing the transmitted signals.

At the receiver, the proposed MIMO detection adopts an MMSE linear receiver:

$$\mathbf{G}_k^s = \left(\left(\mathbf{E}_k^s\right)^{\mathrm{H}} \left(\mathbf{H}_k^s\right)^{\mathrm{H}} \mathbf{H}_k^s \mathbf{E}_k^s + Q\frac{\mathbf{N}_k^s}{\varepsilon}\mathbf{I}\right)^{-1} \left(\mathbf{E}_k^s\right)^{\mathrm{H}} \left(\mathbf{H}_k^s\right)^{\mathrm{H}}, \tag{3}$$

where Q is the number of data streams and ε is the transmit symbol energy. The number of data streams in this work is assumed to be limited by $\min(N_r, N_t)$. In the case of SU-MIMO, both spatial streams go to the same UE. The MMSE filter is chosen because it has the ability to mitigate self-interference without adversely amplifying the received noise. The MMSE filter is also able to separate the spatial subchannel of the MIMO structure, as shown by Jang and Lee [12]. The received signal is multiplied by the MMSE filter (3) to obtain the detected data stream, $\mathbf{D}_k^s$:

$$\mathbf{D}_k^s = \mathbf{G}_k^s * \mathbf{Y}_k^s = \hat{\mathbf{X}}_k^s + \mathbf{N}_k^s. \tag{4}$$

For each data stream q at each RB, UE k then computes the SINR for every subcarrier (the subcarrier index s is omitted for ease of reference):

$$\mathrm{SINR}_k^q$$
$$= \frac{\left|(\mathbf{G}_k\mathbf{E}_k\mathbf{H}_k)_{qq}\right|^2 \varepsilon}{\left|(\mathbf{G}_k\mathbf{E}_k\mathbf{H}_k)_{qj, j \neq q}\right|^2 E_s + \left(|\mathbf{G}_k|_{qq}^2 + \sum_{j \neq q}|\mathbf{G}_k|_{qj, j \neq q}^2\right)\mathbf{N}_k^s}, \tag{5}$$

where q is the spatial subchannel at every subcarrier and $|X|_{qj}$ denotes the element located in row q and column j of matrix X. The SINR metric aims to compute the self-interference from the data stream component $|Y|_{qq}$ and the self-interference component $|Y|_{qj, j \neq q}$ from the other transmitted data streams within the same subchannel. In this work, it is proposed that the allocation will be based on the sum of the achievable capacity of both spatial streams.

In an SU-MIMO system, for RB c, denoting the index of starting subcarrier by n and the finishing subcarrier by m, the average rate of user k is given by

$$r_{k,c} = \frac{1}{m-n+1}\sum_{s=n}^{m}\sum_{q}^{\min(N_t, N_r)} \log_2\left(1 + \mathrm{SINR}_{k,s}^q\right). \tag{6}$$

The eNodeB allocates each RB to user according to the selected resource allocation algorithm. The scheduler then uses this feedback information to allocate the RB to the UE with the highest achievable data rate, r_k^q. Compared to SU-MIMO, the scheduling for the decision to choose the best precoding matrix is slightly complicated in MU-MIMO. To maximize the system capacity of MU-MIMO, the most suitable precoding matrix must be selected from the codebook to transmit on each RB. Based on the chosen precoding matrix, a dynamic subcarrier allocation is employed to select the user with the best channel condition. The selected users are then precoded to share the same time and frequency resources to maximize the system capacity.

Because each of the spatial streams can be allocated and scheduled independently in MU-MIMO, the UE k calculates the data rate of each spatial layer and feeds it back to the BS. The user k calculates the data rate of each spatial layer q on a RB basis.

$$r_{k,s}^q = \frac{1}{m-n+1} \sum_{s=n}^{m} \log_2\left(1 + \text{SINR}_{k,s}^q\right). \qquad (7)$$

Again, for every RB, the scheduler allocates each spatial layer to the UE that has the best channel conditions for the corresponding layer.

4.2. Subcarrier Allocation. The interference-aware subcarrier allocation scheme uses the SINR as the performance metric to determine the allocation. The SINR metric has the knowledge of a particular subcarrier that is affected by self-interference, especially when the correlation is high inside the spatial subchannels.

The allocation ranks users from the lowest to highest SINR metric in each spatial subchannel. Consequently, the next best subcarriers are allocated to users in rank order, allowing users with the lowest SINR at that particular spatial subchannel to have the best SINR that is available for the next transmission. Each MS provides SINR information to the BS, and the subcarrier allocation algorithm then allocates subcarriers to the MSs.

The nomenclatures are set first as references. In the following algorithm, $q = \{1, \dots, Q\}$ represents the effective spatial subchannel considered for the allocation algorithm. Σ_k^q represents the average SINR metric for user k in the qth spatial subchannel, K is the total number of users, and S is a Q by N_q matrix in which each row is a vector containing the indices of the useable subcarriers for the particular spatial subchannel (i.e., $N_q = \{1, \dots, N_{\text{sub}}\}$, where N_{sub} is the total number of useable subcarriers). $\text{SINR}_{k,s}^q$ is the SINR matrix for user k at subcarrier s and spatial subchannel q, and $\mathbf{C}_{s,k}$ is a matrix that stores the subcarrier indices (subcarrier location) of the allocated subcarriers for user k and subcarrier s.

The following algorithm performs the proposed interference-aware subcarrier allocation.

(1) After the eNodeB transmits the data matrix $\mathbf{X}_k^s$, the kth UE computes the MMSE filter (3).

(2) The kth mobile station then computes the **SINR** (5) of the qth spatial subchannel.

(3) With the feedback information from UE, eNodeB allows the user with the lowest data rate to have the next choice of best subcarrier as follows.

    (a) Generate short list of users and start with the user with the least SINR, $\boldsymbol{\Sigma}$ (For the first iteration in the allocation scheme, when no subcarriers have been allocated, all users assumed to have equal SINR value; thus the list appears entirely arbitrary). Find user k satisfying

$$\Sigma_k^q \le \Sigma_i^q \quad \forall i, \, 1 \le i \le K. \qquad (8)$$

    (b) For the user k in (a), find the subcarrier s satisfying

$$\text{SINR}_k^q \ge \text{SINR}_j^q \quad \forall j \in N. \qquad (9)$$

    (c) Update SINR_k^q, N_q, and $\mathbf{C}_{s,k}$ with k and s in (b) according to

$$\Sigma_k^q = \Sigma_k^q + \text{SINR}_{k,s}^q,$$
$$N_q = N_q - s, \qquad (10)$$
$$\mathbf{C}_{s,k} = s,$$

    where N_q is the allocated subcarriers at spatial subchannel q and $\mathbf{C}_{s,k}$ is the allocation matrix to record the allocated subcarrier s for user k.

    (d) Go to the next user in the short list in (a) until all users are allocated another subcarrier, $N \ne 0$ in (c).

In this algorithm, users are not allowed to share subcarriers, thus reducing the complexity of the algorithm. In the SISO case, Jang and Lee [12] show that the capacity can be maximized if a subcarrier is only assigned to one user because the interference from other users' signals that share the same subcarrier is reduced. This paper extends the theory presented in [12] into the MIMO case, in which the number of users sharing the same subcarrier is limited to the number of available spatial subchannels (two subchannels in this case).

5. Simulation Environment and Parameters

This paper aims to apply the feedback schemes to spatially correlated subchannel environments. In an MU-MIMO downlink environment, the effect of self-interference must be considered because the spatial correlation experienced by the UE in a real channel environment can vary from an ideally uncorrelated channel to a fully correlated channel.

This study considers an urban microenvironment with a 500 m cell radius, outdoor terminals, and 2 GHz frequency band. This environment is represented by the 3GPP-SCM Urban Micromodel [13], with an RMS delay spread of 251 ns, an excess delay of 923 ns, and a Nonline-of-Sight (NLOS) propagation scenario. The total number of available subcarriers depends on the overall transmission bandwidth

TABLE 4: OFDMA parameters.

Parameters	Value
Downlink bandwidth	10 MHz
Time slot/subframe duration	0.5 ms/1 ms
Subcarrier spacing	15 kHz
Precoding codebook size, L	2
FFT size, N_{FFT}	1024
Useable subcarrier, N_{sub}	600
Number of OFDM symbols per time slot (Short/Long CP)	7/6

TABLE 5: Correlation scenarios.

Correlation modes	R_{MS}	R_{BS}
Uncorrelated	0.00	0.00
Fully correlated	0.99	0.99

of the system. For this simulation, the representations of the LTE-OFDMA downlink parameters are summarized in Table 4.

The proposed interference-aware subcarrier allocation is simulated in QPSK, with a 1/2 rate modulation and coding scheme (MCS). This combination is one of the available MCS, as specified in [1]. QPSK modulation is chosen in the simulation because of its robustness and its ability to tolerate higher levels of self-interference, which makes it suitable for transmission in lower SNR region at the expense of lower transmission bit rate.

The performance of the subcarrier allocation in combination with the partial feedback scheme will be simulated against different spatial correlation MIMO environment, that is, self-interference effect. Therefore, the Urban Microchannel model is further extended into two correlated channel environments: (i) an uncorrelated channel that represents ideal channel conditions, in which the effect of self-interference is minimal and (ii) a "fully" correlated channel, which represents a worst case spatial correlation scenario. In a fully correlated channel, the effective MIMO channel is similar to a SISO system. The spatial correlation matrix of the MIMO channel, $\mathbf{R}_{MIMO}$, is the Kronecker product of the spatial correlation matrix at the BS and the MS, $\mathbf{R}_{MIMO} = \mathbf{R}_{MS} \otimes \mathbf{R}_{BS}$, as proposed by Beh et al. [14]. The proposed correlation scenarios are summarized in Table 5.

Three different feedback schemes are considered: (i) full feedback, (ii) partial feedback (both of these are applied to the MU-MIMO case) and (iii) SU-MIMO, which represents a case without any form of feedback. A set of 2000 independent identically distributed (i.i.d.) quasi-static Rayleigh distributed time samples per user are used in the simulation. A single CQI, which is based on the average SINR of the 12 grouped subcarriers, is fed back for each resource block (RB), and it is assumed to be perfectly known. The result is simulated based on 10 users, unless otherwise stated. A 2×2 antenna configuration is considered for the simulation. Because of the increased computational complexity and the insignificant power control gain in the frequency domain

dynamic allocation, equal power allocation is assumed throughout the simulations.

6. Error Performance Analysis

6.1. *Comparison between Different Feedback Schemes.* The proposed interference-aware subcarrier allocation scheme is compared against another subcarrier allocation scheme, known as the Dynamic Subcarrier Allocation (DSA), as proposed in [15]. In the DSA scheme, the subcarrier allocation at each spatial layer is treated independently, and channel gain is used as the performance metric to determine the subcarrier allocation.

Figure 2 illustrates the BER performance in both the uncorrelated and fully correlated channel. MU-MIMO shows significant improvement over SU-MIMO; the margin of difference is approximately 4 dB at BER = 10^{-3}. This result confirms the multiuser benefit that MU-MIMO can offer. For the SU-MIMO case, the poor performance can be explained by the spatial correlation coefficient (R_{MIMO} = 0.99); in this case, the effective channel in the SU-MIMO system is similar to a SISO (i.e., a single data stream). The increase in the BER gain between MU-MIMO and SU-MIMO is significant, especially at higher SNR. The DSA offers better performance when simulated in the uncorrelated channel; however, it suffers from severe BER loss as the channel achieves full correlation. This loss occurs because there is no knowledge of the channel condition from the subcarrier allocation scheme because channel gain is used as the performance metric. Consequently, the results from SU-MIMO are not considered in this paper.

The advantage of the interference aware allocation scheme is significant in a fully correlated channel, as illustrated in Figure 3. Full feedback MU-MIMO offers higher BER performance than SU-MIMO, for which the margin of difference is approximately 2.5 dB at BER = 10^{-3} in a fully correlated channel. In the case of the MU-MIMO feedback schemes, full feedback offers superior BER improvement to partial feedback, for which the margin of difference is approximately 2 dB at BER = 10^{-3}.

Nevertheless, MU-MIMO has been shown to achieve more BER gain through the additional dimension of diversity in the spatial domain in both correlation environments by exploiting the spatial subchannel as an additional dimension for allocating resources. By utilizing the interference-aware allocation scheme at each spatial dimension, the effect of self-interference is further reduced. MU-MIMO also has a large wavelength separation between the UEs, thus allowing a higher degree of decorrelation.

6.2. *Performance of Different Codebook Sizes.* In this section, four codebook sizes are compared, $L = \{1, 2, 4, 8\}$. In a fully correlated channel, the advantage of larger codebook sizes over smaller ones is obvious, particularly for the partial feedback scheme, as shown in Figure 4. However, in an uncorrelated channel, the BER performance for $L = 8$ is only marginally better than that of $L = 2$. This lack of improvement occurs as a result of the lower multiuser

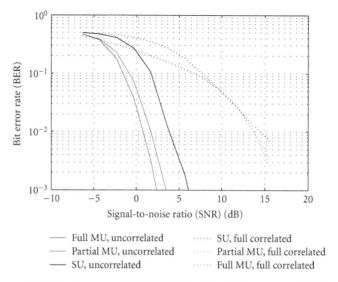

FIGURE 2: BER performance for DSA, for $L = 2$ in different types of feedback.

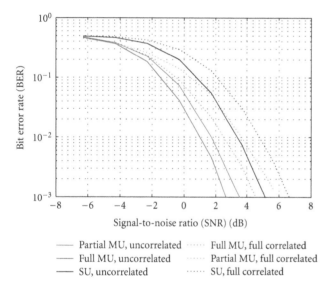

FIGURE 3: BER performance for interference-aware allocation, for $L = 2$ with different types of feedback.

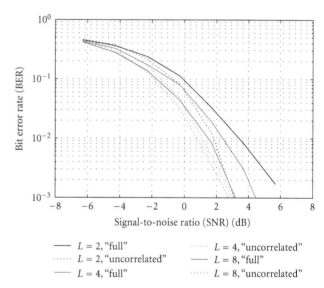

FIGURE 4: BER performance between different codebook sizes (partial feedback MU-MIMO).

diversity gain that can be achieved by the partial feedback scheme because the feedback information has been limited at the scheduler. In the case of the full feedback scheme, a higher BER gain can be achieved by larger codebook sizes, as shown in Figure 5. As an example, the codebook with a size of $L = 8$ achieved 3 dB gain over a codebook with a size of $L = 2$ in a fully correlated channel at BER = 10^{-3}.

From these results, it can be generally stated that a larger codebook size leads to better BER performance in the full feedback scheme, which helps to reduce the effect of self-interference. This improvement occurs because of the greater selection of precoding matrices. A larger codebook contains more distinct codewords, which increases the possibility that each spatial subchannel can find a better codeword match during encoding. Thus, larger codebooks are more

likely to have a lower BER loss, allowing a more accurate representation of the channel condition. Further, the use of DFT-based codebook precoding effectively reduces the impact of self-interference in a highly correlated channel.

The results published by Ravindran and Jindal [16] also confirm these findings, showing that, in a fully correlated channel, the DFT-based codebook can reduce the channel information amplitude difference between different transmitting antennas, while a constant modulus DFT codebook produces less quantization error than nonconstant modulus Grassmannian-based codebook precoding. A recent publication by Yang et al. [9] also demonstrated that the DFT-based codebook is effective against spatial correlation in an MU-MIMO system.

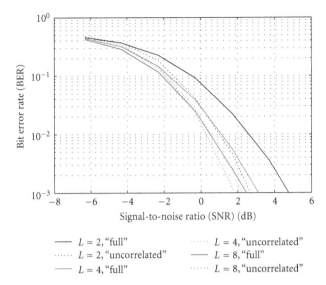

—— $L = 2$, "full"   ⋯⋯ $L = 4$, "uncorrelated"
⋯⋯ $L = 2$, "uncorrelated"   —— $L = 8$, "full"
—— $L = 4$, "full"   ⋯⋯ $L = 8$, "uncorrelated"

FIGURE 5: BER performance between different codebook sizes (full feedback MU-MIMO).

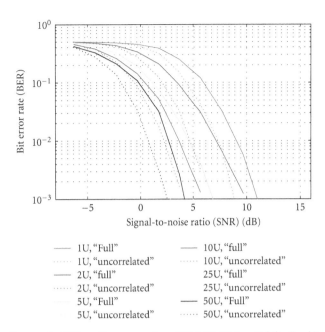

—— 1U, "Full"   —— 10U, "full"
⋯⋯ 1U, "uncorrelated"   ⋯⋯ 10U, "uncorrelated"
—— 2U, "full"   25U, "full"
⋯⋯ 2U, "uncorrelated"   25U, "uncorrelated"
—— 5U, "Full"   —— 50U, "Full"
⋯⋯ 5U, "uncorrelated"   ⋯⋯ 50U, "uncorrelated"

FIGURE 6: BER performance of an MU-MIMO (partial feedback) with different number of users.

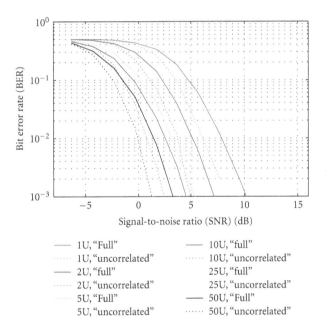

—— 1U, "Full"   —— 10U, "full"
⋯⋯ 1U, "uncorrelated"   ⋯⋯ 10U, "uncorrelated"
—— 2U, "full"   25U, "full"
⋯⋯ 2U, "uncorrelated"   25U, "uncorrelated"
—— 5U, "Full"   —— 50U, "Full"
⋯⋯ 5U, "uncorrelated"   ⋯⋯ 50U, "uncorrelated"

FIGURE 7: BER performance of an MU-MIMO (full feedback) with different number of users.

The BER performance of the MU-MIMO feedback schemes is expected to increase further with larger codebook size. However, using a codebook size that is too large can also pose a few issues. First, a larger codebook size decreases the spectral efficiency of the uplink channel because the feedback information increases considerably. Increasing the codebook size incurs exponential complexity in quantizing the CQI, as shown by Beh in [17], thus defeating the main purpose of channel feedback, particularly in the partial feedback scheme. At the time of writing, only a codebook size of $L = 2$ is supported by the 3GPP specification published in [18] because it trades off between performance gain and feedback overhead.

It is also shown that in a fully correlated channel, larger codebook sizes ($L \geq 4$) offer superior performance to small codebook size ($L = 2$). This result suggests that the size of the codebook has implications for the tradeoff between the numbers of signaling bits required to indicate a particular matrix in the codebook and the suitability of the resulting transmitted beam direction. It is shown by Tse and Viswanath [19] that the codebook size $L = 4$ has a marginally better multiuser diversity gain than $L = 2$ when simulated in the partial feedback scheme. This improvement is observed because the number of users selecting the same codebook matrix is reduced for the larger codebook size, causing a smaller number of users to be scheduled on the same time-frequency resource. For these reasons, it is important to select a suitable codebook size for the MU-MIMO downlink transmission.

6.3. Performance Comparison between Partial and Full Feedback Schemes. Figures 6 and 7 compares the BER performance between the partial feedback and full feedback schemes for different numbers of users in uncorrelated and fully correlated channels, respectively. As the number of users increases from 1 to 25, the BER performance significantly

increases as a result of the richer spectral multiuser diversity gains. When the number of users is increased (e.g., from 10 to 50), the gain of multiuser diversity can be observed to increase slowly, suggesting that the multiuser diversity gain achieves saturation as the number of users increases. This result is consistent with theoretical observations made by Tse and Viswanath [17], in which greater gain can be achieved through the additional dimension of diversity in the spatial domain. MU-MIMO can achieve a similar level of diversity gain, even with fewer users in the system.

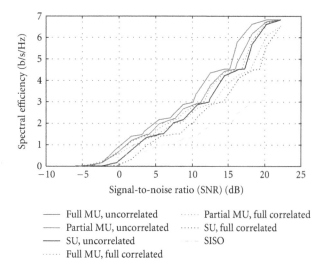

FIGURE 8: Average bandwidth efficiency comparison between the uncorrelated and fully correlated channels in the partial feedback scheme.

This result also confirms that, in addition to the ability to mitigate the effect of self-interference, the proposed interference-aware allocation scheme also considers the effect of multiple access interference (MAI) when simulated in MU-MIMO. In MU-MIMO, the resulting multiuser interference is handled by the multiple antennas, which provide the degrees of freedom necessary for spatial separation of the users, as well as link diversity. For a higher number of users in a full feedback scheme, a larger codebook size can further improve the result.

6.4. Throughput Analysis. Figure 8 compares the average bandwidth efficiency in uncorrelated and highly correlated channel environments. The bandwidth efficiency of a SISO system is plotted as a reference. The simulation result considers 10 users in both correlation cases.

From the figures, MIMO systems in the uncorrelated channel have better bandwidth efficiency than those in "fully" correlated channels. With the additional spatial diversity that can be exploited, MU-MIMO can provide almost double the throughput across the entire SNR range. In the case of "fully" correlated channels, MU-MIMO achieves significant bandwidth efficiency gain over SU-MIMO. The partial feedback scheme is marginally inferior to the full feedback scheme in both uncorrelated and correlated channels.

At lower SNR, the bandwidth efficiency of MU-MIMO is similar to that of uncorrelated MU-MIMO and other feedback schemes because the use of QPSK modulation is robust against the effect of channel imperfection (especially channel correlation) in this case. At higher SNR, the higher level of MCS is vulnerable to channel degradation. By employing an adaptive modulation scheme, the proposed interference-aware allocation is also able to reduce the self-interference effect across all SNRs.

Considering the correlation environment simulated in a fully correlated channel (correlation coefficient of 0.99), the proposed interference-aware allocation scheme is expected to offer higher throughput gain in practical applications based on the results presented in this paper.

7. Conclusion

In this paper, it is shown that the proposed interference-aware allocation scheme (frequency diversity), in combination with the feedback schemes from MU-MIMO (spatial diversity), can improve the BER performance when simulated in a rapidly time-varying channel, which suffers from severe spatial correlation between the transmitting and receiving antennas.

There are two types of MU-MIMO feedback: (i) full feedback and (ii) partial feedback. Full feedback offers superior performance compared to partial feedback, but at the expense of high uplink overhead, while partial feedback offers a tradeoff between multiuser diversity gain and a reduced feedback requirement on the uplink.

In general, a larger codebook implies more accurate knowledge of the MIMO channel at the transmitter, which leads to improved diversity. There is no significant difference in BER performance between codebook sizes when the channel is uncorrelated and operating under single user (SU-MIMO) transmission. The DFT-based codebook adaptation enables the quantization to exploit the spatial correlation inherent in the channel.

These results show that the combination of a codebook size of $L = 2$ with the partial feedback scheme achieves marginal BER performance compared to higher L sizes with full feedback scheme. The utilization of dynamic subcarrier allocation helps to reduce the effect of self-interference by exploiting the frequency diversity. A tradeoff between self-interference reduction and performance gain justifies the selection of the codebook size and feedback scheme in LTE downlink environment.

Acknowledgment

The author would like to thank the National University of Malaysia for the financial support of this work, under the Grant scheme UKM-GGPM-ICT-032-2011. The author also would like to thank the anonymous reviewers for their valuable feedbacks.

References

[1] 3GPP Technical Specification 36.213, "Physical layer procedures (Release 8)," http://www.3gpp.org/.

[2] D. Gesbert, M. Shafi, D. S. Shiu, P. J. Smith, and A. Naguib, "From theory to practice: an overview of MIMO space-time coded wireless systems," *IEEE Journal on Selected Areas in Communications*, vol. 21, no. 3, pp. 281–302, 2003.

[3] H. Weingarten, Y. Steinberg, and S. Shamai, "The capacity region of the Gaussian multiple-input multiple-output broadcast channel," *IEEE Transactions on Information Theory*, vol. 52, no. 9, pp. 3936–3964, 2006.

[4] S. Sanayei and A. Nosratinia, "Exploiting multiuser diversity with only 1-bit feedback," in *Proceedings of the IEEE Wireless Communications and Networking Conference (WCNC '05)*, pp. 978–983, March 2005.

[5] D. Gesbert, M. Kountouris, R. W. Heath, C. Chan-Byoung Chae, and T. Sälzer, "Shifting the MIMO paradigm," *IEEE Signal Processing Magazine*, vol. 24, no. 5, pp. 36–46, 2007.

[6] D. J. Love, R. W. Heath, V. K. N. Lau, D. Gesbert, B. D. Rao, and M. Andrews, "An overview of limited feedback in wireless communication systems," *IEEE Journal on Selected Areas in Communications*, vol. 26, no. 8, pp. 1341–1365, 2008.

[7] H. Rohling and R. Grünheid, "Cross layer considerations for an adaptive OFDM-based wireless communication system," *Wireless Personal Communications*, vol. 32, no. 1, pp. 43–57, 2005.

[8] Philip RI-062483, "Comparison between MU-MIMO codebook-based channel reporting techniques for L TE downlink," 3GPP TSG RAN WG I Meeting #46bis, october 2006.

[9] D. Yang, L. L. Yang, and L. Hanzo, "DFT-based beamforming weight-vector codebook design for spatially correlated channels in the unitary precoding aided multiuser downlink," in *Proceedings of the IEEE International Conference on Communications (ICC '10)*, pp. 1–5, May 2010.

[10] B. Mondal and R. W. Heath, "Channel adaptive quantization for limited feedback MIMO beamforming systems," *IEEE Transactions on Signal Processing*, vol. 54, no. 12, pp. 4717–4729, 2006.

[11] S. J. Kim, H. J. Kim, and K. B. Lee, "Multiuser MIMO Scheme for Enhanced 3GPP HSDPA," in *Proceedigs of the 11th European Wireless Conference*, February 2005.

[12] J. Jang and K. B. Lee, "Transmit power adaptation for multiuser OFDM systems," *IEEE Journal on Selected Areas in Communications*, vol. 21, no. 2, pp. 171–178, 2003.

[13] J. P. Kermoal, L. Schumacher, K. I. Pedersen, P. E. Mogensen, and F. Frederiksen, "A stochastic MIMO radio channel model with experimental validation," *IEEE Journal on Selected Areas in Communications*, vol. 20, no. 6, pp. 1211–1226, 2002.

[14] K. C. Beh, C. Han, M. Nicolaou, S. Armour, and A. Doufexi, "Power efficient MIMO techniques for 3GPP LTE and beyond," in *Proceedings of the IEEE 70th Vehicular Technology Conference Fall (VTC '09)*, pp. 1–5, September 2009.

[15] J. Zhu, J. Liu, X. She, and L. Chen, "Investigation on precoding techniques in E-UTRA and proposed adaptive precoding scheme for MIMO systems," in *Proceedings of the 14th Asia-Pacific Conference on Communications (APCC '08)*, pp. 1–5, October 2008.

[16] N. Ravindran and N. Jindal, "Limited feedback-based block diagonalization for the MIMO broadcast channel," *IEEE Journal on Selected Areas in Communications*, vol. 26, no. 8, pp. 1473–1482, 2008.

[17] K. C. Beh, *Resource allocation for the long term evolution (LTE) of 3G [Ph.D. thesis]*, University of Bristol, Bristol, UK, 2009.

[18] E. Y. Kim and J. Chun, "Random beamforming in MIMO systems exploiting efficient multiuser diversity," in *Proceedings of the IEEE 61st Vehicular Technology Conference (VTC '05)*, vol. 1, pp. 202–205, June 2005.

[19] D. Tse and P. Viswanath, *Fundamental of Wireless Communication*, Cambridge University Press, New York, NY, USA, 2005.

17

ILP Model and Relaxation-Based Decomposition Approach for Incremental Topology Optimization in p-Cycle Networks

Md. Noor-E-Alam,[1] Ahmed Zaky Kasem,[2,3] and John Doucette[1,3]

[1] *Department of Mechanical Engineering, University of Alberta, 4-9 Mechanical Engineering Building,*
  Edmonton, AB, Canada T6G 2G8
[2] *Department of Electrical and Computer Engineering, University of Alberta, Edmonton, AB, Canada T6G 2V4*
[3] *TRLabs, Edmonton, AB, Canada T5K 2M5*

Correspondence should be addressed to John Doucette, john.doucette@ualberta.ca

Academic Editor: Maode Ma

p-cycle networks have attracted a considerable interest in the network survivability literature in recent years. However, most of the existing work assumes a known network topology upon which to apply p-cycle restoration. In the present work, we develop an incremental topology optimization ILP for p-cycle network design, where a known topology can be amended with new fibre links selected from a set of eligible spans. The ILP proves to be relatively easy to solve for small test case instances but becomes computationally intensive on larger networks. We then follow with a relaxation-based decomposition approach to overcome this challenge. The decomposition approach significantly reduces computational complexity of the problem, allowing the ILP to be solved in reasonable time with no statistically significant impact on solution optimality.

1. Introduction

High-availability networks have become integral to our everyday lives, used for banking, financial transactions, voice and data communications, entertainment, and so forth. While much effort has been made to make them as reliable as possible, failures and, more critically, service outages still occur with alarming frequency. The vast majority of such failures are a result of fibre cuts, with most of those failures due to cable digups and similar construction accidents [1].

As the frequency of failures has increased, researchers have developed many approaches for ensuring survivability of the network even in the face of cable cuts or other equipment failures, including a number of mechanisms that allow the network to actively respond to a failure by rerouting affected traffic onto one or more backup routes. Survivability mechanisms are often thought of as being either *restoration* or *protection* [2]. Although the differences between the two are often blurred, and some mechanisms can be considered to be either type, the general idea is that restoration techniques are those in which a backup route is formed after failure, while protection techniques are those in which a backup route is formed before failure. Each individual survivability mechanism has its own advantages and disadvantages and requires differing amounts of spare capacity distributed throughout the network to accommodate backup routes.

One particular protection mechanism that has received a lot of attention in recent years is *p-cycles* [3, 4]. A p-cycle is a cyclic structure of preconfigured spare capacity, as illustrated in Figure 1, for example, where a six-span p-cycle is shown in the leftmost panel. In the event of failure of an on-cycle span (a span that is a part of the cycle), traffic on the failed span can be rerouted around the surviving portion of the p-cycle, as illustrated in middle panel. Each unit of capacity on the p-cycle can be used to protect one unit of capacity on each on-cycle span. However, in the event of failure of a straddling span (one whose end nodes are on the p-cycle but which is itself not a part of the p-cycle), traffic on the failed span can be rerouted around the p-cycle in either direction, as illustrated in the rightmost panel. In this case, each unit of capacity on the p-cycle can be used to protect *two* units of

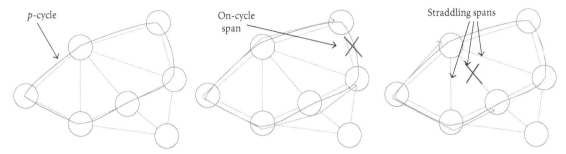

FIGURE 1: *p*-cycle protection.

capacity on each straddling span of the *p*-cycle. So a single unit capacity copy of the *p*-cycle in Figure 1 (i.e., comprising a single unit of protection capacity on each of the six spans of the *p*-cycle) is capable of protecting a total of twelve units of capacity, one on each of the six on-cycle spans and two each on the three straddling spans.

As a special case of *p*-cycle protection, one can use Hamiltonian cycles to provide protection (a Hamiltonian cycle is a cycle that passes through all nodes in the network) [5, 6]. In the most extreme case, a single Hamiltonian cycle of sufficient size can actually protect all single-span failures in the network, as all spans will either be an on-cycle span or a straddling span for that cycle. While this can result in simplified switching scenarios (nodes need only a switch to a single *p*-cycle, rather than localise the failure and make switching decisions for multiple cycles independently), it is merely a special case of *p*-cycle protection. The interested reader can refer to prior literature in [5–7].

Subsequent work in the literature has extended the *p*-cycle concept to *node-encircling p-cycles* (NEPC) [4], *path-segment protecting p-cycles* [8], *failure-independent path-protecting* (FIPP) *p-cycles* [9], and two-hop segment node protection *p-cycles* [10]. There has also been a number of network design approaches developed in the past decade. Such approaches can be classified as either *spare capacity allocation* (SCA) or *joint capacity allocation* (JCA) approaches. In the typical SCA approach, working routing is performed in advance, often via shortest path routing (but not necessarily so), and restoration routing is performed afterwards through some optimal or near optimal method. The objective is typically to minimize spare capacity requirements such that the network is 100% restorable to single-failure events [11, 12]. In JCA approaches, working routing is performed hand-in-hand with restoration routing; working and spare capacity is jointly minimized such that the network is 100% restorable to single-failure events [13, 14]. In general, JCA is significantly more capacity efficient than SCA. While there have been several heuristic methods developed to design *p*-cycle networks [15], we will focus on *integer linear programming* (ILP) techniques, which can be classified as either *arc-path* or *node-arc* models. *Arc-path* models derive from the original span-restorable network design model in [16], where working and restoration routing is carried out over a set of preenumerated eligible routes. In contrast to the arc-path approach, *node-arc* models (also called *transhipment*

models) do not utilize eligible restoration routes [17], rather they are assembled on the fly by the ILP solver.

In addition to *p*-cycles, many other survivability schemes have been proposed in the literature, including various automatic protection switching (APS) techniques, span restoration, path restoration, and shared backup path protection (SBPP). Comparative analyses were carried out in [2] to compare and contrast major restoration and protection schemes in terms of capacity efficiency. Although it is perhaps the simplest form of protection available, 1 + 1 APS was shown to require considerably greater spare capacity than the other schemes. Span restoration and *p*-cycle protection are the next most costly survivability schemes, with span restoration generally serving as a lower bound on *p*-cycle capacity requirements (in fact, *p*-cycles can be shown to be a special case of span restoration). The end-to-end protection schemes (path restoration and SBPP) are the most capacity efficient, requiring the least amounts of spare capacity. In extreme cases, path restoration can approach zero spare capacity requirements because of stub release (releasing surviving portions of failed working paths to be reused as spare capacity), [2].

In most of the work in the literature, the underlying network topology is known in advance, but there have been several approaches developed that include at least some aspects of an unknown or variable topology in the network design process [17–20]. In [19] and [21], the design methods for tree topologies optimization in communication and data networks did not consider restoration or reliability. In [18, 20–22] biconnected network topologies were considered as a transition from tree topologies. In [17–20], survivability itself was included in the design approach. In these approaches, fixed costs are typically associated with establishment of a span as well as with placement of working and spare capacity on those spans. Fixed establishment costs represent rights-of-way and lease acquisitions, excavation, duct installation, amplifiers, and so forth that are not generally dependent on the capacity or bandwidth of the spans.

Relatively little effort has been made on the investigation of the incremental topology optimization problem. Therefore, the goal of the present work is to develop a JCA *p*-cycle network topology optimization ILP formulation that will minimize the overall design cost (capacity and fixed span establishment costs) of a *p*-cycle network along with its underlying topology such that all single span failures are restorable. Due to the significant computational complexity of this problem (as will be discussed later), we will consider only incremental topology design, where a preexisting initial topology already exists but which is amended through span additions. Even this less complex problem becomes intractable for large networks, and so we further develop a problem-specific relaxation-based decomposition technique to solve this large scale ILP.

The outline of this paper will be as follows: an ILP formulation for topology optimization p-cycle design problem is developed in Section 2. It also discusses our experimental setup (i.e., solution approach). Section 3 describes our ILP results. Our problem-specific relaxation-based decomposition technique is proposed and described in Section 4, with results summarized in Section 5. Finally, we wrap up the paper in Section 6 with a concluding discussion.

2. ILP Model

In this section, we present and develop our ILP formulation for incremental topology optimization for p-cycle network design problem. Prior to topology optimization ILP models generally make use of the node-arc approach as enumeration of eligible restoration routes becomes a challenging combinatorial problem when the underlying topology is not known; a separate set of eligible routes is needed for every combination of selected eligible spans. And while we will utilize a node-arc approach for our ILP with respect to working routing, our overall approach will be a hybrid, with the p-cycle selection placement done via an arc-path approach (i.e., selection from amongst an enumerated set of eligible p-cycles). There has been a few notable works in recent literature that develop methods for p-cycle network design without enumeration of eligible cycles, [23, 24], but these approaches have proven challenging to incorporate into our topology-optimization ILP. In order to formulate our ILP model, we first define the following notation:

N: set of all nodes in the network topology, indexed by n or m,

P: set of all p-cycles in the network topology, typically indexed by p,

S: set of all spans in the network topology, typically indexed by i or j. This includes eligible spans as well as existing spans,

S_n: set of all spans incident on node n, indexed by i or j,

Q: set of all eligible spans that can be added to the network, indexed by i or j,

D: set of all demands in the network, indexed by r,

d_r: the parameter that represents the number of demand units for demand r,

$O_r \in N$: the origin node of demand r,

$T_r \in N$: the target node of demand r,

c_j: the incremental cost of adding one unit of capacity on span j,

f_i: the fixed establishment cost for eligible span i,

$x_{j,p} \in \{0, 1, 2\}$: a parameter that enumerates eligible p-cycles by representing the relationship between span j and p-cycle p, where $x_{j,p} = 2$ if it is a straddling span, $x_{j,p} = 1$ if it is an on-cycle span, and 0 otherwise,

$w_{n,j}^r \geq 0$: a decision variable for the number of working capacity units assigned for demand r on span j and flowing out from node n,

$w_{j,n}^r \geq 0$: a decision variable for the number of working capacity units assigned for demand r on span j and flowing into node n,

$w_j \geq 0$: an integer decision variable for the total amount of working capacity units assigned to span j,

$s_j \geq 0$: an integer decision variable for the number of spare units deployed on span j,

$\delta_i \in \{0, 1\}$: a binary decision variable that equals 1 if the eligible span i will be used in the design, and 0 otherwise,

$n_p \geq 0$: an integer decision variable that represents the number of copies of p-cycle p that will be used in this design,

M: a large number (in our case, the summation of all demands plus one).

Note that strictly speaking, the $w_{n,j}^r \geq 0$ and $w_{j,n}^r \geq 0$ decisions variables are integer variables. However, as was shown in [17], as long as the capacity variables themselves are integer, integrality can be relaxed on the underlying flow variables. We then define the problem as follows: minimize

$$\sum_{\forall j \in S} c_j \left(s_j + w_j \right) + \sum_{i \in Q} f_i \times \delta_i \quad \forall i \in Q, \ \forall j \in S. \quad (1)$$

subject to

$$\sum_{\forall j \in S_n} w_{n,j}^r = d_r \quad \forall r \in D, \ \forall n \in N \mid n = O_r, \quad (2)$$

$$\sum_{\forall j \in S_n} w_{j,n}^r = 0 \quad \forall r \in D, \ \forall n \in N \mid n = O_r, \quad (3)$$

$$\sum_{\forall j \in S_n} w_{j,n}^r = d_r \quad \forall r \in D, \ \forall n \in N \mid n = T_r, \quad (4)$$

$$\sum_{\forall j \in S_n} w^r_{n,j} = 0 \quad \forall r \in D, \; \forall n \in N \mid n = T_r, \tag{5}$$

$$\sum_{\forall j \in S_n} w^r_{n,j} - \sum_{\forall j \in S_n} w^r_{j,n} = 0 \quad \forall r \in D, \tag{6}$$
$$\forall n \in N \mid n \notin \{O_r, T_r\},$$

$$w^r_{n,j} = w^r_{j,m} \quad \forall r \in D, \; \forall j \in S_n, \tag{7}$$
$$\forall j \in S_m \mid n \neq m,$$

$$w^r_{j,n} = w^r_{m,j} \quad \forall r \in D, \; \forall j \in S_n, \tag{8}$$
$$\forall j \in S_m \mid n \neq m,$$

$$w_j \geq \sum_{\forall r \in D, \forall n \in N \mid j \in S_n} w^r_{n,j}$$
$$+ \sum_{\forall r \in D, \forall n \in N \mid j \in S_n} w^r_{j,n} \quad \forall j \in S, \tag{9}$$

$$w_j \leq \sum_{\forall p \in P} x_{j,p} \cdot n_p \quad \forall j \in S, \tag{10}$$

$$s_j \geq \sum_{\forall p \in P \mid x_{j,p}=1} n_p \quad \forall j \in S, \tag{11}$$

$$s_i + w_i \leq M \times \delta_i \quad \forall i \in Q. \tag{12}$$

The objective function in (1) seeks to minimize the total cost of the network, including the variable costs incurred for placing working and spare capacity on all spans, and the fixed costs incurred by adding any additional spans to the existing topology (i.e., selecting one or more of the eligible spans). Equations from (2) to (9) are the node-arc constraints that determine working routing and working capacity placement, similar to the approach in [17]. The constraints in (2) ensure that, for any demand, the total number of working capacity units flowing out from the origin node must equal to the number of demand units for this demand, while constraints in (3) ensure that all network flows into the origin node for a particular demand equal zero. Equations (4) and (5) are the related target node constraints. The constraints in (6) ensure the conservation of flow requirement for all transhipment nodes (i.e., not the origin or target nodes) for each demand, while constraints (7) and (8) ensure conservation of flow for all spans (i.e., any traffic flow into a span for a particular demand equals the flow out of that span for that demand). Equation (9) guarantees that the total number of working capacity units deployed on any span will be sufficient to accommodate all of the working traffic routed through it.

Equations (10) and (11) are the arc-path p-cycle placement constraints like those in the original p-cycle paper, [26]. Constraints in (10) ensure that, for each failed span, the total number protection routes available from p-cycles deployed in the network will be sufficient for restoring the working capacity on each span; each copy of a p-cycle copy can restore one working capacity on each of its on-cycle spans and two units of working capacity on each of its straddling spans. Constraints in (11) place sufficient spare capacity to accommodate all deployed p-cycles. Finally, the constraints in (12) force all span selection variables to equal one if the associated span is assigned any working and/or spare capacity.

3. Experimental Methodology

We used a set of seven test case networks of 10 nodes, 15 nodes, 20 nodes, 25 nodes, 30 nodes, 35 nodes, and 40 nodes. The base networks we used herein (i.e., defining the existing topologies) are the most sparse members of the network families from [2], while their so-called master networks (i.e., those with average nodal degree $\bar{d} = 4.0$) represent the set of eligible spans for each of our respective networks. The set of demands for each of those networks were also used herein; each node pair in a network exchanges a number of lightpaths drawn from a uniform random distribution. While one might argue that demands in reality are not known in advance with any precision and are not static, this treatment of demands is common in the literature, as the demands used can represent upper limits on the expected demands.

Eligible p-cycles were enumerated via a custom-designed $C++$ algorithm that performed a depth-first search type of algorithm to enumerate at least the shortest 10 thousand possible cycles that can be drawn in the graph to protect each single span failure, including eligible spans.

We solved all instances of the problem on an 8-processor ACPI multiprocessor X64-based PC with Intel Xeon CPU X5460 running at 3.16 GHz with 32 GB memory. The ILP models were implemented in AMPL [27] and solved with the CPLEX 11.2 solver [28]. We used a CPLEX *mipgap* setting of 0.001, which means that all test cases solved to full termination are provably within 0.1% of optimality.

4. Preliminary Result Analysis

Figures 2, 3, 4, 5, 6, 7, and 8 show the relationship between total network design cost and the number of eligible restoration routes with various establishment cost multipliers. Each square, diamond, and triangular data point represents the normalized total cost (working and spare capacity plus fixed span establishment costs) of the network indicated with the specified number of eligible spans and with the specified span establishment cost multiplier. The cost multiplier is the ratio of the spans' fixed establishment cost to its per-unit capacity cost (i.e., it equals f_i/c_i); the same cost multiplier is applied uniformly on all spans in the network. In our case, we used cost multipliers of 10, 20, and 50, denoted in the charts as low, medium, and high, respectively. We remind the reader that the fixed establishment costs represent rights-of-way costs associated with the span's fibre facility route, installation of the conduit and fibre cables, and all other one-time costs that might be incurred to establish a new span. The network design cost curves for the medium and high establishment cost factors are not shown for the three larger networks, as problem

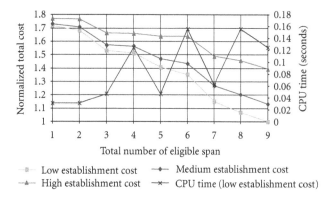

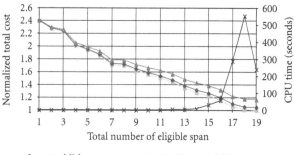

FIGURE 2: Total network costs and CPU time versus the number of eligible spans for the 10-node network.

FIGURE 4: Total network costs and CPU time versus the number of eligible spans for the 20-node network.

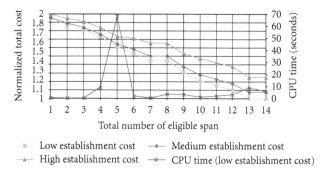

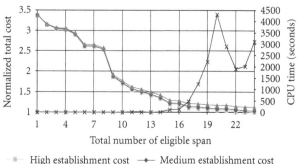

FIGURE 3: Total network costs and CPU time versus the number of eligible spans for the 15-node network.

FIGURE 5: Total network costs and CPU time versus the number of eligible spans for the 25-node network.

complexity becomes exceedingly problematic for these test cases (see further discussion below).

As we expect, the ILP model is better able to perform working and restoration routing and allocate the associated working capacity and p-cycles as we introduce more eligible spans, so that overall capacity costs are reduced as the eligible span set gets larger. The rate of the cost reductions varies from network to network, but the trend spears to be that cost reductions slow as the number of eligible spans becomes large. The interpretation here is that as we provide the network with a greater and greater number of eligible spans to select from, it becomes more difficult for the network to make use of these eligible spans.

We can also note that the establishment cost factor does not appear to have a significant bearing on the behaviour of the relationship between network costs and the number of eligible spans. For each network, the differences between the three curves themselves (corresponding to the low, medium, and high establishment cost factors) is primarily due to the fact that the sum of the selected spans' fixed costs will be larger with a higher establishment cost factor (i.e., the second summation in the objective function), irrespective of the actual number of selected spans. In addition, as will be discussed later, the differences between the three curves are partially a function of the differences in the spans selected by the solver for the various cost factors. However, since the higher establishment cost factors generally result in

selection of fewer eligible spans (see the discussion below), this will have a negative effect on the design costs at higher establishment costs. The total network design costs tend to become closer (i.e., the differences between them become less, relatively speaking) as the networks become larger, though this is primarily due to the fact that the capacity costs represent a proportionally greater share of the overall network cost as the networks become larger. In hindsight, this suggests that perhaps our establishment cost multipliers is likely too small to adequately demonstrate the effect that is seen in smaller networks. This should not be interpreted as suggesting that the objective function itself is flawed, rather, there will be a degree of uncertainty in establishment cost factors that will need to be selected based on observed (i.e., actual) costs and perhaps also artificially through a desire to drive rich or sparse topologies (through low cost multipliers and high cost multipliers, resp.).

In any case, the ILP effectively permits a network designer to select an optimal set of span additions (i.e., incremental topology optimization) on which to design a p-cycle network. Strictly speaking, this problem is NP-hard [29, 30], but like many NP-hard problems, specific instances are solvable in reasonable times. That is the case for small instances of this problem. However, we can also observe in Figure 2 through Figure 8 that the solution runtimes become prohibitively high for large test case network instances and

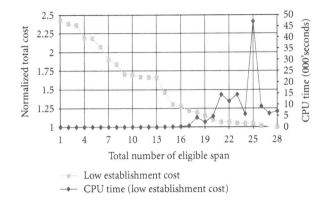

FIGURE 6: Total network costs and CPU time versus the number of eligible spans for the 30-node network.

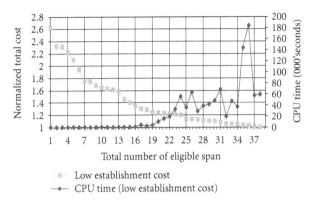

FIGURE 8: Total network costs and CPU time versus the number of eligible spans for the 40-node network.

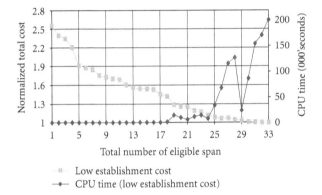

FIGURE 7: Total network costs and CPU time versus the number of eligible spans for the 35-node network.

generally also increase with the number of eligible spans provided to a network. In those figures, the curves with cross (×) data points (read against the right hand side y axes) show the runtime required by the solver when running the corresponding low establishment cost factor results to optimality. Each data point represents the actual processor time used in total amongst all 8 processors (as recorded by CPLEX) to solve the ILP for the indicated test network with the indicated number of eligible spans using the low establishment cost factor (though in most cases, only a single processor was utilized).

As one can observe, runtimes are quite short (from fractions of a second to a few minutes) for the smaller test case networks, but become exceedingly high for larger test case networks reaching nearly 200 thousand seconds (more than two days) for the 40-node network with 78 eligible spans. While there is a general increasing trend in runtimes as we provide a greater number of eligible restoration routes, we can notice that they often exhibit an irregular nature. Although it would be interesting if some useful insight could be gained from this observation, the cause is simply due to peculiarities in the network topologies and the nature of the solution approach. For instance, when the 15-node test case network is solved with 5 eligible spans (Figure 3), inclusion of that 5th eligible span results in the enumeration

of a specific set of eligible p-cycles which happens to be more computationally complex to solve than the test case with only 4 eligible spans or with 6 eligible spans. It might also be interesting to note that the number of branch-and-bound nodes produced by CPLEX's internal algorithm rises quite substantially in test cases corresponding to those instances with irregularly high runtimes, suggesting that simple peculiarities in the branch-and-bound tree contribute to these high runtimes. We suspect that the highly irregular nature of CPU times for those test-case networks was due to a complex interaction of the large number of spans in the network and topological effects (addition of a single span can often provide an obviously beneficial routing option that the solver takes advantage of). Such instances of the problem can create much tighter LP relaxations than other instances, and/or algorithms used by CPLEX's internal branch-and-bound procedures might be better suited to some of those specific cases. As a result, these instances see fewer branch-and-bound nodes when solving the ILP problem. It is these artifacts (i.e., the irregular nature of the runtime increases) in smaller to midsize test case networks, and, more importantly, the extremely high runtimes in the large test case networks that motivate us to develop an alternative solution method for the p-cycle network topology optimization problem, as discussed later in Section 5.

A closer look at the numbers of spans selected by the solver adds some additional interesting insights. As we can observe in Figures 9, 10, 11, and 12, the number of spans selected decreases quite as we increase the span establishment cost factor (i.e., as spans become more expensive, relative to the per-unit capacity costs). However, for larger networks there is almost no variation initially (i.e., as we provide only a few eligible spans), regardless of span establishment factor, but a small degree of variation arises when we provide a greater number of eligible spans. While this may initially seem indicative of some underlying phenomenon, the truth of the matter is that we happened to have selected span establishment factors that produce a lopsided objective function that is dominated by the span capacity costs in the larger networks. In hind sight, a smarter approach would have been to set higher stand establishment factors for these larger networks, so that the objective function is more

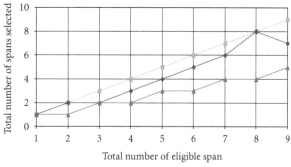

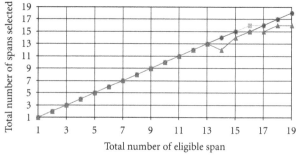

FIGURE 9: Variation of total number of selected spans for 10-node 20-span network.

FIGURE 11: Variation of total number of selected spans for 20-node 40-span network.

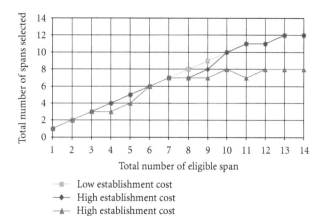

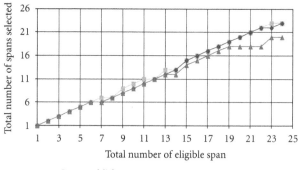

FIGURE 10: Variation of total number of selected spans for 15-node 30-span network.

FIGURE 12: Variation of total number of selected spans for 25-node 50-span network.

balanced, with respect to the span capacity costs and the fixed establishment costs. With the span establishment factors we have used, the solver sees little disincentive to select quite a large number of the eligible spans (i.e., there is only a small cost to add extra spans, relative to the reductions in capacity that result).

5. Relaxation-Based Decomposition Technique

In order to be better able to solve the p-cycle network topology optimization problem in large test case networks, we now propose and develop a problem-specific relaxation-based decomposition technique for the ILP developed above. From the investigation of a hard ILP instance, it is sometimes observed that the computational complexity arises from a set of constraints or integrality properties of specific sets of variables. For the first scenario, we can dualize these hard constraints and create an easy subproblem [25, 31], and the solution of this subproblem can be used to solve the main problem. Our proposed technique is different from this approach in a sense that we decompose the original problem into two easy subproblems by relaxing the integrality

property of some variables rather than relaxing the set of constraints. While most advanced solvers, including CPLEX, utilize some form of relaxation-based approaches to speed up solution of ILP problems, such general approaches often have difficulty properly selecting the best specific relaxations and subproblem decompositions. With some insights into the problem at hand, insights that a general approach might not have, we can decompose the ILP problem into two subproblems. First, we use a partially relaxed version of the original, which is more easily solved. We can then use the solution from that problem to set fixed values for a subset of integer variables and resolve the original with that subset of integer variables acting as parameters. This relaxation-based technique is known as *relax-and-fix-based decomposition* (RFBD) [32]. While the solution is not guaranteed to be optimal in the RFBD technique, the proper selection of the integer variables to relax in the first subproblem and of the integer variables for which we can fix their values in the second subproblem can permit near-optimal solutions. As with most near-optimal algorithms, quality of the solution (in terms of both the objective function value and the runtime improvement) will depend on careful selection of those subsets of variables.

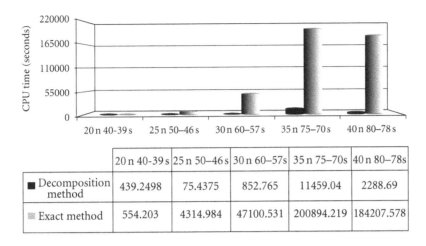

	20 n 40–39 s	25 n 50–46 s	30 n 60–57s	35 n 75–70s	40 n 80–78s
■ Decomposition method	439.2498	75.4375	852.765	11459.04	2288.69
▨ Exact method	554.203	4314.984	47100.531	200894.219	184207.578

FIGURE 13: Comparison of CPU time between decomposition method and exact method.

With the particular ILP problem we developed above, we felt that if we could use a partially relaxed version of the problem to first identify which specific span additions to select, then we could fix that topology and solve the original unrelaxed problem with a known topology. We therefore decompose our problem as follows:

Step 1: relax working capacity (w_j), spare capacity (s_j), and p-cycle placement variables (n_p) and solve the original ILP problem. In other words, all of the integrality requirements on those decision variables are removed and the ILP solved.

Step 2: fix all span establishment variables (δ_i) to the values obtained in Step 1. In other words, take the resulting values for all span establishment variables as solved in Step 1, and convert those variables to parameters with the same values.

Step 3: solve the original ILP, resetting integrality requirements in all relevant variables (but where all δ_i variables are fixed to the values in Step 2).

The main rationale for the above decomposition approach is that the span establishment variables are binary, and so fractional values would have very little meaning; if $\delta_i = 0$, then the span is not selected, and if $\delta_i = 1$, then the span is selected, but $\delta_i = 0.5$, for instance, is difficult to interpret in a manner that has any real physical meaning. The three sets of variables noted in Step 1, however, can be permitted to take on fractional values, and the solution can still impart some physical meaning. For instance, $w_j = 7.8$ would mean that 7.8 units of working capacity are placed on span j, which might not strictly be feasible (one cannot place a fractional unit of capacity) but is still conceptually understandable. In addition, the span establishment variables will still be driven to $\delta_i = 0$ or $\delta_i = 1$ whether the w_j, s_j, and n_p variables are integer or not. Then when we resolve the ILP in Step 3, with the span establishment variables fixed in Step 2,

the resultant ILP is equivalent to the basic p-cycle network design problem.

The branch-and-bound technique is widely used to solve ILP models, as there is no known polynomial time algorithm. This technique applies an intelligent enumeration scheme that can cover all possible solutions by only evaluating a small number of solutions [33]. However, in the worst-case situations, it requires complete enumeration, and in practice, the solver can require a very long time to reach optimality. For our model above, if the solver needed to enumerate all possible nodes in the branch-and-bound tree, the total number of nodes is $m_1^{|Q|} + m_2^{|Q|} + m_3^{|Q|} + 2^{|P|}$, where m_1, m_2, and m_3 are number of integer working capacity variables, spare capacity variables, and p-cycle variables. More specifically, $m_1 = |S|$, $m_2 = |S|$, and $m_3 = |P|$. However, in our proposed decomposition method, even in the worst-case scenarios, the total number of possible nodes in the branch-and-bound tree for Step 1 is only $2^{|P|}$ due to the relaxations of the integrality property of the first three variables. Furthermore, the resulting model in Step 2 becomes much easier to solve, as very tight LP relaxations arise due to the "known" values of the span establishment variables. As a result the proposed method reduces the overall computational complexity of the model significantly, which we'll discuss in more detail in a moment.

6. Results for Decomposition Method

To test the performance of this above technique, we selected the most computationally complex instance of the problem for each network (though we skip the 10-node and 15-node networks, as their solutions are already trivial). More specifically, we tested the decomposition technique on the 20-node network with 18 eligible spans, the 25-node network with 20 eligible spans, the 30-node network with 26 eligible spans, the 35-node network with 24 eligible spans, and the 40-node network with 37 eligible spans. And as stated earlier,

TABLE 1: Comparison of normalized total cost between decomposition method and exact method.

Networks	Normalized total cost		Percentage difference
	Exact (full ILP) method	Decomposition method	
20n40-39s	1	1.000137	0.013776
25n50-46s	1.76266	1.762942	0.01603
30n60-57s	2.834284	2.833077	−0.0426
35n75-70s	3.634334	3.633292	−0.02866
40n80-78s	4.468206	4.466802	−0.03142

our ILP models were implemented in AMPL and solved with the CPLEX 11.2 solver. We used a CPLEX *mipgap* setting of 0.001, which means that all test cases solved to full termination are provably within 0.1% of optimality.

Figure 13 compares the CPU runtimes of the decomposition approach with the original ILP solution. The general trend is that runtime improvements are greater in larger test cases. As we can observe, we see only moderate runtime improvements for the midsize networks (a 21% reduction in the 20-node test case) but significantly greater runtime improvements in the largest networks (a 99.99% reduction in the 40-node test case).

Of course, the tradeoff when implementing a heuristic approach is often a reduction in optimality of the resulting solution, so we also need to compare the solutions we obtain with the decomposition approach with the solutions from Section 4. As we can see from Table 1, the solutions obtained with the decomposition technique are at worst only 0.016% more costly than the full ILP, and in three of the five cases the decomposition approach provides a less-costly solution than the full ILP. This is counterintuitive, as the cost of the full ILP solution should serve as the lower bound on the cost of solutions obtained via our heuristic approach. The explanation is that the differences are smaller than the mipgap setting of 0.1%. In fact, we can note that in all cases, the difference between the solutions obtained from the decomposition approach and the full ILP are within the optimality gap setting of 0.1%, which means that the two approaches effectively provide equivalent solutions.

7. Conclusion

We have developed a new ILP model for incremental topology optimization in a *p*-cycle network that is capable of selecting an optimal subset of eligible spans to add to an existing *p*-cycle network. While the ILP proves to be relatively easy to solve for small test case network instances, it is computationally complex to solve for larger networks. We then developed a relaxation-based decomposition heuristic that significantly reduces runtime of the ILP in large networks, while having no statistical impact on optimality. In the most computationally complex instance, the ILP runtime of over 184 thousand seconds (more than two days) was reduced to less than 2300 seconds (less than an hour), while the objective function value remained within the optimality gap. In fact, the heuristic solution was slightly better than the

full ILP (though again, we note that it was not provably better since the difference was smaller than the optimality gap).

References

[1] W. Grover, *Mesh-Based Survivable Networks*, Prentice Hall, Upper Saddle River, NJ, USA, 2004.

[2] J. Doucette, *Advances on design and analysis of mesh-restorable networks [Ph.D. thesis]*, University of Alberta, Edmonton, Canada, December 2004.

[3] D. Stamatelakis and W. D. Grover, "Theoretical underpinnings for the efficiency of restorable networks using preconfigured cycles ("p-cycles")," *IEEE Transactions on Communications*, vol. 48, no. 8, pp. 1262–1265, 2000.

[4] D. Stamatelakis and W. D. Grover, "IP layer restoration and network planning based on virtual protection cycles," *IEEE Journal on Selected Areas in Communications*, vol. 18, no. 10, pp. 1938–1949, 2000.

[5] H. Huang and J. Copeland, "Hamiltonian cycle protection: a novel approach to mesh WDM optical network protection," in *Proceedings of the IEEE Workshop on High Performance Switching and Routing*, pp. 31–35, May 2001.

[6] H. Huang and J. A. Copeland, "A series of Hamiltonian cycle-based solutions to provide simple and scalable mesh optical network resilience," *IEEE Communications Magazine*, vol. 40, no. 11, pp. 46–51, 2002.

[7] L. Guo, X. Wang, J. Cao, W. Hou, J. Wu, and Y. Li, "Local and global hamiltonian cycle protection algorithm based on abstracted virtual topology in fault-tolerant multi-domain optical networks," *IEEE Transactions on Communications*, vol. 58, no. 3, pp. 851–859, 2010.

[8] G. Shen and W. D. Grover, "Extending the *p*-cycle concept to path segment protection for span and node failure recovery," *IEEE Journal on Selected Areas in Communications*, vol. 21, no. 8, pp. 1306–1319, 2003.

[9] A. Kodian and W. D. Grover, "Failure-independent path-protecting p-cycles: efficient and simple fully preconnected optical-path protection," *IEEE Journal of Lightwave Technology*, vol. 23, no. 10, pp. 3241–3259, 2005.

[10] D. P. Onguetou and W. D. Grover, "A new approach to node-failure protection with span-protecting p-cycles," in *Proceedings of the 11th International Conference on Transparent Optical Networks (ICTON '09)*, July 2009.

[11] H. Sakauchi, Y. Okanoue, and S. Hasegawa, "Spare-channel design schemes for self-healing networks," *IEICE Transactions on Communications*, vol. 75, no. 7, pp. 624–633, 1992.

[12] C. Wynants, *Network Synthesis Problems*, Combinatorial Optimization Series, Kluwer Academic Publishers, 2001.

[13] R. R. Iraschko, M. H. MacGregor, and W. D. Grover, "Optimal capacity placement for path restoration in STM or

ATM mesh-survivable networks," *IEEE/ACM Transactions on Networking*, vol. 6, no. 3, pp. 325–336, 1998.

[14] J. Doucette and W. D. Grover, "Influence of modularity and economy-of-scale effects on design of mesh-restorable DWDM networks," *IEEE Journal on Selected Areas in Communications*, vol. 18, no. 10, pp. 1912–1923, 2000.

[15] J. Doucette, D. He, W. D. Grover, and O. Yang, "Algorithmic approaches for efficient enumeration of candidate p-cycles and capacitated p-cycle network design," in *Proceedings of the Design of Reliable Communication Networks (DRCN '03)*, pp. 212–220, Banff, Canada, October 2003.

[16] M. Herzberg and S. Bye, "An optimal spare-capacity assignment model for survivable networks with hop limits," in *IEEE Global Communications Conference (GlobeCom '94)*, pp. 1601–1607, San Francisco, Calif, USA, December 1994.

[17] W. D. Grover and J. Doucette, "Topological design of span-restorable mesh transport networks," *Annals of Operations Research*, vol. 106, no. 1–4, pp. 79–125, 2001.

[18] A. Kershenbaum, *Telecommunications Network Design Algorithms*, McGraw-Hill, New York, NY, USA, 1993.

[19] R. R. Boorstyn and H. Frank, "Large-scale network topological optimization," *IEEE Transactions on Communications*, vol. 25, no. 1, pp. 29–47, 1977.

[20] A. Z. Kasem and J. Doucette, "Incremental optical network topology optimization using meta-mesh span restoration," in *Proceedings of the Design of Reliable Communication Networks (DRCN '11)*, Krakow, Poland, October 2011.

[21] H. Dirilten and R. W. Donaldson, "Topological design of distributed data communications networks using linear regression clustering," *IEEE Transactions on Communications*, vol. 25, no. 10, pp. 1083–1092, 1977.

[22] R. S. Cahn, *Wide Area Network Design: Concepts and Tools for Optimization*, Morgan Kaufman Publishers, San Francisco, Calif, USA, 1998.

[23] D. A. Schupke, "An ILP for optimal p-cycle selection without cycle enumeration," in *Proceedings of the Optical Network Design and Modelling (ONDM '04)*, Ghent, Belgium, February 2004.

[24] H. Li, B. Jaumard, and X. Fu, "Scalable design of p-cycles for node protection without candidate pre-enumeration," in *Proceedings of the International Conference on Multimedia Technology (ICMT '10)*, October 2010.

[25] S. Rajagopalan, S. S. Heragu, and G. D. Taylor, "A Lagrangian relaxation approach to solving the integrated pick-up/drop-off point and AGV flowpath design problem," *Applied Mathematical Modelling*, vol. 28, no. 8, pp. 735–750, 2004.

[26] W. D. Grover and D. Stamatelakis, "Cycle-oriented distributed preconfiguration: ring-like speed with mesh-like capacity for self-planning network restoration," in *Proceedings of the IEEE International Conference on Communications (ICC. Part 3 (of 3)*, pp. 537–543, June 1998.

[27] R. Fourer, D. M. Gay, and B. W. Kernighan, *AMPL: A Modeling Language for Mathematical Programming*, Duxbury Press, 2002.

[28] ILOG, *ILOG CPLEX 11.0 User's Manual*, ILOG, 2007.

[29] B. Gendron, T. G. Crainic, and A. Frangioni, "Multicommodity capacitated net-work design," in *Telecommunications Network Planning*, B. Sanso and P. Soriano, Eds., pp. 1–19, Kluwer Academic Publishers, 1999.

[30] H.-J. Kim and J. N. Hooker, "Solving fixed-charge network flow problems with a hybrid optimization and constraint programming approach," *Annals of Operations Research*, vol. 115, no. 1–4, pp. 95–124, 2002.

[31] L. A. Wolsey, *Integer Programming*, Wiley-Interscience, Toronto, Canada, 1998.

[32] M. Noor-E-Alam and J. Doucette, "Relax-and-fix decomposition technique for solving large scale grid-based location problems," *Computers & Industrial Engineering*, vol. 63, no. 4, pp. 1062–1073, 2012.

[33] D.-S. Chen, R. G. Baton, and Y. Dang, *Applied Integer Programming*, chapter 2, John Willey & Sons, 2010.

Permissions

The contributors of this book come from diverse backgrounds, making this book a truly international effort. This book will bring forth new frontiers with its revolutionizing research information and detailed analysis of the nascent developments around the world.

We would like to thank all the contributing authors for lending their expertise to make the book truly unique. They have played a crucial role in the development of this book. Without their invaluable contributions this book wouldn't have been possible. They have made vital efforts to compile up to date information on the varied aspects of this subject to make this book a valuable addition to the collection of many professionals and students.

This book was conceptualized with the vision of imparting up-to-date information and advanced data in this field. To ensure the same, a matchless editorial board was set up. Every individual on the board went through rigorous rounds of assessment to prove their worth. After which they invested a large part of their time researching and compiling the most relevant data for our readers. Conferences and sessions were held from time to time between the editorial board and the contributing authors to present the data in the most comprehensible form. The editorial team has worked tirelessly to provide valuable and valid information to help people across the globe.

Every chapter published in this book has been scrutinized by our experts. Their significance has been extensively debated. The topics covered herein carry significant findings which will fuel the growth of the discipline. They may even be implemented as practical applications or may be referred to as a beginning point for another development. Chapters in this book were first published by Hindawi Publishing Corporation; hereby published with permission under the Creative Commons Attribution License or equivalent.

The editorial board has been involved in producing this book since its inception. They have spent rigorous hours researching and exploring the diverse topics which have resulted in the successful publishing of this book. They have passed on their knowledge of decades through this book. To expedite this challenging task, the publisher supported the team at every step. A small team of assistant editors was also appointed to further simplify the editing procedure and attain best results for the readers.

Our editorial team has been hand-picked from every corner of the world. Their multi-ethnicity adds dynamic inputs to the discussions which result in innovative outcomes. These outcomes are then further discussed with the researchers and contributors who give their valuable feedback and opinion regarding the same. The feedback is then collaborated with the researches and they are edited in a comprehensive manner to aid the understanding of the subject.

Apart from the editorial board, the designing team has also invested a significant amount of their time in understanding the subject and creating the most relevant covers. They scrutinized every image to scout for the most suitable representation of the subject and create an appropriate cover for the book.

The publishing team has been involved in this book since its early stages. They were actively engaged in every process, be it collecting the data, connecting with the contributors or procuring relevant information. The team has been an ardent support to the editorial, designing and production team. Their endless efforts to recruit the best for this project, has resulted in the accomplishment of this book. They are a veteran in the field of academics and their pool of knowledge is as vast as their experience in printing. Their expertise and guidance has proved useful at every step. Their uncompromising quality standards have made this book an exceptional effort. Their encouragement from time to time has been an inspiration for everyone.

The publisher and the editorial board hope that this book will prove to be a valuable piece of knowledge for researchers, students, practitioners and scholars across the globe.

List of Contributors

Jia-Liang Lu and Wei Shu
Department of Computer Science & Engineering, Shanghai Jiao Tong University, Shanghai 200240, China

Min-You Wu
Department of Electrical & Computer Engineering, The University of New Mexico, Albuquerque, NM 87131-0001, USA

Hanane Houmani
EAS Group, ENSEM, Hassan II University, Casablanca, Morocco

Mohamed Mejri
LSFM Group, Laval University, Quebec, QC, Canada

Yasmin Hassan, Mohamed El-Tarhuni and Khaled Assaleh
Department of Electrical Engineering, American University of Sharjah, P.O. Box 26666, Sharjah, UAE

Ammar Zafar and Mohamed-Slim Alouini
Electrical Engineering Program, KAUST, Al Khawarizmi Applied Mathematics Building 1, Mail Box 2675, Makkah Province, Thuwal 23955-6900, Saudi Arabia

Yunfei Chen
School of Engineering, University of Warwick, Coventry, CV4 7AL, UK

Redha M. Radaydeh
Electrical Engineering Department, KAUST, Thuwal 23955-6900, Saudi Arabia
Department of Electrical and Computer Engineering, Texas A&M University, Texas A&M Engineering Building, Education City, Doha, Qatar

Lina S. Mohjazi, Mahmoud A. Al-Qutayri, Hassan R. Barada and Raed M. Shubair
College of Engineering, Khalifa University of Science, Technology and Research, UAE

Kin F. Poon
Etisalat-BT Innovation Centre (EBTIC), UAE

Bartosz Polaczyk, Piotr Cholda and Andrzej Jajszczyk
AGH University of Science and Technology, Department of Telecommunications, Al. Mickiewicza 30, 30-059 Krak´ow, Poland

Vinay Kumar and Sudarshan Tiwari
Department of Electronics and Communication Engineering, Motilal Nehru National Institute of Technology, Allahabad 211004, India

A. Drigas and S. Kouremenos
National Center for Scientific Research "DEMOKRITOS", Institute of Informatics and Telecommunications, Agia Paraskevi, Attici, 15310 Athens, Greece

Victoria Sgardoni
Department of Electrical and Electronic Engineering, University of Bristol, Bristol BS8 1UB, UK
Department of Aircraft Technology, Technological Educational Institute (ATEI) of Chalkis, Psachna, 34400 Evia, Greece

David R. Bull and Andrew R. Nix
Department of Electrical and Electronic Engineering, University of Bristol, Bristol BS8 1UB, UK

Mohd Faisal Ibrahim, Masita Jamal, Saadiah Yahya
Faculty of Computer and Mathematical Sciences, Universiti Teknologi MARA, 40450 Shah Alam, Malaysia

Mohd Nasir Taib
Faculty of Electrical Engineering, Universiti Teknologi MARA, 40450 Shah Alam, Malaysia

Zsolt Kollár and Péter Horváth
Department of Broadband Infocommunications and Electromagnetic Theory, Budapest University of Technology and Economics, Budapest 1111, Hungary

Fabrizio Iacopetti, Sergio Saponara, Luca Fanucci and Bruno Neri
Department of Information Engineering, University of Pisa, Via Caruso 16, 56122 Pisa, Italy

F. Javier Rivas, Almudena Díaz and Pedro Merino
Department of Languages and Computer Science, University of Malaga, UMA, Campus Teatinos, 29071 Malaga, Spain

João Paulo Pereira
School of Technology and Management, Polytechnic Institute of Braganc̦a (IPB), 5301-857 Braganc̦a, Portugal

Pedro Ferreira
Institute for Systems and Robotics, Technical University of Lisbon (IST), 1049-001 Lisbon, Portugal

Fidel Liberal, Ianire Taboada and Jose-Oscar Fajardo
University of the Basque Country UPV/EHU, Faculty of Engineering of Bilbao, Alameda Urquijo s/n, 48013 Bilbao, Spain

Rosdiadee Nordin
Department of Electrical, Electronics and System Engineering, Faculty of Engineering and Built Environment, Universiti Kebangsaan Malaysia, 43600 Bangi, Selangor, Malaysia

Md. Noor-E-Alam
Department of Mechanical Engineering, University of Alberta, 4-9 Mechanical Engineering Building, Edmonton, AB, Canada T6G 2G8

Ahmed Zaky Kasem
Department of Electrical and Computer Engineering, University of Alberta, Edmonton, AB, Canada T6G 2V4
TRLabs, Edmonton, AB, Canada T5K 2M5

John Doucette
Department of Mechanical Engineering, University of Alberta, 4-9 Mechanical Engineering Building, Edmonton, AB, Canada T6G 2G8
TRLabs, Edmonton, AB, Canada T5K 2M5

Printed in the USA
CPSIA information can be obtained
at www.ICGtesting.com
JSHW051437221024
72173JS00006B/1502